T0267932

HARVARD SQUARE

Praise for *Harvard Square*

"Catherine J. Turco brings a novelist's subtle sense of character, place, and pacing to an incisive, truly new consideration of a universal, though often invisible, fact of life: how we relate to where we live. And, on a deeper level, how we relate to change. A twenty-first-century Jane Jacobs, Turco's intellect, compassion, and commitment come through on each page."

—Lea Carpenter, author of *Eleven Days*
and *Red, White, Blue: A Novel*

"A lovely, well-told story that will change how you think about markets, market-places, and perhaps even your own shopping."

—Joseph L. Badaracco, author of *Step Back:*
How to Bring the Art of Reflection Into Your Busy Life

"Turco's history will forever change my daily commute of walking through Harvard Square. She provides amazing insight into the changes that have happened and will continue to happen and demonstrates that those who observe that the Square is changing are repeating a claim that has been made for centuries."

—Max H. Bazerman, Jesse Isidor Straus Professor of
Business Administration, Harvard Business School

"*Harvard Square* is an emotionally gripping historical ethnography, powerfully connected to both the archive and to the lived experience of our attachments to a real street-level market and the people within it."

—Peter Bearman, coauthor of *Working for Respect:*
Community and Conflict at Walmart

"This book is an intellectual and emotional revelation about why street-level marketplaces—the places where people dine and shop, meet others, and feel part of the scene—mean so much to them and why this 'love story' is inherently fraught. It is original and insightful about both markets and people."

—Cecilia L. Ridgeway, author of *Status:*
Why Is It Everywhere? Why Does It Matter?

"Turco uses the example of Harvard Square, a neighborhood she knows well and loves dearly, to examine the role of marketplaces in our lives. She shows how we develop affective ties to these dynamic markets and then deplore the changes that market forces bring about. This book raises important questions about the tensions between markets and communities and the extent to which we both crave and resist change."

—Mary Waters, Harvard University

"You will simply fall in love with how Turco draws you in and how she guides you to appreciate the paradox that markets are both source for and threat to what is sacred and intimate in our lives."

—Ezra W. Zuckerman Sivan, MIT Sloan

Harvard Square

A LOVE STORY

Catherine J. Turco

Columbia University Press
New York

Columbia University Press
Publishers Since 1893
New York   Chichester, West Sussex
cup.columbia.edu

Copyright © 2023 Catherine J. Turco
All rights reserved

Library of Congress Cataloging-in-Publication Data
Names: Turco, Catherine, author.
Title: Harvard Square : a love story / Catherine J. Turco.
Description: New York : Columbia University Press, [2022] |
Includes bibliographical references and index.
Identifiers: LCCN 2022021031 | ISBN 9780231209281 (paperback) |
ISBN 9780231557863 (ebook)
Subjects: LCSH: Harvard Square (Cambridge, Mass.) |
Central business districts—Massachusetts—Cambridge.
Classification: LCC HT177.C27 T87 2022 | DDC 307.3/42097444—dc23/eng/20220802
LC record available at https://lccn.loc.gov/2022021031

Columbia University Press books are printed on permanent and
durable acid-free paper.
Printed in the United States of America

Cover design: Noah Arlow
Cover image: Philip Borden

For my father and all our Sundays in the Square

CONTENTS

Details concerning the contemporary Harvard Square marketplace were current as of June 2022 when I submitted my final manuscript to the publisher. One challenge of writing about an inherently dynamic phenomenon such as the market is that some details will undoubtedly be out of date by the time this book reaches you. As I hope the book will convey, however, the lessons we derive from all that change may well be timeless.

Introduction

Out of Town News kiosk, 1985. Courtesy of Cambridge Historical Commission.

PROLOGUE

Sacred Sundays

The fence along Cambridge Common was broken in one spot. That became our spot. Every Sunday morning, my father and I would pull up alongside those two downed wooden rails, leave the old Chevy Malibu behind, and make the rest of our pilgrimage by foot. During the Revolutionary War, Minutemen had encamped on the Common's lush green expanse, and in the late 1960s thousands of antiwar protestors demonstrated there. To us it was just a convenient passageway. Each week, we would step over the busted beams and onto the path that led to Harvard Square.

To be clear, this was no mere stroll. My father reserved the walk through Cambridge Common and up Massachusetts Avenue for serious discussion. By my teens, this meant politics and current events. In 1985 when I was seven years old, it meant drills.

"Massachusetts," he'd start off, easing into things with our home state.

"Boston," I'd reply.

"California," he'd continue, as we skirted around some of First Parish's first arrivals and crossed Church Street.

"Sacramento," I'd respond while glancing down the street to an alternate house of devotion, the Harvard Square Theater. I liked how its new pink and teal mural looked three-dimensional. In a few years, when the artist expanded the piece, Charlie Chaplin would tip his hat at us as we passed by each week.

"Colorado," my father would say as we made our way further up Mass Ave. I remember how his voice echoed when we passed the cavernous, columned entrance to the "Coop," the campus department store and textbook vendor known more formally as the Harvard Cooperative Society.

"D-Denver," I'd reply with slight hesitation after giving Boulder passing consideration. Reaching the heart of Harvard Square, we'd follow the street's bend and the distinctive red awning of Nini's Corner around to Brattle Street, then stop in front of Nini's open-air racks.

With my dad momentarily distracted by the latest issues of *Time*, *Scientific American*, the *Economist*, or the like, I'd scan the Square and check in on some of its denizens. The Square has long been home to a diverse population of otherwise homeless individuals. Over the years, many of these residents grew familiar to me, from the man who held his Bible aloft and screamed of damnation to the one who sat on the sidewalk and quietly read his scripture of choice, the Sunday *Times*. Apparently, I became familiar to some as well, a fact I gleaned years later when the charismatic man who sold copies of the homeless periodical *Spare Change* in front of Au Bon Pain complimented me on a new haircut. From those early years, however, I recall most clearly the woman with the tattered skirt and the wild beehive of gray dreadlocks. We saw her every Sunday for months in a row and worried when she wasn't there.

"Florida," my father would resume the drill, stepping away from the magazines and continuing our walk up Brattle Street.

"Tallahassee." The woman with the beehive was back a few weeks later, ministering to a flock of pigeons in front of the Tasty Sandwich Shop across the street.

"Oregon," he'd say, stepping in front of me to open the door of the Greenhouse.

"Salem," I'd say, scooting under his outstretched arm and into the restaurant, grateful we'd made it to the end of the drill before getting to Alaska or, God forbid, the Dakotas.

With several houseplants lining its windowsill and faux greenery painted onto its mirrored walls, the Greenhouse Coffee Shop & Restaurant was more greasy spoon than botanical paradise. But it was our greasy spoon.

Over the years, we were happiest when we found a breakfast spot like the Greenhouse that we could return to over and over. What earned our loyalty was simple: an adequate cream-cheese-to-bagel ratio and how seriously its staff took this most serious matter. To this day, my father has strong views about what constitutes sufficient cream cheese coverage for a bagel, and it is more than what any rational, experienced server ever assumes on the first go. Whether due to nature or nurture, I share the predilection. So, when we found a diner or café that would indulge our idiosyncratic preference and expand the Overton window on cream cheese (or butter and jam, if we were in a muffin kind of mood), we felt uniquely seen and understood, and we would settle into a comfortable routine with the place.

The Greenhouse was quiet that early in the morning, and we could almost always secure our favorite table by the window. Soon the twenty-something waitress, whose white Reebok high-tops I coveted, would approach. I liked her for her shag haircut and the confidence that made me think she had been one of the popular girls in high school, but I liked her most for how expertly attuned she was to my father's temperament. He has a keen sense of humor but a radical directness that can make his red hair, blue eyes, and left-handedness seem his most ordinary attributes.

"The usual for you two?" she'd ask, pleasantly to the point. We'd smile and nod.

"Extra cream cheese," my father would invariably add, with a no-nonsense tone but a wry grin telling Reeboks he knew she'd seen it coming.

Thanks to Reeboks we enjoyed a nice run with the Greenhouse. We were thrown the week we arrived expecting our comfortable routine to unfold as usual but instead had to explain cream-cheese-to-bagel ratios to a frazzled neophyte, the priestess to our breakfast ritual having moved on. A few weeks later we moved on too. Not long after, we embarked upon a brief but intense love affair with a place called Mrs. Miller's Muffin Shop on Eliot Street, whose staff let us take as many pads of butter as we wanted. Then one day Mrs. Miller's disappeared. At some point along the way, we made a go of it with a place called the Left Bank at the corner of Eliot and JFK Street, and over the years we ate our share of egg sandwiches at the even greasier spoon, Lee's Beehive. By the time I graduated from high school in 1995, however, we had settled into a long-term, committed relationship with the Bruegger's Bagels shop on Mount Auburn Street thanks to an exceptional weekend manager who understood us instantly and who, years later when I had just moved back into town to attend graduate school, recognized me on the street and told me she had my dad's extra cream cheese waiting if we were coming back that Sunday. We were. Sometimes you have to weather a lot of change to sustain the things you cherish most.

"Want to see what's going on in the world?" my father liked to ask, nodding in the direction of Out of Town News as we stepped outside Greenhouse.

We'd look left then right for oncoming traffic then cut across the intersection where Mass Ave, JFK Street, and Brattle Street all curve and converge. Just as the state capital drill drew my mind to places beyond Wakefield—the town twelve miles north where both my parents had grown up and where now my brother and I were growing up—so did some of our favorite Sunday morning spots, and none more so than Sheldon Cohen's newsstand. Cohen began his career as a boy hawking local newspapers outside the Harvard transit station in the 1930s and '40s, opened Out of Town News in a low, boxy structure next to the station in the mid-'50s, and was still there in the '80s and early '90s to greet us many Sundays, having by then earned the affectionate nickname, "unofficial mayor of Harvard Square."

The mayor had recently moved his business a few feet over, and it now occupied the old copper-roofed subway headhouse. I loved this cramped little kiosk for how it reminded me of the phantom tollbooth in Norton Juster's children's story—a tiny portal that transported me to faraway places. Its racks and shelves were crammed with major dailies like the *Washington Post* and *Los Angeles Times*, sophisticated periodicals like *Foreign Affairs* and the *London Review of Books*, women's magazines such as *Grazia* and *Frau*, and everything from obscure southern literary journals and midwestern philosophy ones to hobby publications on weightlifting, coin collecting, equestrianism, knitting, and more. Also, though not a tollbooth, Out of Town News did have a ticket booth that listed all of the concerts and plays and events coming to town.

Cohen's mashup of global and national content did not just whisk one away to distant lands like the magic tollbooth, however. It also drew the world in. The diversity of reading material attracted a diversity of human specimens, and in those early years I found the newsstand's patrons as exotic as its titles. I was fascinated to see how often the two ran together—*Le Monde* for the tweedy old codgers and *BYTE* for the new-age techies; *Mother Jones* for the pretty earth mamas and *Vogue Italia* for the sexy edgy ones; the *New York Times* and a carton of cigarettes for the hurried grad students with their to-go coffee cups.

Before the internet made easy cosmopolitans of us all—before we could call up the whole world by typing a few keystrokes or clicking on a Twitter icon—local icons like Cohen and hubs like his Out of Town News did that work for us. Standing next to my father each week as he explained to me headlines about glasnost, the famine in Ethiopia, and a new computer called the Macintosh, I began to appreciate just how wide this outside world was, and I started to imagine myself in it someday.

Each week, depending on who and what intrigued me the most at Out of Town News, I would decide anew which publications I'd read once I grew up. The search for who I was going to be based on what I was going to read continued at our next stop, WordsWorth Books. When we began our Sunday morning ritual, there were at least twenty bookstores in the Square. However, not all were open on Sundays; even fewer were open early enough for us; and only WordsWorth had just the right siren call to lure my famously frugal father: discounts (10 percent off all paperbacks, 15 percent off all hardcovers). So, WordsWorth became our bookstore.

As luck would have it, the shop's owner, Hillel Stavis, was not just a local disruptor in the discount game (other Harvard Square bookshop owners resented him for undercutting their prices); he was also a technological innovator. Stavis had invested in a computerized inventory system before anyone else, and once my father and I discovered this marvelous fact, we peppered whichever poor soul was manning the information desk that Sunday with query after query about what was in stock and what could be ordered if not. A few decades later we would be typing all our queries into a search engine ourselves, and WordsWorth, once the disruptor, would close its doors, a victim to Amazon's industry-wide disruption. But my dad and I weren't thinking about any of that at the time. We just loved having access to so many cheap books in one place and people to help us navigate it all. When my father decided we should know something about computer programming, the staff helped us find an introductory book on the topic. (I recall some mention of bits and bytes but little else.) Later, when my own radical directness on the pages of Wakefield High's student newspaper, the *Warrior Times*, prompted some editorial "softening" by the paper's faculty advisor, I felt called to become a First Amendment warrior, and the WordsWorth staff armed me with a copy of Shiffrin and Choper's hefty, green casebook on the subject. More than even the books, however, what I remember most about that bookshop is the freedom I felt following my instincts and interests, whether aided by its information desk or simply wandering its labyrinthine aisles.

"Let's go to the Charles," I'd suggest, after we were shaken out of our book-browsing trance having somehow wound our way back to the shelf where we'd started. I didn't mean the nearby Charles River but, rather, its recent namesake, and we'd set off for it.

Construction of the Charles Hotel and its courtyard of restaurants and retail shops was completed in 1985, not long after my father and I began our

Sunday ritual, and it quickly became a staple of our route. We would cut through the hotel's lobby, climb its tall, wide staircase, glance at the faculty types settling in for brunch, make a pit stop at the second-floor bathrooms, and then exit into its red brick courtyard before heading on toward John F. Kennedy Park, which lay just beyond. I liked the fresh, clean newness of the hotel in contrast to some of the Square's longer-lived institutions, whose shabbiness I would come to see as chic only later. The hotel had a restrained newness. Early American quilts, Shaker furniture, and an upstairs jazz bar gave the place the same sort of understated but upscale New England glamour that a weathered Nantucket cottage or Beacon Hill brownstone has—impressive not for its ostentation but its implied connection to some longer, weightier historical narrative.

Its connection to one specific historical narrative mattered most though. One day when the hotel was still under construction, my father walked me past the site and explained that years earlier the bus yards of the Massachusetts Bay Transit Authority (MBTA) had been located there. His father, my grandfather, was an MBTA bus driver whose route took him through the Square each day, and earlier in my grandfather's career, those yards were where hundreds of buses and streetcars were stored and repaired.

In fact, my first trip to Harvard Square was not a Sunday morning, and it was not with my father. It was the afternoon I visited my grandfather at his work. I was only five years old, and I do not recall what brought my mother, brother, and me into the Square that summer day. (My mom thinks it was the promise of air-conditioning. The Harvard museums had it; our house did not; and there were only so many times she could stand taking us to the YMCA pool.) What I do recall is waiting in the hot sun outside Harvard Yard for Papa Turco's bus to arrive. Eventually, the bus sidled up to the curb, came to a stop, and let out its loud pneumatic hiss. When my grandfather pulled the inside lever and the accordion door opened to reveal him in the driver's seat, I was so excited to see him I threw myself up the bus's steep steps and immediately face planted.

We traveled just a few stops that day, but the view out the bus window captivated me. The crazy carnival of street musicians and jugglers, tour groups and shoppers and summer school students all weaving in and out of one another on the narrow sidewalks convinced me that my grandfather had one of the most exciting jobs in the world. It would be some years before I understood that he had hoped to take a different route in life. Born with perfect pitch but a terrible sense of direction and so colorblind he could not differentiate red from green traffic lights except by their position on the lamppost, he had been called to the clarinet and jazz, not the Massachusetts transit system. However, his father lost his North End factory job during the Depression, and my grandfather had to pass up a spot at the music conservatory. Then came the war, and he went off to fight. After all that, I imagine a steady gig with the MBTA had its appeal.

Over his thirty-five years on the job, my grandfather made thousands of loops through Harvard Square. I once asked him what that had been like, and he told me, "I saw a lot of the same and a lot of change." As a little girl walking through the Square and passing through the Charles Hotel each Sunday, I liked the feeling of traveling a path I knew he'd once traveled. I liked conjuring what the old "bus barn" might have looked like, imagining where in relation to the hotel's lobby he might have parked his bus or stood talking to colleagues between shifts. Years later when he attended my wedding reception at the Charles Hotel, I looked over at him and wondered if he was doing the same and what he thought of the long route that had brought us all to that day.

Now when I look back at my own many loops through Harvard Square— all the ones I took with my father those Sunday mornings—I think of what my grandfather said, and I, too, see "a lot of the same and a lot of change." I see the reassuring consistency and continuity of our weekly routine—the parking spot we staked claim to, the drills that built confidence through repetition, the breakfast order that never altered, the familiar faces and favorite haunts, the family history. We were two heathens in an otherwise devout Catholic family, but even we had our sacred rituals. At the same time, I see that change was perhaps the most consistent feature of those mornings. The Square was always a little bit different each week, and so were we. Coffee shops and servers we became attached to came and went. We welcomed new, new things like WordsWorth's inventory system while seeking personal transformation from its aisles of discount books. We read of distant lands and the changing world at Out of Town News. We walked through time at the Charles Hotel. I grew up.

The first Sunday after I moved out of my parent's house in Wakefield and into my freshman dorm at Harvard, my father parked in our spot by the broken fence and made the walk into the Square on his own to meet me. He did this again every Sunday for the next four years. Our walk route and breakfast order stayed the same, but our conversation topics changed. Now I would report on what I learned in class that week. Now when we talked politics it was less didactic, sometimes even contentious. It never crossed my mind to stop just because I was in college or our opinions had begun to diverge. I loved our Sunday mornings. Our relationship was evolving, as all relationships do.

~

Several decades later, on a bitterly cold night in February 2017, I sat in a basement meeting room on Brattle Street and watched a New York real estate investor roll his eyes and check his iPhone. He worked for Equity One, a $4 billion real estate investment trust that had recently invested $85 million in Harvard Square property. Equity One had scheduled this meeting with the community, but as far as I could tell, Harvard Square was the last place on earth this Equity One guy wanted to be that evening.

In 2015 Equity One had acquired a set of commercial buildings in the heart of Harvard Square from a local family trust that had owned and operated the properties for nearly a century. Shortly after the sale was complete, Equity One revealed its plan to evict all the existing business tenants, gut two of the buildings, and then "re-tenant" the renovated complex with all new businesses, presumably the sort of national and global chains that populated their other developments around the country.

This plan did not go over well with the local crowd. Harvard Square has long served as a sort of beloved Main Street/urban village for the greater Boston area, and it occupies a special place in many people's hearts and lives. There are the people like my grandfather who forge bonds with the Square because of their work with the MBTA or Harvard University or one of the many restaurants and stores in the marketplace. There are the small-business entrepreneurs like Sheldon Cohen who set up shop and stake their claim to the American dream in it. There are the hippies and activists who came for the protests and music in the '60s and '70s and stayed for the bookstores and coffee shops in the '80s and '90s. There are the college students who, one generation after another, pass through at a formative period in their lives and never forget the times they had there (even if those times are rendered slightly hazy for some of us by late-night scorpion bowls at the Hong Kong Restaurant). There are Cambridge kids who come to the Square to hang out after school and suburban kids who come on the weekends to wander around and get a taste of city life. (My high school friend and I are not the only people whose first time inside a bar was in Harvard Square at age sixteen courtesy of some poorly made fake IDs and an indulgent bouncer.)

There are the wealthy professionals and faculty members who live in the expensive homes surrounding the area and constitute the Square's permanent residents. There are the buskers, writers, and artists who come for the culture of the place and, in the process, create the culture of the place.

Equity One saw profit potential in a market beloved by so many. I don't know if they saw what was coming next. When the firm first appeared before the requisite city boards to gain approval for its redevelopment plan, Harvard Square loyalists of all stripes flooded the meetings and delayed proceedings, using public comment periods to voice their outrage and opposition. Thousands of citizens signed onto a petition asking the city to save one of the local businesses facing eviction, a toy store that specialized in Curious George paraphernalia. Several city councilors spoke out in the press to say that Equity One didn't understand Harvard Square and that the firm's plans seemed focused solely on how to "maximize profit within their purchase" and "harvest the highest rents possible."[1] (In Equity One's defense, that was what their investors were paying them to do.)

The city sent Equity One back to the drawing board. The firm revised its plans and was now begrudgingly—based on the body language emanating from its representatives that cold, February evening—holding public meetings like this one to preview those plans and hopefully win favor with the community before returning for final approval. These out-of-town investors had private property rights on their side and would eventually get their redevelopment project going, but they were still far from having the public on their side. At an earlier meeting like this one, a disgruntled Cantabrigian left early and hurled a snowball against the window on the way out.

Mind you, hurling snowballs and insults at developers was nothing new to Harvard Square. For decades, the local neighborhood association called itself the "Harvard Square Defense Fund." Its mission was to preserve and protect the Square from overdevelopment in the same way an environmental defense fund tries to preserve and protect an endangered species or forest. Over the years, the Harvard Square Defense Fund brought numerous lawsuits against commercial property owners, corporations, and even the city to try to block various projects.

As much as I loved the Square, I had always been a bit perplexed by the heightened emotions some people had around changes in the marketplace there. On our walk over to the meeting that night, I'd told my husband, Philip, that we should just listen, not talk. We might have concerns about the project, but we weren't like these "overly emotional Harvard Square types," I said. Philip gave me a sideways glance but said nothing.

He and I had moved back to Harvard Square two years earlier, in 2014. In many ways living there was exactly what I'd hoped it would be. We became instant loyal patrons of the Harvard Book Store, rekindling a bond I'd formed in college when I would wander the shop's aisles between economics classes. We became attached to a new bagel shop, Black Sheep Bagel Café, whose owners, Manny Ramirez and Shoshanah Garber, asked no questions and passed no judgment when I ordered a tub of cream cheese to go with my one bagel. We caught some shows at Club Passim, where my folks had gone on dates in the '60s when it was still called Club 47; we took in the annual Valentine's Day showing of *Casablanca* at the Brattle Theater; and the waiter at the Charles Hotel asked where we'd been if we didn't show up for brunch a few weeks in a row. The Square felt like ours. It was where we had met in grad school, where we had gotten married, and now it was home.

But I had also been upset almost as soon as we'd moved back, and that's why we were at the meeting that night. The truth was, I'd found myself getting a bit, shall we say, "overly emotional" at times, and I knew that's why Philip had given me that sideways glance. Harvard Square wasn't what it used to be, I'd heard myself say with increasing frequency these past few months. I wasn't alone in this sentiment. Almost every week it seemed one of the local papers ran a piece on the death of Harvard Square and the local shops and restaurants that had always made it special.

It wasn't all about Equity One either. Other real estate investors with national and global portfolios were gobbling up properties all around the Square. Rents were rising to levels many long-standing merchants could not afford, forcing some to shut down or relocate. Some property owners were leaving their buildings vacant for months—even years—at a time while they held out for the highest paying replacement or merely pondered their redevelopment options. The Harvard Square Theater on Church Street had been shuttered and vacant for the past five years; the mural on its facade that I'd loved as a kid was now tagged with graffiti.

In the meantime, online shopping and Amazon.com were taking a toll on brick-and-mortar retailers everywhere, and the Square was no exception. Sure, the Harvard Book Store was still open, but twenty or so other bookshops had closed since my high school and college years. WordsWorth was long gone; a Citizens Bank branch was there instead. Everywhere I turned deep-pocketed national and global brands seemed to be moving into places once occupied by local merchants. Greenhouse had closed in 2007 after its owner died, and a venture capital–backed national pizza chain was about to move into its old spot.

If all that weren't enough, the city had recently announced plans to evict Out of Town News from the kiosk and repurpose the space for public use. Sheldon Cohen had gotten out of town and out of the news racket years before, selling his business to Hudson News, a chain that operated hundreds of airport newsstands; then Hudson News, citing declining demand in print sales, let its lease expire in 2009, at which point a local newsstand operator stepped in to take over. For the time being, Out of Town News remained open, but these days more of its patrons were coming for the lottery tickets than the periodicals, and the city had just slapped an expiration date on it.

I hated all these changes. And that Equity One guy rolling his eyes like he'd prefer to be anywhere but here—who had no attachment to the place and who thought everyone in this room was being overly emotional—he was really starting to piss me off. A microphone was now making its way around the room. I listened as one member of the community after another critiqued Equity One's plans. There was talk of the dangers of unchecked global capitalism, the soullessness of chain stores, and the sanctity of Harvard Square and its local businesses. At some point, my anger began to morph into sadness. I felt a sense of loss. The changes people were describing were overwhelming. They were right, I thought: Harvard Square *wasn't* what it used to be. I found myself mourning for the Square I had known and loved and now felt slipping away from me.

When Philip and I returned to the Square, my grandfather, ninety-three, was visibly moved. He said he thought it was "real cool" we were living there and that he couldn't wait to see our new place. A month later, he died before making that one last trip to the Square. Around that time, I began to worry about my father driving into the city so much. I started to make more trips out to Wakefield than the reverse. Sometimes we don't stop to think about our most important relationships until we start to feel them slipping away.

"The Square isn't what it used to be," someone at the meeting said, snapping me back to the present discussion. Hearing my own words thrown back at me, I began to interrogate them, and I grew skeptical. What exactly did we mean when we said the Square wasn't what it used to be? What did it used to be? Could it have possibly been the same thing to all the different people of all different ages and inclinations in this room? Why were we all acting like this was hallowed ground being desecrated, when we were really just talking about a marketplace that was changing—a marketplace that had always changed?

How many changes must my grandfather have seen over his thirty-five years of loops through the Square, I wondered? How many had I seen over a similar time span? I hadn't hated all those changes—I'd liked a lot of them; others I probably hadn't even noticed. I'd lived through stores coming and going before, old buildings getting torn down and new ones going up. Hell, I'd even shut down a Harvard Square shop myself once: when I was in college I led a student-run business called Harvard Student Agencies (HSA); when the internet tanked our travel agency's sales because customers began ordering their Eurail passes and budget flights online, I directed the agency to close and felt pleased with myself for leading HSA into the future. Why was I so focused on looking back now? We were talking about a marketplace, and markets change.

I wondered if there was something different about these recent changes. Was the Harvard Square Defense Fund's environmental analogy more apt than I'd been willing to credit: Had I been focused on daily weather fluctuations when there had been fundamental climate change going on all along? Or was I the one that had fundamentally changed? Was I experiencing change differently now than when I was younger?

The more I thought about these questions the more rattled I got. I loved a good chain-store bashing as much as the next local these days, and I myself often partook. But things were more complicated than some of the easy epithets being thrown around the room that night—"soulless" and "heartless." Hadn't my father and I found bliss in a Bruegger's Bagels shop? In college, hadn't I wandered the aisles of HMV and Tower Records looking for the latest Elliott Smith or Pearl Jam CD to soothe my tortured, twenty-year-old soul? I knew better than to get sentimental about all this, I told myself.

So why was I reaching out for one of the microphones? Why was I—in a decidedly "overly emotional" sort of way—telling the Equity One folks that they didn't understand Harvard Square or the relationship the people in this room had with it? I was all over the place that night.

Later in the evening when I was back at home, I tried to make sense of my wild, scattered thoughts. I thought of my father's favorite Christmas movie, *The Godfather*, and saw that from Equity One's perspective this was "business, not personal." I didn't love the eye rolls, but I empathized with the perspective: I'm a business school professor in a department focused on innovation, technological change, and creative destruction. I'd just written a book about social media and the Millennial generation and how those new tools and that new generation were reshaping the future of business. I knew markets changed all the time, and I knew it was often disruptive. However, I could also see that for those who loved Harvard Square, this was deeply personal.[2] The business of it all felt almost like an affront. Given my own attachment to the Square and my emotional reaction that evening, I clearly empathized with that perspective, too.

In a sense, I had been wildly swinging between those two perspectives my whole career, not just that evening. I'd worked in investment banking and high tech after college and got an MBA, but then took a hard left to get a PhD in sociology to study culture and meaning, then a hard right back out to teach at a business school. The field I chose to specialize in, economic sociology, I chose because it helped me see both sides—to look for the personal in the business and the business in the personal. I tried to do that now.

I laid the two puzzle pieces side by side: Looking at that night's meeting through a basic economics lens, I saw a group of individuals discussing a dynamic market. Looking at it through a conventional sociological lens, I saw a community defending a cherished place. Both perspectives made sense. After all, Harvard Square is a marketplace. What did not make sense from either perspective, however, was this: The thing people seemed so deeply, emotionally attached to in this place *was* the market. Everyone that night had been talking about something they loved—something maybe even sacred to them. And everyone had been talking about a market.

I thought I understood markets and market change pretty well up until then, but I'd never thought about how we develop emotional relationships with the markets in our lives. I'd never thought about why these might be particularly tricky attachments for us all to navigate given the nature of markets and market change. The Equity One guys didn't fully get the relationship people had to Harvard Square, that was true. But did anyone else in that room? Did I?

Part of living in a capitalist society is that we create a lot of our lives in and around markets. We call them soulless yet we assign them sacred duties: So many of the routines and rituals that ground us unfold in market settings— are market transactions, even—like my bagels and cream cheese. So many of the meaningful bonds we form with one another are mediated by and forged in markets, like mine was with my father. So much of what defines the neighborhoods and places that we feel define us are the particular shops and stores in those places at a particular moment in time. How could we not get attached? We don't often think about it this way, but it turns out markets are surprisingly good at offering one-half of what my and my father's Sunday ritual gave me each week—what sociologists call a sense of "ontological security," a stabilizing sense of continuity—the sense that the world is as it appears and that we have a secure place in it.

Yet—and here's the tricky part—markets are also inherently unstable settings. And that is also a part of our relationship with them. The markets we participate in change on us all the time—sometimes quite rapidly, sometimes quite profoundly, for all sorts of different reasons that can be hard to understand or control fully once we notice them. Sometimes we welcome these changes. Sometimes we invite the changes ourselves. Sometimes these changes directly undermine the sense of ontological security we'd previously derived from a market, and so we feel profoundly destabilized. Sometimes we mourn and rage at the desecration this feels like. Oftentimes we do all of these things at once. Change is a tricky thing to navigate in any relationship.

We live more and more of our lives in markets these days. It can feel like things are changing on us faster and faster. A lot of us feel more destabilized than ever. If we're honest, a lot of us are more emotionally reactive than ever. Why is that? If our relationship with markets has always been characterized by "a lot of the same and a lot of change," why are some of us finding today's changes so upsetting? Are the changes unfolding now different from those in the past? Are we? Or do we just think this time is different because this is our time?

Walking down our hometown Main Streets or through our urban shopping districts, many of us look around and, with a sense of sadness and sometimes even moral indignation, think to ourselves: "It's not what it used to be." The recent coronavirus pandemic only amplified these concerns. During the shutdown, many of us were as socially distanced from our local street-level marketplaces as we were from our family and friends. We got a glimpse of what it might look like to no longer have these marketplaces in our lives. Our daily rituals and routines were pulled out from under us. In Harvard Square, the bustling streets I had delighted in from the window of my grandfather's bus were eerily empty. The shuttered shop doors with their "Closed for COVID" signs looked like gravestones. The whole place felt like a ghost town. During the slow, painful reopening that followed, many began to ask whether the worrisome changes unfolding before the pandemic had been accelerated by it. The truth is, for a while now a lot of us have been wondering whether the special relationship we've had with the street-level marketplaces in our lives is nearing its end. In my neck of the woods, people have been asking: Is Harvard Square dead and lost to us forever?

We can't answer these questions until we first understand our relationship with markets and market change. What does this relationship give us, and how have we navigated it in the past? How does it stabilize us, and how does it destabilize us? When does it comfort us? When does it excite and transform us? When does it sadden us? When does it absolutely infuriate us? Only then can we start to understand what sort of changes this relationship can weather and what sort of changes—in the market and in ourselves— might break it forever. Harvard Square is an extreme case of market love and outrage, and it has been for at least a century. That makes it a good place to start looking for some answers. It turns out we can learn a lot from those "overly emotional Harvard Square types."

Chapter One

A LOVE STORY TOLD FROM THE STREET LEVEL

Harvard Square was not "Harvard Square" until the mid-nineteenth century. For the two hundred years before, it was known simply as "the Market-place."[1] In the early 1630s, the area of Cambridge, Massachusetts, that historians now call Old Cambridge was brand new Newtowne to the Puritans who had just arrived from England. They named Newtowne capital of their Massachusetts Bay Colony and designated it one of just four market towns in the settlement.[2] Ever since that time, a commercial marketplace has sat nestled into the low hill that rises off the north banks of the Charles River.

Today, that marketplace is one of several squares—small commercial districts that cater to the surrounding area—in Cambridge, a city of approximately 120,000 people. "The Square," as it has become affectionately known over the years to the sometimes-chagrin of those whose loyalties lie in the city's Porter, Central, Inman, or Kendall Squares, now covers about forty-four acres of land. Up until the recent pandemic, it consisted of a bit over three hundred shops, stores, restaurants, entertainment venues, and offices.

Stories set in Harvard Square, from iconic Hollywood films to local television news segments, often begin with an aerial shot of those forty-four acres.[3] The camera carries us up and overhead to situate us in the setting. We gaze down and see the winding, tree-lined Charles River, sculls skimming swiftly across the water's surface. We see several elongated streets coursing toward a small central meeting point, then fanning back out, leaving a confused jumble of short side streets and alleyways behind. We see the tops of

Aerial view of Harvard Square, ca. 1978. Photo by Spencer Grant.

boxy, brick and concrete buildings sitting at odd angles like the haphazardly placed pieces of a child's board game. We see the tops of the tall leafy oaks and honey locusts that rise from the grassy lawn of Harvard Yard, and, in its center, we see the pointy white spire of Memorial Church aiming toward something above even our vaulted vantage point.

An aerial view of the colonists' Harvard Square would show us something different. The absence of seventeenth-century drones or helicopters (not to mention time travel) renders this a somewhat speculative exercise, but Susan Maycock and Charles Sullivan's comprehensive history of early Cambridge, *Building Old Cambridge: Architecture and Development*, gives us a sense of what we might see.[4] The Charles River would, of course, still be there for us to spy from the sky, but so would a lot of marsh surrounding it. Where today paved roads are etched into the ground and give the landscape its form, we would instead gaze down upon quiet Town Creek, gently bending and curving with the land. It would be another three hundred years before Memorial Church's white spire arrived on the scene to make its ascent to the heavens, but the gabled roof of the Puritans' first meetinghouse would testify to similar celestial aspirations. As today, we might spot some leafy treetops peeking out of the open expanse that would soon be Harvard

Yard. However, where brick and concrete boxes now jut from the ground, we would see only flat pastures and cow pens and the low, slate rooftops of small wood-frame houses. And, if we could fly low enough, we might just be able to make out the contours of a small, open-air market sitting right in the middle of it all.

Aerial shots are clarifying. They help orient us. Cinematically, however, they are almost always followed by the camera swooping down to the street. In classic Harvard Square movies like *Love Story* (1970), *The Paper Chase* (1973), and *Good Will Hunting* (1997), street-level shots plunge us into the bustling, pulsating human activity below. Here we see crowds of people pouring out of the subway and crowds of people flowing across the Square's narrow streets headed to and from who knows where. We see people selling newspapers and people buying newspapers; people ducking into shops empty-handed and people ducking out of shops with arms full of groceries or books or tiny gift bags concealing secret treasures within. We see the number 1 bus and the number 77 bus and the number 73 bus pull up and deposit new batches of people to replace those waiting to be carried away. Through streaky windows we see people standing behind counters serving coffee to people sitting at counters drinking coffee. We see shopkeepers sweeping entryways, police officers on patrols, young parents pushing strollers. We see old men sitting and talking in pairs, students in a rush, couples in love.

The soundscape is different here, too. Whereas classical overtures and instrumentals typically accompany aerial shots in the movies, at the street level we hear the din of passing conversation, snippets of language flowing in and out of earshot, each one layering over the next. We hear the hiss of buses coming to their stops then starting back on their way. We hear the beep, beep, beep of trucks backing up to make their deliveries. We hear exhaust pipes and engine roars, and, because it is Harvard Square, we hear incessant, impatient honking horns. So many horns.[5]

The French philosopher Michel de Certeau argues that the aerial, scopic view of a city works like abstract academic theory: it turns something exceedingly messy into something more comprehensible to us. Yet de Certeau cautions that this abstraction is always part fiction. The totalizing, orienting view we get from above is a simplification born from distance. It is a simulacrum of the messy, disorienting, buzzing reality of the life transpiring below. That "swarming activity on the ground," de Certeau says, is the more "anthropological"—as well as the more "poetic and mythic"—level at which we humans actually live our lives.[6] This is why the cinematographer's camera always, inevitably, has to descend and land at the street level: you cannot tell a love story from the clouds.

This book is a love story told from the street level. It is an unconventional, complicated, and messy love story—but it is a love story all the same. It starts almost four hundred years ago in that seventeenth-century market we glimpsed from above.

∽

This early market sat in the center of Newtowne in what is now Winthrop Park—a 145-foot by 90-foot rectangular speck of green that sits atop a low rise at the present-day intersection of JFK Street, Mount Auburn Street, and Winthrop Street.[7] *Building Old Cambridge* is our best source for what this original market was like and how economic life around it evolved over the next two centuries.[8] Minimal physical description of the original marketplace survives, but it seems not to have had permanent stalls. Markets at this time were traditionally held on set days of the week. Like the meetinghouse, which had its own weekly cadence and where people gathered for worship and town meetings, the market was a natural center of village social life.[9] A street-level view would have revealed people gathering there each market day to trade things like produce, wood, hay, and furs, as well as current news and gossip. In time, some permanent shops began to open up around the market, usually in the home of the storekeeper and his family. After the founding of Harvard College in 1636, businesses catering to the university began to appear on the scene as well, including the area's first printing press. By the mid-1600s there was a variety shop, a tailor, a woolen draper, two inns, a bakery, and several other artisans and tradesmen hard at work, including a village blacksmith.[10] In 1651, a local man opened what would become the village's most popular "public house," the Blue Anchor Tavern. Having apparently passed Puritan muster, it was allowed to sell "beer and bread" to students, visitors, and townspeople.[11]

The village was compact, and intentionally so. In what sounds like an early instance of Cambridge zoning, the people of Newtowne adopted an order that required houses to be built within the town's narrow boundaries until all the available spaces were filled. Another order required houses to be set back no more than six feet from the street. The tiny little town the colonists imagineered for themselves did not always impress outsiders, however. Growth was slow; nearby Charlestown had proved the bigger draw from the start, and a larger market flourished there. Even with the building order, the few houses scattered about the marketplace felt thinly spaced. In 1680 a Dutch visitor arrived expecting to be impressed by the town now called Cambridge and "the only college or would-be academy of Protestants in America." Instead, he found, in his words, a "not very large village" and a piddly little print shop with a broken paper sash.[12]

One hundred years on, in the years leading up to the American Revolution, the Market-place was a bit bigger and a bit more developed, but it would likely still have left the Dutchman unimpressed. Trade remained light; housing in the village, sparse. A few things were different. During the mid-1700s, a number of wealthy Anglican families loyal to the Crown had built homes nearby, including a row of impressive mansions just west of the village along what is now called Brattle Street. Harvard College had expanded, and it now drew over a hundred students and faculty to the area. Nevertheless, the market that had grown up over the past century was not the major trading center early settlers had perhaps envisioned. It was still a small, quiet village marketplace that served the local residential and college populations. The Blue Anchor Tavern remained a popular watering hole where townsmen liked to gather and talk politics. A local blacksmith still toiled nearby, as did other tradesmen and artisans common to the period, such as a glazier, a tanner, a hatter, and a currier.[13]

This is not to say the quiet little eighteenth-century village lacked excitement. For a brief period each summer, it was neither quiet nor little, in fact. The days surrounding Harvard commencements were wild, drunken, carnival-like spectacles that drew people of all types from all over. Andrew Schlesinger's history of the university, *Veritas: Harvard College and the American Experience*, lists as among the event's rowdy revelers: farmers, craftsmen, tradesmen, Native Americans, women with babies, schoolboys, servants, slaves, paupers, blind men, "cripples," "lunatics," gentry and "grand seigneurs," and, of course, the graduating students and their families.[14] Just as the early market provided a weekly rhythm to village life, commencement provided an orienting ritual for the annual calendar, only it brought an even wider assortment of social and commercial diversions with it.[15] During the celebration, Cambridge Common—the large green lying just north of the Market-place—was transformed into a chaotic amusement park with tents and stands featuring wild attractions that anticipated in even more eccentric fashion some of the eclectic street performers Harvard Square would become known for in the late twentieth century. There were jugglers and fortune-tellers, pantomimes and organ grinders, rum sellers and sword swallowers, along with "singing dwarfs," itinerant fiddlers, monkeys, dancing bears, and, at least one year, an elephant.[16]

As the American Revolution approached, frivolity gave way to gravitas. Gone from Cambridge Common were the hucksters, hustlers, and revelers (though the festivities would resume for a while after the war). Now the area buzzed with revolutionary activity.[17] By spring 1775, hundreds of Minutemen from around New England were encamped in barracks on the Common. Still more troops occupied the college after Harvard dismissed its students early that year. Thousands more soldiers were quartered throughout Cambridge. The "Tories"—those wealthy loyalists who had built mansions for themselves along Brattle Street—fled early in the uprising, and the military confiscated some of their homes. When George Washington arrived in July 1775 to take command of the revolutionary forces, he set up his residence—and the military's headquarters—in one of the abandoned mansions. He and his aides-de-camp worked out of that location until they and the troops departed Cambridge in spring 1776.

In the fifty years following the Revolutionary War, the population of Cambridge almost quadrupled, rising from 2,115 in 1790 to 8,409 in 1840.[18] Harvard was now a nationally renowned university with a medical school, divinity school, and law school. Nearly a third of its matriculants hailed from outside New England, and its students and faculty numbered several hundred. Every day, horse-drawn stagecoaches and omnibuses made dozens of trips back and forth to Boston, hinting at the metropolitan transportation hub the Square would soon become, first with the advent of the horse-drawn street railway, then with the electric streetcar, and, finally, the subway. However, those changes were still on the horizon, and most of Cambridge's industrial growth was taking place in other parts of the city. For the first half of the nineteenth century, a street-level view of the village would have revealed a marketplace not so different than that of the early settlers. Taverns, shops, and trades composed the local economy and catered to the small surrounding population, which included wealthy merchants, artisans, and tradesmen, some remaining descendants of the early Puritan families, a few African Americans, and the university and its students and faculty.[19] The marketplace offered its share of both staples and exotic enticements to this crowd. Little children liked to sneak in after school to explore the mysterious aisles of the East and West Indies goods stores, groceries that sold imported items like molasses, rum, and dates alongside more conventional local produce.[20]

Change was in the offing, however. From 1840 to 1850, Cambridge's overall population nearly doubled, to 15,215, and that was just a taste of what was to come. By 1900, due in large part to immigration and rapid industrialization,

Cambridge's population would soar to over 90,000, and the city would be outfitted with modern water, gas, and sewage lines and electrified street railways.[21] Perhaps because the scent of rapid growth and development was already in the air, perhaps because of pride in the role this little village had played in the young nation's storied birth, a few people began to glance backward during the early to mid-nineteenth century, as if to ensure the swiftly receding past had at least been properly marked for posterity. Around the 1830s, Cambridge changed the Market-place's geographically descriptive street names to those referencing some of the village's early leading men. Water Street became Dunster Street; Crooked Street, now straight, became Holyoke Street.[22] "Tory Row," those stately mansions the British loyalists had fled, became a part of local and national lore by midcentury, now preserved as physical reminders of the colonists' victory.[23] Harvard Square started to be called "Harvard Square."

As the nineteenth century unfolded, perhaps no one was more captivated by the historical romance of the place—and perhaps no one did more to create the historical romance of the place—than the poet Henry Wadsworth Longfellow. Born in 1807 and a descendant of early Puritan colonists, Longfellow was enthralled with the nation's founding story from an early age. Shortly after he arrived in Cambridge in 1836 to begin teaching at Harvard, he rented a room in the house George Washington had used as his headquarters early in the Revolution.[24] By then, the Brattle Street mansion was owned by a widow who took in boarders from the college. Longfellow was so keen on the Georgian-style residence and its ties to the past that when he married Fanny Appleton in 1843, his wealthy father-in-law bought the home as a wedding gift for the newlyweds. The poet continued to live and write there until his death in 1882.

During those years, Longfellow became a fixture of village life, his fame contributing to the mystique the place had for others. He was known for taking regular strolls through the Market-place. He would often stop in at Amee Brothers, the newsstand and bookshop that doubled as a popular gathering spot for faculty, students, and townspeople looking to catch up on the news of the day.[25] Longfellow loved the village's character and atmosphere, and he was not always keen on the idea of it changing. In 1868 he purchased some nearby marshland in order to prevent it from being developed for slaughterhouses.[26] When horsecar service from Boston dropped off dramatically during the Great Epizootic of 1872 (a devastating equine influenza epidemic that felled horses in urban centers throughout Canada and the United States, suspending streetcar service in many areas), Longfellow delighted in the temporary peace and quiet. It reminded him of the marketplace he'd known nearly forty years earlier, when it seems to have held even more charm for him. "Our City has become once more a remote and quiet village," he wrote. "To me the feeling is delightful. I think of the army of invaders unable to cross the bridge, and enjoy their discomfiture and my repose. Alas! It is only a momentary triumph."[27]

Momentary triumph or not, Longfellow had already captured the essence of that earlier marketplace for time immemorial. It was right there in his 1839 poem "The Village Blacksmith."[28] In iambic tetrameter and trimeter, the poet expressed appreciation for many of the same things other Americans would come to appreciate about their own beloved Main Streets and urban villages. The blacksmith and his shop were cherished institutions, as stable and rooted in place as the stately tree that stood beside them (*"Under a spreading chestnut tree / the village smithy stands"*). The local merchant was known and admired by all for his hard work and independence (*"His brow is wet with honest sweat / He earns whate'er he can / And looks the whole world in the face / For he owes not any man"*). The market's regular routines, as dependable as the church bell's hourly chime, brought a comforting consistency to life in the village (*"Week in, week out, from morn till night / You can hear his bellows blow / You can hear him swing his heavy sledge / With measured beat and slow / Like a sexton ringing the village bell / When the evening sun is low"*). Commerce and community cohered there (*"And children coming home from school / Look in at the open door / They love to see the flaming forge / And hear the bellows roar"*). Human beings and their very human feelings (*"Toiling,—rejoicing,—sorrowing"*) mattered there.

Like the camera that descends from above to land us on the street, Longfellow's verses throw us right onto that poetic, mythic, anthropological street level. More than a century before de Certeau would advocate for this perspectival stance in his philosophical essay "Walking in the City," a poet with a penchant for daily strolls captured it for us. Of crucial note for this book, Longfellow saw straight into the beating heart of village life at the street level: He saw a market at work. He saw the poetry in market life. He delighted in its rituals and traditions. It held a sort of Tocquevillian charm for him. He felt the romance of America in it. In a place whose historical narrative had been attached to the idea and ideals of American democracy from the start, it was probably hard not to. Longfellow cherished this little marketplace and all that it meant to him.

He is not the only American to have fallen in the love with his local street-level marketplace over the years. He is also not the only person to have fallen in love with this particular street-level marketplace—the one we now call Harvard Square.

THE REALITY AND THE ROMANCE OF HARVARD SQUARE

André Aciman's 2013 novel *Harvard Square* is set in the bars and cafés of its namesake. Most of the story unfolds in one particular establishment—a real-life coffeehouse called Café Algiers that operated in the Square for fifty-seven years and closed in 2017. The book tells the story of two North African émigrés who meet there in 1977. One is a Harvard graduate student struggling to get his PhD in literature; the other, a cantankerous, sharp-tongued taxicab driver. For a brief time, the two men find in their "little world" of Café Algiers, and in one another's companionship, the sort of community and culture for which they have been yearning—the sort of community and culture they often call to mind in reminiscences of their homelands and, especially, the city they both love, Paris.[29]

People have long found companionship, community, and culture in places like Café Algiers and street-level markets like Harvard Square. This is true whether we turn our gaze to the streets of a large European city like Paris, France, or a small American town like Peru, Indiana. Although we often contrast suburban or rural Main Streets and downtowns with their more urban counterparts, the street-level markets most of us know personally—and, in particular, what we value most about them—have a fair bit in common with one another regardless of their locale.

And yet there is no "typical" or "average" street-level market, either.[30] There is no perfectly "representative" American downtown shopping district from which we could generalize to the entire population of street-level markets across the United States, no modal Main Street we could probe to ascertain what defines these things for us or what changes have been unfolding in them in recent years. Even if there were, it would not help us with this book's larger agenda of trying to understand the relationships we develop with these markets. None of us loves just any market. We love the one we love.

This book will not try to tell the story of all those other Main Streets. It will tell the story of just this one small street-level market and the intense but complicated relationship a range of people have had with it over the past one hundred years. In some ways, Harvard Square is like a lot of other local street-level markets around the country. It has been characterized as a "busy Main Street" and, by one local partisan who sounds like local partisans everywhere, as the "best little downtown in America."[31] In others ways, both obvious and not so obvious, it is unique. Regardless, certain attributes of it are apt to remind you of a street-level market you know or perhaps one you once knew and now miss. The things Harvard Square has been known and loved for are the things many "squares" have been known and loved for over the years.[32] The hope of this book is that in the finely rendered details of this one quirky little case we will uncover insights that transcend it. As literature and poetry teach us so well, sometimes we come to understand ourselves and our relationships best through the truths revealed by the radiant particularities of a story that is not ours yet ignites in us the sparks of recognition.

~

So, what are some of Harvard Square's radiant particularities? What are the details that have, over the past century, come to define it in all its unique peculiarity yet speak perhaps to more?

The feature that typically strikes new arrivals to Harvard Square most immediately is its small size. Sweeping aerial shots can convey a larger-than-life persona that belies just how human-scaled the Square is at the street level. It is tiny by comparison to many urban shopping districts in larger cities. The entire thing could fit within a block or two of some neighborhoods in New York or Chicago.

It is also rather cramped. Those early Newtowne settlers who wanted their first structures to be densely situated in the village center would perhaps be quite pleased with the feeling one gets today walking through the Square's short, narrow streets. It can feel almost cozy. The tallest building is a ten-story concrete, brutalist outlier that the university erected in the 1960s. Surrounding it are far more modest brick and wood structures of various ages and in various stages of disrepair or renewal. Most are no more than a few stories high, and they give the appearance of having been jammed in together, each one bumping up against the next. The Square's notoriously narrow sidewalks replicate this feeling in human, bodily form.

Yet it is the density and diversity of small shops, stores, restaurants, and cafés within those buildings and lining those sidewalks that have most defined this marketplace over the years. During the twentieth century, Harvard Square evolved from a sleepy village market into a thickly concentrated, hyper-agglomeration of small shops and restaurants, most of them locally owned, independent operations. Within the space of a few minutes, someone walking through this commercial menagerie would, depending on the year into which we decide to drop our perambulator, pass by stores specializing in such miscellany as: candles, tea, cameras, typewriters, music (sheet music, sound systems, used records, new records, discount records, CDs), wine, classic men's suits and tailored Oxford shirts, clothes made all of hemp, Harvard insignia, Russian crafts, tennis rackets, modern furniture, world maps, miniskirts, and, of course, books—comic books, rare books, Marxist books, Christian books, textbooks, poetry books, and more. Along the way, our street-level stroller would also wander by barber shops, copy shops, tailors, cobblers, dry cleaners, travel agencies, foreign-language centers and test-prep centers, convenience stores and pharmacies, small groceries, cheap diners, fancy French restaurants, and a whole lot of burger joints.

The longevity of some of the Square's businesses has been as noteworthy a feature of the marketplace as its overall commercial density and diversity. A number of establishments still in operation today date back to the late nineteenth century and early twentieth century. Cambridge Savings Bank was founded in 1834, and the Harvard Cooperative Society, which sits cattycorner from it, was founded in 1882. The tobacco shop Leavitt & Peirce opened in 1884. Its neighbors on Massachusetts Avenue—Cambridge Trust and the clothing shop J. August—opened in 1890 and 1891, respectively. Felix Shoe Repair, just a bit further down Mass Ave, dates its origins back to 1913; the Brattle Square Florist, to 1917; the Harvard Book Store, to 1932; Cardullo's Gourmet Shoppe, to 1950; Charlie's Kitchen, to 1951.

The market's long-lived establishments are also long loved. Harvard Square denizens have been known to grow quite fond of their shops and eateries. Favorite haunts often acquire affectionate nicknames, passed from one generation of patrons to the next. More than a century's worth of thirsty Harvard students procured their booze at "the Pro" (Harvard Provision Co., est. 1895). Suggesting a visit to the Harvard Cooperative Society has outed many an unsuspecting outsider, for it is "the Coop" (and not pronounced "Co-op," either) to those who know it well. For decades, people have ordered pizza at "Noch's" (Pinocchio's Pizzeria, est. 1966) and Chinese food and drinks at "the Kong" (the Hong Kong Restaurant, est. 1954). Certain cherished institutions have been honored with more than nicknames; they've had entire documentaries dedicated to them. Olivia Huang's 2017 film *Grolier Poetry Book Shop: The Last Sacred Place of Poetry* profiles the Grolier, a cherished little literary hole-in-the-wall that has operated in the Square since 1927.

Treasured Harvard Square institutions have not all been of the brick-and-mortar variety, either. Along the way, certain proprietors have, like Longfellow's blacksmith, become defining and beloved features of the market themselves. For decades, many more people than just me and my father came to expect Sheldon Cohen—"unofficial mayor of Harvard Square"—at Out of Town News each morning. At a celebration of Cohen's career in 2012, community members came together to share stories about his role in their lives and the life of Harvard Square.[33] Long-standing merchants like him have become deeply embedded and widely adored on account of their constancy and their commitment. Cohen, for instance, did not just hawk newspapers every day for decades. He also invested time and energy in the success of other merchants and the marketplace's overall vitality by serving as president of the Harvard Square Business Association, a group of business and property owners founded in 1910 to promote commerce in the Square.

Before Cohen was elected "mayor," Felix Caragianes was the "president" of Harvard Square.[34] A Greek immigrant, Caragianes opened his shop shortly after arriving in the United States in 1912, and he shined shoes and sold newspapers there for thirty-seven years. Early in his tenure, he earned favor among freethinkers and fans of the First Amendment when he was arrested for selling copies of H. L. Mencken's controversial *American Mercury* magazine.[35] Over the years, he also lent more than $10,000 to Harvard students of Greek descent to help them pay their college bills. A year before Caragianes's death in 1951, more than one hundred people, including multiple Harvard faculty and students, attended a Greek Orthodox celebration of his "name day," St. Felix Day.[36] When he passed, the *Cambridge Chronicle*'s headline read: "A Harvard Square Celebrity Dies."[37]

The most well-known and well-liked merchant in Harvard Square history, however, may have been Max Keezer. Keezer—who gave flyweight boxing a shot first but who, as best I can tell, never acquired a title in either pugilism or Harvard Square lore—started peddling secondhand clothes in the Square when he was eighteen years old and kept at it for fifty-five years, remaining a fixture in the marketplace until his death in 1941. When not at his shop, Keezer could be spotted walking about the Square in his long polo coat and soft cap, greeting most passersby by name. He was known to waive the bills of students short on cash, and in at least one instance he quite literally bailed a student out of trouble with the law. The *Harvard Lampoon*, a student humor magazine, immortalized him as the smiling "Keezer Cat" in a parody of *Alice in Wonderland*, and the university issued him an official invitation to sit among dignitaries at its commencement ceremony one year.[38] After his death, former customers recalled him for his steadfastness and his generosity: "Max and his grin were always there, on the corner, ready to do business," read one remembrance.[39] Another was titled, "If You Get Into a Jam at Harvard, See Max."[40]

Affection has always run deep in this marketplace. Like the loyal customers of Bailey Brothers Building & Loan in *It's a Wonderful Life*, loyal patrons of Harvard Square have even stepped in to rescue long-loved establishments and proprietors during tough times. In 1991, the restaurant and bar Casablanca, an iconic haunt since the 1950s, came under financial pressure. Thirty-seven individuals with a deep attachment to the place, and whom the bar's owner Sari Abul-Jubein called "the usual suspects," put up $280,000 to become partial owners and keep it going.[41] In 1996, members of the community flooded into public meetings and lobbied city officials to try to block a redevelopment project that threatened to shutter the Tasty Sandwich Shop, a 210-square-foot, one-room, fourteen-stool greasy lunch counter that had been operating in the same spot in the Square since 1916. "The Tasty" could not be saved, but the community's efforts were so fiercely fought they were memorialized in a 2005 documentary, *Touching History: Harvard Square, the Bank, & the Tasty Diner*.[42] Outpourings of support for embattled businesses continue to this day. In October 2020, after navigating months of diminished sales during the coronavirus pandemic, the owners of the Harvard Book Store (est. 1932) emailed customers about the business's precarious financial situation. The following Sunday, the store had the largest single sales day of its eighty-eight-year history.[43] As in personal life, so it seems in market life: some relationships are worth fighting for.

It is important to pause and consider further what relationships people are really fighting for in these examples. Markets are relational phenomena, sociologists tell us, and they are conventionally defined in terms of the buyer-seller relationship. When we look at Harvard Square through that lens, we see what we just saw: a set of shops and shopkeepers transacting with a set of customers and the connections formed between them. These are genuine connections, for sure. However, the sort of intense displays of devotion we see here stem from more than just fondness for a particular business or business owner. People's idea of Harvard Square—and people's love of it—has always been about more than its quirky, cramped shops and larger-than-life merchants. This is because markets like the Square offer more than the goods and services traded in them. They are defined by more than one single relationship. They *are* relational phenomena, absolutely—but they are relational in a far more profound way than we tend to think.[44]

Markets are a setting for a whole range of relational experiences we have in life. The shops and merchants, through their commercial venues and offerings, create opportunities for us to make all sorts of connections *with one another*. As this book will show, what a market like Harvard Square really means to people is what all the different human connections they've made in it have meant to them. People's attachment to the market is tied up with all these other attachments. Those are its most radiant particularities of all.

For some people, Harvard Square is where they have formed some of their most intimate, personal connections—the ties that have nourished and supported them, the ties that have sometimes even defined them. When I think of what Harvard Square means to me, I think of Sunday mornings with my father at the Greenhouse restaurant. I think, too, of that first time my best friend and I sneaked into "the Grille" with fake IDs and of late nights at "the Kong" with my college friends and of the first date I had with my husband and every Friday night date with him since. More than bagels and newspapers and booze, these intimate personal experiences are what the Square's commercial establishments and offerings have given me. This is true for thousands of other local residents and students who have at some point in their lives considered themselves a "regular" there. It is true, too, if in a different way, for some people who have simply passed through but, while they were there, caught a show they'll never forget or had a night to remember. It is true for those on the other side of the conventional buyer-seller interface as well. When I asked a private equity investor, who grew up in a suburb outside Cambridge and whose firm had just paid millions of dollars for a large commercial property in Harvard Square, what it was about the Square that appealed to him, his first instinct was not to talk in terms of net present value and cash flows. He told me, instead, about how when he was growing up, he and his parents came into the Square every December to do the family's holiday shopping and attend the annual Christmas Revels music concert. The co-owner of Black Sheep Bagel Café, Manny Ramirez, offered a similar answer when I asked why he had wanted to open a business in Harvard Square versus some other location. Ramirez said he had loved the Square since he was a teenager, when he and his friends made regular trips there to shop for CDs at Tower Records and HMV.

For some individuals, Harvard Square is where they have found a group to which they belonged. Market offerings allow people to connect around shared interests and experiences, and many a distinctive subculture has located a unifying tradition or favorite meeting spot in the Square's commercial landscape.[45] For Harvard students of a certain era, for example, the Bogart Film Festival was a cherished rite, one many still look back upon fondly. Starting in 1957 and continuing for years after, the Brattle Theater played *Casablanca* like clockwork every exam week.[46] (The film, considered by many the greatest love story of American cinema, now plays at the Brattle every Valentine's Day, supporting more personal, romantic connections for couples in the area.) Grolier Poetry Book Shop is considered hallowed ground for poetry lovers, and its regular poetry readings have long been a sacred ritual in the Boston-area poetry scene, bringing poets of all types and skill levels together. In 1984, the Harvard Square Theater began hosting a slightly more irreverent tradition, but one just as treasured to its faithful followers: every Saturday for twenty-eight years, the movie theater ran a midnight showing of the *Rocky Horror Picture Show*, including live cast, fishnet stockings, and all.

These sorts of market offerings do not just foster tight ties among the devoted; they have helped make the Square into a sort of cultural crossroads over the years, a place where people are exposed to a wide range of human creative endeavors. Its shops, theaters, and cafés have been known to support an interesting mix of high and low culture, capturing—and, at times, even creating—the contemporary zeitgeist. The Brattle Theater started to show foreign films in the 1950s when few theaters in the United States did. It was one of the first theaters to introduce Americans to the work of Fellini, Antonioni, Truffaut, and more.[47] In the early 1960s, the coffeehouse Club 47 became a central node in the emerging blues and folk music scenes. Audiences were introduced to the likes of Muddy Waters, Jackie Washington, Joan Baez, Joni Mitchell, and Bob Dylan. Decades later, Club 47's successor, Club Passim, hosted independent singer-songwriters like Tracy Chapman and Suzanne Vega, and it remains a vital folk music venue to this day.[48] Meanwhile, just outside its coffeehouses and theaters, the Square's sidewalks have long supported a cultural market of their own, serving as a stage for all kinds of buskers. Before she played Club Passim, Tracy Chapman played on the streets of Harvard Square and, on cold days, on its underground subway platform.[49] Performing alongside street musicians like Chapman has been a cast of characters including painted human statues, mimes, magicians, puppeteers, fortune-tellers, chess masters, and, for several years, a player of a two-stringed Chinese opera fiddle, the *jinghu*, known for its distinctive shrill.[50]

As these examples suggest, Harvard Square has, perhaps most of all, been a place where people have been exposed to and come into contact with individuals quite unlike themselves. In this small, tight space in which an elite university sits in the midst of a public transit hub, the marketplace as a whole and some of its most iconic businesses have been known to serve as what sociologists call "third places"—those spaces outside of home and work, like a local pub or diner, in which people of all backgrounds and walks of life can meet and mingle as relative equals.[51] Many of these are just passing encounters. People simply see and sense the human diversity about them as they go about their own, individual activities in the market. Other times the market may throw them in closer quarters with one another. Perhaps no business ever signified this feature of the Square more—and perhaps no business in the Square was ever more cherished by so many for all that it meant to them—than the Tasty, that little diner people tried to save. Federico Muchnik, the filmmaker whose documentary profiled the Tasty and who was a regular customer there in his teens, described it as the sort of place where, "You could walk in at any time of day and you could sit down and on your right you would have a Harvard professor and on your left you would have a homeless person and you could have a conversation."[52]

The Tasty was so known for these sort of cross-class connections that it was featured as a date spot in both *Love Story* and *Good Will Hunting*, two iconic Harvard Square movies in which people of different classes meet and fall in love. In fact, the Square's local identity as a third place where all kinds of people are thrown together has been picked up on and sentimentalized in more than a few Hollywood films set there. *With Honors* (1994) tells a story about the friendship that forms between an ambitious Harvard student and an older, wiser (and feistier) homeless man played by Joe Pesci.[53] In real-life Harvard Square, it is common to come to know some of the Square's homeless by face if not name, and common also to find oneself standing in line for coffee alongside Cambridge cops on the beat, construction workers on break, Harvard deans darting between meetings, students caffeinating for class, and local attorneys on the clock.

The market's annual festivals and fairs have fostered similar connections. One weekend every October, for example, the banks of the Charles River overflow with the preppy parents, siblings, and friends of rowers who have come to town for the Head of the Charles Regatta. Those who have come for the races (and who, to borrow a line from another movie set in the Square, the *Social Network*, often look like they are about to try to sell you a Brooks Brothers franchise) are joined by hundreds of students and local residents who turn out less for the sport and more for the crisp air, people watching, and food stands selling hot cider, donuts, and baked potatoes along the river's edge. On other weekends during the year, hundreds turn out for the Square's various street fairs, some of which are now decades-old traditions. In 1979, the Harvard Square Business Association began holding an Oktoberfest. In 1984, the group added a Mayfair to the market's annual calendar. In 2018 and 2019, the Thai Association of Boston hosted a Thai Festival in Winthrop Park, right where the original seventeenth-century market sat. Thai restaurants from around the area set up stands and sold food alongside vibrantly costumed performances of traditional Thai dances and exhibitions of Muay Thai boxing.[54] At events like these, individuals connect with the community writ large. Most attendees remain anonymous to one another, but in the same way that walking through the marketplace or riding the subway can make one feel more connected to others, coordinating with a mass of diverse human beings around shared rituals like these makes people feel more connected to their shared humanity. Over the years, that experience, that feeling, has become a part of many people's notion of this marketplace.

Finally, as the Thai Festival demonstrates, the Square has served not just as a venue for connecting with the local community but also as a portal through which local residents and shoppers can connect with the much wider world. Its reputation for being a sort of cosmopolitan hub for the greater Boston area really took off during the 1960s. At the same time that the Brattle Theater was introducing locals to arty foreign films, Out of Town News was one of the only places in the region where an individual could buy a copy of the *Washington Post*. A few blocks over, Design Research—a retail concept dreamt up by the architect Ben Thompson and known for its sleek modern furniture and housewares—was the first store in the United States to carry Marimekko prints from Finland, sparking a fashion craze that soon swept across the country.[55] Hungry diners came to Harvard Square to sample a wide variety of international fare at places like Cardullo's Gourmet Shoppe and restaurants such as the Wursthaus and Henri IV. Others channeled their inner Hemingway by sipping coffee at Café Pamplona or their inner Bogie by grabbing a drink at Casablanca or the Blue Parrot. Looking back at this period of Harvard Square history, one individual said of the 1960s and '70s: "Its charm lay in its basement bookstores and cafés, in its tiny alleyways, in the vaguely bohemian and continental atmosphere it had at a time when the only croissant to be found in the Western Hemisphere south of Montreal and north of Guadalupe was at Patisserie Francaise on JFK Street."[56]

But the market in Harvard Square was a platform for accessing the world well before and well after the 1960s and '70s. Ever since trading began in the settlers' early seventeenth-century marketplace, the Square's merchants, traders, and shopkeepers have served a sort of bridging function, bringing goods from around the region and around the world to local consumers. That was true during the era of East and West Indies goods stores. And it was true years later when my father and I came to Harvard Square seeking figurative passage to parts unknown through the wide assortment of books, music, and food sold there, as others came seeking literal passage to faraway places in one of the Square's multiple travel agencies.

To be sure, Harvard Square may be unusual in just how much it has bridged the local and global. Universities in general promote a cosmopolitan orientation. Large, elite universities like Harvard attract students, faculty, and visitors from all over the country and all over the world. Harvard's international stature also makes it a popular destination for thousands of foreign and domestic tourists each year. It is not surprising that the local market would carry goods and services from afar. That said, all street-level markets bridge the local and the global in one way or another, and Harvard Square may just be an extreme case of this. Ever since the earliest bazaars and open-air markets, street-level markets and the local traders, peddlers, and merchants doing business in them have served this sort of bridging role to at least some extent.[57] Stanley Milgram's classic 1967 sociological study of the "small-world" phenomenon showed this quite concretely.[58] Milgram gave a letter to a set of individuals on one side of the country and asked them to get it to someone they did not know and whose address on the other side of the country they were not given. In the end, it was a local clothing merchant who most frequently directed the letter to its final destination, connecting the target recipient to the larger world.

The street-level markets most of us know have more in common with Harvard Square than just their bridging function. So many of the features just described, so many of the connections formed, are apt to feel familiar. Whether we find ourselves recalling a quiet suburban Main Street or a bustling urban village, most of us recognize the sense of stability and continuity afforded by a market's long-lived institutions. Perhaps we are reminded of a local hometown bank that was in business for decades before we arrived on the scene looking to open an account for our babysitting or paper-route earnings. Or maybe it's an ice-cream parlor whose owner sponsored our Little League team and always remembered that our favorite flavor was black raspberry. Or maybe just a longtime restaurant owner who greeted us with a smile every Friday night. Most of us also recognize the routines and traditions of market life and the orienting stability that comes from all the connections we have formed around them. Not every market has a Bogie Festival or an Oktoberfest, but they all have their own rites and rituals that comfort us in their consistency and strengthen bonds of community, whether Fourth of July parades or holiday tree lightings or local farmers' markets. When we stop to think about street-level markets we have known, many of us cannot help but think of things that have nourished and defined us through our lives, like our first dates and first kisses, family dinners and friendly reunions.

∾

And yet even if you feel the sparks of recognition firing, you are probably also starting to feel like this is all a bit too much. Unless you are besotted with Harvard Square yourself, the earlier description may have come across as too sentimental for your taste. Even if parts of that description called to mind a street-level market you once knew, your rational self is likely, in this very moment, trying to shove aside your emotional self in order to remind you that, really, it was not all apple pie and ice-cream parlors and Fourth of July parades. Your rational self has a point. It turns out that part of the nature of these markets or, at least, part of our relationship with them is that we tend to romanticize them.

A number of historical and cultural scholars argue that, over the course of the twentieth century, Americans came to embrace an idealized conception of street-level markets, which now clouds our memories of the real thing. These scholars deconstruct the culture's sentimental notion of "Main Street" and "downtown."[59] They note how the image of welcoming "third places" belies the actual segregation and inequality that has often occurred in these settings. There is a reason civil rights protestors picked lunch counters as the place to make their stand, after all. These scholars further note that continual change has characterized these markets every bit as much as the continuity and stability we like to associate with them. Some argue that the wholesome image we have of local shops and their friendly proprietors merely diverts our attention from the more pernicious forces of global capitalism in which those commercial actors are embedded. They point to how this wholesome image has been commoditized and sold around the world, most explicitly in Walt Disney World's ersatz "Main Street U.S.A."[60] According to this academic literature, the idea so many of us have when we call to mind street-level markets of our past owes more to the work of American storytellers than to our actual lived experiences. We think we are recalling our home-town Main Street, but what we are actually picturing is Thornton Wilder's creation in *Our Town* or the charming downtown of Bedford Falls in *It's A Wonderful Life*. When it comes to our street-level markets, it turns out we are, all of us, romantic poets like Longfellow.

Notably, the novel *Harvard Square* wades right into this scholarly conversation. Aciman's characters constantly contrast the authenticity they associate with their beloved Paris—and the authenticity they feel they have at least somewhat found in Harvard Square's Café Algiers—with what they consider to be the "jumbo-ersatz" nature of most American culture.[61] At the same time, though, the story is told from the perspective of the graduate student who is now an adult, visiting Harvard Square years later with his teenage son. He admits to the reader that his recollections of that earlier time and place may owe more to sentiment and nostalgia than to anything else. He catches himself romanticizing the Harvard Square of his youth just as he knows he and his friend had romanticized Paris all those years ago: "We blamed Cambridge for not being Paris, the way over the years I've blamed many places for not being Cambridge."[62] He knows that he came to love his time at Harvard and in Harvard Square only "after, not during" his time there, but it is that "magical after love" he wants to convey to his son now. It is through that "magical after love" he now looks back and contemplates what it all meant to him and his life.[63]

That a novel by the name *Harvard Square* concerns itself so directly with the human tendency to sentimentalize tells us something about its name-sake. What scholars say about Americans' relationship with "Main Street" is perhaps especially true about the relationship people have had with Harvard Square over the years: It is a market that for multiple reasons lends itself to being romanticized. For starters, a university's presence intensifies the attachments certain people form with the local marketplace and the establishments in it. Like the narrator in Aciman's novel, students passing through Harvard Square do so at a unique moment in their lives. They are forging formative bonds and opening themselves to new experiences. For some, Harvard Square is their first home away from home. It is a period they are apt to recall vividly and look back upon fondly. Every year come reunion time, there is a crop of alumni walking the streets like Aciman's character, reminiscing about the times they had in the places they once frequented.

What's more, it is easy to be enchanted by the sense of history in a place with a nearly four-hundred-year-old institution sitting in the middle of it. The Boston-area architecture critic Robert Campbell has said that when you walk through Harvard Square, you can sense "the richness and depth of time. . . . You feel you're in a place with a past. You sense an ongoing narrative." He's not wrong. Of course, every street-level market—every small-town Main Street and every urban village—is a sort of palimpsest in brick and mortar. When we stroll along the sidewalk or step into a shop, we also step back in time to what was there before and assume a role in an ongoing narrative. Part of our attachment to these places is an attachment to that past—to the particular narrative of which we have become a part. Harvard Square's narrative is perhaps an especially rich and compelling one to step into. Scholars tell us that part of the appeal of "Main Street" in our culture is that we have linked it to fundamental American values of democracy and community.[64] How much more connected to the story and romance of American democracy can a street-level market be than one around which thousands of Minutemen and George Washington himself encamped during the early months of the Revolution? Longfellow saw the story of America in this little village marketplace, and it was a large part of its appeal for him.

Even for those who stroll through Harvard Square unaware of that legacy, it is almost impossible to miss the narrative thread of the place. Harvard Square's savvy merchants have always known how to tell and how to sell a good story. It is hard not to feel at least some mystique stepping into shops and restaurants in which framed black-and-white photographs on the walls and chatty proprietors behind the counters are quick to remind you of the famous individuals who once sat or stood exactly where you are now sitting or standing. In a single afternoon of shopping in Harvard Square, one can learn where, back in the day, JFK or Teddy Roosevelt or Julia Child or the Aga Khan or Barack Obama liked to have their clothes tailored or their hair trimmed or their pints filled.

Something people often like to say about downtowns is that "the faces change but the people stay the same." That statement is more false than true for many communities. It is especially untrue for communities that have undergone rapid residential turnover and demographic change. However, the presence of a centuries-old institution like Harvard may make it more true in Harvard Square than in a lot of places. For hundreds of years, the market there has been catering to more or less the same customer set: the university and its students, faculty, and staff; a small number of wealthy residents living nearby; and the many commuters and visitors from around the area and around the world who pass through and stay a while. Even as the people occupying these roles have turned over continually, the roles themselves have been mostly stable.

In 1956, a man named Joe McCarthy (but not the one you're thinking of) wrote a piece about Harvard Square for *Holiday* magazine. McCarthy had grown up there in the 1920s and recently returned for a short visit. After noting that, sadly, one or two "characters" from the old days were no longer there, including the secondhand clothes peddler Max Keezer and an always-dependable taxicab driver named Nappy Williams, McCarthy continued: "But everybody else is still there—the Radcliffe girl reading Kafka as she waits for her date in front of the Coop, the squash player on his way to the courts with this topcoat flapping against his bare legs . . . the visiting chemist from Cal Tech, the visiting mathematician from New Delhi . . . the two sophomores discussing the French movie they saw the night before at the Brattle Hall."[65]

McCarthy did not know that Radcliffe girl reading Kafka, obviously. But he recognized her for the role she was playing in the ongoing story of Harvard Square, and he was grateful to find the story of which he had once been a part still there, still recognizable, still unfolding. McCarthy concluded his walk down memory lane by recalling the "perennial graduate students" who never appeared to him in any great hurry to acquire their degrees and disembark on their careers. "The truth of the matter, of course, was simply they could not face the thought of leaving Cambridge," he wrote.[66]

In nostalgic magazine profiles like this and in best-selling novels like Aciman's, in devotional documentaries and in Oscar-winning blockbusters, over countless drinks among old friends and roommates and on countless strolls through its crooked little streets, Harvard Square has, probably more than most street-level markets, been recalled with a certain sentimental flair. Yet if it is true that Americans have always romanticized their street-level markets to some extent—and if it is true that that is a part of our complicated relationship with these markets—well then, isn't Harvard Square just the "best little downtown" to study if we want to understand that relationship? It may have one of the most intense love stories of them all.

THE STREET-LEVEL PERSPECTIVE AS ANALYTICAL STRATEGY

My original motivation for this project was personal and exploratory. I wanted to understand the changes I saw happening in the street-level market outside my front door, a street-level market I had long adored. I also wanted—felt I *needed*—to understand my own complicated feelings about those changes. Something told me that was going to be as important for making sense of what was going on.

In my early musings, I came across Mo Lotman's 2009 book, *Harvard Square: An Illustrated History Since 1950*. In it, Lotman presents stunning street-level photographs of Harvard Square from the 1950s through the early 2000s, along with vivid descriptions of many of the businesses that operated during those years. Lotman's thoughtful commentary on the Square's evolution raised some of the same questions I had been mulling: What had changed? What was the same? What did it all mean? The book inspired me to pursue those questions further. I wondered what I might learn about all markets were I to do an even deeper dive into this particular one, and I was curious to see what might be gleaned by applying a theoretical lens to the inquiry.

I quickly encountered a problem, however. The academic theories of markets I knew from economics and economic sociology rarely bring the camera down to the street level. They tend to see and theorize markets at the industry or commodity level, offering their version of the aerial shot.[67] To understand the markets in our lives, we are taught to analyze the market structure of the publishing industry or the insurance industry or the pharmaceutical industry. We learn to see the dynamics of supply and demand, substitution effects, creative destruction, and capital flows at that level of the economy. These theories help us be more informed market participants. But they don't tell us much about the anthropological—let alone the mythic, poetic—experiences we have as we make our way through the markets of our lives.

Like the philosophical writings of de Certeau, the work of the economic historian Fernand Braudel suggests an alternative approach. Braudel saw economic life as layered. "One might say that the economy of the entire world is a succession of different altitudes as in a relief map," he once wrote.[68] In his sweeping, three-volume history, *Civilization & Capitalism, 15th–18th Century*, he chronicled not just the emergence of multinational capitalism at what he considered the highest level of the economy but also the hustle and bustle of market activity that lay closer to what he called the "ground level" of people's material lives.[69] Braudel, in short, brought his gaze to the local street-level markets of the period he was studying. He profiled the open-air markets, bourses, and fairs, as well as the peddlers and traders who circulated through them and the shops that popped up around them.

As soon as one begins attending to the hustle and bustle of life at the ground level, of course, it becomes instantly apparent that this plane is not so one-dimensional itself. It is composed of multiple perspectives, and it must be seen from these vantage points to be fully understood. One of my favorite books is Peter Bearman's *Doormen*, in which Bearman brings his and his readers' gaze down to the ground floor of New York City high-rises where doormen, building managers, residents, and visitors come together in intricately complex choreography to form the small social world that is the lobby. By looking at the lobby up close and from these different perspectives, Bearman is able to use this little world as a powerful lever for understanding the much larger social structures in which we are all embedded. Instead of a residential lobby, in this book we will take one, small, street-level market and look at it from the perspectives of the different actors who make it up. We will see it through the eyes of its consumers, including the long-term residents who live nearby and the shorter-term students and visitors who pass through, as well as from the perspective of its merchants, its commercial property owners and developers, and more.

Existing work in urban and cultural sociology has contemplated the vagaries of life at the street level outside its building lobbies. However, this work has often overlooked the commercial market there. A typical sociological treatment of Harvard Square would be to tell the story of Harvard Square the *place* or Harvard Square the *neighborhood*. Harvard Square *the market* would receive a chapter or two about how its shops and stores contribute to the character of the place.[70] In most sociological accounts, if the market is seen at all, it is seen through the lens of other important topics that have captured the scholar's interest more—topics like urban politics, gentrification, small-town decline, racial inequality, consumer culture and mass consumption, or global capitalism.[71] Rarely do scholars in this tradition assign commercial markets a leading role. Rarely do they theorize those markets directly.

To their credit, a number of these studies do expose the deep attachments people form at the street level. However, because they are not focused on the commercial market, they do not attend to its emotional registers either. The scholar's analytical lens trains our attention on the emotions and moral sentiments that arise from things like residential displacement, racism, and socioeconomic inequality. The commercial market sitting at the street level may appear as a background character in, or a product (oftentimes, victim) of, other cultural and economic dramas unfolding. Never, though, is it the central love interest of the story.

This book casts the market in a leading role. It privileges the *market* in the *market*place. Like any other, this view will be a partial one, highlighting certain things at the expense of others. However, because so few studies have made the street-level market so central to their inquiry, it will reveal things that have been obscured or overlooked from those other vantage points. As we zoom in on the particular human actors who have been a part of this little shopping district over the years, the human emotions of market life will pop into sharp relief. Part 1 will use the case of Harvard Square to reveal a first layer of the relationship we have with our street-level markets, exploring why these markets so often provoke the disquieting sentiment that they are not what they used to be. Part 2 will dive into key moments in Harvard Square's history to probe the deeper ways we attach to these markets, unraveling why, at times, they can provoke extreme expressions of love and outrage.

The perspective offered will be a new one. Economics has left us empty-handed when it comes to making sense of the complicated feelings so many of us experience in relation to the markets with which we interact. Not only do most economic theories of markets hold their gaze high above the street level, but they also fail to contemplate our emotional attachments to markets at any level. Meanwhile, sociology has contemplated people's emotional attachments to place but missed the market and, along with it, all the tricky attachments people have to the market in the place, the market that helps make the place. Both fields lack a theory for why someone might compose a poem about a market. Both miss the complicated love story that lies at the heart of their subject matter. This book heads straight for that love story.

PART 1

A Lot of the Same, A Lot of Change

Chapter Two

NOT WHAT IT USED TO BE

On a cold March night in 2019, I made my way across the icy grounds of the old Episcopal Divinity School on Brattle Street. I was headed to yet another basement meeting about the fate of Harvard Square. Forecasts predicted a foot of wet snow that evening, and the gothic spire of St. John's Chapel was already fading into the gathering gray as I arrived.

The divinity school had operated on this land from 1867 until 2017 when it closed. In the years leading up to its closure, the school struggled financially and sold some of its property to nearby Lesley University, which bought the remainder of the campus in 2018. Despite its new owner, the campus was largely unchanged from its theological days. The tree-lined grounds still had an ethereal hush about them, especially on a night like this.

About seventy other people—mostly longtime Cambridge residents in their sixties or beyond but also some younger blood and a few city officials mixed in—had come out for the meeting that evening. After stomping off the slush from our boots and shaking off our damp coats, we settled into the rows of assembled folding chairs and waited for the Harvard Square Neighborhood Association meeting to begin.

The Neighborhood Association was a recent reincarnation of an earlier neighborhood organization, the Harvard Square Defense Fund.* The Defense

---

* In this book, organizations with "Harvard Square" in their names (e.g., the Harvard Square Neighborhood Association) will be introduced by their full names but often abbreviated by dropping the "Harvard Square" (e.g., the Neighborhood Association).

Fund's activities had petered out about a decade earlier as its original members became too old to carry on their fight against overdevelopment in Harvard Square, although its most spirited leader, a feisty octogenarian named Pebble Gifford, had remained an outspoken critic of various development projects over the years. In 2016, amidst growing concerns about the Square, a small group of concerned citizens including a Harvard professor, a local architect, and a Cambridge activist with a past in movement politics decided it was time to pick up the torch and begin the fight anew.[1] With Pebble's blessing, the Harvard Square Defense Fund was reborn as the Harvard Square Neighborhood Association.

It was now three years since the Neighborhood Association's founding and two years since the Equity One meeting that had so rattled me. During that time the worrisome changes in Harvard Square had only accelerated. Another large, outside real estate investor had entered the commercial property market in 2017 shortly after Equity One. It soon began raising the rent in its buildings to levels some local business tenants could not afford. Larger corporate entities that could afford those rents were moving in. Crema Café, a popular coffee shop run by two local women and known for its cozy, crunchy vibe, closed its doors in 2018.[2] A few months later, Crema's old space was leased to a different coffee shop with a different vibe—the New York–based coffee chain Bluestone Lane that described itself as a "coffee, café, and lifestyle brand" and which, at the time, had more than thirty other locations across the country and $19.5 million in venture capital financing to fund its further expansion.[3] A few doors down, a locally owned clothing boutique closed, and a Patagonia store was rumored to be opening in its space next year.

Not surprisingly, these changes rattled a community already on edge. The fate of the Square's local independent businesses seemed increasingly uncertain. Many worried this harkened the end of the Harvard Square they had known and loved for years. The local press kept a steady beat on each property sale and business closure, speculating on the meaning of it all in pieces with headlines such as "More of the Square for Sale" (*Boston Globe*) and "An Uncertain Future for Harvard Square" (*Harvard Magazine*).[4]

Harvard College's student newspaper, the *Harvard Crimson*, ran features on the topic. One piece, titled "The Transformation of Harvard Square," lamented that many of the defining features of the Square could not withstand the monetary pressure developers and national chains were bringing to the marketplace. It was impossible to preserve the Square's historic character, "when rising rents and exorbitant land values force out businesses that are decades-old mainstays in favor of trendy coffee shops," the student jour-nalists wrote.[5] The loss of "unique establishments with decades of history in the Square" was the loss of "the unique charm" they and others cherished about the place.

In a separate feature that ran just a few weeks prior to the meeting I was now attending, *Crimson* reporters interviewed local merchants about the current climate of rising rents and large, deep-pocketed competitors. The paper concluded: "As the face of the Square changes, small business owners have no choice but to confront a version of the neighborhood's future that may no longer save space for them."[6]

That was not a version of the Square's future the Neighborhood Associa-tion wanted to see. Its members were distressed by what was being lost, and tonight's meeting had been called to discuss the situation. The group's board had grown especially frustrated in recent years by what they saw as the Har-vard Square Business Association's position that market-driven change was inevitable and simply had to be accepted and adapted to. From the Neigh-borhood Association's perspective, something had to be done to stop exist-ing businesses from being driven out of the market. To raise awareness and help start a conversation, the group had invited a panel of local merchants to talk to its membership that night and share their experiences in the current environment.

Susan Corcoran, owner of the Black Ink gift shop, spoke first. A lithe, graceful woman with long, striking gray hair, Corcoran looked like a former ballet dancer ("trapeze and yoga," she would later tell me), and her store's aesthetic had the same blend of grace and whimsy that she did. Black Ink carried what Corcoran called "unexpected necessities"—things like beau-tiful wrapping papers, letterpress and silk-screened gift cards, ceramic tea sets, and old-timey toys such as Guillow's balsa wood model airplane kits and Kewpie dolls. In the '60s, Harvard Square had supported numerous quirky small gift shops whose wares reflected the tastes and personalities of their proprietors, but that model was mostly a thing of the past, and in 2019 Susan's shop stood as one of the few callbacks to it.

That night, Corcoran introduced herself to the audience as the owner of Black Ink but also "its chief buyer, bookkeeper, maintenance worker, and janitor," referencing the number of roles she played each day as an indepen-dent proprietor.[7] Black Ink was her life, she told the crowd, and it was now facing an existential crisis. She could not afford the rent her new landlord was asking.

As she spoke, Corcoran's poise gave way to passion. She took aim at the Square's commercial property owners and the big-name brands they seemed to prefer as tenants. Representatives of some of these entities had recently been quoted in the press, saying they wanted to help Harvard Square by "activating" retail in the shopping district while also maintaining the Square's authenticity.[8] Corcoran bristled at such talk. "The Square has a wealth of experienced retailers. We don't need their 'activation,'" she said. "What we need to do is activate ourselves and our voices to tell people what we are losing because of [them]." And, as for authenticity, that was precisely what local shops like Black Ink offered Harvard Square, she said. Only now, "it's becoming impossible for us" because of the decisions of these larger players.

Most of all, Corcoran was sick of hearing that the changes affecting her business were just the result of natural market evolution, she told the crowd. "Some individuals would have us believe that these changes are inevitable, that we just have to embrace them—that it's our fault if we can't survive them." That's not the right way to think about it, she argued. The changes were "not coming as a result of real choice, but because our choices are being taken away from us by big corporate entities and their investors."

Tom Brush addressed the crowd next. Brush owned the small, no-frills burger joint Flat Patties, as well as Felipe's Taqueria—a low-cost burrito bar so popular with students that its primary aesthetic was deafening noise, and whose hyperefficient staff made burritos and tacos to order so rapidly that customers often arrived at the cash register unsure of what they were holding.[9] Brush was also a co-investor in Crema Café alongside his daughter and her friend, who had run it before it closed. All three businesses had the same private equity firm as their landlord that Corcoran did.

I had not met Brush before this meeting, but I had heard of him. He'd been described to me by several individuals as a "serious businessman," and looking at him now, he struck me as the sort of highly competent individual who would be as comfortable in front of a financial model as a table saw. Compared to Corcoran's emotional appeal, Brush cut a more stoic figure that evening, though he too expressed concern. He told the crowd that small businesses like his face a lot of ups and downs. Larger, well-capitalized firms might be able to pay high fixed rents, Brush said, but in his experience small independent operations like his needed flexibility. That's why he preferred leases with a lower base rent in exchange for sharing a percentage of sales with the landlord. Explaining Crema's closure, Brush acknowledged that the café's sales had "slipped a bit" in recent years. When it came time to renegotiate, the café's new landlord wanted an overall rent that was beyond what the business could generate.[10] In a matter-of-fact tone, Tom said that Flat Patties might meet a similar fate when its lease expired within the next year: "I would love to stay, but it is what it is. I don't know what will stop all this."[11] He understood that landlords like his had their own investors to satisfy, he said, but he also wondered where things were going. Would the Square be all national chains at some point? Would the only businesses willing to pay the market's rising rents be "big brands who are using these spaces as billboards—as a place to establish their brand"?

As the night wore on, other local business owners stood up one after another and shared their experiences and their concerns. The co-owners of Karma Yoga Studio, located on the other side of Harvard Square from Black Ink and Felipe's, spoke of the vulnerability they felt in the current market. Even though their building hadn't yet changed hands, their rents had risen with the market, and they worried that any day they might wake up to learn they had a new landlord. One of them said, "We've seen our rents go up and as a local business there is nothing to protect us. We know our building is a desirable developer opportunity, and we have no idea if we will be here in another year. . . . It feels like the market is pushing this and there's no stopping it. How do local businesses survive? What levers do we have?"

Other merchants, including Laura Donohue, expressed their frustration and anger. Now in her fifties, Donohue had an undergraduate degree in economics from Harvard and an MBA from MIT. Sick of the corporate world and wanting to be her own boss, she'd bought Bob Slate Stationer in 2011 from the family that founded the business back in 1933. She had loved the store ever since her student days when she would go there to stock up on her favorite pens and notebooks before the start of each semester. Running the business in 2019 was a different story though. Bob Slate's building was still held by the family trust that had owned it for decades, so Donohue did not have a new landlord to contend with directly; but, like Karma Yoga, her business still had to contend with all the market externalities those other new landlords were creating. She worried, for example, that the major redevelopment project starting next door to Bob Slate would depress foot traffic and cut into her sales and that the soaring rent in the nearby buildings in which Black Ink and Felipe's operated would eventually put upward pressure on her rent as well.

Most of all, like Corcoran, Donohue was hurt by the narrative she kept hearing that businesses like hers were relics of the past and that all of this change was just a reflection of creative destruction and the natural evolution of a market economy. "I hate the term 'creative destruction,'" she told me on a break after learning I studied economic and cultural change at MIT. To the crowd, she defended small-business owners like herself: Some people "act like we are afraid of change, like we are failing. Let me tell you, I'm not failing. I've been competing with big businesses like Staples and Blick [Art Supplies] for years. I'm working hard. I'm fighting. But I can't also fight with a huge developer."

After the last of the business owners spoke, the panel's moderator opened discussion to the audience. Several people asked about the feasibility of collective or community ownership of real estate as well as land trusts. Might that protect small-business owners better than the open market, they wanted to know? Several others asked about the political viability of commercial rent control. One individual asked whether the Neighborhood Association might somehow encourage more ownership by nonprofit trusts or Harvard University. There was talk of forming a committee to look further into these issues.

As I listened, it seemed to me most of the comments were made with an air of somber resignation. It was as if no one was taking their own suggestions entirely seriously—as if they knew the ideas were likely unrealistic, but they had no better ones to offer themselves or the business owners facing them. It was as if everyone was thinking what the Karma Yoga owner had said: "It feels like the market is pushing this and there's no stopping it."

∼

I left the meeting that night depressed. In subsequent months, reports of Harvard Square's imminent demise were hard to escape. Residents and business owners despaired over the "mallification" of the Square, while the local press continued to cover each new business closure and empty storefront. Even city officials sounded powerless and defeated by the situation. In June 2019, Marc McGovern, then-mayor of Cambridge, voiced his concerns publicly, saying he was worried the Square was being taken over by "large national and international chains that can pay top dollar for a spot in the busy square, at the expense of quirky independent stores."[12] That same month, a local TV show called *Greater Boston* ran a segment titled "The Changing Face of Harvard Square."[13] After ticking through a list of cherished cornerstones that had closed, the host put the question to viewers: "Is the historic neighborhood losing its personality? . . . Is it the end of Harvard Square as we know it, or just a new chapter?" Most people I ran into were saying it was the end.

Something else happened during these months, too, however. I began to dive into the historical archives. The Cambridge Room of the Cambridge Public Library has an impressive collection of old Cambridge newspapers dating back more than a hundred years. I started to read all the articles on Harvard Square I could find from the early 1900s on. I also began visiting the Cambridge Historical Society to make my way through the archives of the Harvard Square Business Association and the Harvard Square Defense Fund. Almost as soon as I started, the depression I'd felt leaving the Neighborhood Association meeting was replaced by a new feeling: *deja vu*.

It first hit me when I stumbled upon some news articles from the late 1910s and early 1920s and the minutes to the Harvard Square Business Association's (called the Harvard Square Business *Men's* Association at that time) 1920 annual meeting. By all accounts, rents were on the rise throughout the market at that time. Prominent properties were changing hands among both local and outside developers, all eager to capture more income from their investments. Long-standing businesses were being displaced in the process. In March 1920, for example, a set of properties located on the corner of Massachusetts Avenue and what is today JFK Street was sold to a syndicate of New York real estate investors.[14] These properties were home to several Harvard Square mainstays, and, almost immediately, the new landlord began raising the rent, in some cases to double or more what the tenants had previously been paying.[15] Among those affected was the grocery firm J. H. Wyeth & Co. It could not afford the rent hike and was given a thirty-day order to vacate to make way for a new tenant that could.

Wyeth & Co. had been in the Square for more than half a century. In 1898, a devastating fire had almost destroyed the business, but its owners moved the shop to the corner where it now stood and rebuilt it. In the years after the fire, it became known for its quality produce and the "high ideals" of its proprietors.[16] By 1920 it had become a Harvard Square institution in the minds of many shoppers. However, when Wyeth & Co.'s new landlord raised the rent that year, the firm's owners did not look for a new location like they had after the fire. This time, they just closed up shop. James Wyeth, the firm's founder, was ninety years old by then, retired and spending much of his time in Florida, sitting amidst his beloved orange trees. His partner, Herbert Shepherd, had been with the business for forty-five years and remained active, but Shepherd knew the grocery business was not what it used to be. Like many other local grocers at the time, Wyeth & Co. had been struggling of late.

J. H. Wyeth & Co. Grocers, 1907. Courtesy of Cambridge Historical Commission, Boston Elevated Railway Collection.

A new market innovation was upending their industry: grocery chains that leveraged their scale to outcompete small shops like Wyeth.

Wyeth & Co.'s closure came as a blow to the community. Some families had been getting their groceries there for generations, and customers knew the shop's owners personally. The *Cambridge Tribune* took a moment to mourn the store's passing in April 1920. Wyeth was one of those businesses that helped make Harvard Square such a special and "unusual" place, the *Tribune* observed.[17] Although no one yet knew what business would move into Wyeth's former space, it was thought likely to be a chain store. The paper's staff conceded that even as "the closing out of this business comes about as one of the almost inevitable changes in business life," they felt "a personal sense of loss" all the same.

For a while it looked like Wyeth's neighbor, Amee Brothers, might meet a similar fate. Amee Brothers had been one of Longfellow's regular stops on his strolls through the marketplace. It was a newsstand, stationer, and bookshop—and, like Wyeth, a Harvard Square institution. Brothers John and Bert Amee were the second set of Amee brothers to run the business, and they had been working side-by-side in the shop since they were boys.[18] Local residents, prominent faculty, and students followed Longfellow's footsteps, making it a habit to stop by the shop each day to browse, catch up on the latest news, and visit with the popular proprietors. When academic or political debates broke out in the store, as they often did, the two brothers were known to jump right in (John, quietly, gently; Bert, directly, bluntly). They and their shop were a part of the community, a stable part. Come reunion time, alumni always swung by to check in and visit, confident they would find John or Bert behind the counter.[19]

Yet now it was unclear whether Amee Brothers would be around for the next reunion. The new landlord was asking for double the shop's prior rent, and the business could not afford it. Just in time, the unexpected departure of a restaurant on nearby Brattle Street opened up an alternative. Grateful for the reprieve, John and Bert quickly relocated the shop and carried on. Even still, the move was unsettling and marked a meaningful change for some Harvard Square denizens. The business had been in its prior location with its familiar sign hanging over the door for decades. A May 8, 1920, article in the *Cambridge Chronicle* noted, "Without the sign of Amee Brothers staring them in the face, Harvard Square will look queer to most people."[20]

Amee Brothers and Wyeth & Co. were not the only businesses sent reeling from soaring rents in this period, and residents and merchants alike were concerned. In April 1920, the Harvard Square Business Men's Association decided to dedicate its annual meeting to discussing the Square's considerable "rent problem."[21] Opening the meeting, one of the group's leaders spoke about the "enormous increases" seen around the market. He admitted he did not know what was a fair rent for stores in the locality, but he thought it was an important question that needed to be tackled.

After a number of members shared their thoughts on the rent situation, Edwin Sage, another Harvard Square grocer, spoke up. Alluding to the fate of his former competition, Wyeth & Co., Sage broached the chain-store issue that was compounding the rent problem for shopkeepers like himself. Sage's own grocery store would remain in Harvard Square (and in his family) until 2000 when—amidst that later era's own discussion of chain stores and rising rents—it finally closed. That spring evening in 1920, however, he was already detailing the frustrations of competing against these new large-scale entities. In his words, chains "took the cream of the trade, leaving the skim milk for the local merchants."

Not everyone in the Business Men's Association shared Sage's perspective. Several of the businessmen argued that it was local merchants' responsibility to adapt to the constantly changing market environment, whether that meant new competitors or rising rents. Thomas Hadley, a realtor and property owner, said that he had sympathy for the men up against chain stores, but, even so, change was inevitable and everyone must adapt to it: "We must face the situation as it is. We cannot do business as we did even ten years ago but must constantly study and devise new methods." Hadley believed in the disciplining power of the market, arguing that the "invasion of Harvard Square by the chain stores" would drive businessmen such as himself to study their businesses more closely.[22] "Few men who really study the conditions and then give their customers what they want fail to succeed in business," he asserted.

Echoing Sage's concerns, however, was the druggist Charles Stover. Stover insisted that while some members might foolishly welcome the coming of the chain stores, the chains would "get what they wanted" of members before they were through. "Those who are up against the chain stores go through hell!" he cried out impassionedly. "They have hundreds of branches and if each pays a net profit of $1 a day, that is all they expect." Sage agreed with Stover and warned his fellow members: "Just wait until the chain stores get you . . . and then see what they do to you!"

The discussion that evening wove back and forth between the emerging threat of chain stores and the rising commercial rents in Harvard Square. The painter J. Leo McDonald took the rent issue to heart and seemed particularly concerned that more outside developers might try to enter the market and gain control of it. He suggested that the businessmen join together and protect their interests by buying up some of the land bordering the Square's main streets, "or else some 'smart man' from New York" would come along and buy it and raise the rents on them all even more.

Hadley, the real estate man who had argued for the disciplining force of market competition from outside chains, appeared to share McDonald's concern with outside real estate investors. Like McDonald, he suggested the local businessmen unite to buy up property and secure their footing. Noting that there was one big piece of property in Harvard Square for sale at that time, Hadley tried to rally the group, declaring they should all "get together and take it!"

There appears to have been no movement on Hadley's proposal. At the end of the long evening, the membership voted to form a committee "to consider the rental question" further.

∽

As I read the 1920 meeting notes and news clippings, it was impossible not to be struck by the parallels to what I was seeing and hearing in the present market. Nearly one hundred years had passed, but the conversations were so similar. In both periods, citizens and merchants expressed concern about the transformation of Harvard Square in the face of rising rents, chain stores, and even outside real estate investors. In both periods, the community mourned the loss of long-lived local establishments and despaired about what that meant for the Harvard Square they had known and loved for years. In both periods, local capitalists grasped for seemingly anti-capitalist solutions such as collective ownership of property.

I didn't yet know what to make of these parallels, but one obvious question came to mind right away: What had transpired in the meantime? At the outset of this project, I had intended to study the changes unfolding in contemporary Harvard Square. I always knew that inquiry would need to be informed by the historical context, but I did not expect to find myself going down a rabbit hole of historical research chasing a puzzle I now felt compelled to unravel. Yet that's exactly what happened the further I dove into the historical materials.

Soon I came across a discussion in the mid-1930s that echoed that of the 1920s and the current market. In 1936, sixteen years after Wyeth's closing and the businessmen's meeting about chain stores, property ownership, and rising rents, Amee Brothers bookshop joined Wyeth in the graveyard of Harvard Square establishments. The local developers of the building to which Amee had relocated in 1920 were now planning to raze that building to make way for a new one and for new tenants who could pay higher rents.[23] The situation disturbed a number of people in the community. Unlike the waning James Wyeth in 1920, Bert Amee was a "hale and hearty" seventy-two-year-old with no desire to retire.[24] However, his business could not afford the higher rents it would have to pay going forward. So, he made the difficult decision to close the store that had been his and his (now late) brother's life's work. Those who knew Bert personally felt the loss acutely. "The march of progress has cut him off untimely," the *Boston Herald* mourned.

Despite the ravaged national economy during these years, Harvard Square was seeing a fair amount of new development projects and new businesses owing to the university's expansion. Other long-standing businesses like Amee Brothers were getting squeezed out of the changing market. "Harvard Square is a different place today," the *Herald* observed: "The old stores, the old friends are gone. Restaurants and liquor stores crowd the landscape and one-arm lunchrooms are elbow-to-elbow with [the new university buildings]."

Amee Brothers had been a part of the fabric of Harvard Square for more than six decades. The community lamented the store's passing and worried about what it meant just as they had sixteen years earlier when Wyeth & Co. closed. In an obituary of sorts, the *Boston Globe* memorialized the beloved bookshop recalling its "unique blend of commercialism and sociability."[25] Striking a similar note, the *Cambridge Tribune* remarked that Amee's closing represented the loss of an "institution rich in tradition" and yet "another change for the Square."[26] As it had when reporting Wyeth's closing, the *Tribune* expressed a sense of wistful acceptance, concluding: "This firm rich in its associations is going out of business. . . . It will make a change in the Square, but in a few years the old will be almost forgotten, so readily do we adapt ourselves to change."

Do we adapt ourselves to change so readily? Comparing the discussions of the 1920s and 1930s to today's, I wondered. Weren't people getting upset about many of the same things over and over again? The deeper I dove into the historical archives, the more I had to confront that question. In the coming weeks, as I continued to make my way through the old newspaper clippings and organizational files, I discovered that for a long while now public dialogue about Harvard Square has had a distinctive leitmotif. Again and again, people have lamented that Harvard Square is "not what it used to be." Again and again, they have attributed this upsetting development to the loss of the Square's beloved local establishments at the hands of rising rents and powerful outside economic forces closing in on the marketplace. Harvard Square has suffered many deaths over the past century.

I came across the leitmotif in the 1950s. In remarks prepared for the fortieth anniversary gala of the Business Men's Association, one of its founding members, Fred Olsson, looked out at the current market and didn't like what he saw.[27] Gone were the "lovable shopkeepers" who had once operated in the Square but were now departed. In the old days, Olsson told the association's membership, "the character of the people who traded there, as well as that of the merchants, marked the Square as unique." That smaller, simpler, quieter marketplace of years past was plagued by fewer problems than their current "rocket powered" one. In Olsson's opinion, the Square just wasn't what it used to be.

I came across the leitmotif again in the 1970s. Now, however, the Harvard Square of 1950 that had so upset Olsson was the golden age to which some people wanted to return. In the early '70s, residents were mobilizing against several new development projects they feared would displace existing businesses and destroy the Square. A 1972 *New York Times* article about community opposition to one of these projects suggested people's fears were especially acute because the Square's "character has already been changed in the last year or two as many small businesses have been forced out by rising rents and the financial muscle of chain restaurants."[28]

That same year, Cambridge's city manager, John Corcoran, appointed a volunteer citizens task force to address these concerns. Five years before I was born and twelve years before my and my father's Sunday walks through the Square would begin, Corcoran expressed regret that, "Many years ago, the people of Cambridge would spend many of their Sundays walking and relaxing at the Common and along our riverbank. Harvard Square was an interesting location where business flourished and the people of Cambridge enjoyed many leisure hours."[29]

The student staff of the *Harvard Crimson* agreed with the city manager that the Square wasn't what it used to be, although they mourned the loss of something slightly different than Sunday morning strolls. In a July 1972 piece, the *Crimson* reported that Harvard Square had been so "commercialized" over the past several years that "modern facades of state or nationwide retail chains" now stood where old storefronts and restaurants had, only three or four years ago, served as the staging ground and gathering place for "movement culture" and "New Left politicos."[30]

The beat went on. By the late 1980s, people were looking back to those supposedly dark days of the early '70s and recalling *them* as golden ones. A 1987 *Boston Globe* article titled "Harvard Square Losing Its Funky Look" quoted a local resident and business owner who recalled: "In the 70s, we had all these nice stores, restaurants, and coffee shops and every one of them was successful. Then, the landlords started to get greedy and raised their rents every other year and things started to change."[31] Gone were the places that had given Harvard Square the "fabric and charm" it once had, the article reported; the loss of such establishments was "destroying the uniqueness that attracted people from all over."

Another article in 1987 speculated about "The Death of Harvard Square." Pondering whether there was any hope, it asked, "Can Harvard Square be saved?"[32] It then went on to describe the community's outrage that real estate developers and property owners were destroying the Square's unique "charm" with exorbitant rents such that only national chains could afford to operate there. A group of residents and shopkeepers were once again busy lobbying the city and taking developers to court to try to stop this desecration of their beloved Square. Others, however, felt the battle was already lost. Sari Abul-Jubein, owner of the Harvard Square restaurant Casablanca, told the *Globe* reporter, "Forget it! It's too late. The Square is gone, the developers have killed whatever charm it had."[33]

More than a decade later, Harvard Square was still with us—albeit on life support, according to some. In 2000, the owner of Cardullo's Gourmet Shoppe warned that rents were going up, and "there may well be a day when the only places that can afford to be in Harvard Square will be the chains."[34] A Cambridge city councilor told the *Cambridge Chronicle* that she felt a sense of "profound loss and disappointment" looking out at Harvard Square. In recent years it had lost its character and become "clearly an outdoor mall."[35]

Five years on, in 2005, the Associated Press ran a piece: "Denizens Decry Harvard Square Decline: High Rents, Chains Drive Out Tenants."[36] A local shopkeeper made a dire prediction: "Harvard Square, unless something drastic is done, is dying." The Square's death was even appearing in children's literature now. In Ann Downer's 2003 *Hatching Magic*, a wizard named Gideon laments: "In the olden days before the Gap and its ilk took root in Harvard Square, you really could find a decent substitute for eye of newt."[37]

During my first pass through the historical materials, I became so fascinated by what I began calling in my notes the Harvard Square "Death Discourse," I pinched a nerve in my neck from sitting in the same position reading for so many days in a row. Of course, one person's fascinating can be another person's tiresome. I hired an undergraduate research assistant to do her own pass through the historical records and worried she might quit from boredom. After a month or so of work, she told me in a twenty-year-old's exasperated tone, "It's just so much of the same."

She was not the only one to feel this way. Another puzzling thing I was discovering in my research was that denizens themselves seemed increasingly aware and weary of the recurrent nature of all this talk—and yet still the talk persisted. Ever since starting my fieldwork, I had noticed that present-day residents, business owners, and city officials would often begin their expressions of concern with qualifiers such as, "I know we've been saying this for years but . . ." One long-term property manager told me that he was living through "at least the fifth death of Harvard Square that I can remember." He joked about how worked up some members of the community got over changes in the Square. A few minutes later, though, his tone turned serious and he began to tell me about the changes in today's market that he said were eroding the traditional culture of the place.

I observed this sort of tired meta-discourse in public hearings and local press coverage as well. In 2016, when City Councilor Jan Devereaux convened a hearing to discuss concerns over Harvard Square, she prefaced her remarks by saying, "I know this is a perennial conversation, but I think we've reached a point where we need to have that perennial conversation again."[38] A *Boston Globe* article that same year began: "The endless skirmish over the soul of Harvard Square is heating up again. . . . Griping that Harvard Square is not what it used to be is a virtual right of residency. More than one generation has lamented the loss of its favorite stores and restaurants."[39]

Whether it is a right or not, it certainly had become a rite. However, my research was also revealing that this was not a universally endorsed rite. I was discovering in the historical record that almost every time the Death Discourse broke out, at least some members of the community spoke up to contest it. The Square was not dying, the counterargument invariably went; it was merely evolving, as all markets naturally do. Getting upset was simply a failure to accept the inevitability of market change in our lives and the need to adapt to it.

Thomas Hadley had articulated this view in that April 1920 meeting of the Harvard Square Business Men's Association. He expressed sympathy for local merchants who were up against new chain-store competition but argued that those merchants must adapt or perish, for such was the nature of markets. Each era's Death Discourse prompted some version of Hadley's response. In 1987, before market change began decimating the print news business, Sheldon Cohen, owner of Out of Town News and then-president of what was now called the Harvard Square Business Association, was the one to voice it. Frustrated by lamentations about Harvard Square's imminent demise, Cohen offered his theory of all the constant cathecting: "It's the growth, the growth of business, the growth of Harvard Square, the growth of life. You have to look on it like the growth of a child. But some people don't like it, they just don't like change."[40] More than thirty years after that, it was the Business Association's and others' continued insistence on the inevitability of market change that prompted the Neighborhood Association to call its meeting on that gray, snowy night in 2019.

I had started this research project out of concern that Harvard Square wasn't what it used to be. It turned out Harvard Square had *always* been not what it used to be. I had been personally rattled for months because I could not reconcile my emotional reaction to the market changes I was seeing with what I knew intellectually about markets and how they work. It turned out that the internal debate I was having with myself had been simmering in this marketplace for at least a century.

Just like I had done the night of the Equity One meeting, I tried to lay the two puzzle pieces side by side: In the Harvard Square Death Discourse, everyone was talking about something they loved—something they wanted to hold onto, something they wished would not change; but they all were also talking about a market, and markets always change. Papa Turco had been right: Harvard Square had had "a lot of the same" over the years, but "a lot of change," too. Before I could make sense of what I was seeing in the current period, I would have to unravel the puzzle of why Harvard Square had always been not what it used to be and what that meant. To do that, I realized I would first need to look more carefully at all that change.

Chapter Three

THE TIMES THEY ARE (ALWAYS) A-CHANGIN'

When we walk down the streets of our local markets and pass by the signs and storefronts we have come to expect—when we peek into shop windows and see scenes unfolding that we have seen unfold many times before—it can feel as if this is how it has always been and this is how it always will be. Longfellow captured that feeling in "The Village Blacksmith." To the villagers who strolled through this little marketplace in the 1830s and '40s, it probably felt as if Dexter Pratt, the real-life blacksmith who inspired the poem, and Pratt's Brattle Street workshop were fixtures of village life, as dependable as the church bell's regular chimes, as rooted and enduring as the spreading chestnut tree that stood beside the shop.

And yet if we step out of our present moment to consider the broader sweep of time, we are apt to feel something quite different. Temporal shifts in perspective are often revealing. What would we see if we could situate ourselves at the street level and observe the passage of time? It would not be constancy, but change after change after change.

Let's start by lingering outside one single street address. What a different poem Longfellow might have written had he been able to see not just Pratt's home and workshop but also all that followed there. The building that stands at 54 Brattle Street today is a humble, wood-frame structure with two stories and a hipped roof.[1] It looks almost exactly as it did when Dexter Pratt lived there. In fact, it looks almost exactly as it did when the blacksmith *before* Pratt lived there.[2] That's probably why it felt as if a mighty smith had been there forever and would be there forevermore. But, of course, that's not how things went.

In 1847, not long after Longfellow composed his poem, Dexter Pratt died, and his blacksmith shop along with him. The workshop that stood next door to his residence was soon demolished. It was replaced first by a small house and then a larger Victorian house, which would itself be demolished a century later and replaced by a commercial building that, at various points, would be home to a dry cleaner, an antiques shop, several different clothing boutiques, a chocolate confectionery, an Indian restaurant, and an Italian restaurant.[3] Oh, and the spreading chestnut tree—that symbol of strength and endurance that stood beside the shop—it didn't make it out of the 1870s.[4] It was felled (over Longfellow's and others' objections) during a municipal street-widening project.

The smith's small residence did endure, though. It is the building we still see today from the street. Yet its story is as much about change as it is about stability. In 1870, Dexter Pratt's daughter sold the house to a Cambridge man who immediately transferred it to a woman named Mary Walker.[5] Walker knew all about change—what it was like to have unwanted changes forced brutally upon you and what it was like to spend a lifetime fighting for the change you wanted. She was a former slave. Born into bondage on a North Carolina plantation in 1818 and pregnant by age fourteen, Walker escaped in 1848 while on a trip to Philadelphia with the plantation owner and his daughters.[6] Once in Massachusetts, she found work as a dressmaker and caretaker, all the while trying desperately to free her mother and three children who remained enslaved in North Carolina. After the Civil War, she was finally reunited with two of her children. However, life in Cambridge was hard for a family of former slaves, and they were forced to move several times. When Walker saw that the old blacksmith's house at 54 Brattle Street was up for sale in 1870, she saw what Longfellow had seen in it, albeit from her very different vantage point—the promise of stability. Walker secured the property and soon had a will drawn up so that it would remain in trust, unable to be sold, until her youngest grandchild reached at least his twenty-first birthday.[7] For the next several decades, her family lived in and ran a small boarding business out of the house. The boarding business offered a stable source of income as the family found its footing in Cambridge, and in 1912, Mary Walker's youngest grandchild, by then a full-time mail carrier for the Harvard Square post office, sold the property and used the proceeds to buy a new home for himself and his wife.

At this point, a different enterprising woman stepped onto the scene at 54 Brattle Street and began running a tea room out of the property called the Cock Horse (a reference to the wooden toy horses children often played with). Born in Kentucky, Frances Gage was a slender, single woman who dressed smartly in long gowns and attractive ties and was said to "radiate efficiency" wherever she went.[8] The Cock Horse began modestly enough as a single room where five or six Harvard students would come to eat, smoke, and while away some hours of the day. However, Gage had bigger plans for her venture. By the 1920s she had built the business into a thriving restaurant that filled four rooms and drew more than two hundred patrons a day. Gage did all the menu planning and buying herself, and she oversaw a large staff of one assistant, ten waitresses, and fifteen helpers in the kitchen. Just feet from where once there had been a flaming forge and bellows blowing, and in rooms where Mary Walker's family had lived and passed through on their own journey, there now stood cooling racks for warm loaves of brown bread, an ice chest to keep salads crisp, and a pastry room of floury mist where all the restaurant's cakes and pies were prepared.

54 Brattle Street, the Cock Horse Restaurant, ca. 1937. Courtesy of Cambridge Center for Adult Education.

Gage retired in 1930, first turning her restaurant's management over to another single woman, then selling the business and property to a new owner in 1939.[9] The Cock Horse continued to operate at 54 Brattle Street throughout the 1940s, changing hands (and menus) several more times. In 1943, the then-owner asked the city whether he might be allowed to build an addition on the property so as to handle all the increased business resulting from the wartime stationing of WAVES (Women Accepted for Volunteer Service, the U.S. Navy's Women's Reserve) at nearby Radcliffe College.[10] Not long after, events around the world found their way to 54 Brattle Street even more directly.

In 1946, the Window Shop, a gift store, coffee shop, and bakery that provided employment to European refugees, moved in and took the place of the Cock Horse. The Window Shop had been operating elsewhere in the Square since 1939, when four faculty wives with $65 in pooled capital and a desire to help families fleeing Nazi Europe opened a small, one-room shop.[11] The idea was to give refugee women a place to work and sell their own hand-crafted goods. The business quickly expanded and soon moved from its original location to a larger space in the Square, but in 1946, its then-landlord refused to renew its lease citing complaints about the cooking odors from its busy restaurant. With 54 Brattle Street back on the market at the time, members of the Window Shop's board (the organization had since incorporated as a nonprofit) realized they could finally give their enterprise a stable home. They bought the village blacksmith building, and the shop operated there for the next twenty-six years.

During its tenure, the Window Shop offered not just income but also support and community to its staff, some of whom had lost their entire families to the Holocaust and spent time in Nazi prison camps themselves, and all of whom had been uprooted from their prior lives. When the shop finally closed in the early 1970s, it was devastating for some of the longtime staff members, but by then there were fewer refugees seeking a place like the Window Shop, and the organization had begun to buckle under its labor expenses, having committed itself to very generous employee and retirement benefits relative to most retail businesses.

Facing mounting losses, the board sold 54 Brattle Street to the Cambridge Center for Adult Education (CCAE) in 1972.[12] The CCAE was looking for additional classroom and office space, and 54 Brattle was ideally located just down the street from its main building. As part of the sale, the CCAE agreed to keep the shop's bakery open until the last refugee employee retired.

It turned out the CCAE knew a bit about stability and change itself. Founded in 1871 as the Cambridge Social Union, it almost went bankrupt during the Great Depression and had had to repurpose and rename itself to survive.[13] The CCAE kept its promise to the Window Shop, and the renamed "Black-smith House Bakery" stayed open until 1996, when finally it closed.

Then, as always, time marched on. The next year a new local bakery moved in, renting the Window Shop's former space and running a small coffee shop out of it for the next fourteen years.[14] Today, the CCAE occupies the building. Nearby, a stone marks the spot where the chestnut tree once stood, and a modern sculpture of the tree, cast in iron, memorializes it. A few doors down on Brattle Street, in the place where Café Algiers once sat, a hipster hangout called the Longfellow Bar serves fried shishito peppers, orange wines, and a rum and madeira cocktail called "Sea Change."[15]

Sea change, indeed. If Longfellow could have traveled through time, he would have seen what we just did—that the blacksmith's modest, little dwelling, which had seemed such a beacon for stability, was in fact a vessel for, and reflection of, all sorts of changes in individual lives and the culture at large. By standing on the street corner outside 54 Brattle Street and watching time fly by, we have seen local merchants thrive, local merchants die, and families arrive with hopes for a better future. We have seen the rippling effects of financial crises, civil wars, and world wars. Most of all perhaps, we have seen how massive social transformations altered who walked through that little building's front door and took a seat at the kitchen—or the tea room, or the coffee shop—table.

ONE BLOCK, OVER TIME

Instead of focusing on just one address over time, what if we pan back and expand our view to take in an entire block of Harvard Square? Perhaps we can get an even clearer understanding of the sorts of changes that define (and constantly redefine) a marketplace like this.

To do this, let's move from the outskirts of the Square where Dexter Pratt and Mary Walker's house sits to the very center of the commercial district. In the heart of the Square, Massachusetts Avenue, Brattle Street, and JFK Street all converge around a triangular brick plaza. This is the main plaza from which one descends into and ascends out of the Harvard subway station. It is the plaza on which the kiosk, which was once the subway headhouse and then the Out of Town newsstand, now sits empty, for the time being at least.

From this central point, the three streets all head off on their separate ways. Brattle curves west. Mass Ave bends east. Only JFK Street travels straight off. It makes a beeline southwest to the Charles River. On its short trip there (it reaches the Lars Anderson Memorial Bridge in less than a half a mile), the first street it crosses is Mount Auburn. There, on the corner of JFK and Mount Auburn, is where the colonists' seventeenth-century market sat, now called Winthrop Park. Let's settle into this first, short block of JFK Street for a while and make it ours—this 450-foot stretch that runs from the heart of modern Harvard Square to the location of the original village market, on route to the Charles River.

JFK Street was originally called Wood Street by the colonists from England.[16] Then, for more than a century, it was Boylston Street. Its 1981 renaming in honor of the late president was the culmination of one of most intense spats in Harvard Square's messy, complicated love story, and we will get to that later in the book. For now, however, we will focus on the businesses that have lined our one block of this street during the many years before and the many years after that spat; and for the sake of simplicity, in this chapter we will refer to it as JFK Street regardless of what year we visit.

Our block of JFK Street, 1973 (when it was still named Boylston Street). Photo by Ernst Halberstadt. Boston Public Library and Digital Commonwealth.

As far as its businesses are concerned, there is nothing especially unique about our block relative to any other in the Square. We could just as easily look down a stretch of Massachusetts Avenue or a short side street like Dunster and extract similar lessons. However, some of the Square's most beloved stalwarts have sat along this stretch of JFK, and we have already met a few of them. If we dropped ourselves onto this block in the 1700s and early 1800s, we would come upon the popular early watering hole, the Blue Anchor Tavern. If we traveled forward in time a bit to, say, the late 1800s or early 1900s, we would find, near the very start of the block where Mass Ave and JFK Street intersect, the cherished Amee Brothers bookshop.[17] Next door is where the respected grocer Wyeth & Co. relocated after its 1898 fire and where it stayed until closing in 1920. Along that same side of the street, the Tasty Sandwich Shop served coffee to devoted patrons from 1916 until 1997. Just across the street, the Curious George toy store operated for more than twenty years until the real estate investment trust Equity One bought its building in 2016 and set off a process that resulted in petitions, hurled snowballs, and, in a few years' time, the displacement of all the building's tenants.

So many other businesses have come and gone along this block, too. Drawing on a variety of sources including Cambridge Directories from the late nineteenth through late twentieth centuries, Maycock and Sullivan's *Building Old Cambridge*, Lotman's *Harvard Square*, and old newspaper articles and advertisements, it is possible to reconstruct which establishments we would find along this stretch of JFK Street over the past 125 years or so.[18] The number and variety of businesses that have come and gone is staggering. At one time or another, establishments such as the following (and many, many others) have appeared on the scene, stayed a while, then disappeared: Anderson's Express, promising to carry your parcels safely around the world though their connections "with all principal expresses, baggage checked to steamboat wharves and stations"; a Western Union telegraph office; Universal Collection Agency, "bonded under Mass. Laws" and ready to make collections wherever needed so their customers can "have more money in the bank and less on ledger"; Cosmos Printers; University Typewriter; the Harvard Bowlaway; 20th Century System auto rentals; a multistory parking garage; Young Lee's Restaurant; Howard Johnson's Restaurant; the independent apothecary Billings & Stover; the chain pharmacy CVS; Minuteman Radio; Discount Records; Helvetia European Tours; a large, two-story American Express travel agency; the second- and third-story offices of various real estate brokers, insurance agents, lawyers, architects, and several Christian

Science practitioners; the cobbler Antonio Cammarata and the tailor John Brennan; Corcoran's Department Store; Abercrombie & Fitch; a farrago of barbers and hairdressers and dentists and opticians; and alongside eateries that remained for decades, a revolving door of other small taverns, lunchrooms, delicatessens, and pizza joints.

What causes the death and disappearance of businesses like these? By conducting some autopsies of the establishments that have come and then gone along this single block, we can further sharpen what we began to see when we time-traveled through the old blacksmith's house. That is, we can begin to delineate the sources of change that play out at the street level and the sorts of changes that define a street-level market like this. Then, we can return to the recurring Harvard Square Death Discourse and start to unravel why Harvard Square has always been not what it used to be to those who have loved it.

The Liability of Newness

Cardullo's Trattoria is as good a place as any to start our inquest. It was an Italian restaurant and oyster bar that opened on our block of JFK Street in 1955, and it was gone eighteen months later. New businesses like the Trattoria come and go all the time. Sometimes an entrepreneur's clever new idea is ahead of its time or just never quite catches on. Sometimes an idea is flawed from the start or simply requires more capital than the entrepreneur has access to. It is hard work to get an enterprise off the ground, and a high percentage fail in the first few years. What economic sociologists call the "liability of newness" is especially acute for small restaurants and retail shops that operate on thin margins and whose owners often lack the cash reserves to fund early losses or overcome initial missteps.[19] Even talented, seasoned entrepreneurs like Frank Cardullo can run into these issues.

Frank Cardullo was born in 1915 into a family of entrepreneurs.[20] His grandparents owned lemon groves and olive orchards in Messina, Sicily, where Frank was born, and his father ran saloons in Providence, Rhode Island, until the Temperance Movement shut them down. Undiscouraged, Frank's father regrouped and moved his family to the town of Frostproof, Florida, where he went on to own a grocery, a restaurant, and what Frank later described as a "drugless drugstore" with a large tobacco department, a soda fountain, and an ice-cream parlor.[21] As a child, Frank helped his father make wine at home on the weekends and worked after-school jobs at all

three of the family businesses during the week. He washed dishes at the restaurant, and potatoes and onions at the grocery, and he served sodas at the
drugstore, standing on a Coca-Cola crate so he could reach the fountain.
When his father passed away in 1929, Cardullo was just fourteen years old
but already had years of work experience to his name.

After moving to the Boston area with his mother and brother, Frank got
a job at a drugstore and enrolled in a pharmacy course thinking he might
make a career of it. Within a few years, however, he felt called back to his
roots in the food business. In 1936, at the age of twenty-one, he bought his
first restaurant in Boston.

It wasn't until 1942 that Cardullo entered the Harvard Square market by
buying the Wursthaus. The Wursthaus was a German restaurant that had
been operating on this block of JFK Street, next door to the Tasty, since 1917.
Eight years later, in 1950, Cardullo opened a second business in the Square
just across the triangular intersection on Brattle Street. This one was his own
creation, and he called it Cardullo's Gourmet Shop.[22] He had the idea for a
high-end food store that would sell imported goods like canned sardines and
fancy teas and candies, along with fine meats and cheeses, and sandwiches
made to order. While perhaps not such a novel concept today, it was the
Square's first gourmet food shop, and the business almost failed in its early
years. Customers were skeptical of its high prices and exotic products, and
Cardullo had to experiment with his marketing and merchandising. Years
later, Cardullo recalled that had it not been for the successful Wursthaus
keeping him solvent, he would have lost the store. After five years of uncertainty and hard work, however, the new business finally began to prosper.

That was when Cardullo decided to launch his next venture, the Trattoria.
He opened it in a building at the very start of our block just feet from his
other two enterprises. Unlike his gourmet shop across the street, however,
Cardullo's Trattoria did not survive its troubled infancy. In his 1990 self-
published autobiography, *Peeking Through the Hole of a Bagel or Behind a
Hot Pastrami: The Life and Times of a Restauranteur*, Cardullo wrote that
Americans were not yet ready to accept, or at least pay for, truly authentic
Italian food. The oyster bar might also have been a bit too exotic for Harvard
Square patrons of that time; Cardullo had gotten that idea from an oyster
bar in New York's Grand Central Station. Most of all, though, his costs were
just too high. He wanted a top-notch trattoria so had hired the best Italian
chefs he could find, encouraged them to prepare multiple different sauces,
each with its own expensive base, and put a lot of money into the restaurant's

décor, from fine table linens to Italian-themed uniforms for the waitstaff. Despite all his experience, Cardullo launched too big, too fast, and the Trattoria succumbed to an early death.

Over the years, Cardullo's Trattoria was not the only new business on the block to come and go so quickly. However, it helps explain why some others did: Street-level businesses have a very high infant mortality rate.

The Liability of Humanness

The Wursthaus had a far longer run, but it too eventually closed—in 1996 after seventy-nine years on the block. Cardullo was eighty-one years old by then and ill. Business was down, and he had overextended himself trying to expand to a second Wursthaus location.[23] The original JFK Street restaurant had been operating under bankruptcy protection for several years, and its creditors finally forced the closure. Few may have noticed when Cardullo's short-lived Trattoria disappeared in the 1950s, but the Wursthaus had had a long life, and patrons mourned its 1996 death for years after. Known for its predictably bad food, wide beer selection, and monstrous sign whose six kitschy tiers spanned two stories and jutted perpendicularly off the building for all to see, it had been a local landmark, a popular gathering spot for generations of students and residents, and part of the Square's distinctive cultural fabric.[24] But, as the saying goes, nothing lasts forever.

Every business enterprise is a human enterprise. Even those ventures that survive their infancy—even those that have lived long, rich lives like the Wursthaus—remain vulnerable to all of the things to which their very human operators are vulnerable. Creations that owe their birth and longevity to human ingenuity and grit fall all the time because we humans are imperfect, mortal creatures. Business owners can get distracted, or overextended, or greedy, or simply old and tired and frail. And, inevitably, they die.

Frank Cardullo died in 1997, a year after the Wursthaus did. However, his Gourmet Shop survived his passing. Frank's child, Frances, had taken over the store in the 1990s when Frank fell ill; and Frank's grandchildren, in turn, kept it going after their own father died.[25] In 2015, the Cardullo family finally sold the business, and a new family stepped in to run it. Cardullo's Gourmet Shoppe (by then spelled with the old-timey flourish) had become an institution unto itself.

Not all businesses are so lucky. Many small businesses perish when their proprietors do. We saw how Dexter Pratt's blacksmith shop died along with the smith. The same happened to Mandrake Books, which operated for many years on our block, just across the street from the Wursthaus.

Irwin Rosen began operating Mandrake Books on JFK Street in 1951, and he ran it single-handedly until his death in 1997.[26] Born in the Bronx, Rosen graduated from Harvard College in 1925 with a degree in classics and literature, took doctoral classes in psychology at Columbia, worked as a high school English teacher and social worker, and, in 1939, traveled to Europe with a Jewish philanthropic group to help Jews flee the Nazis. Then he became a bookseller in Harvard Square and stayed at it through the end. Exceptionally well-read and uncompromising in his taste for serious works of nonfiction, Rosen stocked Mandrake's shelves with the sort of art, architecture, philosophy, and psychology books he personally enjoyed. Under his charge—and with the air of erudition that parlor lamps, throw rugs, and stacks of weighty tomes emit—the bookshop was a haven for the highbrow. Rosen was known to Harvard Square regulars as much for his recall of obscure texts as his prickliness with undiscerning customers. He also had no use for modern developments in bookselling, whether paperback books, discounting, or even the cash register (he used a drawer). Yet the business endured so long as Rosen did, and both were beloved fixtures in the Square. After Rosen's passing in 1997, the store never reopened. With no one from the next generation ready to step in and amidst the increasingly competitive bookselling market, there simply was no Mandrake without Rosen.

By the time Rosen and his shop died, Mandrake was actually no longer on our block of JFK Street. In 1971, Rosen had been forced to move the bookstore to a different location in the Square after his JFK Street landlord gave him a fifty-day eviction notice.[27] The landlord had found a new commercial tenant who was willing to pay double the rent. That experience reveals yet another source of frequent business upheaval, and sometimes even death, at the street level.

The Property Market

Every street-level market is embedded within a commercial property market. What happens in that underlying property market has repercussions for the businesses built atop it. Prior work has helpfully shown how macro-level forces such as the incentives of global capitalism or regional competition for growth can draw capital into a local market and spur real estate development in ways that transform the residential and commercial landscape.[28] However, when we swoop down to the street level, we see that many of the business closures attributed to those larger forces still have, as their proximate cause, something far more mundane and down to earth: a landlord.

Regardless of whether a property is owned by a local individual, a global firm, or anything in between, when a tenant's lease expires it is usually the landlord's right to raise the rent or find a new tenant.[29] The property rights of landlords are generally strong; we saw how the Window Shop had to move when its lease was up because a landlord claimed not to like its cooking odors. Such rent increases and re-tenanting decisions are especially common, though, after a property changes hands. Stores that are alive and operating one day can be sentenced to death the next day when in steps a new landlord who plans to redevelop the building or demands a higher return on investment.

This has happened again and again throughout Harvard Square and along just our short stretch of JFK Street. In the previous chapter we saw how J. H. Wyeth & Co. Grocers closed in 1920 after its building was sold and the new landlord raised the rent. That property was the same one from which the Tasty Sandwich Shop would later be pushed out by its landlord in the 1990s. For a vivid midcentury example on the block, we can look at what happened to the multiple commercial tenants of a local landlady named Bertha Cohen.

Cohen was a Polish immigrant who came to the area around 1914 at the age of twenty-two.[30] She took a job in a hat shop in downtown Boston and began saving what she could. Cohen took frugality seriously—to an eccentric extreme, some said. Lotman's *Harvard Square* recalls her as a "Dickensian" figure who dressed in tattered clothes and who, even after having amassed a fortune, worked out of a dirty basement workroom lit by a fifteen-watt bulb to spare the utilities expense.[31] Yet it was these habits that helped her build a local real estate empire. Cohen used her savings from the hat shop to acquire her first property in Harvard Square. During the 1930s and '40s, she amassed even more property throughout the marketplace, including several commercial buildings toward the Mount Auburn Street end of our block on JFK Street, not far from where the old village market once was. By the 1960s, Cohen, a woman barely five feet tall, had become the largest individual property owner in the Square, and she wielded considerable market power. The *Harvard Crimson* described her as a "thorn in the side" of the university after she refused to sell a few of her buildings to the school; the feisty woman took pride in the designation.[32] She was criticized by some for keeping her buildings in dilapidated condition, but beloved by others because those dilapidated conditions kept her rents low. A number of the popular establishments and cheap eateries that gave Harvard Square its bohemian vibe in the early '60s were tenants of hers.

When Cohen died in 1965, a Boston real estate developer named Max Wasserman bought her properties from the estate. He began increasing rents and emptied some properties entirely to begin redevelopment, driving many of Cohen's old tenants out in the process.[33] Years later, some would look back and say that the disposition of Bertha's properties after her death and the ensuing business turnover caused by Wasserman was the single greatest turning point for Harvard Square—the moment it began to lose its unique character and charm, the point after which it was never again itself.[34] Interestingly, however, one of the businesses Wasserman forced out was the Harvard Square Garage located at the very end of our block. Shortly after Cohen's death, Wasserman repurposed the garage building for retail but got into financial trouble around that time.[35] The property changed hands once again, and, in the coming decades, its new landlord filled "the Garage" (as it was still called) with many of the funky, grungy businesses that would come to define Harvard Square for all the Gen-Xers now on the scene.

The case of Bertha Cohen and her properties on this block reveals just how important landlords are to the fate of street-level businesses and just how unpredictable a source of market change this can also be. Neither merchants nor shoppers can predict a landlord's death, and they often have little or no transparency into property owners' decisions to sell their buildings. Yet the lives and whims and deaths of landlords can make whole establishments disappear from the streetscape and new ones appear in their place.

In 2016, when the Dow Family Trust sold their properties along this block of JFK Street, all of the businesses within them were displaced. Residents like me were quick to cast the new owner, Equity One, as a heartless disruptor of a once-stable marketplace. Some saw Equity One's presumed plan to replace unique local establishments like the Curious George toy store with seemingly generic but well-capitalized chains or banks as an example of unrestrained global capitalism. Later in the book, we will consider that criticism, but our present exercise in time travel offers a more straightforward lesson for now: landlords of all kinds have been evicting businesses from the street level for ages.

Time buries details. In 2017, when I sat in that basement meeting, growing angry at Equity One for its plans, what I did not know was this: Richard Dow—whose Dow Family Trust was the ostensibly stable, reasonable landlord that greedy Equity One replaced—had himself evicted a dozen small shops from this block in 1948 and 1949 to make room for a department store.[36] Then, he did it again in 1971: Dow was the landlord who evicted Mandrake Books for a higher-paying tenant. That same year, he also evicted a local apothecary called Billings & Stover from a building at the start of this block—and replaced it with a bank.[37]

Creative Destruction

At the start of our block, not far from where the apothecary and then the bank and then the Curious George toy store would all eventually operate at one time or another, there was a very different sort of business operating in that spot just before the turn of the nineteenth century: stables.[38] By the 1920s, the stables were gone, and at the opposite end of the block on the corner of Mount Auburn Street, there sat the three-story automobile garage that Bertha Cohen would later own. That garage was itself the result of the conversion of some earlier railway stables around the corner on Mount Auburn Street, but now it was a fully outfitted garage that held over three hundred cars as well as a car rental agency called 20th Century System.[39] Stables, carriage houses, and blacksmiths had once been some of the most common businesses in the Square, but in the span of just a few decades they were wiped off the map. According to *Building Old Cambridge*, by the 1930s Harvard Square was home to five other parking garages, eight repair shops, two gas stations, and even a Ford dealership.[40]

In his 1942 book *Capitalism, Socialism, and Democracy*, Joseph Schumpeter argued that capitalist markets are in constant turmoil, forever being revolutionized from within as new products, new modes of production, and new organizational forms emerge and displace old ones. Recognizing the inextricable relationship between the birth of the new and the death of the old, he called these forces the "gales of creative destruction."[41] Most people who have taken up Schumpeter's ideas and studied creative destruction have done so at the industry level, examining how new technologies regularly disrupt established industries and unseat once-dominant firms. A recent example is how the internet and streaming technology have upended the entertainment industry. Yet creative destruction does not just unfold at the industry level. It is one of the greatest sources of change at the street level.

When we stand on our block of JFK Street and watch the years pass by, we see gale after gale blowing through, carrying new establishments in and existing ones out. For decades there were multiple tailors working through-out the Square and a number along just this block—men like John Brennan, an Irish immigrant who made and altered suits for fifty-six years' worth of students and faculty including both Presidents Roosevelt.[42] In time, how-ever, and following advances in the manufacture and distribution of cloth-ing, independent haberdasheries and tailor shops began to disappear from the streetscape, their demand having been cut by larger clothing retailers and ready-to-wear fashion trends. By the middle of the twentieth century, Corcoran's Department Store had moved into Richard Dow's building in the middle of the block.

Corcoran's had been operating in Cambridge for several decades, but its 1949 expansion into Harvard Square marked a new era of growth for the company. Its JFK Street branch had two floors and seven thousand square feet of sales area, was outfitted with air-conditioning, and was described at its opening as "modern in every respect."[43] Of course, one era's modern disrup-tor is the next era's lumbering dinosaur. By the 1980s, Corcoran's Harvard Square store was the company's only location, and profits had declined to a point where it could no longer afford the rent. At the end of 1987 Corco-ran's announced it was closing for good, and in early 1988, a fast-growing retail chain out of Philadelphia called Urban Outfitters moved in.[44] Urban Outfitters' youth-oriented products were not just more appealing to the cur-rent generation; they also yielded a higher margin than the products sold by traditional department stores like Corcoran's because many were made in Urban Outfitters' in-house wholesale division, which designed, produced, and marketed private-label merchandise.[45]

Developments in manufacturing, distribution, and merchandising fueled by technological advances have spurred the death and life of more than just clothing merchants. Consider the case of optical stores and opticians' offices. Students and professors are a good bet for the optical market, and for much of the twentieth century Harvard Square was home to multiple eyeglass stores and eye doctors' offices, including several on just our short stretch of JFK Street. Yet even astute opticians such as Andrew Lloyd or James Lowry who set up shop there in the early 1900s could not see the gales of cre-ative destruction that would come to wipe out some of their predecessors a century later.[46] Soft contact lenses, online contact lens distribution, and Lasik surgery all reduced demand for traditional spectacles. Then came new options for even those who still preferred glasses. With its clicks-to-bricks strategy and its in-house design and manufacturing of eyewear, Warby

Parker unsettled the optical world when it emerged in 2010. In 2017, as a number of small optical houses struggled, a large Warby Parker showroom opened up at the end of our block, right across the street from Winthrop Park where the original village market had been.[47]

The drugstores that have come and gone along this block offer yet another example of creative destruction at work. Billings & Stover, the apothecary evicted by Richard Dow in 1971, initially relocated to a smaller space on Brattle Street just across from where the sturdy chestnut tree once stood. However, the drugstore, like the tree, was eventually felled by modern developments. As the twentieth century unfolded, innovations in science and manufacturing led to more and more medications being mass produced and a decline in pharmacies' traditional (and traditionally quite profitable) compounding businesses.[48] Those changes, coupled with developments in distribution and retailing, created scale advantages that helped chains like CVS rise to dominance. By the 1990s, Billings & Stover had given up on the drug business altogether and converted itself into a nostalgia shop, harkening back to the "drugless drugstore" of Frank Cardullo's family.[49] Meanwhile, CVS opened a small store on our block, a few doors down from where Billings & Stover had been in its heyday. In 2002, Billings & Stover closed for good, and in 2015 the small CVS left our block to make room for a massive, two-story CVS, which took up residence across the street in the building where Wyeth & Co., the Tasty, and the Wursthaus had all once lived.[50]

The gales of creative destruction are relentless and they appear to spare none. University Typewriter used to be on this block, and then the PC emerged, students and faculty adopted it, and University Typewriter departed. Throughout the twentieth century, there were multiple photography studios on this block (and several camera shops throughout the Square). With the emergence of digital photography, these establishments began to die off.

Technological and organizational transformations in the music industry have also swept through and reordered the street level. In the early 1900s, our block was no music mecca. The main music store in Harvard Square was Briggs & Briggs located over on Mass Ave. It sold sheet music and instruments, which it also repaired. But then record sales took off midcentury. By the 1970s, there were multiple record stores throughout Harvard Square and as many as eight shops specializing in the sale and repair of sound systems.[51] Along just our one short stretch of JFK Street, we could have bought stereo equipment at Tech Hi-Fi or Audio Lab and albums at Strawberries or Discount Records (located where the Western Union telegraph office had been).[52]

The opposite end of our block, 1973. Courtesy of Cambridge Historical Commission.

By the late 1990s, however, Discount Records and Strawberries were gone.[53] Just around the corner, crowds flocked to HMV and Tower Records to shop for CDs. When those larger chains first opened, they were bemoaned by people who missed the days of going store to store to browse for records. A decade later, HMV and Tower were themselves gone. Music was increasingly being distributed online and on iPods, and people like me bemoaned the change, missing the days of browsing for CDs.

Finally, let's not forget bookstores. Ever since Harvard University's early days there have been bookstores in the Square and bookstores on this one block of the Square. Over the years, our block was home to Amee Brothers (1868–1920), the Harvard Book Store (1932–1950s), Mandrake (1951–1971), a Barnes & Noble (ca. 1960s), a science-fiction bookstore called Science Fantasy (ca. 1980s), and multiple small second- and third-story rare bookstores and binderies.[54] Some of these, like Amee and Mandrake, moved off the block to new locations in the Square before closing for reasons unrelated to creative destruction in the book industry (e.g., rent increases or evictions, the aging or death of the owner). At least one that moved off this block remains in the Square today: the Harvard Book Store relocated to Mass Ave years ago and is still there. To make it this long, however, the Harvard

Book Store has had to weather gale after gale of creative destruction that have swept through its industry and swept away so many of its brethren booksellers—disruptions that included large chain stores such as Barnes & Noble and Borders and, more recently, Amazon.com and ebooks. At the start of the 1990s there were more than two dozen bookstores in Harvard Square.[55] Only a handful remained by 2011, which Maycock and Sullivan point out was the same year Amazon.com announced that Cambridge had the highest online book purchases per capita of any large U.S. city.[56]

Cultural Change

Buying books online instead of in a store doesn't just happen because technology enables it. People's tastes, preferences, and habits have to evolve, too. Cultural change in general is another major source of disruption at the street level, continually ushering new street-level establishments into a marketplace and old ones out. Let's consider Sweetgreen's 2016 arrival on our block and some of the businesses that came before it.

Sweetgreen is what today's food industry insiders call a fast-casual, farm-to-table restaurant chain.[57] It sells salad and grain bowls prepared to order. Founded in 2007, the company raised more than $300 million from venture capital and institutional investors to fund its early growth, and it has locations across the United States.[58] Its menu shifts seasonally, and its ingredients are sourced from local farmers. All of its takeout bowls and utensils are compostable. More than half of its orders are placed through a mobile app by customers who want to pick up their bowls "on the go" or have them delivered. The company's business model and operations owe a great debt to waves of creative innovation and destruction in everything from mobile technology to recycling technology, supply chain logistics, capital markets, food storage, and food preparation. However, Sweetgreen's strategy, marketing, and popularity reflect something else as well: evolving cultural beliefs about personal health and the health of our planet.

In 2016, Sweetgreen opened a store on the Mount Auburn Street end of our block. Over the years, this same stretch of JFK was home to a tavern, two different pizza shops, and two different deli's (as well as, in the early 1900s— and admittedly only indirectly related to this discussion of food and health— an undertaker).[59] The Square still has its share of pizza and burger joints (and then some), but around the 1980s the health food movement began to make inroads into the marketplace.[60] At the time, some customers grumbled that their favorite greasy spoons were being edged out by restaurants that served such offenses as "watercress garnish or a side order of sprouts" (offerings one local restaurant reviewer found so appalling she turned them into an epithet).[61] Nevertheless, eating habits and tastes were changing. It was only a matter of time before wrap places, fro-yo shops, and smoothie joints arrived, and that they did.

Some of those establishments had short lives, lasting only as long as their specific gastronomic fad did. Fashion cycles and fads are often at play at the street level, fueling the rise and fall of frozen yogurt shops or the sudden popularity of grain bowls. And yet what lies behind such seemingly trivial trends are often broader transformations in cultural beliefs and understandings. Absent Americans' increased focus on health and wellness, Sweetgreen and its grain bowls may never have appeared on our block.

What's more, were it not for significant cultural changes in gender relations, King's Tavern might still be across the street. King's Tavern, and its sign reading "Men's Bar," first appeared on JFK Street in the late 1930s.[62] Harvard Square sported several men-only establishments in those years. However, by Christmas Eve 1969, when King's closed its doors for the final time, it was the last remaining men's bar in the area. Times had changed. The owner of King's soon opened a new venture in the same building, but this time it was a co-ed cabaret where, according to the *Harvard Crimson*, "young girls and bearded students" could hang out together.[63]

Some of the same cultural changes that led to the death of King's "Men's Bar" and the birth of King's co-ed cabaret paved the way for Good Vibrations to open one block up on JFK Street in 2017.[64] Founded in San Francisco in the late 1970s by a feminist and sex educator, Good Vibrations had expanded to eight branches by the time it arrived in Harvard Square.[65] Carrying a wide selection of vibrators, dildos, and anal toys and offering workshops on sexual health and pleasure, its appearance in the marketplace reflected the continued evolution of beliefs about sex and sexual empowerment, including the rise of the sex-positivity movement.

Good Vibrations is also a good reminder that the perceived morality of products and activities can shift and, when that happens, the street level shifts. This is especially true when we institutionalize our evolving moral consciousness in the law. Frank Cardullo's father had already begun to lose some of his saloon licenses in Providence, Rhode Island, as the Temperance Movement grew, but once Prohibition was enacted via the Eighteenth Amendment, saloons and taverns disappeared from street-level markets across the country (and speakeasies appeared, at least for those who knew where to look for them). After Prohibition was repealed, businesses selling alcohol sprouted up once again, including Varsity Liquors in Harvard Square. It opened at the top of our block in 1937, right on the corner of Mass Ave and JFK Street, not far from the Wursthaus.[66] Since then the Square has had no shortage of bars and liquor stores. Although it might have had even more: from the late 1970s through early 2000s, the Harvard Square Defense Fund lobbied against the city's issuance of new liquor licenses in the Square, even winning a cap on licenses in the late 1980s, arguing that such establishments degraded the Square's environment and led to crime.[67]

More recently, Massachusetts citizens voted to decriminalize the sale of marijuana, first for medical uses in 2012, then for recreation in 2016. In 2017, Harvard Square's first medical marijuana dispensary opened on a short side street off JFK, not far from Good Vibrations and its neighbor, a smoke shop that sells bongs and vaping paraphernalia.[68] Reflecting growing awareness of racial stigmatization and the disproportionate impact racial minorities bore from the War on Drugs, the Massachusetts Social Equity Program began prioritizing the issuance of cannabis licenses to minority-owned businesses, and in 2020 two local black entrepreneurs, Leah Samura and Sean Hope, were granted approval to operate the first recreational cannabis shop in Harvard Square on nearby Church Street in a space once occupied by a Starbucks.[69]

Cultural evolution is a complex process. Sometimes the changes we see at the street level reflect a shift in the beliefs of the entire population. Sometimes they reflect the beliefs, habits, and styles of a new generation. When King's Tavern closed and the co-ed cabaret opened, not everyone welcomed the change. One of the tavern's older, longtime patrons had liked the all-male refuge and grumbled about the new place, "I went down there once and that's it."[70] But, of course, the cabaret wasn't really for him. It was for those "young girls and bearded men" who wanted to hang out together now.

Those bearded young men were implicated in a whole wave of business deaths, in fact. Since at least the early 1900s, the Square supported multiple barbershops, including at least four barbers who back in the 1920s and '30s offered trims and shaves where Sweetgreen now prepares salads.[71] In fact, old Cambridge business directories list barbers working on both sides of our block of JFK up through the early 1960s. Then the references to barbers disappear. The culprit, according to those in the trade? All the '60s and '70s young men who brought beards back into style and began wearing their hair long.[72] Some local barbers tried to "get with it" and adapt, according to news reports at the time.[73] They did away with the black-and-white striped barbers' cloths, straight-backed chairs, and other hallmarks of tradition. However, other establishments, such as University Barbershop that had been in operation since 1880, shut down. Lotman's *Harvard Square* suggests that as many as eight barbershops closed during this period.[74] The market had contracted, and there was simply not as much business to go around.

The new young hippies may not have missed the barbershop rituals of old, but some older people undoubtedly did. Not being able to get their regular shave at University Barbershop—like not being able to get a drink at King's with just the guys—was one of many changes to which older folks in the Square had to adapt. During those decades, the Square became a destination for bohemian youth culture of all forms, not just long hair, and the marketplace began to cater to this new and growing customer base. In came coffeehouses, boutiques, and foreign restaurants that appealed to the young hipsters of the time. Out went some older establishments like those fallen barbershops and men's clubs that had catered to the prior generation.

Yet those new shops and restaurants of the '60s and '70s would, one day, be the old, unfashionable dotards replaced by the likes of Sweetgreen, itself born from a new generation's consciousness. Sweetgreen's founders were seniors at Georgetown University in 2007 when they got the idea of opening a fast-food restaurant that would better cater to their cohort. In a 2018 interview, one of them recalled, "McDonald's did not speak to us, Chipotle, these places did not make sense for us." He said, they wanted to build a "McDonald's of their generation."[75]

As we saw in chapter 1, the Square's commercial landscape has often reflected the cultural zeitgeist. That is part of what so many people have loved about it. But, of course, all street-level markets feel the effects of cultural change, whether stemming from the evolving tastes of the entire population or from one generation succeeding the next and bringing new preferences with it. That said, the market in Harvard Square may be hyper-receptive to cultural change on account of the specific population it serves and how quickly that population turns over.

Population Change

Global and local population flows drive change at the street level all the time. People like Felix Caragianes, the Greek shoe-shiner and newspaper peddler we met in chapter 1—as well as Bertha Cohen, the Polish real estate magnate, and Frank Cardullo, the Sicilian-born restauranteur—all underscore how large-scale international migration flows can lead to new entrepreneurs and new enterprises popping up in local marketplaces like Harvard Square.

In the academic literature, residential gentrification is by far the most commonly discussed type of population-driven change at the street level; so much so, that the other sources of business turnover discussed in this chapter are often overlooked. In *Naked City: The Death and Life of Authentic Urban Places*, sociologist Sharon Zukin documents the death of "Irish bars, Latino bodegas, and black soul food restaurants" throughout New York City as middle-class and wealthier residents have gentrified one "authentic" urban village after another.[76]

Gentrification has also been a popular, go-to explanation for the death of Harvard Square establishments, frequently bandied about in local news articles and casual conversations about why the Square is no longer what it used to be. The City of Cambridge has experienced rapid growth in recent years (although it only recently climbed back to its mid-twentieth-century levels, having experienced population decline from the 1950s to 1990s). Like many growing urban areas across the United States, it has struggled with the displacement of some of its immigrant, minority, and lower-income residents.[77] Nevertheless—and in contrast to many urban neighborhoods studied by sociologists—gentrification is likely not the main source of population-driven business turnover we see in Harvard Square for one simple reason: the area immediately around Harvard Square has been gentrified since at least the early twentieth century.[78] Some might even say it was gentrified before Longfellow's time, when those wealthy Tories began building their mansions along Brattle Street in the 1700s.

In the late 1800s, Harvard Square almost became an immigrant enclave—the sort of neighborhood that would, in other cities, undergo repeated waves of residential turnover and, eventually, gentrification. However, that never came to pass.[79] Around the turn of the nineteenth century, Cambridge had a large and growing population of Irish immigrants. Many of them found work at the railway, coal dealers, carriage houses, and ice tool factory then operating in Harvard Square. But before the area's residential makeup changed to reflect this, most of that light manufacturing and service work went away. Harvard University—then, as now, the biggest influence on the area's population—began to expand. Its enrollment grew from 754 in 1870 to 3,364 in 1909, and because the university offered minimal student housing at that time, investment dollars poured into the Square to build private dormitories.

The luxury dorms that were constructed during these years were so lavish for their era that the path along which most were built—a short stretch of Mount Auburn Street extending east off JFK—became known as the "the Gold Coast." It did not take long for taverns, billiard halls, retailers, and boardinghouses to spring up around the Gold Coast and solidify Harvard Square as a commercial, rather than industrial, district. A 1913 report of the City of Cambridge contrasted the Square with other more industrial parts of the city, suggesting it was well suited to serve as the "center of a high-class resident district" and "collegiate square"—"the natural center of a more expensive residence district, with such shops as serve the neighborhood tributary to it."[80]

Throughout the twentieth century, the university continued to expand, and its presence has had a profound influence on the marketplace. In chapter 1, we saw how the university serves as a stabilizing force for the market because, year in and year out, it brings the same general types of customers into the market in the form of students, faculty, and tourists, who carry with them broadly similar market needs over time (e.g., casual eateries, clothing shops, school supplies, entertainment options, bookstores, etc.). Yet even as the university affords such a stable role structure for the market, it also generates rapid, continual turnover within those roles—and that likely accelerates the pace of culturally driven market change.

Every year a new crop of students arrives to replace those moving on. Whereas a small-town Main Street typically serves a relatively stable local population, the seasonal student population that flows into and out of Harvard Square and the surrounding area numbers approximately twenty thousand each year.[81] The individuals who make up that twenty thousand are continually bringing in their own, new, of-the-moment preferences, habits, and tastes. The university also attracts a large visitor and tourist population from around the world, and that population is constantly turning over as well. In addition, the Square has been a metropolitan commuter hub ever since the first elevated rail lines were laid down in Cambridge. In recent years, about twenty-two thousand people have passed through its subway and bus terminals every day, representing another dynamic population flow of professionals and workers, albeit with less rapid cohort replacement than occurs with the students and tourists.

With such a constant flow of people passing through, carrying in their new and distinct preferences, it is no wonder we see a lot of businesses coming and going on a block like ours. The Square is like an ethnic enclave that has a new immigrant population arriving to unseat the old every few years—only, the land the new immigrants hail from is the future. If enough people arrive preferring frozen yogurt over ice cream, or salads and wraps over roast beef, the market will eventually shift to reflect those preferences, and the shops that line the streets will change; until, of course, the people and their tastes change once again.

Finally, because creative destruction and cultural change often work in concert, the Square's unique population dynamics may accelerate the effects of creative destruction as well. Younger generations are especially prone to adopt, diffuse, and popularize new innovations. Before most people in the country had a mobile phone, cell-phone stores were popping up around Harvard Square. In 2000, one opened up not far from our block of JFK Street. Some people thought these new stores were eyesores and mourned the loss of the retailers they unseated.[82] It is possible some older residents and faculty felt exactly the same when University Typewriter first appeared. Such may be the price of being at the vanguard.

State and Municipal Decision Making

All markets are embedded within and shaped by the rules of the state. As we saw with Prohibition and the legalization of cannabis, local and national regulations can spell the death or life of street-level establishments. So can changes in zoning. Municipal zoning ordinances can prohibit entire tracts of land from having any business establishments at all (e.g., by designating an area a residential, versus a commercial, district). Within designated business districts, the zoning code can specify which types of commercial activities are allowed (e.g., retail, office, or industrial uses). Height limitations, required setbacks, and allowable floor-area ratios can affect the incentives of developers and entrepreneurs and, in turn, which businesses appear in the marketplace. In 2020, an amendment to the Harvard Square zoning guidelines prevented banks from having more than twenty-five feet of street-level frontage, and this change seemed to spur one JFK Street landlord to lease his large retail space to a cannabis shop instead of the bank he'd been contemplating.[83]

Public infrastructure projects are another source of disruption and change at the street level. Cambridge's nineteenth-century street-widening project did not just kill the blacksmith's chestnut tree over on Brattle Street, it also spurred redevelopment on our block, helping transform it from what

Maycock and Sullivan describe as a "hodgepodge of stables, houses, and shops" into the more modern twentieth-century commercial block we have been analyzing.[84]

By far, the infrastructure projects that have most transformed our little stretch of JFK Street have involved the subway, whose entrance lies at start of the block. The original subway construction project in the early 1900s and the massive subway extension project that lasted from 1978 to 1985 were both huge disruptions to the marketplace. Each project entailed years of construction, created gaping holes in the heart of the Square, and necessitated the rerouting of foot and carriage/car traffic in ways that threw-off the everyday shopping routines of Square denizens and cut into the sales of many merchants. In each case, the market that emerged after the project's completion looked different than that which had existed before.

When the subway opened in 1912, some observers complained that "the square has ceased to be the trading center it was before the subway took traffic underground."[85] However, commercial development of the area also took off. George Dow, Richard Dow's father, put up his first Harvard Square building in 1913. As new buildings like that went up and others changed hands, businesses got shuffled around like pieces on a board game.

Years later, some local businesspeople would similarly complain that the 1980s subway extension depressed foot traffic in the Square by allowing more commuters to change subways and buses underground. However, commercial real estate development was robust after that project as well, and a number of new shops and stores entered the market. As Lotman put it, "Once the streetscape's ventral chasm had been sewn shut, a brand-new Square emerged. . . . It was as though the whole neighborhood had been turned over with a hoe, both literally and figuratively."[86]

Local and Systemic Shocks

Finally, unexpected crises and catastrophes take business lives just as they take human lives. Over the years, floods and fires have ripped through buildings on our block and others across the Square. Sometimes a business is destroyed overnight by such an event, never to reopen again. Other times, the catastrophic event displaces a healthy business, which then relocates and sets off a chain reaction of commercial changes that ends with some other business disappearing from the landscape. In the previous chapter, we saw that the Wyeth & Co. grocery shop appeared on our block of JFK Street at the turn of the nineteenth century after a devastating fire forced it to move from its original location. What we did not see then was that, at the time of the fire, our block already had a long-standing grocer. George Wood's family had been running a shop on that corner of JFK Street for two generations. However, Wood was nearing retirement and Wyeth's owners were eager to continue their operation, so they offered to buy him out.[87] Wood accepted, and a sign for "J. H. Wyeth & Co. Grocer" replaced that of "Geo. A. Wood" on the corner of our block.

Crises and disasters even further away can send shockwaves that ripple through a local market. Macroeconomic shocks, financial crises, and distant wars all find their way to the street level. The Cambridge Center for Adult Education, which eventually moved into the blacksmith's house, only barely survived the Great Depression, and many street-level establishments did not.[88] On our block of JFK Street, a restaurant and café called Z Square opened in 2006 but never made it out of the Great Recession of 2007–2009.[89] Reports at the time suggested multiple possible causes for the business's closure, from early missteps and poor planning to a failure to keep its city licenses current. Either way, a drop in revenue from the economic downturn seems to have been something this faltering business could not weather.

The establishments most vulnerable to sudden shocks are usually those already weakened by some of the other factors we have discussed—e.g., evolving tastes, competition carried in by the gales of creative destruction, rising rents, or business owners who simply lack the capital or stamina to rebuild after disaster strikes. Death at the street level can come from many directions, and sometimes all at once.

≈

Perhaps no shock has ever hit local markets like the recent pandemic. The coronavirus has been for street-level businesses the same as it has for human beings: a deadly killer. Businesses with preexisting conditions and comorbidities were the hardest hit, including retailers who were already struggling to compete with online commerce and Amazon.com in recent years, independent restaurants whose razor-thin margins were already being chipped away by new third-party delivery services such as UberEats, and all the new businesses that had been striving to catch on and all the old businesses that had been trying to hang on before the pandemic hit.

We will return to the pandemic later but, for now, the point is this: to most of us, it felt like COVID-19 came out of nowhere, and, along with all the other havoc it wreaked, the turmoil it caused in our local markets was deeply destabilizing. It was destabilizing to landlords whose capital was tied up in properties that could no longer generate much of any rental income. It was destabilizing to business owners who wondered whether their life's work and savings would be wiped away. It was destabilizing to employees who depended on those businesses for their salaries and now found themselves without a job to go to each day. And it was destabilizing to all of us as consumers who saw our daily habits and routines pulled out from under us, who missed being able to come together in the marketplace, and who watched with grief as some of our favorite shops and restaurants disappeared forever.

Yet as shocking and seemingly unprecedented as all that was, the disturbing feelings it set off in us were not entirely unfamiliar. Most of us had felt a lesser version of that shock before, when encountering the unexpected death of some cherished establishment we weren't yet ready to say goodbye to. It is a feeling a *Boston Herald* reporter expressed in 1936 when he wrote forlornly about Amee Brothers' passing: "Harvard Square is a different place. The old stores, the old friends are gone."[90] It is what some bookworms surely felt that late-spring morning in 1997 when they walked to Mandrake only to find it closed, the store having passed on overnight along with its charmingly cantankerous owner. It is related to why there were so many sad testimonials about the Wursthaus when it closed, and why when news got out in the early 1970s that the Window Shop was closing, it wasn't just employees who were devastated. A longtime customer of the store spotted one of the shop's board members in Harvard Square and shouted from across the street, "What do you think you're doing closing the Window Shop?"[91] And it is why so many of us have, at one moment or another, stood on a street corner somewhere and thought, "It just isn't what it used to be."

Longfellow understood this sentiment. He felt it himself. In 1879, for the poet's seventy-second birthday, the children of Cambridge presented him with an armchair made from the branches of the downed chestnut tree—the tree he had tried but failed to save from the city's modernization project.[92] In return, he wrote a poem for the children called, "From My Arm-Chair." In it, he recalled the tree, and the smithy at work, and the "bellows blow" and the "anvil beat," and he wrote, "The Danish King could not in all his pride / Repel the ocean tide / But, seated in this chair, I can rhyme / Roll back the tide of Time."[93]

Chapter Four

A TRICKY RELATIONSHIP

Our adventure in time travel can help start to unravel the puzzle of why Harvard Square has always been not what it used to be. At first, that sentiment sounded like such a trite expression of nostalgia it was capable of boring even the most dedicated college research assistant. Who, after all, hasn't heard someone from the old neighborhood lament that things aren't what they used to be? Who, after a certain age at least, hasn't heard themselves say the same about their own hometown Main Street or favorite urban village? People often get nostalgic for the supposedly more authentic pasts of these places.[1] People often get attached to their favorite old haunts. A college-town square is especially likely to provoke such sentimentality.

Our one-block stroll down memory lane—or JFK Street, in this case—offered additional perspective. Harvard Square is a marketplace, and markets change all the time. As we watched all the different forces continually roll through and transform the marketplace by carrying some businesses in and others out, one thing was clear: Harvard Square has actually, quite literally, always been not what it used to be.

Yet if it were this simple—that markets change and people get nostalgic—why do we see such recurrent upset? Why hasn't everyone absorbed these rather straightforward lessons by now? It is not as if all the smart people passing through Harvard Square over the years have been unaware they are participating in a market or unaware that markets change all the time. The Square has been a commercial district for almost four centuries. Everyone there knows it is a marketplace, just like everyone who has talked about the special meaning of a particular shop or restaurant has known they were talking about a commercial entity and that such entities come and go. In 1920, as the *Cambridge Tribune* mourned Wyeth & Co.'s closing on our block, we saw the newspaper's staff acknowledge, "The closing out of this business comes about as one of the almost inevitable changes in business life."[2] Sixteen years later, as locals mourned Amee Brothers' closing just around the corner, we saw the same newspaper remark that, of course, "in a few years the old will be almost forgotten, so readily do we adapt ourselves to change."[3] Nearly a century of repeated upset later, we saw how the familiar Death Discourse had evolved to incorporate its own relentless persistence so that, now, when denizens lament changes in the Square, they often begin by saying they know theirs is a time-worn lament.

If everyone knows that change is such an inevitable aspect of market life, why do they keep getting so upset about it? Why, in short, do people keep getting upset when a market acts like a market and changes on them? A quick trip back to the blacksmith's old house can offer some perspective.

HOW MARKETS STABILIZE AND DESTABILIZE US

As much as change defined the story of 54 Brattle Street, that little dwelling taught us something else important—it taught us about the preciousness of stability in an inherently unstable world. Why, after all, was it so important to keep the Window Shop bakery going until its last refugee employees retired? Why did Mary Walker, a former slave, want to ensure 54 Brattle Street remained in her family for as many generations as possible?

Walker, her children, and the Window Shop's employees had suffered some of the most incomparable and brutal forms of instability human beings can face. They had experienced the sort of total, existential destabilization that comes from being denied basic human freedom and agency, from being completely uprooted, ripped out of one's existing life and torn from one's closest ties. No single dwelling or employer could give them back what had been taken nor redress all the suffering that had been inflicted upon them. However, life and work at 54 Brattle Street had offered them a small measure of stability after all the wrenching instability they had been forced to endure—and, more than anyone, they knew the value of that. That little house, once shaded by a sturdy, spreading chestnut tree, was a place where they could begin to re-root themselves in the world. It was where Mary

Walker and her family were able to reaffirm and rebuild their connections with one another and where they could begin to dream of a future that, this time, they might control. It was where the Holocaust survivors and refugees who worked at the Window Shop began to reconstruct their lives and forge new ties in a new homeland.

To draw comparisons between the sort of destabilization Mary Walker, her children, and the Window Shop's employees faced and any other sort of instability in life is problematic. However, we can still learn from their experiences, and what they teach us is a crucial lesson concerning the human need for even just a little bit of stability amidst the sea of changes life throws our way.

Although we rarely think of them in such terms, it turns out that street-level markets and the shops and restaurants in them are quite like that little house at 54 Brattle Street. These markets see a lot of change pass through them, but they also offer a lot of stability and, in the process, help us feel rooted in the world at least for a brief period. They are surprisingly good, that is, at providing us with what psychologists and sociologists call a sense of "ontological security"—i.e., a basic trust that our world is stable and as it appears to be, and that our place in it is secure.[4] Without a sense of ontological security, human beings feel unmoored. Without a sense of ontological security, we can feel a sort of existential anxiety and a disconcerting lack of control and agency in our lives.

Part 2 of this book will explore the ontological security we derive from all the different ways a street-level market like Harvard Square brings us together and helps us forge a stabilizing sense of community. For now, however, let's consider a more basic form of ontological security we derive from these markets: the predictable, routine interactions they afford. In the *Constitution of Society*, sociologist Anthony Giddens lays out some of the defining features of stabilizing routines.[5] Giddens is not writing specifically about markets—in fact, his work tends to emphasize the instability, not the stability, of modern market life—yet the image one gets from his description of routines that provide ontological security is oddly familiar: it reads like an account of an everyday visit to your favorite local shop. It reminds me, personally, of the hundreds of trips I made to Crimson Corner to buy a newspaper.

For many years, I set out from home each morning and followed the same path to Crimson Corner, crossing first Mount Auburn Street, then Brattle Street. (*For a sense of ontological security, Giddens says it is important to feel physically situated in time and space and to experience oneself in the flow of action, oriented to a task at hand.*) As I approached, I saw the familiar sandwich board out on the sidewalk. It told me the shop was open, and I could go in to buy my paper. (*Giddens writes that there must be a clear interpretive frame for understanding what the situation is and, thus, what interactional rules will apply in it—e.g., one is about to step into a shop for a commercial transaction, not a date or a party or a class.*) Once there, I pulled the shop's door open and entered. A little bell jingled, and Chris Kotelly, the owner, greeted me. (*There should be clear markers to signal the interaction's beginning.*) I pulled my paper from the rack and approached the counter to hand Chris my cash. (*There should be clear social roles for individuals to assume and orient to—e.g., customer, shopkeeper, clerk. There should also be clear physical rules for how individuals position themselves in relation to one another—e.g., one side of the counter or the other.*) Chris and I chatted as we completed the transaction. I asked how business was or noted that I saw his son working over the weekend; he asked how Philip and the dog were doing or how my research was coming along. New England weather came up a lot. (*There is conversational turn-taking and a shared understanding of what is tactful versus not in the particular setting.*) We said goodbye, and I left with my paper. (*There is a clear end to the interaction.*)

Comparing my regular visits to Crimson Corner with Giddens's recipe for ontological security, it is humbling to realize how much more than a newspaper I got there each day. Yet it's true: on a deeper, psychological level than I ever contemplated when contemplating my morning paper, I really did experience a sense of agency and intentionality as I cut my way across the Square each morning. When I saw the sandwich board out on the sidewalk and spotted Chris standing in the back when I entered, I actually did feel reassured that the world had not changed on me overnight. When I selected my paper from among the options on the rack, if I'm being truly honest with myself, I was not just grabbing something to read once I got back home; I was also, on some level, making a claim (to myself? to the world?) about who I was as a person. And, when Chris asked after my family or my work, it reassured me that my unique presence in this world had, in some small but very real way, been marked. After he and I successfully completed our morning choreography, I felt buoyed by the experience even if I didn't often reflect upon why—that we had just reconfirmed for each other that the social fabric of which we both were a part remained intact.

Once we come to appreciate how a simple commercial transaction like buying the morning paper can provide a meaningful sense of ontological security in our lives, we can start to see how the many routines of market life are constantly stabilizing and grounding us in similar, and similarly profound, ways. When we walk down the same streets each day, the sight of familiar signs and shop windows reassures us that the world is still as we have come to know it. All the small daily, weekly, and seasonal market rituals we develop help lend our lives a reassuring sense of predictability, whether it involves us stopping at the same coffee shop on the way to work each morning, or meeting up with friends for a drink after work at the same bar each week, or buying one's favorite notebooks and pens from the same stationer before the start of each school year.

Most important, we begin to see how all the different attachments we forge in the context of the market's routines and within the market's spaces help stabilize and ground us. The most meaningful of these ties help define our unique sense of self. Sunday bagels with one's father or seeing the same show with loved ones every year offers more than comfort through consistency; these become key scenes and recurring motifs in the compositions that are our lives. They become a part of who we are. More casual connections, like the sort formed across a counter or standing in line, help ground us in the way my daily exchanges with Chris Kotelly grounded me. When a waiter asks if you want "the usual" or a bartender begins to prepare your favorite drink before you've even asked for it, that small gesture reassures you on some level that you have been seen and recognized as the distinct individual you feel yourself to be. Even when we are simply making our way down the street during a crowded weekend street festival or on a Tuesday afternoon errand, the shared co-presence of so many other human beings offers its own form of reassurance. As we make our way through the world, weaving ourselves successfully around each other, we continually, implicitly take one another into account and mark one another's existence.

In short, markets support and call forth all sorts of routine interactions that help us trust in the social world we inhabit, and trust that we are securely rooted in it. Yet we rarely think about them this way. We think of how religious rituals (e.g., weekly Shabbat, Sunday Mass) can provide a stabilizing sense of continuity to life and how they help individuals feel more securely integrated into a community. We think of how large ritualistic gatherings (whether sporting events or rock concerts or religious revivals) can evoke a sort of collective effervescence that builds solidarity and reaffirms people's shared humanity.[6] But markets, too, can help generate feelings like these. They can help us feel rooted in our sense of self, in our community, in our world.

We underappreciate this aspect of markets, but it has been right in front of us all along, both in our daily lives and in the academic literature. Past studies of both urban and small-town life contain all sorts of evidence that street-level markets provide us with the streetscapes we come to expect, the daily rituals that stabilize and ground us, the third places in which we regularly interact and connect with one another. Yet so often these things have been attributed to other important phenomena like the "neighborhood" or the "character" of a place.[7] Such a focus has not been wrong, but it has diverted our attention from the *market's* fundamental role in all this; diverted our attention from the fact that it is the market in the place that is giving us so much of what we have attributed to place over the years.

Once we appreciate the market's role in offering such stability and security, we begin to unravel the puzzle of why people are so continually upset over market change. We understand better why "it's not what it used to be" is such a persistent lament of market life. The answer lies in the very nature of the market itself—in how it offers us *both* a lot of the same and a lot of change. This dual nature creates a deep, abiding tension for us, for it means the very same thing that is so good at giving us all this precious stability is also forever changing on us, destabilizing us in the process. That which gives us such a reassuring sense of ontological security also takes it away. Who wouldn't get upset by that?

Our time-traveling exercise in the previous chapter revealed just how relentlessly unsettled a setting a street-level market can be.[8] Its instability arises from multiple, complex factors. Prior work has tended to train its gaze on one of the many forces at play and give that one thing sustained attention, whether it be residential dynamics, or technological disruption, or the interests of real estate owners and urban elites. However, monocausal depictions overlook just how multiple and complex the forces for change are in these markets and what that implies for the overall instability of the setting. All of these forces interact with one another and amplify each other's destabilizing effects. A business may be in the midst of navigating creative destruction in its industry when an exogenous shock like a financial crisis hits the entire economy or when something changes in the local property market. The proximate cause of Wyeth & Co.'s closing in 1920 was that its new landlord had doubled the rent, but part of why the independent grocer could not afford that new rent was that its sales had fallen in recent years because of competition from chain stores; not to mention that when the rent increase hit, one of the business's two partners was ninety years old and had scaled back his involvement in the business.

Once we appreciate how numerous and layered the changes are that continually transform the commercial landscape, we begin to appreciate more clearly just how difficult—at times, how impossible—it is to predict when those changes are coming and what exact form they will take. We also better appreciate just how challenging it can be to even understand them once they have arrived. Some of what unfolds at the street level is embedded in complex macro-level transformations concerning national and global markets, capital flows, and technological innovations that may initially be obscured from our street-level view or that might at first seem unrelated to our daily lives. One struggling Harvard Square shop owner purchased her business—a woman's clothing boutique—in the early 2000s after having worked at the shop for fifteen years. She was a skilled craftsperson who had developed her own clothing line and had finely tuned instincts for what styles and products appealed to the shop's customers. But she was not much into technology at the time. Within two years of taking over the business, she began to feel the effects of online commerce, and they only grew stronger from there. Looking back, she said, "I thought I knew the business. I'd worked in it. It seemed like not much would change. Little did I know!"

If it is hard for a seasoned business owner like her to see change coming, it can be even harder for us as consumers to see it. Some drivers of change, such as a longtime landlord's or proprietor's death, or a fire, or a global pandemic, are essentially impossible to predict. According to Giddens, if one had a perverse desire to create ontological insecurity in another, one might start by generating unpredictable and hard-to-decipher disruptions to the individual's everyday life.[9] That is to say, one might drop that person into a market.

When I graduated from college, Crimson Corner was still called Nini's Corner, and it was in a different location. It sat just across from the start of our block in chapter 3, right at the busy intersection of Massachusetts Avenue, Brattle Street, and JFK Street. At some point after I graduated, the owner of Nini's Corner, Philip Nini, began to have health issues, and his nephew, Chris Kotelly, took the family business over and renamed it. (Philip's father—Chris's grandfather—had founded the business in 1963.) When I moved back to the Square, I went to Crimson Corner as I'd gone to

Nini's Corner before, and I didn't much mark the name change. The place seemed mostly the same to me as when my father and I had stopped to browse its outdoor racks each Sunday. Then one day the shop was gone. The building's landlord had forced Crimson Corner out so that a new restaurant chain could move in.[10] Chris managed to keep his business going by securing a small space around the corner, but newspaper and magazine sales had been sliding in recent years, so when he reopened, the shop carried more tourist-oriented Harvard insignia than periodicals at its new address. I still went in for the newspapers and magazines, but now they filled just one narrow rack in the corner of the shop. Then one day there were no more magazines at all.

Even when we see and welcome market changes that are coming, like those that bring us exciting new innovations or offer us greater convenience or better prices—even when we as consumers *drive* the market's transformation with our evolving habits and preferences—those very same changes can confront us as exogenous and destabilizing. When the magazine rack disappeared, it's not like I wasn't reading news online myself by then. It's not like my own purchases of print periodicals hadn't declined in the years leading up to Crimson Corner's forced relocation. Yet still I felt shaken when I saw the shop gone from its old corner that first morning; and still I felt a pang when the magazine rack disappeared from the back of the store. And, when Chris closed his shop for good after the business was hit hard by the pandemic, I felt much more than a pang.

In 2011, when Amazon.com reported that Cambridge had the highest *per capita* online purchases of books of any large U.S. city, many Harvard Square denizens genuinely mourned the closing of bookstores and lamented the changing face of the marketplace. Even when reactions like this seem irrational or hypocritical from one angle, they make sense from another: We can still miss routines that we helped hasten the end of, because those routines were a taken-for-granted part of our everyday lives and meant so much more to us than the transaction itself. I missed wandering the aisles of Tower Records looking for CDs even as I embraced the iPod when it came out. Like many patrons of the Harvard Book Store, I hope never to have to miss wandering the store's aisles even though I have at times ordered from Amazon.

We feel even more acutely destabilized when it feels as if market changes have been foisted on us against our will. Think about the profound sense of vulnerability and dislocation a proprietor like Chris Kotelly must have felt when he and his whole life's work were uprooted simply because a landlord decided that higher rent could be obtained from a new tenant. Or, if we can sit with the uncomfortable feeling for a moment, consider the hurt and perhaps even betrayal someone like Chris might have felt when the woman who used to come in every morning like clockwork to get her newspaper started to show up more sporadically. And it's not just proprietors who can feel destabilized. As consumers, the simple arrival of an out-of-town real estate investor and eviction of a few local haunts can drive some of us to rage—or at least to hurling snowballs.

In a chapter titled "Pissed Off in L.A." in his book *How Emotions Work*, sociologist Jack Katz describes an emotional response many of us have had at the street level and which is quite useful for understanding why market change, especially when it feels forced upon us by others, can be so unsettling.[11] Katz investigates the source of road rage. He concludes that it arises from the sudden shock of ontological insecurity drivers experience when they get cut off. Driving along in our cars—like heading out to buy the newspaper or grab our morning cup of coffee—we tend to feel a certain continuity and control over our life's course. We are literally making our way through society, and, as we travel on our respective journeys, we feel a sense of agency and also that our presence is being marked and recognized by all those other drivers with whom we are implicitly coordinating. However, all of this is jarringly disrupted when someone cuts us off. When someone cuts us off—when, say, a fancy investment firm pushes out the businesses we have come to know and expect and replaces them with ones we don't—we are jolted out of our taken-for-granted sense of ourselves and the surrounding environment. We can feel unsettled, temporarily disoriented. Sometimes anxious. Oftentimes angry—after all, the person who cut us off acted like we were not even there, as if our path through the world was not significant enough to be taken into account.

Market change at the street level is a cutting off of sorts—from the streetscape we have come to expect, from the routines that have grounded us, from the ties that have rooted us to one another and to our place in the world. Sometimes it is an even more profound, more existential, cutting off. When the market changes because it has started attending less to us and our preferences and more to the next generation and that generation's preferences, it reminds us of our mortality—and there is nothing that provokes ontological insecurity quite like that. Most of us of a certain age can empathize with what those older men in the 1960s must have felt when they could no longer go to the barbershop they'd been going to for years not because they or their preferences had changed, but because the world had. I felt a bit of that when the magazine rack disappeared from Crimson Corner.

And therein lies the tension and therein lies the trickiness: markets are very good at giving us ontological security, and they are very good at taking all that security away from us. They continually stabilize us and destabilize us. We attach, and they cut the tie. *This* is our relationship with them, and this is why it is so damn tricky. The sort of upset that has recurred throughout Harvard Square's history and which is common to many street-level markets may sound like trite nostalgia or naïve sentimentalism, but it is more aptly seen as the result of the rather poignant, Sisyphean task we set for ourselves when we decided to live our lives in a market society. We continually seek—and momentarily find—stability and security in something that is destined to destabilize us in the very next moment.

PART 2

Crazy Love

Chapter Five

CRAZY LOVE

When my husband and I moved back to Harvard Square in 2014, I took up the habit of wandering into Black Ink every so often to browse. The gift shop appealed to the part of me that has always known with great certainty my life would be perfect if only I could find the right notebook. Or pen. Or pencil case. Or, during one particularly low week in graduate school, binder clip.

The store's tall glass facade framed in silvery gray metal offered a dash of industrial chic next to the old-fashioned red awning of Cardullo's Gourmet Shoppe. Inside, the space was narrow but deep, and it contained multitudes. Along the side walls, green shelves climbed from the floor to the very high ceiling above and held things like delicately crafted ceramic tea sets from Japan and shiny melamine serving trays, next to glass chemistry beakers last seen in Mr. Wizard's laboratory and at least seven volumes of the *Adventures of Tintin*, a midcentury Belgian comic strip about an adventurous boy reporter who travels the world on assignment with his dog Snowy and their friends Captain Haddock and Professor Calculus. One day I discovered a book of witchcraft spells two shelves above a coffee-table book on how to care for succulents. Near that was a thirty-nine-piece toy Steel Works construction kit and a box of animal-shaped erasers, the latter of which I purchased for my niece, whose hyper-focus on school supply shopping that fall had suggested I might have a kindred spirit in the family.

To wander the store was to wend one's way around the multiple tables filling its narrow middle. On those sat gigantic glass jars filled to the brim with huge yellow rubber bands that looked like they could hold a boat to dock, tiny red lobster claw finger-puppets labeled "Clawsome!," and silicone wine-bottle stoppers in every color of the rainbow. On the left side of the store was the cash register. Behind it hung crisp canvas tote bags and vintage-inspired wrapping paper with images lifted from out-of-date world atlases and old textbook charts classifying various types of flora, fauna, and fungi.

I often wondered who had curated this quirky menagerie. It seemed like he or she must possess some sort of wiccan-like sense to know that my brain would develop strong opinions about the attractiveness of different kitchen sponges after coming across an unusually appealing gray circular one on the store's shelves (the yellow, rectangular one I bought at the supermarket having been rendered immediately grotesque by comparison); or that the quadrant of my brain capable of developing such spongely preferences sat directly adjacent to the part that thrilled at seeing red plastic eggs of Silly Putty or packages of freeze-dried Astronaut Ice Cream transporting me back to elementary school field trips to Boston's Museum of Science.

Black Ink's shop floor. Courtesy of Black Ink, Inc.

Yet impressed as I was, I'd never met the store's curatorial wizard until that snowy March night in 2019, when Susan Corcoran and several other local business owners spoke at the Harvard Square Neighborhood Association's meeting about their challenges in the current marketplace. As soon as Corcoran stepped to the microphone, though, I recognized her. She was the striking woman I'd seen working at the shop during some of my visits, and I should have made the connection before. Dressed in slim black jeans, black flats, and a silvery top the color of her long, wavy hair, she reminded me of Black Ink's tall, metal-framed windows—a sleek, monochromatic exterior through which one caught glimpses of the whimsy and warmth lying within. After Susan spoke to the crowd about her frustrations in the market and the sizable rent increase she was facing from Black Ink's new landlord, I went up and introduced myself.

A couple of weeks later, I visited Susan in the store, and we sat gazing down on the shop from a tiny, hidden loft I had never before noticed on my prior visits. The space felt a bit like that perfect notebook for which I had always been searching. It was obscured from below by several large Chinese paper lanterns hanging off the store's ceiling, and it had just enough space for one wooden workbench, two stools, and a small file cabinet that doubled as a perch for Susan's laptop. Scattered across the workbench were sample products sent by vendors and artists, including several beautiful, hand-pressed greeting cards and two miniature teacups, as well as loose sheets of graph paper on which Susan's neat handwriting tracked inventory and product orders, plus invoices and shipping labels and an old fax machine that startled me when it rang.

"I have to close at the end of the year," Susan said quietly.[1] Below us, a handful of customers milled about, and an employee sorted stainless steel hanging clips into small boxes to be sold as sets. Joni Mitchell's voice floated softly through the store.[2] Susan had not yet announced the closure to her staff or customers. She was still holding out hope that her new landlord might come down on the rent so she could stay. But that hope was dwindling.

Susan and her husband, Tim, opened their first Black Ink store in 1994 on a quaint street on the flat of Boston's Beacon Hill neighborhood. Before that, they lived in Chicago, where Susan was an early employee of Paper Source, a stationery, crafts, and gift store founded in the early 1980s by a different Susan, a woman named Susan Lindstrom. In their early thirties, the Corcorans decided to move from Chicago to Cambridge, and Lindstrom suggested they open a Paper Source store for the company out there.

So, "with a van full of paper," as Susan Corcoran put it, she and Tim headed off to the East Coast. When they arrived, she negotiated a lease in Cambridge's Porter Square, a mile down Massachusetts Avenue from Harvard Square, and they opened up shop.

After a few years, Susan said, "We started to ask ourselves, why are we doing this for someone else? We're putting all this time into it, why not do it on our own, and our way?" They had an idea for a shop, and the time felt right. Black Ink was a different concept than Paper Source so Corcoran was able to remain on good terms with Lindstrom, but she knew it still stung her former boss when she left to go out on her own. It was the right decision for her and Tim, though.

Around the same time, Tim went back to Harvard College to finish the undergraduate degree he'd abandoned twenty years before, and Susan became pregnant with their first child. To keep costs down in the shop's early days, they hired no staff and worked seven days a week. Susan and the baby manned the store during the day, while Tim headed to campus and then joined them as soon as his classes ended. From the start, the shop's merchandise reflected Susan's personal aesthetic. It also reflected whatever was going on in their lives at that time. When they had two young babies at home, she began carrying bath toys at the store. When they bought a house in Cambridge, she stocked more home goods. Then, they opened a dedicated furniture and homeware store right around the corner from their house.

By 2001, the couple had a two-year-old, a five-year-old, and two businesses. However, Harvard Square had always had sentimental appeal to Tim, so when a friend at the Harvard Square Business Association told them some space might be coming available in the Square, they decided to go for it. It was a stretch financially, but it was in a prime location right next to Cardullo's, and it would advertise itself. The couple did the entire renovation and build-out themselves, and as quickly as they could. They needed the store to start generating revenue so it would cover the utilities, taxes, insurance, and rent for which they were now responsible. Together, they tore the former tenant's storefront off the building and installed the striking new glass facade that would define Black Ink to passersby. Inside the store, Tim built not only the loft in which Susan and I were now chatting but also the massive, floor-to-ceiling green shelves. It was an exhausting, hectic time. "We were burning the candle on both ends," Susan said. After a pause, she added, "Tim never bounced back from it."

A year after the Harvard Square store opened, Tim was diagnosed with stage 4 cancer. He died the next year. A widow and single mother to two young children, Susan closed the homeware store but continued to operate the two Black Ink shops. "I kept going. I had to. There wasn't any other option," she told me. "I paid our rent, paid our employees, kept the operations going." But it was hard. "I used to come up here and cry," she said, motioning to the loft.

Black Ink's Harvard Square landlord at the time was the Dow and Stearns Family Trust, a legacy of Richard Dow, one of the landlords and developers we met on our block in the mid-1900s. By then, Dow was dead, and the trust had hired a local on-site property manager to oversee the buildings. Susan described the property manager as a kind man, who swung by often to check on her during Tim's illness and after his passing. "That would never happen today," she told me. A few years back, the trust had fired that property manager and replaced him with an international real estate investment management company to help ready the properties for sale. Then, in 2017, the trust sold Black Ink's building to the North Carolina–based private equity firm Asana Partners.

After the sale was announced, Susan received a call from someone at Asana letting her know that members of the firm would soon visit from North Carolina.[3] A few days later, seven people in suits filed into her shop. She recognized several of the young women in the group. She was sure they had come by the store before, "scouting and scoping it out" in the weeks preceding the sale. I could tell from her voice that the visit felt like an invasion to her. "They stood in the middle of my shop," she said, "oblivious" to the shoppers and staff trying to move around the narrow space. One of the individuals from Asana told her that the firm wanted Black Ink to stay; that they knew a business like hers couldn't pay top rates for rent, but they wanted a mix of businesses in the building. "That gave me some hope," she said. "But with time I came to see that wasn't true."

Black Ink's lease was up soon. Contractually, Susan had an option to extend it for 2.5 years "at market rates," and she was hoping to negotiate an affordable rent that would allow her to stay. However, when she tried to reach out to Asana to begin negotiations, Susan told me, she struggled to get responses to her emails and calls. Eventually, she hired a lawyer. It was the first time in her career she'd had to do that. Through her lawyer, Asana conveyed that the firm was willing to make a concession: an 80 percent increase in rent, which was below market by their estimation. But that was still more than what Black Ink could afford. Susan asked her lawyer to see if Asana would let her stay through the end of 2019 instead of having to vacate mid-year. Asana agreed.

I stayed in touch with Susan as 2019 wore on. She seemed, understandably, to be cycling through the various stages of grief over the impending loss of her store. At one point, she thought she might try once more to persuade Asana to come down on the rent. A friend advised she not get emotional when speaking with the firm's representatives. "He told me this is a numbers issue," Susan said. But for her, it had always been a "heart issue," and her heart was breaking. This business was inextricably personal to her. It was just as much her and Tim's creation as their two children, who had grown up keeping their mom company in the shop and who both now worked in it part time. This was the store Tim had always dreamed of, and it is where Susan mourned his passing. When we spoke during those months, I could tell she was, in a way, losing him all over again through the loss of the store. One day, she pointed to the distinctive green shelves he built and said, "I will destroy them myself before I let someone else take them down."

Susan was not just heartbroken. She was mad. Mad at Asana, whom she blamed for taking her life's work from her. Mad at the City of Cambridge and the Harvard Square Business Association, who she felt should be doing more to protect businesses like hers. She wrote a letter to the mayor, and, for the first time since opening her store, she refused to pay her dues to the Business Association. Yet she also knew that what was happening was not just about her and her hurt. Asana was "getting the community piece all wrong," in her opinion. This was a heart issue for the community, too.

Christmas had always been Corcoran's favorite time of year at the shop. That was part of why staying through the end of 2019 was so important to her—she wanted one last Christmas in the Square. In the weeks leading up to the holiday, the store always buzzed with activity, and she loved working out on the floor then. Some families came back every year to do their shopping. "They walk in and grab a basket and head directly to where they're going," she told me. "The store doesn't belong to me during those weeks. It belongs to them—the people coming in. I'm just facilitating their experience."

This was what Asana didn't fully understand, Susan said. They had seen Harvard Square as an attractive market in which to invest. However, they had failed to see that in many people's minds, shops such as Susan's *were* Harvard Square. Black Ink wasn't the only small, independent shop getting swept away by new, outside investors like Asana and the well-capitalized chains they preferred as tenants. With her old neighbor Chris Kotelly's Crimson Corner displaced from its corner and nearby Crema Café having closed, Susan said it felt like a "tsunami" was hitting the Square. "People expect us to be here." She thought Asana was discounting just how upset people were starting to get over the changes. Anticipating the community's response to Black Ink's closure, Susan said, "I think this will be unlike anything Asana is expecting."

⁓

On September 5, 2019, Susan hung a six-foot-tall scroll in Black Ink's front window. It was a letter from her, composed in neat, black typewritten text, interspersed with splashes of bright, colorful script. It told customers that after eighteen years in the marketplace, Black Ink would be closing its Harvard Square shop at year's end. Susan thanked her staff for their talent and dedication, and she thanked the "wonderful community" who had supported her business through the years. She signed the letter simply, "Peace & Love."

That same day, Susan placed another, much smaller sign inside her shop. On the deep windowsill just below the tall scroll, she placed a plain piece of 8½ by 11 printer paper that customers could see upon entering. It read:

Hello friends! Please join us in a project called "Dear Asana Partners." Asana Partners is the real estate investment [firm] that purchased this building and another parcel on Brattle Street . . . They are located in North Carolina and have been purchasing many other commercial properties in [the area]. Please let them know what you think about the displacement of local businesses like Black Ink. This is YOUR Community and we want you to have a way to express your feelings. Write a note to Asana . . . We will be posting this on our Instagram [and] will present the document to Asana Partners when the project concludes.

A lot had happened to Susan that year. Now, she thought, maybe she would make something happen. She left some large, blank sheets of white poster paper and a few black magic markers next to the sign on the sill. Then she waited. It didn't take long for that something to happen.

Within days, hundreds of people had left messages. Some notes were signed by name or initials and the person's city of residence; others went unsigned. Many were love letters to Black Ink and conveyed heartache over its closing. Susan was right—this was a heart issue for a lot of people. "I have been coming to Black Ink since I was a teenager," wrote one Cambridge resident; "I am saddened and angry and betrayed."[4]

The death of Harvard Square was a common refrain. A number of people linked the loss of Black Ink to other recent losses in the Square like that of Crema Café, and they shared what these places had meant to them. Black Ink and local businesses like it were the "beating soul of the city" (Andie, Cambridge). They are "our community . . . We meet and greet and share peace with each other" in them (Marie-Louise, Quincy). These establishments are what made Harvard Square, Harvard Square, people wrote—they represented "the spirit" of the Square (Malden), gave it its "soul" and its "character." Craig of Somerville asked, "What is Harvard Square without shops like this?" Someone else declared it a "travesty" to lose these places. "It has broken my heart," wrote "V.E." of Boston.

Other messages read less like mournful love letters to a dearly departed and more like the angry missives of a spurned lover. People lashed out at Asana. They accused the firm of being "greedy" and "unfair," of "robbing" the community and "ruining" Harvard Square for its own selfish benefit. "You have no soul," read one note. "Shame on you for these unfair practices," read another. "Can you spell moral bankruptcy?" one individual asked. "How do you sleep at night?" asked another. People called Asana "jerks." They called Asana other names. "Thanks a lot for ruining Harvard Square, you sorry flock of bottom feeders." "Thanks for contributing to the creeping soullessness of Harvard Square. I urge you to reconsider, you absolute robber-baron movie villains."

By the end of the first week, local news outlets had taken note and started covering the "Dear Asana Project."[5] As word spread that Susan intended eventually to mail the stack of messages to Asana, even more people stopped by to express their feelings on the page. Susan kept having to add more sheets of blank poster paper to the sill.

Some notes pled for Asana to rethink their decisions and change course—to save Black Ink and the Square. Others lobbed threats. "Rest assured I will never step foot in any business that you impose on our community in your tainted real estate." "Continue to displace local businesses and I will ensure that every college student, family, and employee boycotts anything that moves into your property. No one will want to rent from you." Still others told Asana to get out of Harvard Square entirely. "We don't want your corporate nonsense here. Go back to North Carolina where you came from!!!" One just said, "Fuck You, Asana."

Black Ink's exterior, with pages from the Dear Asana Project hanging in the front window, fall 2019. Courtesy of Black Ink, Inc.

As the holidays approached, some embraced the Christmas spirit. One individual wished Asana, "Happy holidays, Scrooges!" Another let Dr. Seuss's *How the Grinch Stole Christmas* convey his feelings about the private equity firm: "You're a bad banana with a greasy black peel. Your heart's an empty hole. You've got garlic in your soul. I wouldn't touch you with a 39½ foot pole." Someone else tacked on an addendum: "You're a triple-decker sauer-kraut and toadstool sandwich with arsenic sauce."

I stopped by the shop frequently during these weeks to read the ever-growing pile of messages. The closure of this small, idiosyncratic store—a store one might uncharitably describe as selling nothing more than knick-knacks that appeal to the thirteen-year-old girl in some of us—was provok-ing fierce expressions of love and outrage from all corners. The people who poured their hearts out on Susan's poster paper—the people who composed bitter, angry messages to investment professionals working eight hundred miles away—were not just longtime patrons of the shop or local business owners who knew Susan personally. Some merely knew the store from pass-ing it by over the years. Some who left messages were longtime residents of Cambridge; others, more recent Harvard matriculants. Some were students at other colleges in the Greater Boston area. Many were residents of nearby cities and towns that ran the gamut from wealthy to working class.

As the messages accumulated, it struck me that this felt like more than just another case of people being momentarily destabilized by market change. This was not just another mournful lament that Harvard Square wasn't what it used to be. This was some crazy love. And what seemed to be unifying people in their expressions of love and outrage was the feeling that some-thing meaningful—something almost sacred to them—was at stake, and that Asana was in the process of destroying it for the firm's own financial gain. "Black Ink *is* Harvard Square" wrote someone, and Asana was a bunch of "greedy capitalist pigs" about to ruin it. Notes like "Don't let your capitalist greed ruin the history, culture, and sanctity of this area" kept bringing me back to that day in the store, when Susan and I had chatted in her loft and Joni Mitchell sang, "they paved paradise and put up a parking lot."

From one angle, this sort of intense emotional response was not surpris-ing. Scholars across a range of fields have observed that people get upset when they feel that market forces are threatening something sacred. In my own field of economic sociology, Viviana Zelizer's work documents the intense hostility with which the public met the early market for life insur-ance in the early nineteenth century.[6] Such commercialization was thought to erode the sanctity of death. Since then, Zelizer and others have probed a range of cases, including the commercialization of bodily organs, egg and sperm donation, adoption, child care, and elder care, and found that, to this day, many people still get disturbed at the thought of market forces invad-ing personally meaningful, sacred spheres of life.[7] In economics, Alvin Roth has written about the "repugnance" people often express for the market and market actors in such instances.[8] In social psychology, Philip Tetlock and his colleagues have tested and elaborated similar ideas in experimental studies. Their "Sacred-Value-Protection Model" predicts that when market forces threaten to transform something we have traditionally held sacrosanct—such as family, friendships, or votes—we often have strong, negative emotional responses ranging from concern and fear, to intense anxiety, to even anger and moral outrage.[9]

In short, the Dear Asana Project is not the only time or place in which people have lashed out at "capitalist pigs" for desecrating something special. It is not even the first time in Harvard Square's history that such outrage has exploded onto the scene. As a culture, we seem to have a recurring, deep-seeded fear that the capitalist market will contaminate or even destroy what we hold most dear. This sort of market discomfort is probably especially strong in a city that has earned its local nickname, "The People's Republic of Cambridge." (During the 2020 presidential primaries, the *Los Angeles Times* ran a profile of the "liberal bubble Elizabeth Warren calls home"; Warren lives on a side street just outside the Square.)[10]

It might, therefore, seem straightforward to interpret all this commotion as merely a hyped-up, intensified form of the sort of anti-market sentiment that is always simmering just beneath the surface of our culture. The first half of one note scrawled for Asana supports this interpretation. The note began, "I'm Marxist." However, it continued, "Keep our local companies!"—and it is that second part that makes it harder to explain away people's upset in this case.

If all the love notes to Harvard Square and Black Ink strewn across the pages of the Dear Asana Project tell us anything—if all the years of the recurring Death Discourse taught us anything in Part 1 of this book—it is that people in this liberal outpost are quite capable of falling truly, madly, deeply in love with their markets and market institutions. In fact, people in Harvard Square become so smitten they sometimes go completely crazy when they feel their beloved market slipping away. The Dear Asana Project—like other eruptions of crazy love we will explore—is puzzling precisely because it involves a bunch of people lobbing anti-capitalist epithets in defense of a capitalist market they desperately love.

Past studies of moral outrage over the market's encroachment into sacred spaces have focused on cases in which it was easy to think that what was sacred was, at least traditionally, not a part of the market. Drawing on Emile

Durkheim's classic sacred-profane dichotomy, the assumption of prior work—and the assumption underlying so much of our everyday discourse— is that what is sacred to us is that which is set *apart* from the market, and what is profane to us *is* the market. Yet when we look carefully at the messages written to Asana, one thing becomes unmistakably clear: the sacred thing people were so fiercely defending—the thing they were so worried was being desecrated and destroyed by market forces—was itself a market and the market institutions that constituted it.

And *that* is the really tricky part of all this. We so often think and talk in terms of the profane market destroying what we hold dear. But what if the thing we hold sacred is also that which we find profane? No wonder we sometimes go crazy. Our relationship with markets is not just that they stabilize and destabilize us. It is that, ultimately, we both love and hate them; they are both sacred and profane to us.

～

Part 2 of this book heads deeper into Harvard Square's love story to better understand our complicated love-hate relationship with markets. It steps back into the Square's past to explore earlier moments of "crazy love"— i.e., puzzling (and, sometimes, puzzlingly extreme) emotional reactions; moments when people have clung especially tightly to the market they loved, afraid that one or another market change was about to destroy it. These are revelatory moments for our purposes because people often become the most reflective and articulate about what a relationship means to them when they feel it slipping away. As Joni Mitchell put it, "Don't it always seem to go that you don't know what you've got till it's gone."

By unraveling these puzzling instances of "crazy love," we will start to understand why people may attach so deeply to a market that they come to love it, even sacralize it. We will also start to see what sorts of market changes are so destabilizing that they can feel like a profanation of that sacred love. In each case of "crazy love," we will uncover that what's ultimately at stake is some sense of community rooted in the marketplace. Changes that seem to provoke the most intense emotional responses in people are those that threaten the sense of togetherness they have found in the market. In short, what might look like "crazy" behavior from the outside is often just individuals' attempts to defend their cherished attachments to one another and a collective life they share. And that's not so much crazy as it is love.

As we proceed, we will begin to make out the even deeper tension at the heart of life in market society, one that underlies the stability/instability tension we surfaced earlier: markets are both collectivizing and atomizing; they make us feel together and apart. Indeed, the deepest source of ontological security we derive from markets comes not from their stabilizing routines but from the deep and abiding attachments we form with one another in the course of all those routine interactions. As it turns out, markets are very good at providing and destroying this basis of ontological security, too.

Economics has taught us to think of markets as settings where atomistic individuals pursue their own self-interest. Sociology has taught us to think of markets as social, relational phenomena. They are both. This book deepens our understanding of markets as relational phenomena, while exposing the tension their dual nature poses for us all; namely, markets continually remind us of the collective and connected nature of our lives, while at the same time harnessing our self-interest in ways that repeatedly, invariably destabilize whatever sense of togetherness we derived from them.

As we make our way through Harvard Square's crazy love story and work our way back to the present, we will glean lessons that can help us better understand our own times. By allowing the resonances and echoes of the past, as well as the differences, to surface along the way, we will be better positioned to explore what the market means to a range of present-day market participants, why recent changes may be provoking such acute feelings of destabilization, and what it all might imply in general for Americans' relationship with street-level markets like Harvard Square.

By the end, we will see that our relationship with markets is so damn complicated and can drive us so damn crazy because it is ultimately about our relationship with ourselves and one another—with how we come together and how we come apart. We fall in love with our markets when they make us feel a part of something shared, when we feel securely tethered to one another in our ever-shifting world. At the same time, we wring our hands and rage at the market—even scream about the desecration of it all—when market changes roll through and rip apart those sacred ties.

Chapter Six

EVERYBODY GET TOGETHER

On a dreary March afternoon in 1910, thirty or so men met in an office on our block of JFK (to them, Boylston) Street to discuss the possibility of forming a Harvard Square business association.[1] The week before, several respected business owners, including Albert "Bert" Amee of Amee Brothers Book Shop and Thomas Hadley of the hardware store Moore & Hadley, had circulated a letter proposing a group whose mission would be to work together to "bring about conditions beneficial to the whole trade" in Harvard Square.[2] The Square's merchants had always been an independent lot, but many were reeling from recent changes in the market. Some felt it was time to set aside their differences and navigate the challenges together.

As the meeting got under way, most were excited about the possibility of working together. Some, however, cautioned that it might not go seamlessly. The men were used to thinking about themselves and their firms first. Some were direct competitors. A local painter with an office down the block spoke up to say that if the group was to succeed, it would be necessary to "eliminate every vestige of jealousy and suspicion among members."[3] Disputes would inevitably arise, and all agreed that the organization's leaders would have to mediate them when they did. Somehow, everyone would have to be convinced that a "spirit of fraternity would benefit all financially."[4]

No one in the room seemed better able to make that happen than George G. Wright. In his sixties, Wright was one of the older men at the meeting and the most respected. He had a track record of bringing businessmen together. Twenty years earlier he had helped found the Citizens' Trade Association, whose mission was to promote "friendly and social" relations among Cambridge's businessmen, and whose original offices were furnished with a billiard hall, parlor room, and large dining hall to support that.[5] Although Wright had not been a part of calling this March 1910 meeting in the Square, he was everyone's choice to lead the new group.

On the one hand, Wright's life had unfolded rather typically for a local merchant of his time, and he had much in common with the other businessmen. Born in 1848, he had grown up in a small, second-floor residence above his father's Harvard Square bakery.[6] He attended Cambridge's public high school and, after graduation, took a job as a clerk for a Boston pharmacy. When that work failed to inspire him, Wright returned to Cambridge to open a firm of his own. For the next three decades, he ran a grain business out of the same building as his family's bakery. Then, at the age of fifty-four, he turned his attention to real estate and became a property manager and insurance broker in the Square. Over his more than forty years of doing business there, Wright had forged deep ties throughout the marketplace.

On the other hand, Wright was not your usual businessman. With bushy eyebrows, an irrepressible cowlick, and a haphazardly tied bow-tie that was often askew, he looked more like a disheveled poet than corporate leader, and he was a romantic at heart—especially when it came to his hometown.[7] It would be hard to find someone who loved Cambridge and Harvard Square more than he did. Wright never married and seems instead to have given himself over fully to the community he cherished. As early as his teens, he began to hold onto printed material relating to the city—pamphlets, newspaper clippings, brochures, etc.—believing these would be important documents for future generations. He liked to quote the poet James Russell Lowell, a friend and contemporary of Longfellow, who penned his own paeans to the Square.[8] Most of all, Wright demonstrated his deep devotion through service to the community. He was an active member of nearly two dozen civic groups. Some, like the Cambridge Historical Society, were devoted to preserving the city's past. Others, like Library Hall, which sought to root out corruption in local elections, were devoted to strengthening the city for the future.

By 1910, Wright had become known about town as the "Sage of Cambridge," and he had an unmatched reputation for civic engagement and rectitude.[9] When the Harvard Square Business Men's Association was officially formed in April of that year, the forty-four charter members elected him their first president.[10]

At the time, there was plenty to unite these men. In 1910, the Square was in the midst of the greatest street-level disruption it had ever seen. Contractors for Boston Elevated Railway were building the new subway there, and work crews were literally digging up the streets.[11] A film of dirt and dust covered store merchandise and shop floors. In the time it took a shopkeeper to sweep, a new layer of filth would form. Streetcar traffic was diverted and detoured. The few brave souls still willing to shop in this mess found their normal footpaths obstructed and had to wend their way around gaping holes. One day, an explosion intending to break up a five-ton boulder belowground sent rock and timber shooting into the air above.[12] Some days the railway workers broke out in violent strikes.[13]

Before all this, the introduction of electric streetcars had already been sowing chaos on the streets of Harvard Square. Thousands of people now changed cars there. Pedestrians, express teams, bicyclists, delivery wagons,

Subway construction in Harvard Square, 1910. Courtesy of Cambridge Historical Commission, Boston Elevated Railway Collection.

and trolleys all had to navigate around one another, prompting the *Cambridge Chronicle* to remark just before the turn of the century that "the turmoil in Harvard Square these days is sufficient to send a good portion of Cambridge citizens to the lunatic asylum."[14] The new subway posed an even graver threat for local commerce, however. The Square's merchants were not merely concerned with the short-term disruption of all the digging and construction; they worried that the shoppers driven away during this period might never return. Aboveground streetcars had wreaked havoc, to be sure, but at least they kept people at the street level when passing through, and that often spurred business for the shops. The subway, on the other hand, might keep people entirely underground. To change lines, many would never need to emerge from below. Those who wanted to come up to the street for a quick errand or stroll would have to pay a second fare to return.

Meanwhile, Cambridge's population was soaring from immigration and development. In the market's immediate vicinity, Harvard University had been expanding in recent decades. The businessmen knew there were opportunities in all this growth and change. However, they also knew that some of their old ways of doing business were starting to crack under the weight of it all. Selling on credit, for instance, was proving far more challenging in a market filled with thousands of new, unfamiliar faces.[15] What's more, all this modern, rapid transit was allowing residents to reach other markets with ease. The merchants' fates were more tied to one another's than ever before. If even a single shop delivered poor customer service—or kept its prices higher than those in a competing market, or was consistently out of stock on popular items— customers might well depart to those other markets for all their shopping. A recently formed Boston Chamber of Commerce was at work on behalf of its retailers, and Cambridge shoppers were being lured across the Charles River.[16]

The men who formed the Harvard Square Business Men's Association and chose Wright as their leader were driven together by these common threats and by the common hope that once the subway was complete, the Square might regain its footing and become a competitive, bustling, modern marketplace. The past few years had persuaded them that perhaps market life was best approached as a shared endeavor. As their president, George Wright took it upon himself to ensure that happened.

～

The early years of the Business Men's Association were busy, heady ones.[17] Under Wright's leadership, the group formed a Credit Committee to share information on delinquencies, so that members knew who not to extend credit to.[18] They formed an Advertising Committee to coordinate marketing and boost the entire market—not just their individual shops—to local customers. A 1911 advertising bulletin they created included promotions for every member and the tag line, "Harvard Square, a more important centre with completion of Subway."[19] They undertook street-cleaning projects to make the market more appealing to shoppers and reverse the reputation for filth it had deservedly acquired during the subway project. To modernize and beautify the Square, members chipped in $2,800 (just under $80,000 in today's dollars) to fund the installation of fifty-three electric lamps.[20]

While tackling these immediate challenges, they also contemplated the market's more distant future. In 1912, the Business Men's Association lobbied the mayor of Cambridge and the president of Harvard University to appoint a committee of experts to help draft a plan for the future development of Harvard Square. Wright encouraged this sort of long-term thinking. Ever since childhood, he had felt fortunate to live in a place so rich in history, and he believed it was his generation's responsibility to steward their unique inheritance for the next. During his years with the association, he liked to stroll through the area's old burial grounds to reflect on the contributions of those who had come before, and in his speeches to the group, he urged members to think about the collective legacy they would impart to those who would follow.[21] The 1913 report of the Committee on Future Development reflected this sensibility. It advocated for modernization projects such as street widening as well as preservation initiatives such as zoning and building restrictions that would protect the Square's unique historic character.[22]

Through all these early endeavors, the businessmen were not just investing in their market and boosting it to the outside world. They were boosting their own communal spirit, too. As with the Citizens' Trade Association, Wright felt it was important for members of the group to socialize and become friendly with one another. Only by getting to know each other personally could they develop what he liked to call "a fuller appreciation of the community of their interests."[23] So, not long after its founding, the Business Men's Association began holding regular meetings at the Colonial Club, a men's social club located just off the Square.

Each meeting began with a large dinner, followed by a round of hearty singing and piano playing.[24] Self-appointed toastmasters led the group in round after round of toasts. By the time members turned their attention to the evening's business, feelings of fraternal brotherhood wafted through the air, carried along by the plumes of cigar smoke and peaty aroma of expensive scotch. A sort of collective market effervescence had started to bloom. The group, which quickly grew to about seventy-five members, was always trying out some new unifying motto at these events. One month it was, "In union there is strength."[25] Another month it was, "Each for all and all for each."[26]

During the early evening festivities, George Wright tended to sit back and give the members space to form the ties that would bind them. After a good round of fun, however, he would reinforce the sense of brotherhood in his own, earnest way. Following dinner, he would call the official business meeting to order and then deliver impassioned remarks. He felt it was his duty to remind them of their shared fate. "None can receive benefit without in some measure sharing it with his neighbor," he said in prepared remarks at one of the group's early meetings.[27] "Every man should consider carefully whether he is working in the interests of the community which is really his own interests," he declared at another.[28] Many nights he invited speakers to talk about the benefits of groups like theirs, further reinforcing his message. One such talk, delivered by a director of the Boston Chamber of Commerce, was titled "The Advantages of Concerted Action for the Retail Trade."[29]

There was a reason Wright felt these reminders necessary. For all the fraternal fun, initial concerns about corralling a bunch of independent entrepreneurs had been warranted.[30] It was hard to get members to agree to uniform store hours, something the group hoped to achieve. Others continued to advertise in ways that undercut fellow members. Some grumbled and asked what they, personally, were getting from it whenever the Advertising Committee came around to raise money for joint promotions. Most of all, some merchants were still stuck in their old ways of doing business, and this was alienating customers who had other options for where to shop. If Harvard Square was going to become the attractive commercial district the group hoped it would be, this was not the time to be "blinded by tradition," as Wright once put it.[31] This was the time to shake things up and do things differently.

Wright thought the businessmen needed some frank feedback. In 1912 he pushed the group to survey female shoppers in the area to ascertain their impression of the market.[32] The wife of John Amee, Bert's brother, helped organize a women's luncheon, and Wright dispatched two members—Fred Olsson, who owned an art and crafts shop in the Square, and Thomas Hadley of the hardware store—to attend and collect their impressions.[33] The women did not hold back. A report summarizing their feedback characterized it as, "unhesitatingly and almost vehemently in the negative."[34]

According to the women, the whole marketplace was old and dated. One described it as "a veritable Rip Van Winkle" that "hadn't been awake for twenty years."[35] Their criticisms were many: Prices were too high. Nothing was ever on sale. Stock was too limited. "They never have what you want," explained one woman. "It's always 'Just out' or 'We expect a supply from New York next week'" she said, parroting the merchants' common refrain. Most of all, the service stunk. "It is a work of art to get a clerk to wait upon you," one frustrated woman said. If she finally was able to get someone's attention, she was made to feel she should apologize "for taking up his valuable time."

The women wanted Harvard Square's businessmen to know that shopping was not always fun. Many days it was just a tedious, tiresome duty they had to perform. Anything that made it easier or more pleasurable was valued. In contrast to Boston shops, the stores in Harvard Square felt designed for the shopkeepers' convenience, not the customers'. In addition, the Square's merchants were not engaging in any of the clever advertising with which Boston retailers had recently been experimenting—newspaper ads with little ditties or gimmicks the whole family could get a kick out of or simple promotions and discounts that allowed a woman to feel, after a long day of shopping, that at least she had gotten a bargain. To top it off, the Harvard Square subway station had no escalator, whereas the Park Street station in Boston did. Who, the women asked rhetorically, would climb up sixty steps "for the doubtful pleasure of shopping in Harvard Square?" Harvard Square's businessmen might be having fun at their dinner meetings, but the women of Harvard Square let them know their market reflected "the pathetic dignity of a decayed gentility."

To their credit, the men seemed to absorb the message. Although no references to the women's feedback appear in the Business Men's Association records after 1912, the fingerprints of that feedback are all over the group's subsequent activities. Both the street-cleaning and street-lighting projects intended to update the Square's dated, grungy atmosphere were launched soon after. The association began actively lobbying the railroad company for an escalator at the subway station. Fred Olsson, in particular, took a keen interest in advertising and promotion after his and Hadley's fateful lunch with the women. Olsson went on to organize Square-wide "Bargain Days" and "Dollar Days."[36] He took the helm of the association's Advertising Committee and enlisted about eight other members to join him in offering cash-back coupons to shoppers.[37] The newspaper ads he placed for his own shop became more clever, whimsical, and quirky over time.

～

Fred Olsson was more than twenty years Wright's junior, and the two men could not have been more different. However, they were united by a deep commitment to the mission of the Business Men's Association. They just had very different ideas about how to achieve it. Wright made moral, sometimes grandiose appeals to member's sense of collective duty; Olsson went straight for their self-interest. In 1914, when Wright was growing tired of hearing members complain about one another, he told the assembled group an impassioned story drawn from one of his recent cemetery strolls. Recalling how he came across the graves of two Union soldiers lying side-by-side, Wright described being moved by the thought that these two men had set aside all the petty faults and deficits of their comrades to press on together to save their cherished Union. Like a battlefield general rallying his troops, Wright commanded, "So our members with courage, perseverance, and loyalty join heartily together at all times and in all places to advance the interest of Harvard Square."[38] Meanwhile, Olsson rolled out a sticker campaign that motivated merchants to advertise the entire Square as they advertised their own businesses.[39]

Likewise, in 1915, when both Wright and Olsson were irritated that some members were not even keeping their store windows clean, let alone investing in appealing displays that would improve the overall look of the marketplace, Wright called on members to have pride in their community and think of one another before their own pocketbooks. "Believe me," he pressed, "you will find, when life's struggle is nearing its close, more satisfaction in the work you have done to benefit and improve the community . . . than you can possibly derive from any account of money."[40] Olsson took a different tack. He channeled the men's animal spirits by pitting merchant against merchant in window-display contests. Soon they were all competing to see who had the best, most creative display.

Olsson knew something about animal spirits. The son of a Swedish immigrant, he looked the part of a buttoned-up Swede with straight cravats tied tight against his throat and blond hair parted straight down the middle.[41] In reality, he could be wild, and his life was often messy and tumultuous. In 1900, his marriage to a striking young woman ended salaciously with accusations of adultery and abuse fired back and forth across the pages of the *Boston Globe*. One headline ran, "In Night Robe: Thus Clad, F. A. Olsson Fled from Home."[42] He remarried almost immediately after the divorce was granted.[43] In 1906, he left his father's Harvard Square shop—J. F. Olsson's, which specialized in picture framing and art sales—to start his own, directly competitive shop just around the corner.[44] J. F was an early member of the Business Men's Association too, and when he died in 1915, Fred pounced on the opportunity. Fred's sister Marie Louise was set to take over their father's shop, and Fred assumed she would not be allowed to join the group. He immediately took out an ad in the local paper, declaring his shop "the only art store member of the Harvard Square Business Men's Association."[45] Olsson had misread his fellow businessmen, however; although the association's by-laws were not officially amended to allow women members until 1919, a majority voted to allow women into the group soon after J. F.'s death, and "Miss M. L. Olsson" was listed on the membership rolls thereafter.[46] Fred Olsson was undeterred. He ran another ad shortly after the first, this one instructing shoppers to "be sure you get the initials right" lest they mistakenly go to J. F. Olsson's instead of F. A. Olsson's.[47]

Even if he was nothing like reserved, upright Wright, Olsson's killer instinct did not make him a poor fit for the association. He believed it was in his and others' best interest to come together and promote Harvard Square every bit as aggressively as they promoted their own individual businesses. He found an outlet for his creative impulses there, too. Over the years, he was a font of bold, sometimes even brash ideas and schemes. The next few years momentarily tempered those impulses, however.

~

The United States' entry into World War I in 1917 posed new challenges for the Business Men's Association. For perhaps the first time since the group's founding, their attention was drawn to events outside the immediate vicinity of the Square. New England faced food and fuel shortages. John Amee, now president of the association, took charge of enforcing fuel limits among the membership.[48] Enrollment in the university declined, and so did business in the Square. The association purchased Liberty Bonds.[49]

George Wright remained an active member during all this. After his term as president ended, he became chair of a newly formed Committee on Municipal Affairs. While Amee and others focused on navigating all the wartime changes, Wright kept his focus where it always had been, on the local. He worked tirelessly to promote public-improvement projects that he felt

would benefit the Square—from new traffic rules, to street-widening projects, to the installation of a public sanitary station. With so much else going
on in the world, however, it was hard to command people's attention, and
Wright seems to have grown frustrated with the group. After a disappointing
1918, Wright wrote a report for the association in which he asked with evident irritation: "Is it not worthwhile to make an effort to encourage a better
development of our Square?"[50]

Things had been even more challenging that year, however. In the fall of
1918, a deadly influenza (what would eventually be called the "Spanish flu")
hit Cambridge.[51] The city temporarily closed its ice-cream parlors, billiard
halls, bowling alleys, and theaters. Local schools were closed and converted
into field hospitals. Although the worst had ostensibly passed by early 1919,
citizens and students were still being advised to avoid churches, theaters,
movies, and crowded streetcars. At least one member of the association died
as a result of the pandemic.

In December 1918, thirty-four-year-old Harold Moore of the Moore &
Hadley hardware store succumbed to pneumonia after contracting the flu.[52]
His store had been in the Moore family for years, and Thomas Hadley, one
of the association's founding members, was Moore's brother-in-law. By the
time of Moore's death, Hadley had moved into real estate, and the family
hardware store did not survive Harold's passing. By the next spring it was
operating under new ownership and a new name.[53]

Upon his death, the Business Men's Association paused to honor Moore's
memory, as they did whenever a member died.[54] Despite the occasional
bickering and squabbles, these men were forming deep bonds of mutual
respect through their work together. During Wright's tenure, the group
began a practice of memorializing each member's passing, a tradition carried
on through the years. After news of a death like Moore's, the businessmen
would lower their shop's shutters or dim their store's lights for the afternoon.
At the start of the group's next dinner meeting, before any entertainment
and festivities, they would hold a moment of silence for the departed. One
member would then be assigned to draw up "resolutions"—a formal, written
tribute to the individual's life and contributions—which would then be read
at the next meeting and entered into the official record.

~

By early 1919, several merchants in the Square were still struggling to recover
from the flu, but otherwise a sense of normalcy had begun to return.[55] The

Business Men's Association and its members seemed ready for the next chapter. The group soon voted to change their bylaws to allow women to join officially as "Associate Members" (though they were not yet ready to drop "*Men's*" from the name).[56] Fred Olsson was especially bursting with new ideas. As soon as the war conditions abated, he proposed what he described as a "really radical" new type of advertising.[57] It involved affixing large signs on top of automobiles and sending them to outlying districts with drums and bugles to announce Harvard Square Bargain Days.

Yet Olsson had also been changed by those trying few years. More and more, he found himself appealing to members' sense of communal responsibility. He was starting to sound a bit like Wright, that is. In January 1919, the association held a symposium during which longtime members, including Olsson and Wright, laid out their vision for Harvard Square now that the war was behind them. In Olsson's remarks, he declared, "The old idea of independence is a dead letter, and every man is his brother's keeper to this extent—that he has no right to so act in his own business as to drive a possible customer away from his fellow merchant."[58] This was rich, coming from a man who had left his father's business to open a competing shop around the corner and then pounced on his father's death as an opportunity to steal business from his sister. However, Olsson was older now, and his perspective was evolving. As chair of the Advertising Committee, it was now his responsibility to rally the troops. He grew frustrated when he felt the shortsighted self-interestedness of members stymied his efforts. When the committee struggled to get any joint promotions done in 1921, he suggested it temporarily cease its efforts. He remarked, "We have no apologies to make. There is no reason to spend money at a time that has been far from settled, during which each member has followed his own needs. . . . I believe anything really worthwhile must be backed by all members."[59]

Meanwhile, Wright's perspective was narrowing. Now in his seventies, his mind seemed increasingly drawn toward preserving the collective he had worked so hard to build. At times this crowded out his openness for progress and change. His remarks and writings were now sprinkled with references to Cambridge's growing immigrant population, a development he did not welcome. Despite Wright's own father having been born in England, Wright felt the city's new immigrants could not be as committed to the community as native-born residents such as himself. Large apartment houses had brought to the area "considerable numbers having no interest in our affairs," he said, and he bemoaned the changing "character" of the population.[60]

In his 1919 report of the Municipal Affairs Committee, he quoted an article from *World Work* magazine, a pro-business periodical known for opposing immigration, unions, and socialism. The article described Harvard Square has having degenerated into a "wretched" state, and it commended German cities as the most beautiful cities in the world because, through careful planning, the Germans had solved the problems of crowding, noise, and discomfort.[61] Wright drew from a portion of the article that harped on Harvard Square's transformation from a quiet village marketplace unified by shared interests to a large city center with diverse interests. He warned that the city was falling "prey [to] a thousand selfish interests," and he once more called for the membership to come together—only this time, to "oppose the forces of deterioration."[62] What Wright saw as deterioration was actually the marketplace starting to reflect an evolving and expanded collective and the interests of those in it. He continued to cling to his smaller, narrower collective.

~

Immigrants were not the only "outsiders" to enter Harvard Square in those years. They were also not the only outsiders perceived to be a threat to the businessmen's emerging collective sensibility. As we saw in chapter 2, by 1920, chain stores and outside real estate investors had begun to enter the marketplace and pursue their own interests. The fact that modern, sophisticated enterprises and investors wanted to do business in Harvard Square was, of course, a testament to the Business Men's Association—the group's hard work had succeeded in putting the Square on the map as an attractive shopping district. Yet as we saw, these new outside-owned entities often displaced long-standing merchants and disrupted the market's existing order. They were also hard to bring to heel.

Since its inception, the Business Men's Association had sought "uniform and just principles of trade" across the market.[63] However, chains had little interest in coordinating on things such as consistent closing hours or advertising, and their new "cash-and-carry" business model lured customers away from local firms operating with a more traditional, higher-priced, higher-touch customer service model (which included amenities such as deliveries and charge accounts).[64] To some in the association, the chain stores' aberrant pricing and practices were unfair competition, plain and simple. Meanwhile, there was a general belief that outside real estate investors from New York or elsewhere could not be trusted to think about the best interests of the

Square.[65] Compared to local real estate men like Hadley who were active members of the association, these outside actors had no ties to the market and were felt to view the Square and its properties in purely speculative terms.

No outside entity, however, drew more ire from the association—and Wright in particular—than the one that had helped spur the group's very formation: Boston Elevated Railway. The "El" was a continual thorn in the side of the group, and over the years the businessmen struggled to gain the El's cooperation on much of anything. When the association worked with the city to put most of the Square's wires underground, the El refused to pay the cost of submerging theirs. Wright, as chair of the Municipal Affairs Committee, was furious.[66] Wright also wanted the El to remove or renovate the enormous brick rotunda that served as the original subway headhouse. It sat right in the middle of the Square, had no sidewalks or safety zones around it, and was felt by many in the association and the city at large to be a menace to traffic and pedestrians.[67] The El refused to do anything about it.

The El's rotunda became a personal obsession for Wright.[68] It meant more to him than traffic snarls and pedestrian safety. In his opinion, it had been put there by the "short-sighted actions" of a self-interested actor who failed to think about what was best for the collective.[69] Its presence was a "standing reminder" of how selfish interests could prevail in the market, and he wanted it gone.[70] Yet despite his best efforts, it seemed almost impossible to wrangle this powerful, regional corporation to the group's cause. Frustrations with the El persisted. Years later, when members came together to decorate the Square for Christmas, the El agreed to join the effort and put up some decorations—then sent the association a bill for the labor.[71]

The city and the broader economy grew during this period, and so did the Business Men's Association. With business booming and outside forces solidifying a sense of local solidarity, membership jumped 60 percent during the 1920s; by the end of the decade, there were 176 merchants on the rolls.[72] During this roaring decade, the association's meetings became even more raucous affairs. The "Cigar Budget" was now a formal (and growing) line item in the group's financial records.[73] Entertainment at the meetings was less spontaneous and more of a spectacle. One month, an invited guest performed magic tricks, while another offered "comical impersonations of Italian-American lingo, which kept members in a roar," according to a report of the meeting.[74] Another month, members watched two men known as the "Nadeau Twins" fight a round of "midget boxing."[75] Yucking it up over cultural differences and midget boxing does not age well. For better or

Harvard Square, ca. 1922-1924. Courtesy of Cambridge Historical Commission.

worse—and it is often for worse—groups sometimes bond by highlighting perceived distinctions between themselves and those they cast as outsiders.

Through it all, market change continued to give the association purpose. The rapid increase in automobile traffic became a huge focus. It was proving to be every bit the street-level disruption as the subway had been. The group's leaders were in constant communication with the city's traffic officers, troubleshooting problems as they arose. One of the biggest issues was that people would abandon their cars on the Square's narrow streets and leave them there for hours, creating traffic jams that prevented other drivers from finding short-term parking so as to do their own shopping. A *Boston Transcript* editorial declared the conditions in Harvard Square "a menace to life and limb" for thousands of people.[76]

Fred Olsson showed a growing interest in these issues and would soon step in to lead the association's Traffic Committee, but it was George Wright who took up the cause most passionately in the '20s. He successfully lobbied the city to impose parking limits, something the membership had voted to support. After the limits were imposed, however, several members went around Wright's back and requested permits from the city to allow them to park in front of their stores all day in violation of the new rules. Wright was astounded—and disgusted. The old man had had enough. He appeared before the Cambridge Licensing Commission in 1922 and told them not to allow Harvard Square businessmen to bypass the rules. He was ashamed, he said, to have to go before the commission for this purpose, and he resigned as chair of the Municipal Affairs Committee.[77]

Perhaps out of contrition for having let Wright down—or maybe just out of respect for his many contributions over the years—Wright was reelected president of the association in 1924 and 1925. His health was starting to decline by then, and his messages to the group took on an even more passionate, at times almost pleading, quality during his swan-song presidency. He wanted the younger generation to really understand "the community of our interest."[78] The association should not be judged by what it does for any one individual, he continually reminded them, but what it does for the whole.

∽

When Wright's final term as president ended, Harvard Square was well poised for the future. Street-widening projects first proposed in the 1913 report on the future development of Harvard Square were finally coming to fruition. Thanks to Wright's tireless lobbying of the state legislature and railroad commission, the subway structure they all hated—that irksome reminder of the El's refusal to embrace their shared project—was finally set to be renovated. The merchants' collective will had finally prevailed. (The new structure would be the now-famous kiosk, which future generations have come to know and love and wage their own battles over.)

Members of the group felt optimistic and proud of their accomplishments. One reported, "I note a rumor which seems insistent and gaining ground . . . that the appearance of our Harvard Square—stores, prices, service are all that a discriminating purchaser might desire."[79] Rip Van Winkle had awoken from his slumber.

In the spring of 1928, George Wright lay on his death bed, his final slumber growing near. The grocer Edwin Sage, now president of the Business Men's Association, led the group in a moment of silence to honor the man who had given so much. Then, Sage delivered a speech quite unlike anything

Wright had ever delivered during his years at the helm. Here, there was no grand call back to the past. Sage, who in the early 1920s had railed against chain stores and the threat they posed to traditional grocers, was only looking forward now. "This is the day of change and competition," he declared.[80]

Change was the "immutable law" of the market and "eternal adaptability," the only path for survival, Sage told them.[81] Competition could be cruel, he acknowledged. It could topple century-old businesses and replace them with infant enterprises overnight. But while it spelled the death of traders, competition was the life of trade and the engine of change—so, it must be embraced. As the group's new general, Sage was not asking his troops to set aside their petty differences and come together in brotherhood. He was calling upon them to look ahead, stay alert, and ready themselves for battle:

> Who can read the riddles of production and distribution of tomorrow? Who can measure the possibilities of air transport, of radio, of television, of nitro-cellulose lacquers, of "dry ice," of interconnected power, of the reclamation of industrial waste? The economic battle, inexorable, yet beneficent, provides progress and variety which *is* life. Out of the flux and ferment emerge the victors. Men clear-eyed, alert, resourceful, they win that all of us may live more fully. . . . The world steps aside to let any man pass who can see a year ahead.[82]

A year ahead, in 1929, there would be a spectacular crash. Then, the Depression and another war to follow. The Business Men's Association and its members would face challenges none could yet foresee. But that night, as the group contemplated the unknown future, George Wright was getting ready to depart a world already quite changed from that which he had entered. It was a brave new world he had, in part, helped create by channeling his and his peers' instincts to come together to improve and grow the market they had inherited.

Upon his death, Wright gave one more thing to the community he loved. The man who liked to wander through old burial grounds to remind himself of the unbroken connection between past and future bequeathed all of his life's papers—including his notes and records from the Business Men's Association, his journals and correspondence, and the numerous scrapbooks of Cambridge ephemera he had been compiling since his teens—to the Cambridge Historical Society.

We tend to think of markets as encouraging purely self-interest, but they also encourage—sometimes demand—a sense of communal spirit. This is especially true for the business and property owners who are most directly involved in making the market at any given moment. Wright may have been an unconventional businessman in certain regards, but he was just one of dozens of merchants who saw the value of coming together to address common challenges and pursue a common vision. Sage was not wrong when he declared competition a fact of market life, but even men as fiercely competitive as a young Fred Olsson had been able to see the market for what it also was—a joint production. The early successes and stumbles of the Harvard Square Business Men's Association reflect the same two human instincts that continually push and pull our markets forward. Wright's collectivizing instinct was, in short, every bit the market instinct as Olsson's early animal spirits. And, as we will see, the Harvard Square market—like all markets—would continue to be defined by this tension in the years to come.

Chapter Seven

FOREVER YOUNG

On October 17, 1950, the Harvard Square Business Men's Association celebrated its fortieth anniversary at the nearby Hotel Continental. By then, the association had nearly two hundred members, and more than one hundred thirty people filed into the hotel's ballroom for the celebration that evening.[1]

A committee had been at work for months planning the gala. Flowers donated by a local florist adorned the tables. Longtime member Marie Olsson contributed a collection of picture postcards from 1908 so all could see what the Square looked like before the association's founding. The young Massachusetts congressman John F. Kennedy was set to speak at the event, but a last-minute scheduling mix-up prevented him from attending. Instead, the mayor of Cambridge addressed the group, and a local humorist, the Rev. John Nicol Mark, entertained the crowd with a talk titled "A Bit of Scotch." Seated at the head table throughout the evening's festivities were Fred Olsson and the two other founding members of the association still alive, the grocer Edwin Sage and the printer Edwin Powell.

Those three men had much to be proud of. In 1950 the marketplace was what they and the association's other founders had always hoped it would become—a bustling shopping district with all the marks of a modern American Main Street. Subway and trolley cars brought thousands of commuters and shoppers through the Square each day. Busy men and women could pop in and out of popular eateries like the Hayes Bickford's cafeteria on Mass Ave or stop and sit for a while at the sixty-four-foot lunch counter in the recently expanded Woolworth's on Brattle Street, a retail chain the Business Men's Association had welcomed during the depths of the Depression.[2] Local residents and students came to the Square to shop, dine, pick up their tailoring and dry cleaning, get a shave, or take in a movie. The University Theater played Hollywood pictures, with popular films drawing as many as five thousand people a day.[3] The Square was such a busy shopping destination that the local department store Corcoran's had recently chosen to locate its latest, most modern branch there. At its grand opening, the seven-thousand-square-foot, fully air-conditioned store was heralded by one local reporter for being "as modern as television."[4]

In the weeks leading up to the fortieth anniversary dinner, the program committee named Fred Olsson as the event's "Historian" and asked him to compose a dedication for the event.[5] Perhaps they assumed a man who had worked so hard to modernize and boost the Square over the years would take pleasure in all the progress his efforts had born. That was not the dedication Olsson delivered, however.

The once fiery young man, so full of new ideas and radical marketing plans, was now eighty years old, and his remarks were more an elegy to

University Theater, June 1951. Courtesy of Harvard University Archives.

the Square of old than an anthem to its modern form. It turned out he was not so enamored with the present market. In fact, he missed the "old fashioned methods" of doing business and the old merchants who had "loved the Square as it was."[6]

Scanning the crowd that evening, Olsson did not recognize many of its young faces, but he addressed his remarks to them. He thought back to the marketplace of his youth and tried to describe what it had looked and felt like back then. There were no big office buildings, no movie theater, no traffic problems, he said. It was a quiet little rural shopping center, "but happy and satisfying."

Olsson wished he could tell the crowd about each and every one of the "lovable shopkeepers" from those earlier days. He wanted his audience to know that "the character of the people who traded there, as well as that of the merchants" had made the Square truly unique. He recalled a few of those individuals, including the brothers John and Bert Amee, as well as a soft-spoken grocer named Dean who was "of the Baker's dozen school," always happy to add an extra pinch or two to the scale without charge. The current market felt more cold and calculating to Olsson. It felt more like a typical market. He said it was sad to think the present generation would never know the joy of that bygone era.

Olsson's dedication was heartfelt. It was also riddled with paradoxes for anyone who knew the man's history. How could a man, who spent years lobbying the City of Cambridge for street-paving and street-widening projects so as to allow more automobile traffic through the Square, now mourn the earlier days of "no autos, no traffic problems"? How could a man, who had once wanted to send a fleet of cars around the city outfitted with signs, bugles, and drums to draw more shoppers to the Square, now say he missed the days when the Square was "undisturbed by overcrowding" and when the only sounds of traffic came from the hooves of the horses who pulled the merchants' delivery carts?

What had happened so that an individual who once organized window-display contests to motivate shopkeepers to modernize their storefronts now found all the modern "plate glass and trim, as well as cabinet-made interiors" a bit too much for his taste? Most of all, how was it that a man, who once had so much ambition he left his father's business to start a competing one around the corner and hoped his sister's membership in the Business Men's Association would be blocked, could now look back in time and recall that earlier market as one in which "there was no confusion of ambition with greed, nor was there any high-pressure political contests"?

To those in the audience who knew Olsson, these may have seemed like amusing ironies from a man who had always been a bit of a character—the sort of inconsistencies prone to a temperamental soul in its final years. However, Olsson's remarks expose a profound puzzle. Olsson was someone who had spent his whole professional life agitating for change in this market. He had started out a rebel. He had always been an innovator. As much as anyone, he had worked to transform the once quiet, village marketplace into the busy, modern shopping district it became. Yet all that change and modernization now seemed alienating to him. Why? Why did a man who had helped make the market what it was feel so despondent looking out at it? How had Fred Olsson fallen out of love with his marketplace?

~

Olsson, an active member of the Harvard Square Business Men's Association since its founding, had become an even more a central player in it during the 1930s. He began that decade as chair of its Traffic Committee, was elected vice president in 1934, and, in 1935, became its president.[7] The '30s were a disorienting period to be a business owner, let alone to feel responsible for a group of other struggling business owners. Starting with the stock market crash in 1929 and continuing through the Depression that followed, merchants in the Square, like everywhere, struggled to navigate what was happening in the broader economy and what it meant for them. When Edwin Sage had called on the association's members in 1928 to look ahead and embrace a new era of "change and competition," this was not what any of them had had in mind, but it was the reality they now faced, and somehow they had to make sense of it.[8]

Early in the decade, the group invited outside speakers to their meetings whom they hoped might provide some insight. The titles of those talks convey the uncertainty of the period and people's attempts to find some modicum of clarity in it all: "Some Aspects of the Business Situation (1930), "The Banking Situation" (1933), "The Retail Trade Situation" (1934), "Economics of the Day" (1934).[9] As the extent of the contraction became apparent, local rivalries began to fall away. The group started to hold joint meetings with other business groups in the city. Together, Cambridge's merchants listened to speeches on the National Recovery Act of 1933, signed codes of fair competition and fair pricing consistent with that act, and entered floats in a citywide "Buy Now" parade, which aimed to inspire local consumers to see it as their patriotic duty to keep shopping.[10]

Amidst all the disruption, old challenges persisted. Death and taxes may be certainties of life in general, but by the 1930s traffic and parking problems had become the established certainties of life in Harvard Square.[11] Fred Olsson threw himself into those issues with gusto. As chair of the association's Traffic Committee, he lobbied the city for new parking and traffic regulations and, then, as George Wright had before him, grew irate when members subverted those rules for their own personal convenience.[12] If they could not coordinate on something like this, Olsson wondered how they would ever come together on the larger economic issues dogging the whole market. His Traffic Committee suggested that the names of members who violated the Square's parking rules be read out loud at future meetings of the whole association: if good faith could not keep people in line, maybe a little public shaming would.[13] Meanwhile, Olsson cultivated relations with the city's new traffic officers, who had recently been hired to try to bring order to the Square's never-ending chaos. Under his leadership, the Traffic Committee convinced association members to chip in and pay for a heater (and the ongoing cost of its electricity) for the traffic box in which the officers

Traffic officer in his booth, ca. 1945. Courtesy of Cambridge Historical Commission.

worked.[14] Day in and day out, these officer jacks-in-the-box stood ready to pop out and jolt passersby to attention.

Even Harvard Square's traffic and parking mess could not distract the merchants from the broader crisis, however. With no economic improvement in sight, spirits in the Business Men's Association inevitably sagged. Facing shortfalls in their businesses, some longtime members became delinquent on their dues.[15] In 1934, Olsson and several of his friends in the group seem to have concluded that if they could not boost members' bottom lines, at least they could try to boost people's spirits. They began to hold regular, casual lunches in the Square open to any members who wished to attend.[16] In June, the association held its first-ever golf tournament at a nearby country club. Two dozen members participated in the tournament, and prizes were awarded for so many different categories—including "Duffer class—highest score" and "highest single hole"—that all who played came away a victor (of sorts).[17] After golf, more than fifty other members of the association met up with the group for dinner at the country club. Two local entertainers—a concert soprano named Miss Helen Mahler and a dancer, Miss Joyce Summers—performed. The hit of the evening, however, was a poem composed by the group's very own Fred Olsson. It was a humorous, motivational ditty, and Olsson distributed copies to everyone so that they could sing the verses together, set to the tune of "The Man on the Flying Trapeze."

The golf outing was such a success it was repeated the next year—and the next year, and many after. However, it was also apparent that the merchants' spirits were not the only ones in need of lifting. In November 1934, the Business Men's Association did something else unprecedented: it held a large dinner at the Hotel Continental and, for the first time ever, invited members' employees to attend as well.[18] It was a show of appreciation for their staffs' efforts during this trying time—and perhaps also a way to motivate workers in the face of declining wages. Either way, the dinner was a hit, and it was repeated the next November as well.

Two hundred people attended that second employee dinner in 1935. Gallons of punch and a hefty budget's worth of "dinner smokes" were consumed, and dancing extended late into the evening.[19] As president, Olsson presided over the affair, and he invited a local business college professor to deliver a motivational speech during dinner. The speaker, Bertram C. Larrabee, was a sort of local Dale Carnegie, the self-improvement guru best known for his wildly successful, if hokey, 1935 book, *How to Win Friends and Influence People*. Larrabee spoke that evening about the importance of imagination, optimism, and the courage to try new things.[20]

Olsson was not a self-help guru like Larrabee, but he felt it was his duty to cheer up his fellow merchants. He began composing fun, clever odes. During the 1936 holiday season, he wrote a yuletide poem for the association.[21] In March 1937, after recovering from an illness that winter, which had forced him to miss a few meetings (and was so serious the group had held moments of silence for him in his absence), he returned with a forty-verse poem titled "Boost Your Neighbor."[22] It reminded members to find fellowship in the market and to refer customers to one another, and it included stanzas like this:

> We begin at the top, where a roof may leak,
>   If such a thing happens, just holler for Peak.
> When he's through, you'll find places needing new paint,
>   Fred Hayden will put it wherever it ain't.
> If plumbing goes blooey, there's three you can call,
>   Then your worries are over, they'll attend to it all . . .

The association's first president, George Wright, had had the look and temperament of a poet, but it was Olsson in the 1930s who became the group's unofficial poet laureate. As the Depression deepened, he churned out more and more morale-boosting poems.

He also made sure members were exposed to exciting new market innovations. Just because the economy was stagnating, it did not mean their imaginations had to. In 1936, he showed a film on store modernization produced by the Pittsburgh Glass Company that demonstrated new fixtures and lighting effects for retailers.[23] That same year, Olsson and Sage began exploring the possibility of installing coin-operated parking meters in the Square.[24] Sage had encountered this novelty on a trip to Texas and returned convinced it was the modern solution to the Square's nagging parking problems.

~

Olsson's tenure as president of the Business Men's Association ended in 1937. In the years that followed, World War II drew the group's focus outward just as World War I had earlier in the century. Instead of talks on the economy, the group now heard such talks as: "Present World Conditions" (1938), "A Frenchman Looks at Defeated France" (1941), "Canada's Modern Mechanized Army" (1942), and "The Russia Situation" (1942).[25]

Olsson continued to run his shop, and he remained an active member of the group. However, as he entered his eighth decade, his concerns began to shift. Traffic in the Square continued to draw his attention, but for different reasons than in the past. The Square had been Olsson's lifelong stomping ground, but it was starting to feel overwhelming. He walked a bit more slowly these days, and the hoards of hurried commuters all rushing about, the high-pitched screech of trains, and the thousands of passing cars with their loud, angry horns now made his daily passage through the Square a menacing experience. After one particularly harrowing morning, he brought a suggestion to the next association meeting—the Square needed more safety islands, he said. His fellow members, most much younger than he now, responded respectfully but in the way one might dismiss a grandparent's concerns, not recognizing the wound inflicted in the process: They suggested several detours Olsson might take around the Square so as "to avoid further worries."[26]

The group still adored the old man, however, and they continued to call upon him to compose poems for their events. His verses celebrated the market they all loved and paid tribute to members who had shown unusual commitment to it. Increasingly, though, Olsson was asked to take on another role as well. He became the group's mourner in chief. It seemed every year brought the death of one or more of the association's charter members, the men with whom Olsson had founded the group, men he had worked alongside for decades. As the group's elder statesman, he was one of the few remaining members who had known these men personally. It fell to him to draw up resolutions and tell the group's younger members about the contributions and character of their predecessors.

As time went on, his two roles began to meld. His poetry became mournful. In 1940, Fred was asked to deliver a poem honoring the thirtieth anniversary of the Business Men's Association. As he took to the podium, he knew he was not going to deliver the sort of verses the group expected. So, before beginning, he offered a short caveat: "I presume most of you count on me for facetious remarks," he said, "and although I admit that I think a good laugh often averts a near tragedy, tonight I am in a serious mood."[27] Then, he read his poem entitled "In Memoriam":

> Thirty years have passed since this organization started,
> And tonight we pause to think of those departed.
> Twenty odd names on the original roll,
> And all but six have paid their toll . . .
> Seven times as many now on the member list,

Yet those who have gone still are missed.
Wright, Cox, Carrick, John Amee, too,
Henderson, Stover, Robinson, and Fiske are a few . . .
Soon the word "charter" need no more be printed
And added to those who never had stinted
In service of our organization,
Will be added the names of the six remaining.
So I ask all those who are not abstaining
To toast them on their next libation.
Meanwhile, a final clause,
I propose a short and quiet pause
As a sort of commemoration.

Olsson was right. More of the association's charter members soon passed away. Among the close friends he lost in the ensuing years were Bert Amee and the painter Fred Haydn. Olsson had worked alongside those men for decades. They had had fun together. He had dropped their names into his light-hearted poems. They had also weathered tough times together. In the resolutions Olsson wrote for Amee, he recalled Bert's hearty laugh lifting Olsson out of despondent moments. Bert was a loyal and trustworthy man, Olsson said, and "All who knew him loved him; all who know him will miss him."[28]

With the U.S. entry into war, the association's younger members soon grew busy managing the complexities of the wartime market. They purchased War Bonds, supported United War Fund drives and Red Cross initiatives, and navigated goods and labor shortages and required evening "dim-outs" (to make the city less visible to attack). As he had for decades, Olsson made his way through the Square each day to work in his shop on Boylston (our JFK) Street, but as more of his longtime friends passed away, the market he had known and loved seemed to be slipping away with them.

In his poems, Olsson took it upon himself to speak for the departed and address the younger generation. With so many now gone, he felt it fell to him to pass the torch. One poem he read to the group went:

. . . We who started this organization,
Toast you now in aqueous libation.
We wish to those who will carry on,
A strength of purpose and a clear vision
That Harvard Square will always mean
A place where Trading is ever clean

That future years to all may bring
Success and joy and life worth living.
So here's to all who take our places
Already I see so many faces
Showing their pride in Harvard Square,
The best place to trade you'll find anywhere. . . .[29]

It made sense that Olsson would speak on behalf of his deceased friends through his poetry. His poems about the market had always been poems about his friends. They had been poems about their community and their collective spirit. But now there were new merchants and new relationships defining the market. Olsson mourned his personal loss, but he also hoped this next generation might find the same sense of joy and meaning in their shared pursuits as he and his peers had.

George Wright, the association's first president, had been forced to reconcile similarly conflicting emotions toward the end of his life. In his twilight years, Wright struggled to navigate the two instincts that had always been inside him—the instinct to preserve the community he loved and the instinct to embrace and support its forward progress. In his final report as president of the Business Men's Association, Wright began by quoting 2 Corinthians 5:17: "Old things are passed away / behold, all things are become new."[30] He was talking about the market, and perhaps also about himself. "While some regret the loss of old familiar storefronts and the perhaps primitive business methods," he wrote, "we know they are gone forever, recognizing the younger generation will not tolerate them." This was, he acknowledged, "the price the community pays" for progress.

That price of progress felt even more personal to Olsson by 1950 when he delivered his remarks at the association's fortieth anniversary gala. The year before, Olsson had submitted his letter of resignation to the group. He was nearing eighty, and the time had come to close his shop and retire. However, the circumstances of his departure had to sting. The association's then-president, Richard Dow, was Olsson's landlord at the time. Dow was evicting Olsson's shop (and other businesses in the building) to make room for the new, modern branch of Corcoran's Department Store.[31]

∾

Olsson had begun his professional life striking out on his own, leaving his father's shop to go it alone as an independent entrepreneur. But, over the years, as he invested more of himself in the market, and as he found common cause with his fellow merchants, he forged deep personal bonds in it. Market life became a collective endeavor. It became something he shared with his friends. It became, as sociologists would put it, profoundly relational. So, now, when he thought back to that earlier market, he thought of those relationships. He thought of his friends. His attachment to that market was his attachment to them. Their deaths marked the death of the market he had known and loved.

Market life often calls forth and cultivates connections among us. In the process, individuals can start to see and feel their collectives in the market itself. Like Olsson, we attach to our markets because we are attached to one another. And yet the bonds we form are as timebound and mortal as we are. Olsson's collective, like Wright's, died along with its members. And yet the market forged on, for, unlike us, it is immortal. It stays forever young. It harnesses new energy and new connections and keeps on evolving—right past us.

At the fortieth anniversary dinner of the Harvard Square Business Men's Association, Olsson stood alone at the dais to deliver his remarks. He looked out and saw a sea of unfamiliar faces. He saw a different market. This was their Harvard Square now, and Olsson knew he had lost a great love.

Chapter Eight

OUTSIDE AGITATORS

President John F. Kennedy was beloved in Harvard Square. During his presidency, local establishments from barbershops and pharmacies to tailors and burger joints touted how he had been a regular customer during his student years and even returned for visits while serving in the U.S. House of Representatives and Senate. The young president had affection for the Square as well. He had known the names of all those tailors and barbers back when he was a student, and he did not forget them.[1] While in office, he expressed a desire to house his eventual presidential library at Harvard. In the spring of 1963, he toured several possible locations for it near the campus.[2] His favorite was on the outskirts of Harvard Square at the site of the old Metropolitan Transit Authority yards.

Kennedy came to town again later that year. On October 19, 1963, during what would prove to be his last trip to the Boston area, he slipped out the side door of a Boston hotel, dodging a large crowd of supporters out front, and headed to Harvard Stadium, where Harvard's football team was about to face off against Columbia's.[3] It was one of those spectacular New England fall days, and although the game was not on the president's official itinerary, rumors had circulated all week that he might make an unexpected appearance. When he arrived just after kickoff, the crowd of fifteen thousand roared. The game was already under way, but the Harvard band broke out into "Hail to the Chief." The fans stood and applauded, welcoming their president.

Harvard football games were a big to-do back then. Played in the nation's oldest football stadium to crowds of thousands, they drew not only students and alumni but also local fans of the sport and those just looking for something fun to do with the family or a date on a Saturday afternoon. At that 1963 Harvard-Columbia game, however, the *Boston Globe* reported that a different spectator sport captured people's attention. It was called "President watching."[4] JFK and his aids sat high in the stands on the forty-five-yard line, and photos from the day show the hundreds of people surrounding him, all smiling and, almost always, looking at him—not the field.[5]

The president was at ease in the crowd. He chatted with his aids and laughed and, at one point, lit a small cigar. He watched the game even if others were too distracted to, and he cheered for his team when the Crimson scored a tying field goal just before half-time. The crowd seemed at ease around him, too, if a bit starstruck. Two couples from the suburbs sitting directly in front of him sneaked the occasional, gleeful glance back. Behind him, a few rows up, a bespectacled, elderly gentlemen gazed down on him with the sweet grin of a proud grandfather. Students on all sides beamed. Even the players on the field were affected by his presence. Harvard halfback Scott Harshbarger, who would go on to be Massachusetts attorney general,

President Kennedy at the Harvard-Columbia football game, October 19, 1963. Photo by Cecil Stoughton. White House Photographs. JFK Presidential Library and Museum.

recalled the game fifty years later in a radio interview.[6] More than anyone else, Harshbarger said, JFK had inspired people his age to see public service as a "noble, decent" undertaking. That day, to Harshbarger and his teammates, it felt "classy to be playing football and have the President of the United States, a classy, young, dynamic leader watching."

A month later, the young, dynamic president was dead. On November 22, 1963, as word began to travel around Harvard Square that JFK had been shot, a group of students gathered at the kiosk.[7] They awaited the newspapers' extra editions and shook their heads in disbelief. When their fears were confirmed, most managed little more than a quiet, stunned, "He's dead." Other students huddled around transistor radios in the stairwells and doorways of their dormitories. Restaurants in the Square cleared out. The few diners who remained seemed frozen in place and spoke in hushed tones. Merchants and property owners lowered the Square's flags to half-mast. Catholics from around the city arrived at St. Paul Church to pray. A few blocks away, the bells of Memorial Church began to toll from inside Harvard Yard.

In the days that followed, Sheldon Cohen of Out of Town News carried Dallas papers so his customers could read reports directly from the city where the tragedy had occurred.[8] In response to customer demand, he began selling photographs and recorded speeches of the late president as well. When talk of a presidential memorial started, Cohen sent the proceeds of those sales to the newly formed Kennedy Library Fund.[9]

Yet in a bizarre turn of events, when official plans were finally laid in 1972 to build the JFK library on the site of the old transit yards where the late president himself had hoped it might be, members of the community rose in vehement opposition to the project and, ultimately, defeated it. The opposition seemed almost unfathomable from the outside. Kennedy was a local icon and hero. An attractive national memorial and museum that would likely spur further growth and development is just the sort of project city officials, property owners, and business leaders usually support, even if lower-income residents sometimes resist such developments for fear of being displaced from their homes by rising rents. In Cambridge, however, a cross section of the city opposed the project, and some of the most active opponents were Harvard Square's highest-income, home-owning residents who had no fear of residential displacement. A number of the city's officials and business owners also opposed it.

Debate over the memorial raged for years. Finally, in 1975—after repeated concessions to the project's opponents who remained unappeased—the

Kennedy family and the developers gave up on trying to locate the memorial where the late president had wanted it. The John F. Kennedy Presidential Library and Museum stands today in Boston's Dorchester neighborhood.

How did this happen? Why did a number of residents, public officials, and business owners in Cambridge—a liberal, heavily Democratic city that had adored the president and overflowed with expressions of grief at his death—end up opposing a memorial to their slain, local, Democratic hero? What was so sacred to these people in Harvard Square that this sacred memorial threatened?

THE POSTWAR OPENING OF HARVARD SQUARE

Before we can unravel that puzzle, we need to engage in some more street-level time travel to see what was happening in Harvard Square in the years before the controversy over the Kennedy memorial exploded. At the time of JFK's assassination, Harvard Square was a very different marketplace than the one George Wright and Fred Olsson had built. As far back as the days of the East and West Indies goods stores that sold imported rum and molasses, the Square, like many village markets, had served as a local platform for accessing products from faraway corners of the globe. However, the years after World War II marked a turning point in this regard. For America, in general, and the Square, in particular, the war occasioned a dramatic opening to the broader world. What was a busy, modernizing Main Street in the late 1940s and early '50s was on its way to becoming a fashionable, cosmopolitan hub by the early '60s. In fact, people were starting to talk about Harvard Square in much the same terms they used to talk about the country's popular president—the marketplace felt dynamic and fresh, even a bit classy.

After World War II ended, Harvard's student population grew and diversified. Students who had left Harvard to serve the country returned after their time abroad. The GI Bill brought even more veterans to campus. Many of the new matriculants lacked the prep-school background typical of Harvard students up until then, bringing, instead, a worldliness and curiosity born of their wartime experiences.[10] Veterans were not the only individuals whose perspectives had been widened by the war, either. All those who had stayed back, whether local merchants or housewives or professionals, had followed the events unfolding across the globe and navigated their ripple effects at home. During those years, the refugee-run Window Shop had been a daily reminder of the devastating instability abroad, but it also introduced shoppers to new European foods and fashions, as prior waves of European immigration had already begun to do earlier in the century. When the war ended, many in the country sought stability and comfort in a return to traditional roles and a general turn inward. However, people's tastes and sights had also been forever changed. With the start of the Cold War, it became apparent the world had as well.

Perhaps no Harvard Square business better demonstrated the dueling American instincts of the 1950s—or contributed more to the Square's growing reputation for cosmopolitanism—than Design Research. Ben Thompson opened the homewares store in 1953 in a clapboard house at 57 Brattle Street, just across from the village blacksmith's old haunt. The store capitalized on what Thompson's biographers called the "historic moment-in-time of national human and social need for home making"—but it filled that domestic need with eclectic foreign goods that tapped into the culture's increasingly international tastes.[11]

An architect by trade, Thompson had been one of eight founders of The Architect's Collaborative (TAC) in 1948. TAC had its offices in the Square and began as a response to the postwar surge in demand for single-family homes. Its founders were proponents of European modernism, and the group hoped to transform the American residential landscape with that aesthetic; the famed German architect Walter Gropius, father of the prewar bauhaus movement in design, was a major influence and one of the partners. As soon as they began designing and building modern single-family homes, however, Thompson spotted a new opportunity: homeowners did not often know what furnishings and products to put inside their houses. Thompson believed home goods could simultaneously serve as utilitarian objects and beautiful pieces of art, and he began traveling to destinations such as Greece, Algeria, Finland, Italy, Bolivia, Malta, and more, sending products he liked back to a storeroom he rented on Brattle Street.

The store's name, Design Research, was meant to reflect this intensive approach to finding and sourcing beautiful, interesting goods from all over the globe. It stocked everything from Danish furniture to Swiss glassware, rustic French pottery, and Japanese paper lamps. During the 1950s, its chic modern showroom became a popular local destination. After it began carrying Marimekko fabrics and dresses at the end of the decade, it became a national sensation. Thompson had spotted the colorful hand-printed textile at the Finnish exhibit of the 1958 World's Fair in Brussels and immediately secured an exclusive license to sell it in the United States. In 1960, Jackie Kennedy was photographed on the cover of *Sports Illustrated* wearing a red-and-pink Marimekko shift dress from Design Research, and a trend was born.[12]

By the early '60s, the president of Neiman Marcus and other major department stores were making regular visits to the Harvard Square store to look for merchandising ideas and keep in touch with current fashions. In 1963, Thompson opened a New York branch; and after that, one in San Francisco. Design Research was no longer just bringing the world to Harvard Square: the store and the Square were becoming exporters of a worldliness born and cultivated there.

Throughout the 1950s a number of other new businesses appeared in the Square that both reflected and furthered the market's growing cosmopolitanism.[13] In 1950, Cardullo's Gourmet Shop opened with its international assortment of teas, candies, and cheeses. That same year, Henri IV opened in a tiny wood-frame house on Winthrop Street, just steps from the original seventeenth-century market. Pronounced as it would be in France, "Henri Quatre" introduced French fare and flare—including the concept of wine at lunch—to Harvard Square.

When Henri IV's founder, Genevieve McMillan, set sail from Europe after the war, she was a young GI bride heading to Cambridge to meet up with her husband, architect Robert McMillan, who would go on to found The Architects Collaborative with Thompson and Gropius.[14] The marriage did not last, but "Genou," as she was known to friends, settled in Harvard Square and became a successful business and property owner. As a girl, McMillan had chafed at her provincial village life in the Pyrenees and could not wait to leave for school in Paris. Once there, the world had opened up for her. She became one of the first women to graduate from the Écoles des Sciences Politiques and developed a passion for African and Oceanic art and world travel, interests she would pursue for the rest of her life.[15] Henri IV—as well as a pastry shop she opened around the corner called Patisserie Gabrielle, named after one of Henri IV's mistresses—were Genou's way of bringing that Parisian sensibility into her new life.[16] People in Harvard Square were apparently ready for it in their lives, too. The restaurant was a hit.

To dine at Henri IV was to be transported. Checkered tablecloths and the songs of Charles Trenet coming from a record player in the corner greeted patrons upon entry, as Gallic food prepared by a chef named Jean-Baptiste awaited them.[17] Snails were not a common menu item in the Square's other eateries, but they became Henri IV's most popular dish; the coq au vin, a close second. Yet the mood was not stuffy or uptight as one might suspect, and the restaurant was known affectionately about the Square as the "Hungry Cat" for how its name sounded to American ears. For ninety-nine cents, one could get a glass of wine, soup, salad, bread, and a cup of coffee.

The Hungry Cat attracted its share of famous artists and writers when they came to town—notables such as Thornton Wilder, William Faulkner, and Juan Miro all dined there—and it functioned as a sort of salon for the growing crowd of young ex-pat graduate students, writers, artists, and professionals in the area. However, its appeal was broader than that. It was popular among GIs who had been to Europe, too. A night at Henri IV left local couples with the same feeling of worldly sophistication that browsing Design Research's eclectic product mix did.

More businesses around the Square began to reflect this sensibility. In 1953, the Brattle Theater converted from a struggling repertory theater into a movie house that ran avant-garde European films not shown anywhere else in the country. Club Casablanca soon opened next door, a nod to the 1942 film and its iconic bar, Rick's Café Américain, where refugees from all over Europe gathered, awaiting passage to the United States. In 1955, Sheldon Cohen, until then a hawker of local dailies, opened Out of Town News after noticing growing demand for news from around the country and the world. At the same time, a number of travel companies, including Helvetia European Tours and University Travel, appeared on the scene to cater to people's increasing eagerness for domestic and international travel. The Square was starting to feel a bit like Rick's—small and intimate, but worldly, too.

Some of the Square's new merchants like Cohen and Cardullo became active members in the Harvard Square Business Men's Association. Slowly the group's rolls began to reflect a bit more of the diversity of the Square. For the moment, new and old seemed to coexist rather peaceably in the market.[18] The Business Men's Association reflected the more conservative instincts in the culture, to be sure, but, for the most part, its domestic traditionalism sat unproblematically alongside the newer expansiveness. While Design Research sold imported home goods from around the world to young couples and Henri IV served artists and graduate students a taste of Parisian life, the association kept up its annual golf outings, often inviting the Cambridge police to join.[19] While the Brattle Theater screened foreign films, the association screened a U.S. Chamber of Commerce–funded animated film promoting traditional American values. Called *It's Everybody's Business*, the film promoted free enterprise, included a character named

"Mrs. Consumer," and depicted excessive taxation as a monster with a long vacuum hose that sucked cash out of merchants' cash drawers.[20]

Concerned about domestic safety during the Cold War, the Business Men's Association invited speakers to talk on such topics as "Our Progress in Civil Defense," "Inside the FBI," and "Keeping Abreast of Russia's Nuclear Tests."[21] The group also watched a lot of Harvard football game films and invited the school's football coaching staff to speak on several occasions.[22] These activities surely reflected members' interests, but it was also the case that there was simply not a lot for the association to do at the time. The market was evolving in ways that pleased most people around the Square, and unlike some other times in the past, it did not seem to require the coordinated activism of its existing merchants. The evolving culture was proving force enough. Meanwhile, most of the changes were not major disruptions to the existing order so much as fashionable upgrades of it: the market still catered to the same types of people as it had before the war (the university crowd, local residents, commuters, etc.)—like them, it was just becoming more cosmopolitan.

Without a clear call to action or shared purpose, interest in the Business Men's Association waned. Meeting attendance fell to its lowest levels in years

Harvard Square, ca. 1960. Courtesy of Harvard University Archives.

by the early '60s.[23] Board minutes from this period note frequent absences of even the group's officers and directors. There was some talk of trying to become a "more serious business association" rather than just "a social one," and, at one point, members were asked to come to the next meeting with suggestions for how the group might be improved.[24] It is unclear if any did. The group that had once led change in the market was starting to lag behind it. They could have followed the market's lead this time and opened themselves up to more new voices and influences, but they chose not to for the moment. In October of 1961, the association voted to consider allowing a woman member to join the board of directors the next year and to hold a midwinter social meeting to which women in the marketplace would be invited.[25] By the start of the following year, the social had been postponed indefinitely, and no women appeared on the slate of nominated directors.[26]

This was an early hint that new and old might not always coexist so seamlessly. Other clues lay inside the Square's hip new coffeehouses. These establishments tapped into the emerging Beat culture that had started to take off in Harvard Square in the late '50s. People went to sit, drink coffee, read a book or have stimulating conversation, and listen to live music—sometimes, just someone strumming a banjo or guitar in the corner; other times, a scheduled show.

In 1958, two twenty-two-year-old women, just out of Brandeis, decided to open a coffeehouse of their own. They called it Club 47.[27] The name came from the club's address: despite the two women's lack of experience, Harvard Square landlord Bertha Cohen had been willing to rent them space in a building she owned at 47 Mount Auburn Street. Within a year of opening, Club 47 was a central player in the country's growing folk music scene. This was due in no small part to yet another young woman.

Joan Baez was seventeen when her family moved from California to Massachusetts.[28] Shortly after their arrival, her father took her to Harvard Square to check out the new coffeehouses people were starting to talk about. When they stepped into Tulla's Coffee Grinder, a cramped one-room place on Dunster Street, Baez recalls in her autobiography, "I was entranced."[29] There were young people immersed in intense dialogue and others playing chess, but what captured her attention most was "a guy under the tiny orange lamp, leaning over his classical guitar, his hair a soft yellow in the diffused light, playing 'Plaisir d'Armour.' "[30] Baez decided in that moment that she wanted to get a classical guitar, move to Harvard Square, sing, and fall in love. So, that's what she did. Soon after her and her father's trip to the Square, she was spending most of her time there, had fallen in love with a Harvard classics major, and was aweing crowds with her distinctive voice at recently opened Club 47.

The club began hosting a range of folk and blues musicians. A young Bob Dylan came up from New York to see what the buzz was about. When he could not secure a slot on the formal schedule because it was full, he performed between sets for the packed room.[31] Jackie Washington, the Canadian blues musician, became a regular.[32] The scene had a way of chipping away, at least around the margins, at some historical boundaries. Black musicians like Washington performed, though often had to stay at someone's home in Cambridge instead of a hotel given ongoing discrimination.[33] The crowds were also not just Harvard students anymore. Shows began to draw young people from around the Boston area and across the class spectrum.

As the coffeehouse culture suggested, Harvard Square was starting to change on some more fundamental level than imported home goods and coq au vin. To Baez and her peers, it felt more and more like their stomping ground—they were making it so. Baez often traipsed around the streets barefoot. She caught rides on the back of young men's motorcycles. What undoubtedly looked like strange, perhaps even dangerous (or, at least, performative) behavior to some of the Square's older denizens revealed a change in who was starting to feel most at home in Harvard Square. When Baez's career took off, it was back in the Square where she felt safest. Years later, she would look back and write that the people she knew from the coffeehouse and music scene in those years "were my first second family."[34]

But as Baez enjoyed what she would later call her "love affair" with Harvard Square, a few of the longer-time residents, merchants, and city officials were not so in love.[35] To them, the younger crew and their hip, new scene reflected a set of potentially concerning cultural changes. Some suspected the coffeehouse customers of drug use. Some undoubtedly bristled at the more racially and socioeconomically diverse crowds being drawn into the Square. Some did not like the politics of it all. In the fall of 1961, Club 47 hosted a hootenanny—an informal gathering where folk musicians perform and the audience often sings along—to support the Committee for a Sane Nuclear Policy. SANE, as the group was called, opposed the nuclear arms race and aboveground testing of nuclear weapons, and it had recently been accused of communist infiltration by several U.S. senators.[36] A few days after the event, the Cambridge police tried to shut the club down for supposed violations of fire laws and for not having proper entertainment and liquor licenses.[37] As one coffeehouse regular from the period summarized it, not everyone in town saw Club 47 as the cool, happening place he and his peers did; some saw it as "a den of iniquity full of beatniks, pinkos, and subversives all dressed in black, smoking foreign cigarettes (and who knows what else)."[38]

By 1963, Club 47's landlord, Bertha Cohen, was one of those skeptics, and she kicked it out of 47 Mount Auburn. The club relocated to Palmer Street on the other side of the Square, but that did not satisfy everyone. Not long after the move, the Business Men's Association held a meeting to discuss "the problems resulting from the activities of Club 47" at its new location.[39]

Despite such evidence of brewing tensions, the early 1960s were a period of relative calm in the marketplace. Like the country's young war-hero president, whose popularity seemed to bridge the gap between Americans born and raised before the war and those who came after, Harvard Square felt fresh, exciting, and more open, yet still reflective of a certain stability of traditional American values. In the years after Kennedy's death, the fissures in the culture would break wide open. For now, though, there was a lot for everybody to like and feel proud of in their little marketplace. And their pride grew as their market's reputation did. A 1961 *Boston Globe* article by the paper's fashion editor encouraged local readers to look no further than Harvard Square if they wanted to see the latest fashion trends. The piece highlighted new "off-beat boutiques" that stocked the most up-to-date looks such as madras jackets and mini-coats, and it included a photo spread of stylish young men and women casually strolling about the Square, looking, as the writer put it, like "the kings of the Mod."[40]

The *New York Times* described the Square as a fashion "mecca" known for its "cosmopolitan atmosphere—coffee houses and foreign restaurants, and the ease of buying international periodicals, Gauloises cigarettes and Spanish perfume."[41] Another *Times* piece said the Square had a special elan, credited Cambridge women and Radcliffe "girls" for having discovered Marimekkos "long before Mrs. Jacqueline Kennedy discovered them," and suggested that, perhaps, just maybe, all those biased Cantabrigians who had long claimed Harvard Square was "The Crossroads of the World" might finally be onto something.[42]

A REVOLUTION COMES TO HARVARD SQUARE

By the mid-1960s, Harvard Square was certainly a crossroads for young people in the area. Youth from all around came to check out the scene and take in what was so hip and exciting about the place—other young people.

Initially, this took the form of high-schoolers and college students from surrounding towns coming to hang out and check out the music, the styles, and one another.[43] But as the civil rights and antiwar movements heated up, the Square became a center of—and destination for—countercultural activity. Whereas in the early 1960s, the Square drew comparisons to hip, cosmopolitan enclaves like New York's Greenwich Village and Paris's Left Bank, just a few years later it was spoken of in the same breath as Berkeley and Haight-Ashbury.[44] The social, cultural, and generational conflicts playing themselves out across America played themselves out in sharp relief in and around Harvard Square. Crucially for our purposes, they played themselves out in the market there as well.

As it always had, the market in Harvard Square continued to change with the people and the culture. By 1967 shops like Zecropia were popping up at the street level. Located on Brattle Street, Zecropia sold handmade hammocks, soaps, and candles as well as those psychedelic disks that look trippy when they spin.[45] Designers 3, run by long-haired twenty-somethings, sold handcrafted jewelry on Boylston (not yet renamed JFK) Street. Truc, one of the "off-beat boutiques" previously heralded for its mod fashion sensibility, expanded its product offerings to include buttons with radical messages such as "I am an enemy of the state" and "Sterilize LBJ: No More Ugly Children," some of which so irked local officials that the Cambridge police were dispatched to pressure the store's owner to stop carrying them.[46]

Truc pulled a few of its more controversial buttons, but the surplus clothing store KrackerJacks continued to sell buttons that read "F*ck Censorship" and "Fornicate for Freedom" even after the city threatened to close the shop for several drummed-up signage and licensing violations.[47] Whether people liked it or not, the market was now catering to a younger generation with whom such messages resonated. As an article about the changing Square put it at the time, "the law of supply and demand is what's happening, baby."[48]

To some city officials and longtime merchants and residents, the changes felt like more than that. They felt like a moral threat. "Fornicate for Freedom" was not exactly the slogan of a classy, urbane marketplace. The issue of teen loitering surfaced early. In the fall of 1966, the Business Men's Association invited a district court judge to speak to the group about juvenile delinquency and how it was affecting Harvard Square.[49] After residents and police began voicing similar concerns, *Cambridge Chronicle* dispatched a feature writer to interview some of the young people gathering in the Square.

The reporter (a Radcliffe student herself) found them to be mostly local, suburban teens engaged in harmless people watching, however.[50]

A year on, though, young people from all over had begun to arrive, and, to some in the city, it did not seem like such a harmless situation anymore. In 1967, Cambridge's mayor, Daniel Hayes, spoke out against what he deemed "the great move into the city . . . of hippies, beatniks, and other undesirables."[51] These "barefoot and bearded" people, as he described them, were apparently a far cry from the attractive, well-groomed kings of mod who had made the Square fashionable just a few years earlier. With their "love-ins, pot parties, etc.," the new crowd was creating an intolerable situation for Cambridge citizens, Hayes said, and he asked landlords and rental agencies to exercise greater discrimination in their rental decisions so as to screen out the bad elements. Meanwhile, the new arrivals made themselves at home in not just the city's apartment houses but also some of the Square's businesses. Hayes-Bickford's, the popular twenty-four-hour cafeteria, was thought to be a popular meeting place for radical militants. The restaurant began to close down in the wee hours of each morning to force the undesirables to clear out, at least for a while.[52]

Since the early 1960s—the period when Timothy Leary led his controversial, if short-lived, LSD experiments at Harvard—there had been a growing drug scene in the Square. With the influx of hippies, Harvard Square was now thought to be the center of the city's drug trade, with sales even happening inside some popular eateries. In early 1967, a Cambridge City Council meeting grew heated when councilors criticized the police chief for not doing more drug busts in the area.[53] Additional busts soon followed. At that same meeting, the city council also took up the issue of "smut literature" being peddled in the marketplace.[54] The police chief reported that he had asked several newsstands to remove offensive literature but that within a few days other material "just as bad" had replaced it on the racks.

Later that year, controversy broke out concerning *Avatar*, a new countercultural underground newspaper sold in Harvard Square. *Avatar*'s masthead listed its contributors by their astrological signs and ran articles—often in a satirical, over-the-top tone—in support of things like draft resistance, "balling" (i.e., sex), Communist China, racial equity, and psychedelic drugs.[55] Mel Lyman, head of a New Age cult located in Boston and which called itself the "Lyman Family," contributed poems with lines like, "I'm going to fuck the world."[56]

City officials hated the publication and considered it obscene. At one city council meeting, councilor Alfred Vellucci waved a large envelope above his head. In it, he said, were two issues of *Avatar*, which he said contained "the filthiest junk I've ever laid my eyes on."[57] The city soon pulled *Avatar's* vending permit and succeeded in getting a lower court to declare the newspaper obscene.[58] Newsstands in the Square stopped selling it after that, but unlicensed street vendors continued to peddle it on the sidewalks. Around this time, the Business Men's Association joined the chorus of critics and met with the city manager to discuss the newspaper's continued sale. The association's minutes from that meeting report, "Everyone present was very dismayed at the fact that such a thing could happen in the Square or any other community."[59] Not long after, the peddlers were arrested.[60]

During these years, the Business Men's Association's activities remained largely anemic, but the meetings the group did hold, like the one concerning *Avatar*, tended to focus on the perceived moral decline of the market. In 1968, the group's members invited a local pastor to come speak about the concerning changes he was observing in the Square.[61] They invited the city's police chief and several detectives to discuss pilfering, which was believed to be on the rise.[62] They were especially exercised by all the hawkers and panhandlers who they felt hassled their customers and who, in some cases, represented competition. Once again, they briefly contemplated dropping "Men" from the group's name but decided against it.[63]

In 1969, the association had several discussions about what it felt was the growing filth of Harvard Square. At a time when young people around the country were singing along to "Alice's Restaurant"—Arlo Guthrie's satirical antiwar anthem about the prosecution of a band of "litterbugs"—the association wrote a letter to the city asking for more attention to the litter problem in the Square and requesting more trash barrels.[64] It was not a senseless request—it was hard to keep the place clean with all the activity those days, and the association had always seen it as its duty to maintain the Square's appearance. Nevertheless, this suggests the contrasting mind-sets of the two groups coexisting in the market at this time: a younger crowd beginning to make Harvard Square their own, and an older guard who felt it was theirs to protect and defend.

News coverage of the market during these years seemed to delight in highlighting the cultural and generational changes unfolding in it. Articles reported on the closure of long-standing businesses that did not appeal to the younger generation's tastes and preferences. These articles often played up the morally questionable aspects of newer shops—like a 1969 piece on how occult stores were thriving in the Square—and they quoted longtime residents and merchants who bemoaned the changes.[65]

But if the market was falling out of step with the older generation, that was because it was growing more in tune with the younger one. When young people got together to talk politics and protest at Hayes-Bickford's—or when they listened to folk music at Club 47 or bought buttons and clothes their parents would likely hate—they were not just rejecting the old; they were forging meaningful ties with one another and a shared identity. There was a new collective market effervescence in the air. And the more this younger generation saw itself in the market—the more these young people saw their beliefs, styles, and preferences reflected in it—the more it was beginning to feel like theirs, and the more that destabilized those who had once seen themselves in it.

As opposition to the Vietnam War grew, so did tensions in the Square. In April 1969, Harvard students took over University Hall in Harvard Yard, demanding an end to the school's Reserve Officers' Training Corps (ROTC) program. The university called in the police, and four hundred officers,

Antiwar protestors in Harvard Square, 1970. Photo by Spencer Grant.

wielding billy clubs, mace, and riot shields, forcibly evicted the demonstrators.[66] After that, the police were an even greater presence in the Square. It was not until the following year, however, that violence broke out in the marketplace itself.

On Wednesday, April 15, 1970, thousands of antiwar demonstrators rallied in downtown Boston. It was tax day, and the protestors opposed the use of tax money for the military. After the protest, an offshoot of Students for a Democratic Society called November Action Coalition, along with members of a group called Youth Against War, led more than a thousand people on a march from Boston, down Massachusetts Avenue, toward Harvard Square.[67] The group had an official parade permit for the march, which declared it a protest against the upcoming murder trial of Bobby Seale, national chairman of the Black Panthers. As the marchers passed through Cambridge's Central Square, someone threw rocks at a bank's windows. Once in Harvard Square, the crowd surged to nearly three thousand. Protestors congregated in the center of the Square, blocking traffic and chanting "One, two, three, four, we don't want this fucking war" and "Free Bobby Seale."[68] Some climbed atop the subway kiosk. Others began to set fire to trash cans.

As police arrived to disperse the crowd, things grew more heated. Some people charged the police. Others broke off and began to vandalize and loot businesses. They threw bricks and Molotov cocktails through shop windows and doors. Firemen arrived to deal with the burning buildings, and two thousand cops from seven municipalities, bearing clubs and tear gas, crowded into the tiny, already packed Square. It took four hours to clear the streets. By the end, 35 people had been arrested, 214 injured, and the Square's businesses had suffered more than $100,000 worth of property damage.[69] Rioters had broken hundreds of shop windows, including those of a bank, a jewelry store, the Harvard Coop, and a branch of Saks Fifth Avenue. They left multiple storefronts and walls tagged with graffiti messages reading, "Free Seale," "When Tyranny is Law—Revolution is the Order of the Day," and "Banks Need Fresh Air—Ventilate Them."[70]

Destruction of retail markets is not an uncommon outgrowth of social protest, even when the protests stem from nonviolent impulses such as antiwar sentiment or the desire for equality. Yet nearly all of these cases raise the same puzzle for most of us: Why are people so quick to take out their anger on the market? When we see protests over a war or racial inequality and police brutality turn into looting and vandalism of shops, is it just about convenience—is it just that that the shops are right there and, thus, easy targets for people's frustration? Or is there some deeper meaning, perhaps even unconscious, in these acts of destruction?

A complete answer to these questions lies outside the scope of our discussion, but it is possible to speculate that part of what might be at play in some cases is this: because people see themselves and their collective identities in their markets, they likely also see their conflicts and, at times, their exclusion, in them, too—and that may be why markets make such appealing targets. Because we attach to and even sacralize our retail markets, we know, on some level, that destroying them is rife with symbolism. At the time of the Harvard Square riot, few markets better reflected the cultural wars of that historical moment. There was a power struggle going on between those who had long seen themselves and their interests reflected in the culture at large—and Harvard Square, in particular—and those who felt the time had come for the world to reflect them and their ideas instead. The young protestors were fighting for their racial, class, and generational consciousnesses to be reflected in the world they lived in; the market right in front of them likely seemed a darn good stand-in for the broader culture and the conflicts the rioters felt with that culture.

The owner of a fashionable woman's boutique in Harvard Square, whose store was looted during two different protests in 1970, described how a young man came into her store one day and told her that the shop should be burned down. "Boys are dying in Vietnam while you make money," he said, then walked right back out.[71] To trash the market was to make a strong claim about who the rioters felt should be in control of it—and of the world in general.

For merchants, property owners, and residents who were already feeling like the market they knew—and the culture they knew—were starting to slip away from them, the direct attacks solidified their sense of threat. They attributed the violence to outsiders who had no respect for, or claim to, the Square. In fact, since the mid-1960s, local discourse had attributed most of the Square's problems—whether drugs, panhandling, or offensive literature—to the influx of young "transients" and "outsiders," or "street people" as they were now being called.[72] Even when the transients stuck around—even as the dozens of new shops catering to them attested to there being a market opportunity in their presence and suggested they were perhaps no more outsiders to the market than any other new cohort with new tastes and preferences had ever been—they were considered illegitimate outsiders by those who felt themselves the rightful insiders. Acts of destruction only reinforced this perspective: now, it felt as if these outsiders were taking over something that was not theirs while making those who believed they had a more legitimate claim to the market feel unwelcome and unsafe.

The Square's long-standing merchants were the first to mobilize. The financial impact on their businesses was real, and it was time to defend their market. A month after the April 1970 riot, the Business Men's Association held a meeting with the Cambridge police chief and his lieutenants.[73] There had been a second riot in early May leading to even more property damage, and the group wanted assurances of a continued police presence in the Square to avoid any more incidents. While association members considered it a productive meeting, the recent events had breathed new life into the group and given them common cause around which to unite. As informative as the chat with the police was, members concluded it would not be enough. "It is obvious," the group's secretary wrote after the meeting, "that the Harvard Square Business Men's Association must now work closer together and demonstrate a leadership position in the community."[74]

The association soon teamed up with other concerned merchants in the Square to lobby the city manager and city council for increased around-the-clock patrolmen, bans on large gatherings, and stricter enforcement of the laws against panhandling and unlicensed hawking of goods and newspapers.[75] At the same time, commercial property owners in the Square began to clean house. In June of 1970, Felix's Newsstand, which had a reputation for selling obscene literature, was evicted by its landlord.[76] Hayes-Bickford's, the popular meeting spot for radicals, closed a few months later, driven out by a steep increase in rent.[77]

The summer of 1970 only brought more young people to the Square, however. There were more demonstrations—and more vandalism and property damage to businesses.[78] In early August, the Business Men's Association convened a special meeting to discuss the full set of problems it felt were impeding business in the Square—not just the riots, but also the panhandling, the Sunday concerts on Cambridge Common, and the loiterers and hawkers who congregated each day on the sidewalks.[79] One hundred thirty-two members came out for the meeting, the association's largest gathering in years. Also in attendance were all the members of the Cambridge City Council including the mayor, as well as the city manager and the police chief. The association asked the city to assign police officers "who are best equipped to handle young people."[80] They discussed the creation of a joint police-merchant committee to promote better coordination and communication.

Two days later, the student-run *Harvard Crimson* published an article titled "The Harvard Square Mess."[81] It criticized the vandals, but also took the merchants to task for having gained "a monopoly of violence" and repression through their mobilization of the police. The student reporter reminded the Square's business owners that they were, in fact, partly responsible for their current predicament: after all, they had helped make the market so appealing to young people in the first place, when they had "courted and sought out young people when they were buying fancy clothes" during the Square's mod days.

That summer, another group began to speak up as loudly as the business community, and this group would prove to be the central axis in conflicts soon to come. Residents and shoppers who had become attached to the Square when it was a busy and fashionable Main Street, and who still relied on it for their daily shopping and entertainment, felt they were being driven out of their market. Merchants who had built their businesses catering to such shoppers reported that sales were off 20–40 percent because their customers no longer felt safe coming into the Square.[82] But perceived safety was not the only issue. Shoppers who identified with the marketplace as it used to be were losing the power struggle between new and old. They, too, looked to see themselves in the market, and they could sense their reflection dimming and that of the newer generation and its culture growing stronger.

In late August 1970, a local woman wrote a letter to the editor of the *Cambridge Chronicle* explaining that there was no reason for her to come to the Square any longer. All the boutiques and shops that used to appeal "to the suburban housewife or the Boston secretary" were gone. "Unless a better balance of shopping facilities can be provided for all age groups," she wrote, she saw no hope for the marketplace—or at least for her place in the market.[83]

The year 1970 marked the height of conflict and violence in Harvard Square. In the marketplace, the outcome was something of a temporary stalemate. An older guard had somewhat remobilized. However, the newer crowd was not going anywhere. The market had turned its attention to them now, and it felt more and more like theirs. A postcard from the early 1970s adorned with hippie, psychedelic swirls encircling a photo of the Square had the telling caption: "This is our scene . . . try to get with it."[84]

THE KENNEDY MEMORIAL CONTROVERSY

In 1972, the *Harvard Crimson* observed that certain individuals around Harvard Square seemed to be experiencing "future shock"—a psychological state of distress and disorientation arising from too-rapid change.[85]

The futurist Alvin Toffler had popularized the idea of future shock in a 1970 book by that name, and, to the student journalists at the *Crimson*, it captured the state of mind of many local residents, business owners, and city officials who were spinning from a whole new set of changes rolling through the Square—changes that concerned the proposed Kennedy memorial.

In December 1963, a month after JFK's assassination, family and friends of the late president had begun making plans for a memorial.[86] The first thing they did was form the Kennedy Library Corporation, a private, non-profit entity that would raise money for, and oversee the construction of, a presidential library and museum, after which the federal government would step in to run its daily operations. The corporation was steered by a board of close Kennedy allies and chaired, first, by a former president of the World Bank and, then, by JFK's brother-in-law, Stephen Smith, who managed the family's wealth out of New York. In 1964, they selected New York–based architect I. M. Pei to design the memorial and began raising the funds to pay for it.[87] Wealthy political supporters, foundations, corporations, foreign governments, and thousands of private citizens from around the United States—including Sheldon Cohen of Out of Town News, who contributed the proceeds from his sale of JFK memorabilia—all gave to the cause. Meanwhile, the state of Massachusetts agreed to transfer to the federal government the old transit yards adjacent to Harvard Square that were, by then, owned by the Massachusetts Bay Transit Authority. This way, the memorial could be in the spot Kennedy himself had hoped to build his presidential library once out of office.

Rising costs and delays in relocating the transit yards set the project's timeline back. However, by 1972 the project's managers were finally ready to get things going. In the intervening years, real estate developers had scooped up several tracts of land around the site, sure that the memorial would spur additional commercial activity in the area. One developer had recently announced plans to build a nineteen-story Holiday Inn, hoping to capitalize on all the expected visitors to the memorial.[88]

Concerns from the community surfaced almost immediately. Residents of Cambridge's socioeconomically and racially diverse neighborhoods east of Harvard Square worried that the effects of all this new development might spill out across the city, driving up property values and rents and, ultimately, displacing working-class people from their homes in those areas. The most vocal and vehement opponents of the project, however, focused on its immediate—and, in their minds, devastating—impact on Harvard Square itself. Many who lived, shopped, or worked in and around the Square feared a "tourist invasion of the marketplace."[89]

By the early '70s, as many as three million people visited JFK's grave at Arlington National Cemetery each year. The Kennedy Library Corporation's initial estimate suggested the new memorial might draw a million visitors annually and as many as twenty thousand people on peak days.[90] Longtime shoppers and merchants who were already reeling from the recent arrival of one group of perceived "outsiders" to the Square—younger people—would now have to contend with hoards of tourists as well. The already cramped marketplace would face increased crowds and congestion, traffic, noise, air pollution, and even more parking insanity. Those who lived nearby and used the Square for their regular shopping and entertainment feared their existing routines would be disrupted, their lives inconvenienced, and their physical and cultural environment polluted by the sheer volume of new entrants into the market. Life at the street level would never be the same.

More than traffic and congestion lay an even graver threat in the minds of some. There would be so many tourists flooding the streets that the market would shift to serving those visitors' needs and tastes, and the character of the Square would be forever changed. Fast-food restaurants and souvenir shops catering to tourists would replace existing shops catering to local and regional shoppers. Establishments such as tailors and cleaners that met residents' everyday needs, as well as unique specialty shops like Cardullo's for which the Square had become known, might get edged out of the market for good. The looming tourist invasion was not so different from the earlier hippie invasion: here was yet another group of outsiders about to descend on the Square, wreak havoc at the street level, and rewrite the whole market in their own image.

To some, this felt like just as big a moral threat as the culture wars of the past decade. The head of Cambridge's Department of Planning and Development worried the surge of tourists would "corrupt" the Square.[91] A city councilor characterized the expected congestion as "barbaric." The owner of the Brattle Theater said the flood of visitors could be a "total disaster" for the business district and its nearby residents.

In 1972, in response to community concern about both the memorial project and the commercial developments spurred by it, the city appointed a sixteen-member citizens task force.[92] Among those serving on the Harvard Square Development Task Force (the "Task Force") were local merchants and professionals, including Sheldon Cohen of Out of Town News, the owner of the Brattle Theater, and one of the partners of The Architects Collaborative; commercial property owners such as Richard Dow; and residents from both the wealthy and working-class neighborhoods concerned about the project—most notably, representatives of a group that would ultimately drive the fiercest opposition to it, the Neighborhood Ten Association.

The Neighborhood Ten Association was a group of wealthy, predominately white men and women who lived in the large, historic homes just west of Harvard Square near Longfellow's Brattle Street residence and around old "Tory Row."[93] (Often abbreviated to "Neighborhood Ten," the group derived its name from a numerical mapping scheme used by city government.) Like Longfellow before them, members of Neighborhood Ten were fond of the historic, scholarly character of the area, and that included the historic marketplace nearby. They were lawyers, business executives, accountants, professors, and architects, many of whom had served in World War II and had some connection to the university, as well as the well-educated wives of those men, some of whom worked in education or publishing themselves and most of whom volunteered at one or another community organization around the city.[94]

Neighborhood Ten held its meetings in the Quaker meetinghouse located just off Longfellow Park, a large green lawn directly across from the poet's former residence. Prior to the JFK library controversy, members had concerned themselves with issues they felt threatened the character and charm of their residential neighborhood and the quality of life in it—things such as rising crime rates and high-rise housing developments. In the early 1960s, when the state wanted to construct an underpass at the intersection of Memorial Drive and Boylston Street, they became active participants in the highly publicized "Save the Sycamores" campaign to preserve the quiet, tree-lined green spaces along the banks of the Charles River where many liked to stroll.[95] The trees were actually London plane trees, not sycamores, a fact that was either unknown or overlooked on account of its alliterative deficiencies. Whatever they were, the campaign to save the trees and defeat the underpass was a success.[96] As the JFK library loomed, the group turned its attention to saving the Square.

In early 1972, both Neighborhood Ten and the Task Force developed position statements that did not outright oppose the Kennedy memorial but which insisted that any new developments give priority to the traditional, street-level experience of the marketplace. Both groups felt the Square must continue to serve existing customers and remain "scaled to human use."[97]

This meant ensuring traffic, parking, and general congestion did not over-whelm the pedestrian experience, and it meant that any new market activity spurred by the project must "reinforce and complement" the Square's exist-ing commerce, "rather than be a competitor to it."[98]

A first test of these principles—and of broader community support for them—came from the nineteen-story Holiday Inn, set to go next to the Ken-nedy library. Three hundred members of the Neighborhood Ten Association voted unanimously to oppose the project, and the group's president, Harvard Business School professor Paul Lawrence, wrote a letter to the editor of a local paper stating that the hotel failed to harmonize with its surroundings and would be a "lasting blot on the Harvard Square scene."[99] Along with a group calling itself Human Scale, Neighborhood Ten drew up a petition pro-testing the development and collected thousands of signatures from across the city.[100] A number of other interest groups soon joined the fight.[101] The *New York Times* found the whole controversy remarkable enough to report on it, noting the fervent local opposition and the "unlikely alliance among Cambridge's usually bickering business, conservation, academic, and com-munity-interest groups."[102]

Opposition was so strong, in fact, it prompted one city councilor to quip, "There's going to be a riot in that neighborhood, if that building isn't stopped."[103] In the end, the building was stopped and the riot averted when the hotel's developers gave in and agreed to reduce the building to eight sto-ries. However, the fight over the memorial itself was just getting started, and it would be even more intense.

"There is a gathering storm," the city's director of planning and develop-ment wrote in an early 1973 memo.[104] Given growing unease in the com-munity and the objective burdens thousands of new visitors would place on the Square's infrastructure and environment, he articulated what some were already thinking: "One is tempted to raise the question as to whether Har-vard Square is an appropriate place for the Presidential Library?"

When Pei unveiled his design for the memorial in May of that year, the gathering storm erupted, and many began to answer that question firmly in the negative. The proposed complex included a striking eighty-five-foot glass pyramid in which the museum would be housed, as well as buildings to hold Kennedy's presidential archives, Harvard's new John F. Kennedy School of Government, and an Institute of Politics.[105] Compared to the debate over the Holiday Inn, however, less attention was given to the architectural details or height of Pei's design. Opposition focused far more on the project's impact on that more anthropological, poetic street level of life, to which the philosopher de Certeau directed our attention in chapter 1.

Upon seeing Pei's plans for the first time, Paul Lawrence complained that it would be a "massive tourist attraction" that would inundate the streets of Harvard Square with thousands of visitors every day.[106] Assigned to write a critique of Pei's design, the Boston Globe's architectural critic demurred, writing that the important questions for this project were not aesthetic but rather: "What will happen to Harvard Square? . . . Will these changes forever alter the pedestrian, small-scale, university-oriented quality of the Square?"[107]

Most people supported locating the scholarly aspects of the project in Harvard Square (i.e., the library archives, the school of government, and the institute). Those elements would not alter the Square or their lives in it, and it seemed only appropriate for there to be some memorial to Kennedy in the area. But a museum—and one that promised to draw thousands of visitors from around the country each day—was a whole other matter. A few days after Pei's designs were made public, eight local groups, including Neighborhood Ten, teamed up to hold a joint press conference at Cambridge City Hall demanding that the area remain a place for people to live and shop, "not a tourist mecca."[108] A decade or so earlier, the groups that gathered that day could have been confused for a list of JFK supporters. Among those in attendance were representatives of the League of Women Voters, Citizens for Participation in Political Action (a progressive group focused on social and economic justice), and four of the city's Democratic ward committees, all now aligned to fight off a museum in JFK's honor.

In the weeks and months that followed, the Task Force, Neighborhood Ten, and other concerned groups began circulating pamphlets and opposition literature throughout the city.[109] They shot off letters to the Kennedy Library Corporation, the General Services Administration (the federal agency that would assume control over the memorial after the library corporation built it), and even the late president's brother, Senator Ted Kennedy of Massachusetts, insisting the tourist-oriented museum would have a devastating effect on the Square.[110] When opponents felt those parties were insufficiently responsive to their concerns, they drafted more letters, held more press conferences, and circulated more opposition material.

JFK may have been a local hero, but to some it was starting to feel like the memorial was being forced on them by powerful outside actors in the form of the library corporation and its Washington cronies. This only further solidified the sense of outside invasion and people's motivation to resist it.[111] Taking matters into its own hands, Neighborhood Ten hired technical consultants to study the project's potential impact on the Square.[112] The Task Force did the same.[113]

One member of the Task Force set off to collect her own data. Martha Lawrence, a Smith College graduate and wife of Neighborhood Ten president Paul Lawrence, hit the road and traveled across the country to visit the Truman Library in Independence, Missouri, the Eisenhower Center in Abilene, Kansas, and the Hoover Library in West Branch, Iowa.[114] Introducing herself as a representative of the official Harvard Square Development Task Force, she toured the quiet, scholarly research sections of each facility as well as the busy museum portions. She wandered through their parking lots to count how many different state license plates she saw (twenty-nine in a Truman lot; twenty-one in an Eisenhower lot) and to jot down what sort of vehicles were parked there ("buses, trucks, campers, trailers, and motorcycles . . . elaborate homes-on-wheels, a substantial percentage carrying or towing cars, beach buggies, bicycles, motorcycles, or boats"). She explored the local tourist economies that had popped up around each complex. The highway leading up to the Truman Library was lined with motels, gas stations, fastfood chains, and retail outlets, she noted. Visitors to the Eisenhower Center could head across the street to buy Eisenhower-branded toothpick holders and baby training pants at a store claiming to be "Kansas's Largest Souvenir Shop," and they could check out any number of other kitschy diversions including a nearby wax museum and a "Hall of Fame" for Greyhound dogs. For people like Martha who were already skeptical of the Kennedy memorial, her observations confirmed their worst fears: these library-museums were major tourist attractions, and the local markets around them morphed to serve their tourist visitors.

For others back in Cambridge, however, observations like Martha's sounded like plain old snobbery. Not everyone in the city opposed the museum. In particular, white, working-class citizens in other parts of the city were often more attached to Kennedy than to the Square. These individuals did not, as one woman wrote in a letter to the editor, take kindly to having "Brattle Street . . . tell us what is good for us."[115] City Councilor Alfred Vellucci, who had hated the hippie infestation of the late '60s, was aligned with this part of the electorate, and he was a loyal Kennedy ally. To him, opposition to the memorial stunk of Brahmin elitism. It reminded him of the "Save the Sycamores" campaign, which had so irked him at the time that he had proposed cutting the trees down and giving pieces of their wood to opponents of the highway underpass "as mementoes of their struggle to stop progress."[116] Now, Vellucci teamed up with several former and current city officials to form a counter-group in support of the Kennedy memorial.[117] At various points, he accused opponents of being Brattle Street elitists, liberal radicals, or both.

Of course, it is hard *not* to see a certain snobbery and NIMBY-ism (not-in-my-backyard-ism) in all the talk of a terrible tourist invasion. The fact was, people who had become attached to Harvard Square as it was in the 1950s and early '60s had an image of what the market should look like, and it did not involve millions of Middle Americans streaming into the Square, eating at fast-food joints and buying tourist tchotchkes, any more than it had involved thousands of "barefoot and bearded" folks holding "love-ins and pot parties." Yet if we look past the patina of snobbery at the human emotions underlying and driving people's opposition, we can derive a general lesson about markets and their meaning to us.

At its most basic level, this was a fight over the identity of a marketplace and the collective identity of those who constituted it. The same people who feared opening the marketplace to tourists in the early '70s had, in fact, welcomed the market's earlier openness when it was reflected in a chic cosmopolitanism and when the "transient" college and graduate students were wearing madras and Marimekko. That market had helped give them a sense of place and self they cherished—the very things that now felt so threatened.

In the midst of the controversy, the most eloquent statement of these concerns came, perhaps unsurprisingly, from someone who had helped create that earlier market and whose life and identity were inextricably tied to it. On a spring evening in 1974, the Boston Society of Architects held its annual dinner in Harvard Square and honored architect Ben Thompson, the founder of Design Research, for his work.[118] Thompson devoted a portion of his remarks that night to the topic on many people's minds: the fate of Harvard Square. Like Longfellow, or George Wright after him, or me and my dad after him, Thompson's experience of the Square was tied to his frequent strolls through it. He had walked through the marketplace nearly every day for thirty years, he told the crowd of fellow architects, and he loved it for the sense of intimacy one got from its "walker's landscape." To him, the Square's vitality and intimacy were derived from it having a market so directly devoted to its local users—the families, students, faculty, and workers who all came together there.

Yet the Square was in crisis, in Thompson's opinion. Already, people like him were feeling deprived of the street-level experiences they had once known and cherished. With the Kennedy memorial, the crisis would grow even more acute. When the tourist-oriented museum opened and the crowds descended, all those who felt Harvard Square was their "walker's landscape" would have to share the streets and sidewalks and street-level establishments with thousands and thousands of new visitors. It would never again be the Harvard Square it used to be. Thompson said, "This is the time for Square residents to ask identity questions: Who are we, and what do we want this place to be?"

∼

In 1974, Pei and the Kennedy Library Corporation made several major concessions in response to the community outcry, including a significant decrease in the size of the overall complex. Yet the opposition continued unabated.[119] In December of that year, the Harvard Square Development Task Force issued a sixty-six-page report saying that while they were open to considering a scholarly library on the site, they wanted the tourist-oriented museum to go. They remained deeply concerned with the project and "all that it implies—in terms of competition between the permanent resident and the transient, between the bus-auto traffic and the pedestrian, between Harvard Square's traditional role as a people-oriented crossroads and its possible new dimension as a tourist attraction."[120]

The Task Force saw this competition between old and new at the street level as a threat to the character of Harvard Square. Its members seemed to link the feared tourist invasion to the generational changes that had already transformed the marketplace: in their report, in a section titled "People in Harvard Square," the group called for further efforts to counteract the trend of the Square becoming overrun with a "very transient and predominately young population."[121] The market, they insisted, should continue to serve a variety of people, and "no single type of group should predominate."

In January 1975, the General Services Administration released a much-anticipated Environmental Impact Statement that was based on the work of a third-party consulting firm. Project opponents had long hoped this study would convince everyone that the museum needed to go elsewhere.

Instead, the consulting firm concluded that the hundreds of thousands of estimated visitors each year would have "minimal impact" on the social and physical character of Harvard Square.[122] Opponents were outraged, and they cried foul. The consulting firm had been accused of political cronyism in the past, and, this time, the firm had allegedly supplied the Kennedy Library Corporation with an earlier draft of the study to review and edit before its public release.[123] Even the *Washington Post*'s editorial board, which had been following the hubbub in Cambridge from afar, weighed in to say that the report seemed a "travesty" of the whole idea of environmental impact statements.[124] It was "outright silly" and "either absurdly ignorant or politically motivated," the *Post*'s editors wrote, "to deny that this [project] would drastically change the unique historic character" of the area.

Furious, Neighborhood Ten wrote the General Services Administration demanding to see the underlying data on which the consultants had relied to reach their conclusions. When the request was denied, Neighborhood Ten filed a lawsuit in federal district court seeking the data under the Freedom of Information Act.[125] Facing a long legal battle and frustrated by the continuing opposition, the Kennedy family and the developers finally threw in the towel. After years of bitter debate—and despite having had the support of many local Kennedy fans and Harvard University (which had always been eager to house the library)—the John F. Kennedy Presidential Library and Museum would go elsewhere. In the end, a quiet, tree-lined public park to honor JFK as well as the Harvard Kennedy School of Government were built on a portion of the site originally slated for the memorial. The rest of the land was sold to commercial developers.[126] (And, in 1981, Alfred Vellucci, still angry about all the opposition to the library, put a motion before the Cambridge City Council to rename Harvard Square's Boylston Street after the late president. From then on, it was JFK Street.)

In the years that followed the library controversy, supporters of the memorial accused its opponents of being, what one columnist called, "Brattle Street elitists in camel's hair polo coats who couldn't stand seeing middle-American tourists" in their beloved Harvard Square.[127] As noted, this clearly was a case of NIMBY-ism. However, it was a rather unusual one in which the offending project was not a landfill or hazardous waste facility but a high-status presidential memorial that promised to bring in millions of dollars of commerce, and in which the cherished thing people were fighting to protect was the identity of a *commercial marketplace* and their own identities attached to it.

As beloved a figure as JFK was, it turned out some people's street-level lives were even more dear to them. From the outside, the "Brattle Street elitists" undoubtedly did look snobby—crazy, even—but underneath it all lay the same human instinct that has (for better or worse) motivated many other people in other places and times: the instinct to defend a shared way of life. What this case uniquely demonstrates, however, is just how much of that shared way of life may be rooted in a market. To opponents of the JFK memorial, being cut off from the Harvard Square marketplace meant being cut off from a shared culture and the defining sense of self and community that came along with it. No sacred memorial could ever be as sacred as all that.

Chapter Nine

WHOSE SQUARE? THE BATTLE FOR CONTROL

Early in Federico Muchnik's documentary *Touching History: Harvard Square, the Bank, & the Tasty Diner*, the camera zooms in on a Cambridge citizen standing before city officials at a public hearing.[1] It is the mid-1990s. The man seems agitated, maybe even a bit unhinged. "You are sheep being led to the slaughter," he warns the city officials. He then turns, motions toward representatives of Cambridge Savings Bank sitting nearby, and yells, "These people do not own that building!"

The building in question was located at the corner of JFK Street and Massachusetts Avenue, at the start of the block we visited in chapter 3. It was the longtime home of such Harvard Square institutions as the Tasty Sandwich Shop, Frank Cardullo's Wursthaus Restaurant, and a handful of other small businesses and professional offices—and Cambridge Savings Bank *did*, in fact, own it. In 1994, the bank had paid $7.5 million to purchase four commercial properties on the block.[2] The public hearing Muchnik captured on film was one of many contentious meetings concerning the bank's subsequent proposal to tear those buildings down and erect a new four-story retail and office complex in their place.

Cambridge Savings Bank was itself a local institution. In Harvard Square since 1834, its headquarters was just around the corner on Massachusetts Avenue. By the 1990s, the bank's leadership felt the whole area was ripe for redevelopment. The buildings it acquired were old—the newest had been

built in 1820; the oldest, 1782—and they were in rough shape.[3] The worst was
the one housing the Tasty and the Wursthaus. It sagged. Almost everywhere.

When trolley cars had first come to Harvard Square about a hundred years
earlier, the cars needed a wider corner to accommodate their turning radius.
Urban legend has it that one day, a crew of workers grabbed some saws and
rounded the building's square corner off but never replaced the buttressing
they removed, causing it to slump over time. The 1890s renovations were
probably less slapdash than lore suggests, but, either way, by the 1990s time
had taken its toll.[4] A large billboard sitting atop the building's roof had been
acting as a sail for years: whenever it caught a strong gust of wind, the building shook. Multiple steel posts had been jammed into the Wursthaus's dining
room to keep its ceiling from collapsing. In the basement, a few cement walls
had been slapped together at one point to keep the whole structure from cav-
ing in on itself. For a while, an old refrigerator had even been used to lend
further support to the low ceiling down there.

To people like Pete Ingram, the bank's president, it seemed like a no-
brainer to tear these shabby old buildings down and replace them with
something new and fresh, not to mention more structurally sound.[5] To
make such a project financially feasible and allow for a reasonable return
on investment, the bank would necessarily charge higher rent in the new,
updated complex. Existing commercial tenants would have to move out
for construction to begin anyway, and the bank was unlikely to invite
them back after. The nearly eighty-year-old Wursthaus seemed to be on its
last legs, more popular in people's imaginations than in their actual dining decisions, and the Tasty was a 210-square-foot hole-in-the wall known
for cheap burgers and tuna sandwiches. Although bank representatives
would not disclose their future leasing plans, their architectural drawings
suggested they had new ideas about what to place in this prime retail location: they seemed to be making room for a few large tenants, most likely
national chain stores.[6]

Given the decrepit state of the buildings, it is easy enough to imagine
people might have praised the deeply embedded, local financial institution
for wanting to invest in the area's infrastructure and development. At the
very least, one would assume the bank, having legally acquired the properties, would be able to renovate and lease them as they saw fit. That's not
exactly how things went down. Upon learning of the bank's plans, a local
official warned a "major firestorm" was about to erupt in the community.[7]
He had no idea.

The Tasty, ca. 1996. Courtesy Cambridge Historical Commission.

It wasn't just that people were attached to a bunch of old, sagging buildings (although some were). They were attached to what was inside those
buildings. The Tasty, most of all. The diner had been in that location since
1916. Like the building it called home all those years, the Tasty was not much
to look at by the 1990s. It probably never was. Its most notable physical features were a sticky yellow Formica countertop and fourteen faded green
stools. But the humble little establishment meant something to people.

It meant something that at that sticky counter and on the those faded
stools, professors and homeless people, ex-hippies and high school students,
elderly women on a break from shopping and bus drivers on a break from
work all sat crammed together, shoulder to shoulder, to eat and talk. It meant
something that hanging on the Tasty's wall was a paper map of the world
with dozens of pins noting where its customers had come from and gone
off to.[8] It especially meant something that Charlie Coney, the Tasty's day-
time chef and counterman-philosopher for more than two decades, did not

let a single person cross the diner's threshold without acknowledgment. A middle-aged Black man whose hair tended toward gray over his long tenure, Charlie had the air of someone who had weathered his share of crap in the world but while it had wearied him, it had not broken him, and he made sure everyone felt welcome and equal. Upon entry, you were assured a "Hi, brother" or "Hello chief" or the like.[9] If you ordered the same thing a few times in a row, Charlie noticed, and you became "Mr. Tunafish" or "Regular-and-a-coffee-roll."

It meant something, too, that the Tasty's owners always seemed to understand just what it was the Tasty offered people—and that it wasn't something listed on the menu. In 1983, owner George Avis reflected, "What makes us click, what makes us work is that we acknowledge personalities."[10] Like Charlie, Avis knew his customers and knew why that mattered: "You can buy coffee anywhere in the Square," he said, but remembering that someone takes cream and two sugars, "It makes them feel accepted. It makes them feel you care enough to learn what their choice is. That's what the Tasty's about." A decade later, the Tasty had been passed down from Avis to his son-in-law, Peter Haddad, and he too had that awareness of the diner's role in the community. "I think of myself more as a custodian than the owner," Haddad said.[11]

That's how members of the community wanted Cambridge Savings Bank to behave: as a custodian of something in which they all had a stake—this small corner of the world and the even smaller shop located there. When, instead, the bank seemed inclined to pursue whatever path best suited its own interests irrespective of the community's opinion, the firestorm erupted.

Long-time Cambridge Savings Bank customers began threatening to close their accounts if the buildings were destroyed and tenants like the Tasty evicted.[12] Members of the Harvard Square Defense Fund, a powerful neighborhood group during the 1980s and '90s, called the bank's plans a "disaster" and "menacing."[13] The Defense Fund's president lambasted developers like the bank for always acting "in the name of the profit motive and the bottom line."[14] Local teens from Cambridge's public high school formed a group called "The Harvard Square Liberation Front."[15] They began showing up at public hearings to speak out against the Square being "mallized" by chains and turned into a commercial "wasteland." Hundreds of other citizens joined the fight with them and crammed into meeting rooms at City Hall to oppose the bank's plans.[16]

To some onlookers, the whole situation looked even crazier than the JFK library controversy. Here, people were not just contesting a new, outside, government-sponsored project that might alter the character of the Square. Now, they were trying to tell existing market participants what they could and could not do with their private property. They were trying to regulate the supposedly free market and have a direct say in which businesses should and should not compose it.

In 1996, the *Baltimore Sun* reported on the uproar with an outsider's sense of bewilderment and bemusement. How was it, the *Sun* pondered, that a dingy little diner could provoke in local citizens "a fervor reminiscent of their ancestors who once gathered on Cambridge Common to take up arms under the command of a Virginia planter named Washington"?[17] With some citizens criticizing a bank for acting "in the name of the profit motive and bottom line" and others calling themselves the Harvard Square Liberation Front, some dismissed the hubbub as a liberal enclave's general distaste for the market and market values. However, that interpretation overlooked one key fact: all these people were fiercely defending a business—a business they loved.

Despite the rhetoric, this was less a battle between market actors and anti-market activists and more a battle over who should control a market in which they were all participants and all had a stake. This was a fight over who gets to decide what changes happen at the street level and, ultimately, what definition of community should prevail there. In the years leading up to the blowup over the Tasty, two competing answers to these questions had emerged and, increasingly, diverged.

THE FREE WHEELIN' '80s

After plans for the JFK library were abandoned in the mid-1970s, some of the commercial developers affiliated with the project, including the firm hoping to build the large Holiday Inn, scrapped their plans and left town. A set of local developers quickly stepped in to fill the void. By the late 1970s, the Massachusetts Bay Transit Authority (MBTA) had begun a massive project to extend the subway's Red Line, which ran through Harvard Square Station, and the Square seemed poised for growth once that project was complete. A local developer by the name of Louis DiGiovanni snapped up the Holiday Inn land with plans to build two tall office towers on it. Another local developer acquired one of the former library parcels on the old MBTA yards and planned to build a large, mixed-use complex on it, complete with offices, a hotel, retail stores, and movie theater.[18]

The commercial landscape also began to shift around this time. Since at least the early '70s, suburban and urban malls had begun drawing shoppers away from street-level markets around the United States. Chain stores such as the Gap, which tended to populate those malls, were making inroads into ever more sectors of the consumer economy and drawing a growing percentage of Americans' shopping dollars. Because of the popularity of certain brands and competition from nearby malls—and, because of scale economies and capital structures that often allowed chains to pay higher rent than could smaller, independent establishments—the Square's landlords began leasing to more chain stores. As the 1980s got under way, chains popped up at the street level more so than in the past, and especially in new or renovated properties. In 1980, the Gap opened a large store in a recently renovated building owned by DiGiovanni. A few years later, when the Charles Hotel opened for business on the site of the old MBTA yards, its retail courtyard sported a Laura Ashley store and a Banana Republic, complete with a Jeep sticking out of its window in reference to its then-safari-themed clothing. By the early 1990s, the Limited, Express, and Structure all had clothing stores in the Square.[19]

At the same time, it was becoming obvious that you did not need a presidential monument to draw tourists to this marketplace. The globalizing economy—and the globalization of higher education and higher education prestige—began to attract even more people from around the world to Harvard University and Harvard Square. All those fast-food franchises and chain restaurants that people had feared would emerge to cater to visitors of the JFK library showed up anyway to cater to both local and faraway visitors. By the early '90s, the Square had multiple national and local food chains, including Bruegger's Bagels, Chili's Grill & Bar, Bertucci's Brick Oven Pizza, and Pizzeria Uno.

Not everyone welcomed these changes. Local discourse during these years began to focus more and more on the loss of the Square's unique character at the hands of profit-seeking developers and the homogenizing chain-store tenants those developers seemed intent on inviting into the market. In local and national news articles, and in countless conversations at local haunts like the Tasty, people mourned the death of long-loved establishments and lamented the marketplace's creeping conformity. Harvard

Square was starting to look like any other shopping center in the country, critics said. It was losing its soul.[20]

It wasn't just Harvard Square. The "McDonaldization" or "chainification" of society was becoming a topic of discussion across the United States.[21] Since the country's founding, local merchants and small-business entrepreneurs had featured prominently in American ideas of democracy. The sense of moral community and economic opportunity on which democracy was said to depend relied on all those values Longfellow had prized in his famous poem—the blacksmith's stability, his industriousness, and his embeddedness in local life. (He was the *village* blacksmith after all, not just any blacksmith.) By the 1980's and early '90s, a number of political philosophers, cultural sociologists, and regular citizens across the country began to worry about what it meant that local merchants and the more traditional, community-minded values they represented were increasingly being displaced by distant corporate actors and their values—e.g., efficiency, predictability, and calculability.[22]

Nevertheless, free-market thinking was ascendant during these years, and it drew on equally powerful democratic ideals of individualism and individual rights. The wage and price controls of the 1970s were out; laissez-faire was in. Reagan was president, and the ideas of free-market proponents such as Milton Friedman shaped public policy and economic thinking of the day. From this perspective, market interference—not big business—was what threatened to undermine crucial American values. (The best-selling nonfiction book in the country—Lee Iacocca's 1984 autobiography, which chronicled Iacocca's rise from humble beginnings to Chrysler CEO—offered testimony to the fact that the American Dream was alive and well in the halls of big business.)

To many, the changing commercial landscape in Harvard Square was, therefore, something to embrace, not something to fret over. It was evidence of the free market at work.[23] Popular franchises were the era's new, new thing and what shoppers of the period apparently wanted. Capital was flowing where it should. Upgraded buildings helped the Square remain an appealing shopping destination, better able to compete with malls for both popular chains and their many customers. When I was a kid walking through the Charles Hotel's brand-new courtyard with my dad, the Laura Ashley and Banana Republic stores made the place seem fresh and cool to me. When I was in high school in the early '90s, my friends and I headed into the Square to shop for jeans and the perfect V-neck T-shirt at the Gap.

The Gap was not the Beat culture of the '50s nor the antiwar movement of the late '60s, but it was a cultural phenomenon of its own, and it appealed to young people like us at the time. If anything, the fact that it was a national phenomenon—that I paged through Gap ads in *Seventeen* magazine while my dad told me about articles he read in *Forbes* on the company's business model and stock performance—enhanced its appeal.

THE BUSINESS ASSOCIATION FOCUSES ITS AGENDA

During the 1980s and early '90s, the changing commercial landscape began to pose some interesting dilemmas for the Harvard Square Business Association (the group had finally dropped "Men's" from its name in 1972.[24]) On the one hand, a pro-business group was perfectly in step with the times. On the other hand, what exactly it meant to be pro-business became more complicated in an environment in which being "pro-" one kind of business could be taken as an abandonment of another kind of business. As we have seen, this same issue had already arisen for the group in the 1920s, when the first chain stores appeared on the scene. However, it had receded as a concern in the intervening decades (along with anti-chain sentiment across the country, which petered out after the 1930s).[25] Yet here it was again. In the years to come, the chain-store debate would prove hard for the Business Association to ignore.

The question of what role a group like this could—and should—play in shepherding the market also took on renewed salience. Small, independent operations continued to outnumber chains in the Square through the 1980s and early '90s and remained a large proportion of the association's membership. Yet with a growing percentage of regional and national firms, this was clearly no longer a market in which major decisions could be made by a group of local businessmen bonding over golf, scotch, and cigars. The market was becoming more diverse, and there were too many complicated outside forces now shaping it.

As a result, tensions long present in the Business Association became even harder to navigate. To compete with the growing popularity of malls, for example, some members of the group felt the Square should offer customers similar amenities, such as consistent business hours.[26] However, the association had always struggled to wrangle even local merchants around such common efforts, and a business like the Gap with worldwide operations was not about to take notes on its hours of operation (or window displays or joint promotions) from a local group like this.[27]

Even if the Business Association could effect such controls, economic thinking of the day discouraged that sort of interference in the free market. As in the past, the group was led by a mix of local merchants and property owners who believed the market must evolve to remain vibrant and healthy. More so than some of its activist forefathers, however, the association's contemporary leaders believed it would evolve most effectively if left alone. So, while some members of the community began to lament the death of Harvard Square's soul, Sheldon Cohen, owner of Out of Town News and president of the association during the mid-to-late 1980s, defended the changes as organic market growth, and the group's overall mission became a bit more circumscribed and focused compared to earlier periods.[28]

Specifically, the Business Association doubled down on the part of its original mission it could still control and which all could agree remained legitimate and important for the market's ongoing vitality: it would focus its efforts on promoting the Square as an exciting, appealing shopping district. In the early 1980s, the association hired its first full-time executive director whose job was to boost the Square through advertising, a monthly newsletter, and an increasing number of public events intended to draw people to the Square and its shops and restaurants.[29] To differentiate the Square from suburban malls and new urban marketplaces, including Boston's Faneuil Hall and Copley Place, the group now sponsored annual events like Oktoberfest and Mayfair.[30] Because the Square's new and old attributes alike could make the marketplace feel unique and special to shoppers, newsletters from this period promoted both: one month the group ran a profile of the new Swatch craze and "the world's largest Swatch store" located on JFK Street; another month, it ran a profile of the Square's oldest continually operating store, the tobacconist Leavitt & Peirce.[31] When the World Cup came to Boston in the early '90s, the Business Association sponsored promotions and ran seminars with Cambridge's Office of Tourism to educate merchants on how to attract and cater to international crowds.[32]

With its focus on boosting the market's overall appeal, the group found common cause with the Square's commercial property owners. A landlord's real estate income and property value obviously depended on the Square remaining an active commercial district, attractive to both businesses and customers. By the mid-1990s, the Business Association and its members in the real estate business had launched a joint "block captains" program.[33] Unlike a mall, the Square did not have one single owner incentivized to maintain the shopping center's overall physical appearance. In the past, that responsibility had often fallen to the association, but now the Square's landlords became even more directly involved. On-site property managers took responsibility for identifying things like overflowing public trash cans, broken bricks on the sidewalk, graffiti, potholes, and more, and then coordinating with the association and the city's Department of Public Works on their repair.

Efforts like this reinforced the idea that the free market was self-regulating and best left free. After all, here were private property owners voluntarily assuming a communal responsibility, driven to do so because it served their individual interests in the market.

THE GUARDIANS VERSUS THE FIGHTER PILOT

That question of communal responsibility—and of how free the free market really should be—was far from a settled topic, however. During the 1980s and early '90s, a growing faction came to believe the Square's property owners and business leaders were abandoning their communal responsibility in pursuit of self-interest and that the free market had grown all too free.

In the 1970s controversy over the JFK library, members of the community had used their voices (and the courts) to defend against an outside threat to the marketplace. Their success left them emboldened and also on guard for new threats that might emerge. As it became clear that the Square was poised for more commercial development irrespective of the library's presence, some began to fear that the Square and its unique character were once again endangered—this time, from the unrestrained market.

In 1979, several members of the Neighborhood Ten Association, including a woman named Gladys "Pebble" Gifford, founded the Harvard Square Defense Fund. The Defense Fund committed itself to protecting the Square's urban fabric from "ecological and environmental deterioration" at the hands of "large-scale, rapid, unplanned, and unmanageable overdevelopment."[34] Like other environmental defense funds at the time, the group saw itself as fighting to preserve and protect a precious communal resource—only, in this case, that precious resource was not a forest or wetlands; it was a marketplace. To the group's founders, it was a perfect analogy. In the eyes of Gifford and her colleagues, developers who would displace existing businesses to erect oversized buildings and lease to chain-store tenants might as well have been draining a reservoir for their exclusive use of the water or cutting down trees in a natural forest to sell off the lumber for profit.

The Defense Fund believed the community should have a voice in what was happening in the marketplace, and, with Pebble Gifford often leading the charge, they were not shy about using theirs. I first met Gifford in 2019 when she was eighty years old but still full of fight. "We should talk soon before I kick off," she told me.[35] A 1960 graduate of Smith College, Pebble served as the Defense Fund's president during some of its most active and combative years. As the group was forming in the late 1970s, she went back to school to become a lawyer, and over the years she would be its most frequent and outspoken public representative. On the subject of Harvard Square, "I've always been an open book," she said when we talked, and she encouraged me to dive into the Defense Fund's historical records to learn more about some of its epic battles. Those records turned out to be twenty banker's boxes worth of files meticulously chronicling her and the Defense Fund's activities from the 1980s through early 2000s. They are filled with court filings, memos, letters, and pamphlets aimed at saving the Square and its unique character.

From the start, the Defense Fund trained its sights on large new real estate projects proposed for the Square.[36] Its members went after the city's Planning Board when that board issued special permits for new construction they felt undermined the Square's traditional human scale. They went after Harvard University when it wanted to build a hotel on the lot of an old Gulf Station, arguing the project would create more congestion at the street level.[37] Most of all, they went after commercial developers. They got into a nasty, drawn-out fight over the mixed-use project set to go on the old MBTA yards vacated by the Kennedy corporation. The Charles Hotel that eventually opened there reflected a number of accommodations to the Defense Fund, including its brick exterior versus the developer's preferred concrete, its specific mix of retail versus residential square footage, and its outdoor courtyard instead of an indoor mall-like atrium—details the Defense Fund felt were more in keeping with the Square's traditional character than the developer's original plans.[38]

Not surprisingly, the Defense Fund's activities did not endear the group to the developers of these projects. When the owner of the Charles Hotel tried to embark upon another development nearby and the Defense Fund once again intervened, the developer grew so frustrated he sued the Defense Fund for "maliciously and frivolously" interfering with his contractual rights.[39]

Members of the Defense Fund did not feel they were interfering with property owners' rights. Led by Gifford—whose maiden name was aptly Porter, an old English name meaning the gatekeeper of a walled city or town—they felt they were simply enacting the community's right to safeguard a collective asset from forces threatening to destroy it. And they blamed the Square's property owners and business leaders for unleashing these forces. "The enemy has always been the same group," Gifford told me when we spoke.[40] "It's the business community."

Within that business community, the Defense Fund's biggest enemy and most frequent combatant was the local developer Lou DiGiovanni. DiGiovanni had grown up in a town near Cambridge, one of ten children of a gardener who immigrated from the coastal city of Pescara, Italy.[41] When the United States entered World War II, Lou was eighteen, and he enlisted in the Army Air Force. He went on to fly thirty-five missions over Germany in a B-17 bomber. After the war, he went to Notre Dame for college and law school, then headed back east to practice law. He struggled to secure a job, however, and sensed that Boston's white-shoe law firms were skeptical of hiring an Italian American like himself. So, he went back to school to get an MBA from Boston University and took a job teaching business law in BU's school of management instead. He and his wife went on to have ten children of their own, while Lou taught and practiced law on the side. He familiarized himself with real estate by doing closings for his clients, who were often immigrant entrepreneurs. Years later, DiGiovanni would tell his son John, "I learned real estate from a Portuguese immigrant."[42]

Eventually, DiGiovanni decided to try his hand at real estate himself. By the mid-1980s, he was the owner of multiple properties in Harvard Square, including a parking garage he built across from Harvard's new Kennedy School of Government; *the* Garage (the former garage-turned-retail-mall at the end of our block of JFK Street, which he acquired when its prior owner ran into financial trouble); and several other commercial buildings with a mix of retail and office space. At one time or another, he and the Defense Fund brawled over almost all of them.

Those who knew Lou personally knew him to be quiet and reserved, professorial—but intense, and this former fighter pilot was not about to be diverted from his commercial endeavors, especially not by the same sort of people he felt had not wanted to hire him as a young lawyer. Pebble Gifford was a fighter too, though. When DiGiovanni's projects evicted long-standing establishments or seemed out of scale for the Square, she and the Defense Fund took him on in city hearings, in the press, in the courts— and even in the streets. One morning, when DiGiovanni's contractors were about to raze a building to start a new project the Defense Fund contested, one opponent of the project jumped into the cab of the bulldozer to stop the demolition.[43]

To DiGiovanni, all these theatrics were about Pebble and her crew trying to hold onto a market that was a mirror of themselves. His understanding of the law and markets did not entail private property owners taking advice from community groups, and even the suggestion of such influence drove him crazy. In 1987, when he saw that the Defense Fund's Annual Appeal Letter claimed the group had extracted concessions from him on the design of his parking garage, he dashed off a letter to them saying their fundraising letter was "inaccurate, misleading, and self-serving."[44] They might think they knew what was best for the Square, he wrote, but he had his own thoughts on the subject and, unlike them, the right to effect them: "Bear in mind I will continue to go forward with projects which are aesthetically consistent with what Harvard Square is all about, and not how you and the members of the Harvard Square Defense Fund perceive what should be in your own image and likeness."

DiGiovanni saw this tendency even more clearly in the Defense Fund's attempts to influence his and other landlords' leasing decisions. In the early '80s, the Defense Fund opposed an attempt by DiGiovanni to lease one of his retail locations to a sixty-game video arcade. In the Defense Fund's opinion, there were enough video arcades in the marketplace already and, according to Gifford: "Large concentrations of video games attract young, transient crowds which then tend to hang out in the area, creating a nuisance for merchants, police, and the public at large. Research also indicates that there is a correlation between such arcades and increases in crime and disruptive behavior."[45] The Defense Fund also fought for a cap on the city's issuance of late-night liquor licenses in the Square. As Gifford put it at the time, "there should be fewer intoxicated trouble-makers on the streets after that hour."[46] The group also supported a zoning ordinance intended to limit the number of fast-food joints in the Square by, in part, requiring operators to offer customers nondisposable plates and flatware to encourage in-room dining instead of take-out.[47]

As these examples suggest, it was not always clear what the boundaries were on the Defense Fund's mission. In cases like the video arcade, liquor licenses, and fast-food ordinance, the group was not just contesting the architectural details or scale of new construction projects. They were seeking control over what businesses would operate in the market and how they could operate—decisions they felt defined the Square's character even more than its physical architecture. However, like a condo board that starts off wanting to ensure the property is maintained for the owners' common interest but ends up holding interviews to screen prospective new buyers, such efforts highlighted the complexity of any attempt to exert moral control over a market—it always involves privileging someone's sense of morality over another's.

WHOSE SQUARE IS IT?

DiGiovanni had a point when he criticized the Defense Fund for wanting to preserve the Square in their "own image and likeness." The Defense Fund's first fund-raising call in 1979 asked for donations to help "Save Our Square," the "our" implying perhaps not just a sense of communal ownership but also a particular definition of community. This was a tricky issue to get around.[48] How can you organize around a collective interest without having at least some collective in mind? (And, in defense of the Defense Fund, the Business Association had been grappling with this very same issue ever since its founding, as we've seen.) Nevertheless, once the Defense Fund began to execute its mission of protecting the Square for a common interest, its members could not escape the uncomfortable question of just *whose* common interests they really represented, *whose* Square they were protecting.

For a landlord such as DiGiovanni, the question of whether the Defense Fund should be able to interfere in his business was, on the one hand, a straightforward question of private property rights. However, it was also an issue of market logic—and by that logic, the Defense Fund was defining community too narrowly. The theory of "highest and best use" in real estate says that a property should be put to whatever use will result in the highest feasible value for it.[49] The idea comes out of neoclassical economics' focus on maximum productivity of assets, and by the 1980s it had become the dominant way of thinking about leasing in real estate circles. If a property could yield more in income from a chain store than a local operator, then that was the best use for it. A key assumption held by many landlords was that a chain's ability to pay higher rent reflected, at least in part, its greater appeal to customers, and, so, this approach to leasing necessarily incorporated people's preferences and interests. That is to say, the market was already responsive to the community—the community comprising all the citizen shoppers who were, or might be, drawn to shop there.

From this perspective, the community had plenty of say in what happened in the market. People exercised their voices and revealed their preferences

every time they bought a new pair of jeans at the Gap.[50] Interference from
the Defense Fund was not just unnecessary; it was distortionary. The self-
regulating and democratic market would get things right if left alone. If some
people did not like the direction in which the market was going, that was
simply because their preferences had grown out of step with those of the
prevailing culture.

From 1988 to 2001 the Business Association president was a real estate
agent and property manager named Tod Beaty, who embraced this perspective. As he put it in 1993, "developers are really on everyone's side" because he
felt they would never make decisions that made the Square less attractive for
consumers.[51] Lou DiGiovanni's son, John, who was becoming a more active
participant in the family real estate business as his father grew older, agreed.

John DiGiovanni was as invested in Harvard Square as anyone. He had
been working there since he was fourteen years old. Before he had a driver's
license—before he could even see fully over the steering wheel—he helped
park cars in a lot owned by his dad, and, over the years, he had multiple
other odd jobs around the Square to help maintain their various properties.
John loved the Square from the start, especially the crazy mishmash of people, from dignitaries and students to workers and the homeless, that always
made the place feel so alive to him. The idea that property owners, whose
income depended on a vibrant, healthy marketplace, would do anything to
undermine the market's overall appeal was anathema to him. Accordingly,
he believed a market fueled by consumer preferences and property owner
self-interest could generally be trusted to make the best decisions. Property
owners should consider the quality of the operators to whom they leased, he
said, and "from there, you let visitors decide what will remain."[52]

This, too, was tricky terrain, though. For one, the reason a chain like the
Gap could afford higher rent in Harvard Square than could a local clothing store was not solely about the Gap's ability to attract more *local* shoppers (though in the case of the Gap at this time, that was likely true). It was
also because businesses with national operations and national brands could
leverage their scale across multiple markets. Such a business did not always
need to cover the full operating expenses of any single location in the same
way as an independent operator living off the income of his or her own store
had to. Scale economies and consumers in faraway markets could essentially underwrite a location, and it might well be in the overall business's best
interest to do that if the location happened to be one like Harvard Square
(or Times Square in New York or any other place that attracted visitors from

all over) that helped raise a chain's overall brand awareness. In that case, though, the community of shoppers supporting the presence of that chain store were not just local shoppers—and we find ourselves back again to the question of just "whose Square" it really was and should be.

More important, perhaps, is this: If, as we have seen, markets give us more than goods and services—if they help give us a defining sense of place in the world, help us construct our distinctive personal and collective identities, help us feel connected to one another—are we satisfied with having voice in our markets only through our consumption behavior? Implicitly, that question lay at the heart of the Defense Fund's attempts to grasp for some control over the changing market. In his 1982 book *The Asymmetric Society*, sociologist James Coleman wrote of the sense of alienation people were beginning to experience as more of their everyday interactions were with distant corporate actors and their rationalizing logics.[53] Those who talked of the creeping soullessness of Harvard Square (even as many of them shopped at its brand new chain stores) were operating with a different market logic—a different definition of markets and what they give to us and mean to us—than that held by the Square's property owners and free-market adherents. They were implicitly arguing that the market reflected values beyond consumption and that perhaps some of those values were also worth holding onto.

Yet they, too, were overlooking the deep complexities of their own position—the complexities that arise whenever you try to hold any definition of community and community values constant, and when one group tries to speak for many. Amidst all the talk of Harvard Square losing its soul and all the Defense Fund attempts to stave off development, the Square still bustled with activity during these years.[54] Just as popular chains drew people to malls, they drew people to Harvard Square. When chain stores opened in the marketplace, there were no mass boycotts or pickets; more often there were lines. Was the Defense Fund really speaking for all those people?

Also, even as many of the Square's beloved local institutions endured—including Leavitt & Peirce, Cardullo's Gourmet Shop, the Wursthaus, and, of course, the Tasty—it did not take long for people to adopt some of the new establishments as their own and make institutions of them. Just as my dad and I settled into a long-standing routine at Bruegger's Bagels, other families and friendship groups and work colleagues fell into weekly lunch and dinner routines at places like Chili's and Bertucci's.[55]

In other cases, the replacement of independently operated establishments by larger corporate entities went almost entirely unnoticed. In 1986, the independently owned Harvard Square Theater was bought by USA Cinemas, which operated two hundred other theaters across the country; then, two years later, Loews—itself owned by Columbia Pictures, bought USA Cinemas.[56] Through it all, crowds still flocked to see blockbusters at the theater on Church Street, and the *Rocky Horror Picture Show* ran every single Saturday at midnight, starting in 1984 and continuing for the next twenty-four years, irrespective of the theater's corporate ownership structure.

The Square still had character and, as always, it was reflective of the times. Punk teens with mohawks gathered in the "pit" beside Out of Town News each day and got piercings and products at the funky, grungy retailers inside the nearby Garage. The Square still had vitality, too. Perhaps most indicative of this was the medley of buskers and jugglers, painted human statues and religious fanatics, magicians and puppeteers and at least one "philosopher for rent," who chose to make Harvard Square their theater each day, sure in the belief that there would be large crowds to entertain.[57] It was this carnivalesque sidewalk life that so captivated me out the window of my grandfather's MBTA bus on my first trip to Harvard Square in the 1980s. More than a decade later, on the eve of the Tasty controversy, there were so many street musicians and artists performing in the Square that some merchants and residents had begun to complain that the symphony of human voices was turning into a cacophony, and the city amended Cambridge's street music ordinance, requiring a rotational schedule to bring some order to the busy, chaotic human theater.[58]

That the Square was changing was clear. Yet it was still very much a platform drawing people together at the street level, and its shops, restaurants, and venues—whether locally owned or not—remained central to that function. There was not going to be any easy resolution between those who saw the market as an efficient, dynamic system fueled by private property rights and consumer sovereignty, and those who saw it as a shared communal resource that offered much more than its goods and services—for it was, in reality, both. This also meant there could be no easy answer to the question of who should get to decide what happened in the marketplace when disagreements arose.

THE FIGHT OVER THE TASTY

By 1994, when Cambridge Savings Bank purchased the building in which the Tasty was located, there had already been more than a decade of bitter disputes between the Square's commercial property owners and the Defense Fund. But never had there been a clash like this. The Tasty became the most contentious battleground yet for these warring factions.

How could it not, really? Didn't the bank legitimately own these buildings for which it had just paid millions, and wasn't it the bank's right to renovate them and tenant them as it saw fit? Weren't popular new businesses apt to draw more people to the Square than a 210-square-foot, 78-year-old diner? And, yet, for those who feared the Square was losing its uniqueness, its human scale, its very soul, how could they let the Tasty perish? What was more unique and specific than something that had only ever existed in this single location since 1916? What was more human-scaled than its cramped counter? What better captured the values and soul of the community than a place where people from all corners of it came and sat side by side?

Robert Campbell, the *Boston Globe*'s architectural critic and longtime Harvard Square enthusiast, wrote at the time that the battle over the Tasty was a battle for "just about everything that matters, all the virtues of any good human habitat."[59] He was not alone in this sentiment. Former patrons of the Tasty from all over the world began sending letters to city officials, local newspapers, and the bank. The letters recounted cherished memories of the diner from people's years in the Square and pled for the establishment to be spared. Filmmaker Federico Muchnik began carrying his Hi8 camera around to community meetings and into the Tasty to capture the unfolding controversy and what it meant to people.[60] He loved the Tasty from his teenage years, and he knew a good story when he saw it. His documentary, *Touching History: Harvard Square, the Bank, & the Tasty Diner*, would come out several years later, in 2005.

From the start, the war had two fronts—one concerned the fate of the buildings; the other, the fate of the Tasty. The city had more leverage in the former, but most people cared far more passionately about the latter. To pressure the bank to revise its renovation plans, the Cambridge Historical Commission, an official city agency, threatened to designate all of the buildings historical landmarks, which would severely limit what the bank could do to them architecturally.[61] At the same time, the city began contemplating whether to designate all of Harvard Square a historic preservation district to more directly restrict what property owners could do with their buildings and, hopefully, avoid future situations like the one it was facing now.

The student editors of the *Harvard Crimson* weighed in to keep the focus on what they felt mattered most. So long as the bank agreed to let the Tasty return to its original location at a reasonable rent after construction, the students said they could care less about how the bank renovated its buildings. However, "if Cambridge Savings Bank opts to out the eatery by raising rent to an unaffordable price," the *Crimson* editors wrote, then the bank should be punished for the transgression and "by all means the JFK Street corner should be declared an historic district" to block the proposed construction.[62] The editorial's title—"Keep the Tasty, Gut the Buildings"—left no ambiguity concerning the students' priorities. Like the Defense Fund, they did not seem to think the community's voice stopped at either the property line or the front door.

The Cambridge Historical Commission's threat of landmarking the buildings worked in getting the bank's attention. The bank went back to the drawing board several times, if always begrudgingly. Eventually, after nearly three years of public hearings, debate, and citizen protest—and after the bank had run through three different architectural firms—the bank presented a renovation plan in June 1997 that city officials and citizens could live with.[63] It would preserve the entire facade of the Tasty's building and as much of the interior structures as possible. Before signing off on the bank's plans, however, the Cambridge Historical Commission insisted upon one, last concession: the Tasty's entrance must be preserved.[64] City officials knew they had no formal authority over whom the bank would ultimately lease to, but they hoped this little detail might serve as a symbolic reminder of what so many people wanted—for the Tasty to return to its home after the project was complete.

As move-out day for the building's tenants approached, however, it seemed increasingly clear that the bank had no plans to invite the Tasty back after construction. The bank's president stopped returning phone calls from Peter Haddad, the diner's owner.[65] Haddad spent the fall of 1997 trying to locate other affordable space in the Square. One deal came close, but then fell through.[66] With every passing day, it was more likely the diner would close for good. A sense of desperation started to set in. Local celebrities joined the fight around this time. Tom Magliozzi, host of the popular NPR radio show *Car Talk* (and one-half of the famous "Click and Clack" duo), encouraged his listeners to lobby the bank on the Tasty's behalf. He wrote directly to the bank's president himself, advising, "You don't want to be remembered as The Guy Who Closed the Tasty."[67]

City officials searched for ways to sway the bank. Hoping that further public pressure might work, Cambridge City Council began holding open hearings so that citizens could express their love for the Tasty and their wish for its return.[68] At these meetings—just like at its cramped counter—the Tasty drew people together from across the community. Cheering one another on were working-class and middle-class residents as well as university faculty, feisty old-timers, and earnest teens. They hooted and hollered in common cause after each statement about how the bank was betraying its commitment to the citizens of Cambridge or how the city should discourage "the encroachment into our community of nationwide chains."[69]

To the bank and its allies, this was all too much. Tod Beaty, president of the Harvard Square Business Association, wrote an angry letter to the city, criticizing this market interference as a "disturbing" overstep.[70] It set a dangerous precedent, Beaty said, and the Business Association could not support it.

Despite Beaty's clear stance, the Tasty debate had put the association in a difficult position. The organization once again found itself stuck in the middle. This time there was no obvious way to reiterate its commitment to the interests of Harvard Square's business community without answering the very same questions the Defense Fund was running up against: Which community? Whose interests?

The conflict here was between two groups that had always been a part of the Business Association—the Square's commercial landlords (i.e., the property owners) and its existing merchants. Ever since grain-salesman-turned-property-manager George Wright led the group to modernize the district so that it could better compete with the Boston markets luring away shoppers of that era, individuals in the real estate business had played a key role in the association. However, the association had also always represented the interests of the Square's existing business owners. Whether it was in 1920, when founding member and real estate man Thomas Hadley told the association's grocers that they would simply need to adapt if they wished to compete with the market's new chain stores, or in 1949, when the association's president Richard Dow, a landlord, evicted old Fred Olsson's art shop to make room for a fully outfitted, modern department store, the group had had to grapple with the sometimes-competing interests of property owners, who sought the highest and best use for their assets, and merchants, who wished to preserve their place in the market. Today was no different. But with the battle lines drawn so clearly by the mid-1990s and controversy over the Tasty exploding, there was no easy way to side-step the tension. The Business Association had to take a stand.

As Beaty's comment reveals, the group's leaders landed on the side of the bank. However, they got there as a result of solidifying their commitment to something else: change. No matter what else it was, they believed the attempt to save the Tasty was an attempt to stop change. The question of whether anyone could or should try to stop market change was becoming the central issue in another debate just starting to heat up.

THE CURIOUS CASE OF PRESERVING A HISTORY OF CHANGE

In 1995, in the midst of the fight over the Tasty—and in hopes of avoiding others like it—Cambridge City Council asked the city's historical commission to work with interested citizens on a plan for preserving the Square's remaining historic buildings.[71] By the end of the decade, the commission's Harvard Square Historic District Study Committee, consisting of residents, business owners, property owners, and representatives of Harvard University, was still at work, trying to reach a proposal upon which all its members could agree.[72] That was proving tricky.

The question at hand was whether to rezone Harvard Square as an official Historic District under Massachusetts law.[73] If adopted, the designation would give the Cambridge Historical Commission binding review over the demolition, construction, renovation, and redevelopment of buildings in the marketplace. Everyone involved understood that designating Harvard Square an official Historic District would affect only the Square's buildings, not its businesses. Part 1, Title VII, Chapter 40C of Massachusetts General Law lays out a process for preserving and protecting "buildings and places," not markets or firms.[74] So, while the city could gain more oversight of property owners' construction projects, it would still have no direct say over what commercial tenants those property owners might choose to put inside their properties.

The Defense Fund supported the Historic District designation. It would ensure property owners had to take into account at least some community concerns in any new real estate projects. It would not preserve everything the Defense Fund wanted, however—it would not preserve the market. Documents from the period reveal the Defense Fund's disappointment that the designation would not prevent landlords from leasing to chain stores.[75] The Tasty had closed in 1997, and Cambridge Savings Bank's redevelopment project was now under way. When, at the Defense Fund's annual meeting in 1998, it was reported that the bank had plans to put an Abercrombie & Fitch, the youth clothing chain, into the Tasty's building after the renovation, the crowd booed.[76] At that same meeting, some members of the Defense Fund asked whether a Historic District designation was simply "too little, too late."[77] Nevertheless, most agreed that it was better than nothing, and the Defense Fund became an active proponent of it.

The proposal's most vocal opponent was John DiGiovanni, Lou's son. Lou was sick with cancer by then, and John seemed to come into his own during this debate. He served on the Historic District Study Committee, and in meeting after meeting (and the committee would have over fifty meetings when all was said and done), he argued his case: the idea of a Historic District was misguided because it went too far.[78] Despite what the Defense Fund said, John believed that designating the Square a Historic District *would* preserve the commercial market, and that was the problem. For the Square to remain competitive and relevant—for it to remain a crowded, bustling, vibrant place—its retailers, restaurants, and landlords had to be allowed to change. Buildings needed to be modernized, storefronts updated, signs changed out, spaces remodeled for new uses. Freezing the Square's buildings in time would, John feared, freeze the whole marketplace and destroy what had always made it so special—its ability to evolve with the evolving world.

It would have been easy for John to frame his objection in terms of the private property rights of the Square's commercial building owners. That had been the central axis by which most fights in the Square had previously been fought, and his family's business was one of the largest property owners in the Square. But, instead, he spoke in terms of change. He had grown up learning the ropes of the real estate business from his old man and hearing war stories about the Defense Fund's antics. He believed that if the marketplace had not been allowed to change—had not been open to new ideas and new actors—his dad would never have been able to make a go of it, and his family's situation would be a lot different. Arguing against the Historic District served his and his family's personal financial interests, to be sure. However, he also felt a sense of duty to defend his ailing father's legacy, and he had a deep-rooted conviction of his own about what made the Square special.

At the time, John was becoming more involved in the Business Association, and he would eventually be elected its president in 2001. During the Historic District debate, the group's leadership landed on a similar position to his, solidifying its commitment to change. From the start of the debate, the Business Association used its monthly newsletters to raise what the group's leaders felt to be the central question in all this: "How far should the efforts go to keep what we all now know and love?"[79]

The association's fall 1996 newsletter quoted local shopkeeper Frances Cardullo. The Wursthaus, long owned by Cardullo's father, Frank, had just closed after eighty years in business, but, unlike the Tasty, it was not because of the bank's proposed redevelopment. Frank Cardullo had overextended himself with a second location and let his business fall out of step with the times. "Staying in touch with his customers and the community was the key element in the success [my father] had for the first forty-plus years," Frances said, "but as he got older and the community evolved, he and his business did not."[80] The newsletter ended by asking readers to contemplate: "Why is it, for a community so proud of its developments in every other area— science, technology, government, the arts, etc—that we have trouble accepting change in our day-to-day lives? . . . How can we passionately fight change and [yet] rationally acknowledge that a community needs change to survive?"[81]

The Historic District debate only deepened the earlier fissures in the mar- ketplace. The Business Association's newsletters now included occasional swipes at Pebble Gifford and the Defense Fund for that group's ostensibly anti-change stance.[82] However, not everyone in the Business Association actually disagreed with Pebble and the Defense Fund. In 1999, with debate over the Historic District still raging, the group surveyed its membership, and its leaders acknowledged that some members—presumably existing merchants who identified more with the Tasty than the bank during that controversy—supported the proposed historic landmarking.[83]

Nevertheless, with a number of the Square's property owners and some longtime retailers like Cardullo opposed to the Historic District, the Busi- ness Association's leaders came down on the side of change. According to the group's final position statement on the topic, the risk of designating Harvard Square an official Historic District was that it would "give 'stand- ing' to a range of organizations that might object frivolously to the slightest design detail in an attempt to thwart change and regulate use" (i.e., which businesses went into the Square's buildings, not just the buildings' physical architecture).[84]

Throughout the protracted debate, several parties tried to chart a middle ground between the two opposing sides. These individuals supported the idea of designating Harvard Square a Historic District but acknowledged DiGiovanni's and the Business Association's concerns about change. They took pains to clarify that their intent was neither to stop businesses from

changing, nor to freeze the marketplace in one moment of time. Rather awk-
wardly—though intriguingly for our purposes—they expressed a desire to,
as they put it, *preserve the Square's history of change*. Harvard's representative,
for example, said the university supported the Historic District designation
but attention must be paid "to keep the history of change" alive.[85] Charlie
Sullivan, executive director of the Cambridge Historical Commission, said:
"Harvard Square has been around for over 350 years of history and change.
We want to try and preserve as much of that as we can."[86]

~

Preserving a history of change is a puzzling concept to get one's head around.
Yet it is the precise problem one faces when trying to protect and preserve a
market. If Harvard Square was not just a *place* made up of bricks and mortar
that people wanted to freeze in time for purposes of nostalgia or historic
education like, say, Colonial Williamsburg—if it was, in fact, a living, breath-
ing *marketplace* made up of brick-and-mortar businesses, defined not just by
its particular makeup at any one moment but by its continual incorporation
of new actors and new ideas—then you really did have to preserve its history
of change to preserve the Square, as painfully awkward as that sounded. But
what really is "preserving change" other than "embracing change"?

   In the end, DiGiovanni and the Business Association won the central
argument, though the resolution contained something for both sides. On
December 18, 2000—more than five years after the issue was first raised and
debate began—Cambridge City Council voted not to designate the Square
a Historic District, but to designate it, instead, a less strictly regulated Conservation District.[87] The Cambridge Historical Commission would still have
design review rights over all construction that required building permits,
but community groups such as the Defense Fund would not be guaranteed
legal standing to block new development projects. The voice for which the
Defense Fund had always fought would be limited.

   The Defense Fund's instinct to preserve the Square was not crazy. It is
human to want to hold onto something so cherished, and nothing draws
people to collective action more than the sense that something precious
and shared is under siege. However, the group's position left it with no real
answer for the question of change. The Defense Fund tried to speak on
behalf of the community, but the community was constantly evolving. The
Defense Fund tried to protect certain establishments and the values and

tastes they reflected, but that meant constraining new values and new tastes from emerging. There is just no easy answer to the question of "how far should we go to keep what we all now know and love," when part of what we love is change.

∼

I stopped by the Tasty on its last night. It was the fall of 1997, my junior year at Harvard. Back at my dorm, I had put on the gray pencil skirt, black turtle-neck sweater, and leather jacket that made me feel like a passionate Romance languages and literature major rather than the pre-professional economics major I actually was (and which, in retrospect, in photos, I see made me look like a Gen X Olive Oyl); and then I headed out to pay my respects. It was late, and most of the Square was quiet. However, as soon as I turned the corner onto JFK Street, I heard music blaring and saw people gathered on the sidewalk in front of the diner. I stepped into the crowd.

I recall there being a strange mix of mania and melancholy in the air. Some people were trying to shove their way inside. Others seemed content to linger outside and reminisce. A photographer was making the rounds, offering to take souvenir snapshots.[88] I spied a few people sneaking off with souvenirs of their own—a salt shaker, an old ceramic mug, one flat, dull spoon. They reminded me of a friend who still held onto her high school boyfriend's faded old baseball cap, as a keepsake by which to remember that first, special love.

After a few more minutes milling about in the crowd, a friend inside spot-ted me through the window and waved for me to come in. Catching a break in the crowd, I scooted my way into the diner to say goodbye. I can't recall whether I thought back to that night or not when a few years later I stood at the cash register and paid for a pair of new Abercrombie & Fitch jeans in what was once the Tasty's home.

Chapter Ten

PULLING AWAY

The e-commerce revolution was already under way when Susan Corcoran opened Black Ink's Harvard Square location in 2002. However, it was not until five or so years later with the advent of smartphones that Corcoran really started to notice a shift in customer behavior. It was around this time, Susan recalled, "I had to start asking people not to photograph products in the store."[1]

People had always wandered into the shop just to browse, curious to check out the colorful menagerie of products visible through the shop's tall glass facade. But now that browsing sometimes took a different form. When a product caught someone's eye, the customer might snap a photo of it, to search for it later online. Some googled the product right there in the store, scrolling through their phones to see whether they could locate it at a better price elsewhere. Not everyone did this, of course, and it did not happen all the time. The store still had many loyal customers who came and shopped as they always had, and most people still preferred to be able to purchase the products right there and then. But it happened enough. And when it did, it hurt—in more ways than one.

Ever since opening Black Ink, Susan had gone to New York several times a year to attend the New York Gift Fair and the National Stationery Show, huge trade shows where thousands of vendors, artists, and craftspeople from around the world came to exhibit their products. Back in Harvard Square, Susan's daily duties included everything from stocking shelves and managing staff to sweeping floors and taking out the garbage; her trips to New York were the exciting, creative part of the job, and they meant a lot to her. Even after her husband, Tim, passed away, she kept up the ritual: "I'd leave my kids behind with a babysitter, and I'd go down there to meet all these people and look around. I'd decide what I liked and what my customers would like, and I'd buy it for my store."

It was through these trade shows that Susan forged long-term relationships with her favorite vendors. They got to know her tastes and had products ready to show her when she arrived at their booths. During the year, they would send her samples of new products they thought she might like. She also used the trade shows to connect with individual artists whose intricate, hand-pressed greeting cards and wrapping paper she liked to carry in the store, the artists' appreciation for beauty and detail a kindred match with her own. After a day of perusing exhibits and connecting with sellers and craftspeople, Susan liked to wander through SoHo and Greenwich Village, popping into little shops like hers in search of new ideas and new inspiration.

All the work she put into building the right vendor relationships—all the time she spent trying to find just the right products to delight her customers back in Harvard Square—"that felt like my intellectual property," Susan told me. It was how she put her own, unique stamp on the business. During the store's early years, she and other shopkeepers were secretive about their vendors. "You didn't want others to know who they were," Susan explained, because that was how you differentiated your store from your competitors. However, once competitors could find all the same vendors online, she said, "I had to let go of that feeling."

Eventually, there came a point when any other gift shop could imitate Black Ink's product selection if it wanted. By then, though, there were fewer and fewer of those shops left each year, and they weren't the biggest threat anyway: Consumers' online habits—and the websites and businesses that enabled them—were. The first few times a customer ordered a product from Amazon.com right there in the shop, Susan got angry and asked the person to leave. A couple of negative Yelp reviews later, Susan realized she would have to let go of those feelings too.

When we spoke in 2019 before she closed her Harvard Square shop, I asked whether she still made her trips to New York. She did. Almost everything she did at the trade shows, she could do online by then, and almost everything she sold in her store her customers could find online. But she still went each year to meet with vendors and search for those special products she hoped would draw customers to the shop. "I'm old school," she explained, "I guess I still think the in-person connections matter somehow." She wondered how many other people felt the same.

The rise of the internet and online shopping ushered in one of the biggest disruptions ever to street-level markets like Harvard Square and establishments like Black Ink. Yet this chapter is not about all the ins and outs of that disruption, nor is it about some enormous expression of "crazy love" like we saw in response to other street-level disruptions in Harvard Square, such as the closing of the Tasty or the proposed JFK library. Instead, it is about why, at least at first, this disruption did not provoke such an emotional response from members of the community. As we will see, there is a rather straightforward answer to that puzzle, but that answer reveals a lot about the complicated nature of the attachments we form to the markets in our lives. We seem to feel and behave quite differently when we are the ones pulling away.

When the internet first emerged, it was an exciting new development seemingly rife with opportunities for enterprising individuals, even at the street level. In early 1995, a local entrepreneur by the name of Marshall Smith partnered with software designer Joe Chung to open an internet café in Harvard Square. Called Cybersmith, it offered coffee, pastries, and forty-eight computer terminals where customers could, according to the business's early newspaper advertisements, surf the internet, try CD-ROMs, or experience virtual reality and photo-morphing.[2] (Photo-morphing, according to the *Harvard Crimson*, was the term for superimposing a person's image onto a T-shirt, or mug, or screensaver. During its first year of operation, personalized screensavers were hot items at Cybersmith.[3]) On the day of its grand opening, this novel café was heralded as a "trial marriage of computer and coffeehouse cultures," and it drew lines that wrapped around the block.[4]

There was a climate of tech optimism, and street-level entrepreneurs did their best to embrace the new tools on hand and put them to sensible use in their businesses. In 1996, the Harvard Square Business Association launched harvardsquare.com.[5] The website offered resources for visitors to the Square, including a map, an events calendar, and a business directory. The Business Association's president at the time, real estate agent Tod Beaty, had been into technology since the '80s when he developed a computerized database that aggregated and tracked Cambridge property listings for local brokers like himself.[6] He was excited about the internet and believed it would be a great tool for promoting commerce in the Square. He and the association's other leaders began using the group's monthly meetings and newsletters to encourage members to embrace the new technology and build websites for their businesses. The group even negotiated a member discount for any merchants who wanted to take one of Cybersmith's website design classes.[7]

There was talk that the internet might one day serve as a robust platform for online sales, but in those early years, the Business Association's leaders (like many) concluded it was "best used as a marketing tool" for the time being.[8] Like a newspaper advertisement, a website could help drive people to the marketplace and its stores. When harvardsquare.com went live, its logo spoke to the desired synergy between online visits and in-person ones: the logo was a cartoon rendering of a stout, crowned juggler. The image had been settled upon after a survey revealed that what people liked best about the Square was its busy, crowded streets that gave the place its "carnival-like atmosphere."[9]

With the benefit of hindsight, we know that the internet was already on its way to becoming a powerful sales platform with a tendency to draw commerce *off* the street. But at the time, as people went about their existing street-level lives, it was difficult to see exactly how and when the changes were coming and what they might mean to existing establishments when they did arrive. It was not always clear how one change might imply another, and another after that. Looking back, I see this in my own personal experiences.

One day, not long after the Business Association launched its website, a coworker of mine at the Harvard Square travel agency, Let's Go Travel, rushed in a few minutes late for his shift. He threw his backpack on the ground, plunked himself down at one of the computer terminals, and waved me over, calling out, "You're going to love what I have to show you!" I stood behind him and waited for the noisy dial-up to connect. When it did, he opened Netscape, typed something into the location bar, and I saw the *New York Times* online for the first time. He was right, I did love it. I had no idea that in a few short years I would help close down our student-run travel agency because all the train-hopping, hostel-sleeping, lightly showered budget travelers who used to walk their dusty, beat-up hiking books into our dingy basement offices no longer needed us. They could buy their own cheap flights, Eurail passes, and backpacks online.

I had even less of a clue that Let's Go's publishing arm, which was at the time sending more than one hundred student researcher-writers out every summer to scour the globe and keep the popular, twenty-two-book *Let's Go Travel Guide* series up to date, would, by my twentieth college reunion, be reduced to a skeletal crew of nine researcher-writers, one print title (*Let's*

Go Europe), and a website. Who wanted to lug around and thumb through a bulky book when you could look up everything you needed right there on your phone?

As it turned out, Cybersmith's founders also failed to divine the future. In 1999, a few months after the Let's Go travel agency closed, the internet café went bust.[10] Homes, schools, libraries, and workplaces had gotten wired up quickly. Access to the World Wide Web on personal desktops and laptops was now so ubiquitous that few people were willing (or needed) to pay by the minute for access at a place like Cybersmith.

Technologically driven change kept coming, and kept changing form—from the early dot-coms and the online distribution of music, to Amazon's growing dominance, to digital photography, smartphones, social media, streaming, and more. One wave of creative destruction after another blew through the marketplace, disrupting Harvard Square's traditional brick-and-mortar businesses in the process. Compared to service businesses (such as salons and dry cleaners) or restaurants (whose date with disruption would come later in the form of third-party delivery apps), retailers were the most immediately affected. Shops that had for so long served as local access points for products and content from afar—bookstores, newsstands, music stores, shoe stores, sporting goods shops, hardware stores, gift shops, movie theaters, and more—all began to feel the effects in one way or another.

This is not to say all retail moved online en masse or that all small, local retailers were invariably doomed. In the 1990s, Harvard Book Store had joined a national consortium of independent booksellers to share best practices and new strategies as they faced off against megastores like Barnes & Noble. With the rise of Amazon, Barnes & Noble began to have its own problems, and the independent consortium and its members turned their attention to navigating this newer, even larger disruption.[11] The Harvard Book Store was early to invest in a website (so early, it managed to secure "harvard.com" as its URL, raising eyebrows at the university across the street). It expanded the number of in-store events and book talks it held so as to draw customers into the physical store and build its local brand. It even purchased a print-on-demand machine (and named it "Paige M. Gutenberg") when it seemed e-books might be yet another threat on the horizon.

New independent retailers also continued to emerge during this period. Rebekah Brooks had so much success selling her own personally designed line of jewelry in her Northampton, Massachusetts, store (opened in 2007) that she expanded, opening a Harvard Square shop in 2012.[12] Customers could browse her unique collection on the store's website or in person. Stores like hers that had strong local brands built around distinctive, one-of-a-kind products still had to compete with the plethora of options shoppers could find online, but at least they were not competing with other vendors—or, even worse, with product manufacturers themselves—selling the exact same products online.

Retailers like Black Ink that did stock the products of other companies were not just sitting still, though. Before Susan Corcoran and her husband ever thought about opening a Harvard Square shop, they had built an online store. Customers of their first Black Ink shop in Boston always commented on the vintage, industrial products and furniture on which Susan displayed the store's merchandise. One day, she had the idea of expanding the Black Ink brand by selling just those sorts of functional but beautiful furniture items—and doing it online this time. She and Tim called their online venture "The Museum of Useful Things" and, for a short period, they even operated a brick-and-mortar outpost of it in Harvard Square before consolidating the products under the Black Ink umbrella. Always on the lookout for the next new thing, Susan was also an early and active user of every wave of social media to promote Black Ink's products and build its brand. First, she kept up a blog, then an active Instagram account. Her unique aesthetic and attention to detail were as evident in her carefully curated posts and photos as in the store's product selection.

And yet a number of retailers in the Square did close as the internet age unfolded. Technological change was not necessarily the sole cause of any given closure, but any good detective can see its guilty fingerprints on some of the businesses that passed away during this period. Little Russia, a store founded by Soviet émigrés in the late 1970s that sold imported Russian products such as beaded necklaces and nesting matryoshka dolls, closed in 2004.[13] The seventeen-year-old Globe Corner Bookstore, which specialized in travel books and maps, and which had maintained a synergistic relationship with the Square's multiple travel agencies when they still existed, closed in 2005.[14] Ferranti-Dege, an iconic camera shop located in the Square since 1955, closed in 2006. Its owner said, "Our camera store was wonderful in the '60s, in the '70s, in the '80s, in the '90s, but it's not what people are looking for in the new century. You don't need as many products for digital photography."[15] Chain-store retailers were not immune, either. As already discussed, within five years after the iPod's arrival, HMV and Tower Records were gone from the Square. As online entertainment began to chip away at the crowds lining up for in-person shows, the AMC Loews movie theater closed in 2012.

The Harvard Square Death Discourse, which had reached such heights during the early '90s, continued apace throughout all this. Each successive business closing was reported and—especially when the fallen was a local establishment—lamented. Curiously, though, even as the world changed in so many ways, the discourse did not. The two culprits most consistently blamed for killing Harvard Square remained: landlords, who were said to be driving up rents to levels only chain stores could afford; and those chain stores, which were said to be destroying the unique character that had always drawn people to the Square. No one was ignorant of the internet's effect on people's purchasing habits, but for a number of years it garnered little more than passing reference in public laments about the Square's decline.[16]

It was as if the loss of the Square's character to high rents and chain stores had become a taken-for-granted fact. The concern was so widespread by then, it did not seem to require any particular group or controversy to fan the flames. The most vocal actor in prior years, the Harvard Square Defense Fund, had petered out by around 2008 as the group's founders grew older (though former Defense Fund leaders such as Pebble Gifford continued to speak out about changes in the Square).[17] Yet still the Death Discourse persisted.

It is always hard to disentangle the various forces responsible for changes at the street level. Signals are often muddy and hard to interpret. It is not surprising that chain stores and high rent continued to capture people's attention. Unlike the 1980s and early '90s, when chains like the Gap and Urban Outfitters drew young people to the Square, some of the chains that followed failed and failed quickly. Whenever that happened, it lent credence to the popular understanding of what ailed the Square: first, that chains made the marketplace a less appealing destination by homogenizing it (after all, if they really enlivened the marketplace by drawing more foot traffic, chains would be thriving, not dying, there); and, second, that rents were too high (if even chains couldn't survive, rents must really be out of whack). When Abercrombie & Fitch closed in 2004, less than five years after it opened in the Tasty's old spot, it was a vindication to those who had said it should never have been there in the first place. Abercrombie's neighbor, the clothing chain Pacific Sunwear, had lasted even less time in the Wursthaus's former location.

What's more, news reports at the time—often quoting merchants directly—emphasized unaffordable rent as a precipitating factor in most business closures. When the Globe Corner Bookstore closed, for example, the owner cited Harvard Square's high rents and told a local reporter, "When your rent gets above a certain level everything becomes hard."[18] That was undoubtedly true. But it was also true that the store's core products—travel guides and maps—were becoming a fundamentally harder sell to digitally savvy customers. The fact was, without visibility into a store's financials, it was often difficult for the public to see when declining sales and compressed margins from online competition were (at least part of) the reason why a store like the Globe could no longer afford its rent.[19]

The changes unfolding at the street level were, as always, complex and driven by multiple, intertwined forces. And, unlike earlier shocks to the marketplace, the internet's effects took longer to manifest fully. It was more like the proverbial frog in a pot of water brought slowly to a boil so that the frog does not realize what's going on until it is too late. In short, it was not surprising there was no fully worked-out theory in the local discourse for precisely what was causing each and every business closure, and it is not surprising that chain stores and rents remained a central focus of the theories that did circulate. However, it is also true that a highly plausible but somewhat more awkward theory did not figure prominently in most laments about the death and decline of Harvard Square—that the community's own changing behavior was also to blame.

Eventually, however, even a slow-moving, diffuse disruption becomes hard to overlook as its effects cumulate. And, when it levels a direct hit at something truly dear, we are forced to take note. In 2008, events happening at the long-loved Out of Town News kiosk began to capture the community's attention. That was when Hudson News, the international chain that had bought Out of Town News from Sheldon Cohen in the 1990s, announced it was closing the Harvard Square newsstand. With readers moving online, the sale of print newspapers and magazines just wasn't what it used to be. For a moment, it looked like Out of Town News was about to disappear for good.

Members of the community responded to the news with sadness and grief, but not the anger or outrage the Tasty's closing had prompted a decade earlier. Most observers seemed to take the internet's role in the business's demise as a sad but inevitable fact of life, and a series of mournful tributes followed in the press.[20] One local headline ran: "At Kiosk, Dire News—Plan to Shutter Newsstand Pierces Heart of Harvard Square."[21] For years, the iconic newsstand had been almost inseparable from the idea of Harvard Square itself, and this would be a tough loss for some to bear. The newsstand was the first thing people saw when entering the Square, whether emerging from the subway or driving along Massachusetts Avenue. It was where students had gathered after JFK was shot; where civil rights and antiwar activists had protested; where punk teenagers had loitered, finding communion in disaffection; and where more than a few individuals had spent their weekend mornings or weekday afternoons, lingering and browsing. It was in almost every movie filmed in Harvard Square, and it was on countless postcards and photographs. More than any other establishment, the loss of the newsstand would signify that Harvard Square truly wasn't what it used to be.

Early 2009 brought a reprieve, however. A local retail operator stepped in to take over the business. Those who had been sad to see the newsstand go now breathed a momentary sigh of relief, a sentiment echoed in the headlines: "Good News! Corporation Rescues Out of Town Stand" and "Harvard Square Newsstand Is Saved."[22] Yet the reality of the traditional newsstand business had not changed overnight. Out of Town News continued to operate in the kiosk, but, like most newsstands by that time, it now functioned more like a convenience store, selling a limited selection of papers and magazines alongside higher-margin, better-selling products including soda, lottery tickets, and cigarettes.[23]

Meanwhile, broader changes in the Square were becoming harder to ignore. It wasn't just newspaper sales that were on the decline. Overall foot traffic in the marketplace and the organic street-performance culture that came with it had waned, too. The kiosk had always been a natural gathering spot and focal point for the Square's street life, but it was serving this purpose less and less, especially without a busy newsstand drawing people to its racks and aisles.

By 2013, City of Cambridge officials and the Harvard Square Business Association were in talks to renovate and repurpose the kiosk.[24] And that meant pushing Out of Town News out of the building. (The small structure was owned by the city and leased to the newsstand.) While the internet's effect on business profitability was not always directly visible to consumers, it was certainly becoming clear to the Square's merchants and property owners, and there was growing concern about the marketplace's overall vitality. The Business Association, led by then-president John DiGiovanni, thought it might make sense to convert the kiosk into a public-events space to encourage the sorts of performances, exhibitions, and good old-fashioned people watching for which the Square had always been known.

Few things signified the changing times more than this. The marketplace, once so flooded with teen loiterers, hippies, Hare Krishnas, peddlers, punks, and buskers that it had sparked complaints and attempts to regulate all the human chaos, now needed help if it was going to maintain its "carnival-like atmosphere." For so many years, the Square had been a powerful platform for merchants and performers alike, but platforms thrive through their network effects. Most of us understand the power of network effects in the positive direction, when each new addition enhances the value of a platform to its users. However, the same dynamics can unfold in reverse. Just ask MySpace or the fax machine. As crowds moved off the streets and online to shop and connect there instead, so too did performers, finding new platforms and audiences on YouTube, Facebook, and the like. Each trend reinforced the other.

This did not mean everyone was ready to let the newsstand go, however. Both the Business Association and the city came under fire for proposing to repurpose the kiosk. This time there was more mobilization and even some anger.[25] Now, there was someone else to direct anger toward, someone else to blame. Even though it was the city and the Business Association, not a private landlord, pushing the newsstand out, the situation fit with the familiar narrative of a landlord evicting a cherished establishment.[26] Once again, debate surfaced over who should have a say in the direction of this marketplace.

In 2016, the city responded to the public outcry by asking for community input into the kiosk's fate.[27] It established a working group, whose task was to collect feedback from relevant stakeholders and propose a plan for the little building's redevelopment and reuse.[28] Some members of the community accepted that, sad as it may be, the newsstand's life had come to an end given the decline of print media. A group of Harvard faculty wrote a public letter that conceded the issue of the newsstand and focused, instead, on the importance of preserving the architectural details of the historic kiosk.[29] But others would not let the idea of the newsstand go. At a public presentation I attended several years into the controversy, multiple attendees were still pushing to save Out of Town News.

To Denise Jillson that sort of talk was misguided and self-defeating.[30] Jillson had served as the Harvard Square Business Association's full-time executive director since 2006. A longtime Cambridge resident whose family history dates back generations—Jillson is a descendant of Rebecca Chamberlain, a woman accused of witchcraft who died in a Cambridge jail in

1692—Denise understood the value of history and tradition. However, as the female director of the former Business *Men's* Association, she was also a testament to the positive value of change. And in a market setting like Harvard Square, Denise believed it was counterproductive to cling to the past. Her approach was not to try to stop market change from happening, but to boost the businesses that remained and to look for new ways to revitalize the marketplace, like the kiosk project.

Since stepping into her role at the Business Association, Denise had often been called upon to respond to public concern that Harvard Square was not what it used to be. Most critics despaired the loss of the Square's small independent businesses, focusing on the growing number of chain stores and the market's rising rents. Now, she was having to defend the association's vision for a repurposed kiosk, one that did not include Out of Town News. As time went on, Denise found these sorts of complaints increasingly frustrating. She suspected that all the people decrying the market changes in Harvard Square were—like almost everyone—complicit in those changes through their own online shopping habits.

"Things constantly change. One wave after another and you can't stop it," she told me in a 2019 meeting, reflecting on the disruption of online commerce and the controversy over the kiosk, which was still dragging on years later. To those in the community who protested the loss of the newsstand, Denise's retort was short and to the point. She asked the critics, "When was the last time you went in there?"[31]

~

By the time the North Carolina private equity firm Asana Partners bought Black Ink's building in December of 2017, Amazon and other online sites had been cutting into the margins of small shops like Susan Corcoran's for years. No matter how creative her merchandising or savvy her social media strategy, how could a one-woman operation compete with what was then a $560 billion behemoth that attracted more than 100 million customers a year?[32] Yet that's what Susan had been doing for years, and, although it was not always easy, Black Ink's sales had still been able to cover the rent under the prior landlord. But the business could not afford the rent increase Asana wanted. So, Susan closed the shop.

As discussed, in the store's final months, customers, friends, and fellow merchants stopped by to say goodbye, and, while there, many took a moment to add their voices to the Dear Asana Project—those poster boards Susan had left on the shop's front windowsill so that members of the community could leave messages for her new landlord. Page after page expressed love for Black Ink and outrage at Asana Partners. Page after page accused Asana and its ilk (ostensibly greedy real estate investors and their greedy, homogenizing corporate tenants) of destroying Harvard Square and the quirky little shops like Black Ink that had always made it so special. None of these individuals, however, used this canvas to point a finger at the other culprit for why businesses like Black Ink were struggling and why Harvard Square wasn't what it used to be: themselves.

Without a doubt, Asana's rent increase was the proximate cause of Black Ink's closure. It was only natural that people would blame the private equity firm. But it was not the only cause of the store's death. Consumers had been pulling away from street-level shops like Black Ink and street-level markets like Harvard Square for years. Once our central platform for connecting to the world and to one another, the street level had started to feel a bit less necessary in some of our lives, a bit less exciting, a bit more burdensome even. A sexy new platform had come along and caught our eyes.[33] It could deliver products and information from around the globe directly to our doorsteps (or our desktops or our mobile phones). It brought us together virtually, online.

When we think about it this way, it's not surprising that people directed their rage outward, and not toward themselves, when Black Ink closed. It's hard to admit when a new, exciting relationship begins to draw our attention away from an existing one. It's hard to admit when we have hurt the ones we've loved. It may even be hard to recognize the depth of our feelings until, as we will see next, someone else moves in and seems to steal our beloved away.

Chapter Eleven

DIFFERENT MARKETS, DIFFERENT PERSPECTIVES

Dear Asana Partners . . .

> *"Stop taking away our city."*
> *"Go home. You can ruin your own neighborhood."*
> *"Stop grabbing land that has history and tradition."*
> *"Keep Harvard Square a place for local residents, not exploitable profit."*
> *"Think about the local culture that is displaced in your efforts to make more money.*
> *"COLONIZATION."*

MESSAGES FROM THE DEAR ASANA PROJECT, FALL 2019

By late 2019, when Susan Corcoran announced she was closing Black Ink and invited people to leave messages for her new landlord, Asana Partners, tensions in Harvard Square were already high. Asana was not the only investor with billions of dollars of capital and a geographically wide-ranging real estate portfolio to have recently bought up prime commercial properties in the Square. And Black Ink was not the first local shop to close in the wake of those changes.

It helps to back up a bit. Corcoran and others began to notice activity in the Harvard Square property market around 2012. That was about the time news started circulating that a billionaire named Gerald Chan was acquiring buildings in and around the Square. Chan would eventually purchase more than $120 million worth of real estate in the area.[1] He and his family had built a fortune in the Hong Kong real estate market, and he oversaw a large portfolio of real estate and healthcare-related investments around the world. In a 2014 *Boston Globe* profile entitled "Billionaire Buying into Harvard Square," Chan described himself as a global investor looking for properties that would generate a good return, and he said his Harvard Square purchases fit that criteria.[2]

Although Chan's portfolio spanned the globe, and although his fortune had been made outside the local marketplace, the man himself was no outsider to Harvard Square. He had attended graduate school at Harvard in the mid-1970s and had a personal attachment to both the university and the area.[3] He and his family had maintained a residence nearby for years, and his sons spent some of their childhoods hanging out in the Square like a lot of other local teens.

I first met Chan in 2015 at Parsnip, a restaurant he had just opened in one of his recently acquired buildings. My husband and I had been following the space's slow but impeccable renovation for months, peering through the building's tall windows that ran alongside Winthrop Park, home to the original seventeenth-century marketplace. We noted as one design element after another was added. Rumor had it that Chan was overseeing nearly every detail himself, from the sculptural chandelier that cast warm light onto the herringbone wood floor below to the art deco glassware used to serve cocktails at the marble-top bar. (Rumor also had it that his methodical decision-making at least partly accounted for the project's lengthy timeline.)

When Parsnip finally opened, we were eager to check it out and found our way one evening to a table on the other side of those tall windows. The restaurant's posh interior struck an interesting contrast with the unassuming man in jeans and a sweater sitting nearby, whom we soon recognized as its owner. After introducing ourselves to Chan and congratulating him on the opening, the three of us got to talking about Harvard Square and our mutual fondness for it. He recounted a moment from his past that felt familiar: he described the time his father visited him in Cambridge while Chan was still in school and how the two had shared a special afternoon wandering through bookstores in the Square.

I was not surprised to hear that Chan felt a special connection to his father or his time at the university. In 2014, he had donated $350 million to his alma mater, Harvard's School of Public Health (at the time, the largest gift the university had ever received); and he had used the naming rights that went along with that gift to honor his father—the school was now the Harvard T. H. Chan School of Public Health.[4] Even still, it was disarming to hear a billionaire global investor talk about the Square and his connection to it in such a similar way to how I and many others did. I did not yet know that the question of how Chan saw this market—and, specifically, whether he viewed it more from the perspective of a global investor or a local individual—would become a burning question on some people's minds in the months to come.

That question gained salience as several large real estate investment firms entered the market shortly after Chan. In the fall of 2015, a publicly traded, New York–based firm called Equity One paid $85 million for a set of buildings along the block of JFK Street we know quite well by now.[5] Equity One's controversial renovation plans and imminent eviction of the children's toy store at the start of this block, the cheekily named World's Only Curious George Store, led to the contentious public meetings I attended in early 2017—the meetings that sparked my curiosity about what the hell was happening in Harvard Square and why the hell I seemed to care so much.

Not long after those meetings, Equity One and all its assets—including its Harvard Square buildings on JFK Street—were acquired by an even larger firm, the $6 billion, Jacksonville, Florida–based Regency Centers.[6] Regency was one of the largest operators of grocery store–anchored shopping centers in the United States, and it proceeded with plans to redevelop the JFK Street properties.

Then, several months after Regency moved into the market, Asana Partners did, too. In December 2017, the $2 billion North Carolina–based Asana paid $108 million to buy a set of buildings along Brattle Street.[7]

Within the space of five years, dozens of street-level shops and restaurants as well as second- and third-floor professional offices across the Square found themselves with a new landlord—Chan, Regency, or Asana. All three of these new property owners were what we might call multimarket investors. Harvard Square was just one of numerous geographic locales in which they held real estate. Changes at the street level soon followed their entry.

For starters, all of the businesses located in the Equity One/Regency buildings had to clear out when renovations to the JFK Street properties began. Some tenants, such as the Harvard Square Business Association, whose offices had been on the third floor for years, scrambled and found alternative space in the Square. Others shut down or left the market. Urban Outfitters, the youth-oriented clothing and lifestyle chain, closed its thirty-year-old branch and did not relocate it.[8] After all the commotion, the World's Only Curious George Store was sold to a new owner who hoped to reopen it in Cambridge's Central Square.[9]

Meanwhile, Chan and Asana began re-tenanting several of their properties. As leases came due or spaces opened up, they welcomed into their buildings and the marketplace a number of well-capitalized, highly professionalized businesses with national or global brands. Some local stalwarts such as Cardullo's Gourmet Shoppe (est. 1950), Brattle Florist (est. 1917), and Whitney's Tavern (est. 1953) remained, but they now sat alongside a batch of new entrants, including Warby Parker, Sweetgreen, Bluestone Lane coffee, Blue Bottle coffee, Patagonia, and Ray-Ban.

The community responded quickly and vocally to all the change. As described in part 1 of this book, the Harvard Square Death Discourse went off the charts; local TV, radio, and newspapers ran features on the Square's uncertain fate; and a new group called the Harvard Square Neighborhood Association emerged to take up the mantle of the now-defunct Harvard Square Defense Fund. This was not the first time in recent memory that outside real estate capital flowed into the Square—in the early 2000s an Atlanta-based firm had acquired an office and retail building on Brattle Street—and it was definitely not the first time brand-name chains had entered the market.[10] However, the amount of property and business turnover, and the speed at which the commercial landscape seemed to be changing, made this feel like an inflection point. One local businesswoman told me it felt like a "global shock" had hit Harvard Square.

Over the course of several months in 2019, I interviewed a cross section of people in the marketplace to understand how they were experiencing the changes unfolding around them.[11] During these conversations, I realized just how hard it was to make sense of what was happening from a street-level vantage point—and how that itself was profoundly destabilizing. The new landlords and their new tenants took an aerial view of things: "The market" they saw and operated in crisscrossed the country and the globe. Strategies that made sense to them at that level of the economy often looked nonsensical to those at the street level. Beneath the many expressions of anger and outrage I heard around Harvard Square lay a lot of understandable confusion about who these powerful new actors even were, what was motivating them, and what theory of markets could possibly explain their behavior.

First, even though Chan, Equity One/Regency, and Asana all entered the Square around the same time and were often lumped together in people's minds as deep-pocketed investors who placed similar types of tenants in their properties, they each represented a different sort of actor in the global real estate industry. They had distinct incentive structures and organizational models. This made it difficult to construct a single, coherent theory to explain their behavior.

Regency (like Equity One before it) was a publicly traded real estate investment trust (REIT). Its managers had a fiduciary duty to the firm's public stockholders, who were paid annual dividends out of Regency's operating income. Asana was a private equity firm. Its managers had a fiduciary duty to their limited partner investors—large institutions such as state pension funds and university endowments that placed capital with Asana in hopes Asana's investments would return a profit sometime down the road. Both Regency and Asana restricted their investing to U.S. markets, and their objective was to generate a financial return from a combination of ongoing rental income and the appreciation in value of their properties.[12] Chan was a personal investor, though the scale of his wealth and the geographic scope of his holdings rivaled those of many financial institutions. He had a firm through which he and a hired staff managed many of his investments, and he acquired his properties through a number of different entities, but the money he invested was his own (i.e., unlike Regency and Asana, he was not acting as an agent on behalf of other investors).[13] When he deployed his capital to acquire assets around the globe, it was to meet his own personal investment objectives.

From the street level, the differences between these actors could be hard to parse, and one of the first things that unified them in many people's minds were the prices they paid for their Harvard Square properties. To some longtime merchants and property owners the prices seemed outrageous. They were often well above the assessed value of the properties and seemed out of line with any conventional metrics for valuing property in the local market.

"No reasonable discounted cash flow could justify these prices," one property manager said of the Equity One/Regency and Asana acquisitions. "I've never seen anything like it in my career," said another. To people like them with years of experience in the marketplace, it seemed unlikely that the volume of business in Harvard Square could support the high rents necessary to make such investments pay off. Local developers who contemplated bidding on the JFK and Brattle Street buildings when they were listed for sale found their valuations to be far below what outside firms like Equity One and Asana were bidding. As properties sold at those high prices, the assessed property value in Harvard Square as a whole nearly doubled, rising from $1.8 billion in 2012 to $3.3. billion in 2017.[14]

At the time of my interviews, a number of local business owners and residents blamed Gerald Chan for the market's initial, rapid appreciation. Some of the buildings he purchased were owned by individuals or family trusts that had held their properties for decades. Some were not for sale at the time when Chan made an offer, typically in cash, often at a price above the property's assessed value.[15] In the years prior, few commercial properties in the Square had traded hands, so there was minimal information about what current market prices might be. Some worried that Chan was resetting them at an unrealistic level and spurring even more turnover as longtime property owners saw what their buildings could fetch from a buyer like him.

One local theory circulating was that Chan's purchases had, in particular, "awoken the sleeping giants" of the market—the Dow and Stearns family trusts. The properties that Equity One/Regency and Asana purchased had been owned by the Dow and Stearns families for nearly a century. In the 1920s, Amee Brothers Book Shop relocated to one of Harry Stearns's and George Dow's buildings on Brattle Street and stayed until Dow decided to redevelop the property in the '30s; Richard Dow, George's son, was Fred Olsson's landlord on JFK Street through the late 1940s. After Richard Dow's death in 1988, the two families hired a local on-site property manager to oversee the day-to-day operations of their buildings. That individual was responsible for leasing decisions, and, under his management, the properties generated steady, moderate returns with which the families seemed content—until 2015, that is, when they began selling them off.[16]

It is possible Chan's purchases awoke some long-term holders, but what was going on in Harvard Square was about much more than any one single investor. What was happening in the Square reflected things happening far away in the global capital markets and real estate industry. The market for commercial real estate in the United States and abroad had been "delocalizing" for decades, with sophisticated financial investors amassing portfolios of properties in multiple geographies.[17] By the 2010s, some analysts cautioned that the commercial real estate market was in the midst of a liquidity-driven speculative bubble.[18] Bubble or not, interest rates were at historic lows, and large institutional investors like pension funds were pouring capital into public and private investment vehicles in search of high yields.[19] Firms like Equity One/Regency and Asana were flush with cash and looking for new places to invest.

At the time of the Harvard Square property sales, a Boston-based real estate private equity investor told me, "There are a bunch of sophisticated real estate investors feasting on markets like Harvard Square where you've got sleepy family trusts and local owners that have lost track of the market." The "market" he was referring to was the broader commercial real estate industry in which Harvard Square was embedded, and he was suggesting that some legacy property owners in the Square had grown out of touch with that market, leaving rents lower than what they could be.

There was a logic to this perspective. Property owners, like business owners, can lose focus; or, sometimes, they may simply choose to optimize things other than straight profit. The longtime property manager for the Dow and Stearns buildings was known as a kind, fair man who supported local merchants by charging reasonable rents, offering flexible short-term leases that a proprietor could exit quickly if something in his or her business or life changed, and who generally preferred to use his own local networks to find tenants and negotiate with them directly, instead of working through brokers and lawyers. For years, the family trusts that owned these properties seemed satisfied with the steady returns they earned under his management. From another perspective, however, one could ask whether such practices had kept rents artificially low. Perhaps they screened out larger, nonlocal tenants that may have been willing and able to pay higher rents but which tended to work through brokers and lawyers and were unlikely to be in this property manager's local network.

Once the Dow and Stearns properties were put up for sale, those lower rents and short-term leases made them appealing investment opportunities: investors with the capital to scoop them up could acquire them at attractive valuations (assuming current rents really were depressed) and then quickly re-tenant them (as leases expired) at "market rent," earning a nice return in the process. Indeed, marketing documents for the properties emphasized to prospective buyers that historical rents in the properties were likely well below market and that many tenants were on short-term leases. The sales processes were reported to be competitive, attracting bids from multiple, large investment firms.[20] In short, while Chan may have helped get the changes rolling in Harvard Square, it may also have been that he, Equity One/Regency, and Asana all just spotted the same investment opportunity.

And, yet, there was also a logic to the street-level perspective that questioned whether these transaction prices were outlandish and which doubted that rents could rise enough to justify them. The Square was already known for having high rents relative to other local shopping districts. A number of existing businesses were struggling to afford the current rent levels. For years, the press had been reporting on one after another business closing due to unaffordable rent. How could anyone in their right mind think rents could go higher?

Each side had a point, actually. The fact is, it is incredibly unclear what "market rent" is in a place like Harvard Square—if such a thing as "market rent" can even be said to exist. That, of course, complicates any assessment of a property's overall value, too. Retail real estate (like most real estate) satisfies few conditions of a perfectly competitive market.[21] Consider these few observations.

Buildings and storefronts are not homogenous commodities, even when in the same neighborhood shopping district: one space might be narrow and deep, another wide and shallow; one might be on a prime corner, another on a hidden side street; prior tenants may have renovated a space making it more suitable for one use than another; the building as a whole might be old and dilapidated or recently refurbished. All of those differences and more translate into different rents and different property values. *Commercial real estate is notoriously illiquid*: long-term leases are common, which means some rates are locked in for years at a time.[22] When a vacancy arises, it takes time to find new tenants and negotiate terms. *Market signals, when they come, are difficult to interpret and slow to be incorporated*: if a business fails in a particular location because it proves unable to cover the rent expense, was it because the rent was set too high in general, or because of factors specific to that business, or both? *Transparency is minimal*: like workers uncomfortable sharing compensation data with one another, tenants who think they might have a good deal on rent are often loathe to talk about the topic with others. Landlords who compete for tenants may also be tight lipped on the subject. Finally, and perhaps most relevant to this discussion, it is possible for the "market" to achieve one equilibrium when composed of one set of landlords and tenants—but then be pushed to a new, higher equilibrium when composed of a new set of landlords and tenants.

It was no wonder people had widely divergent opinions about rent. As I tried to get a handle on the market for my research, I was constantly frustrated with how ambiguous it all was. Merchants with whom I spoke wanted clarity more than anyone. When we met, they frequently turned the interviewing arrangement around to ask me what I was hearing about rents in the market: Was theirs a good deal or not? Did I think these new investors could really fetch the rents they seemed to think they could? Rumors circulated as to what those anticipated rates were. Asana was hoping to get $200 per square foot, I was told. Asana was hoping to get $300 per square foot, I was told. This confusion and speculation did not stem from a lack of sophistication. Even the outside real estate industry experts with whom I consulted—individuals I went to hoping they could tell me what market rent might be, because I was as confused as anyone—expressed uncertainty and wavered on whether the new entrants would be able to get the rents necessary to justify their valuations.

One thing everyone at the street level did seem certain of, however, was this: if there was room for rents to go up, it would be achieved by welcoming in more and more national and global chains. Yet still there was room for debate: Would even deep-pocketed chains want to pay high rents to stay in the Square once they really got to know the market? Even if they did, was it a sound long-term investment strategy for the property owners to fill the market with such establishments? Folks at the street level thought not, and they gave several reasons why, in their opinion, the new landlords' tenanting strategy was "irrational," "out of whack," "naïve," and even "stupid."

To some, the new landlords and their new tenants were simply ill informed about the local market and would soon realize that it was not nearly as lucrative as hoped. "The streets of Harvard Square aren't paved with gold," one property manager told me. The Square might sound posh to outsiders given its proximity to the university, but it was divey places like Charlie's Kitchen and the affordable, bohemian basement-haunt Grendel's Den that stood the test of time—"not the Pataguccis of the world," as one merchant put it (making a dig at Patagonia's high price-points by combining its name with that of the luxury Italian handbag maker Gucci). Others pointed out that chains had not always fared well in this little marketplace because of local preferences but noted you had to have been there long enough to see that; and they had examples at the ready to defend the point. A few years back, for instance, there had been five fast-food taquerias in the Square—three were chains, two were locally owned. The two local establishments had always drawn the longest lines, and they were the only two that remained.

But what if Harvard Square was paved with gold for those looking at it from a different perspective? Businesses that operate in multiple geographic markets must decide which markets are worth entering. These firms tend to rely on sophisticated data analysis and financial modeling that takes into account macro-level population and consumption trends (e.g., younger people's preference for urban living) as well as market-specific metrics such as residential density, income level, and education level. On all those metrics, Harvard Square seemed hard to beat. Regency's promotional brochure described their JFK Street properties to prospective tenants by starting with this description: "Located at the entrance to Harvard University in a highly sought-after location with strong demographics."[23] On the same page was a map of the Square calling special attention to existing brand-name retailers and restaurants already there. Next to the map was a data table listing the population (480,089), average household income ($137,848), and average home value ($984,040) within a three-mile radius of the Square.

This was a different way of seeing and knowing the marketplace, and not all residents and business owners accepted it. Some did not like being reduced to data points: "We aren't demographics," one woman told me. Others contrasted this quantitative, data-driven approach to understanding the market with their own street-level, experiential knowledge, which they argued was more accurate. One merchant told me that she heard Ray-Ban had decided to open its store in Asana's building because of how many foreign tourists came through the Square each year: "But did they actually do the work to know whether the tour groups even pass by that location?" she asked. To her, that "work" was best exemplified by a local restaurant owner she knew. Before deciding to open his Harvard Square eatery, he had conducted months of research by standing in front of the prospective location and using a clicker to count how many people passed by at various times throughout the day and various days of the week.

An even more frequent criticism lobbed at the market's new landlords and their tenanting strategy echoed the Harvard Square Defense Fund's earlier critique of chains; namely, that replacing quirky, independent shops with stores that could be found anywhere would destroy what made the Square special and drew people there in the first place. According to one longtime merchant, the new property owners were misguided because they were going to "kill the golden goose" and, in the process, undercut their own investment theses. By destroying the unique identity of Harvard Square, he said, they were "destroying its whole appeal" and the very value upon which they had hoped to capitalize.

Despite using the old language of "chainification" and "mallification," a number of local actors acknowledged that today's chain stores were different than yesterday's—but they believed the Square's long-term character and value would only suffer more from the entry of these new types of establishments. Recent entrants such as Ray-Ban, Patagonia, and Warby Parker had "clicks-and-mortar" strategies. In that model, physical stores served as showrooms—and, as local individuals repeated often, storefronts served as "billboards"—to help a company build overall brand awareness and drive both online and in-store sales.[24] People at the street level worried about what this would do to Harvard Square: Who would want to come to the Square if it was just a bunch of billboards? What would be so appealing about strolling the streets if the experience was no different than scrolling online, one branded pop-up ad after another appearing in your field of vision? Even if these well-capitalized brands could pay higher rent in the short term, a Square like that would eventually cease to attract people, and it would lose its value even to those brands and their landlords.

More than one shopkeeper and resident said the Square's new investors were "missing the forest for the trees." This critique had a sound basis in history. In the terminology of political scientist James Scott, the new investors were "seeing" the Square like the multi-market investors they were; and that did not necessarily mean they were thinking about all the long-term implications of their actions.[25] In his 1998 book, *Seeing Like a State*, Scott argued that, for purposes of state-building and management, modern states had often sought to isolate a single element of instrumental value (e.g., lumber yield, land revenue) from local environments and then reorganize those environments to serve that purpose. Scott used the case of German forestry as an example. Given the value of lumber in the nineteenth century, officials came to see trees as commodities and then set about refashioning old-growth forests into "commodity machines" organized to optimize their yield.[26] This extractive focus led to forest-management strategies that dismissed local ways of knowing, deprived local actors of their use rights to the forest, and ultimately destroyed the underlying ecosystem. The forests lost the diversity and complexity that had made them so valuable in the first place, becoming far less resilient monocultures that could no longer thrive. Scott cautioned that modern corporate actors might be making similar mistakes, noting,

"Today global capitalism is perhaps the most powerful force for homogenization."[27] It was not naïve to worry about what might become of Harvard Square if its new investors missed the marketplace for its short-term rents.

Multiple messages in the Dear Asana Project raised this same concern. People criticized Asana for "exploiting" the Square and having an "extractive" mind-set.[28] They wrote that the new stores Asana seemed intent on renting to were "generic" and "soulless" compared to shops like Black Ink that gave the Square its appealing character. Several notes pled for Asana to "please take a long-term view." One cautioned, "This approach will destroy the value of the special community you bought into." Another warned, "There will be nothing left to sell one day when what you are selling is devoid of sustainable meaning."

From the perspective of Asana's managers, however, they *were* taking a long-term view of the market, and they *were* thinking about the risks of generic retail and the emotional connections people formed in the market. They just saw all those things differently than people at the street level did. When investors like Asana thought about the long term, they thought about macro-level trends in retail. When they thought about generic retail that risked making Harvard Square irrelevant, they thought about stores like Black Ink. When they thought about shoppers' emotional attachments, they thought about brands.

It was no secret that retail was undergoing a massive transformation spurred by the rise of online commerce. Street-level merchants like Susan Corcoran lived the disruption, but industry analysts had been declaring conventional brick-and-mortar retail on the way out for years. What was "generic" from this perspective was all the struggling shopping malls, department stores, and traditional shops like Black Ink that stocked other businesses' branded products that could now be purchased online, either directly from a brand's own website or from Amazon. Stores that sold their own branded products, like Patagonia, could generate higher margins than traditional resellers of the same goods, while also delivering upon those "clicks-and-mortar" strategies that drove sales through the company's multiple channels. Such "own-brand" stores might even boost foot traffic as well. In a world in which the best price and most convenient option could often be found online, the emotional and experiential aspects of in-person shopping seemed to matter even more, and a popular thesis in retail and real estate circles was that consumers were redirecting their emotional attachments away from the old shops and shopkeepers they once relied upon and toward the brands they now engaged with online. *Those* were the connections that seemed capable of drawing today's consumers away from their screens and out to the streets.

And, of course, online commerce was not the only driving force for change. Consumers' tastes, preferences, and values were, as always, evolving as the culture did. New entrepreneurs were inventing new retail and restaurant concepts they believed to be better suited to the current era than traditional establishments were—and financial investors, eager not to miss out, were funneling capital to such ventures. These businesses tended to leverage technology to offer products and services that appealed to young people, while often embracing socially responsible goals in their branding and operations. Examples included Warby Parker, which sold fashionable eyewear at lower prices than those of conventional opticians by bringing product design in-house and marketing directly to customers online (and which donated a portion of its proceeds to eyecare-focused NGOs); and Sweetgreen, the environmentally conscious chain of healthy salad shops discussed in chapter 3 that was founded by recent Georgetown graduates seeking to build "the McDonald's of our generation."[29]

From all these different angles, Harvard Square looked like an attractive, lucrative market that could thrive if it had the right businesses in it. In-person commerce might not survive everywhere it had before the internet, but, the thinking was, it might still flourish in places where people, especially young people, congregated and sought out the emotional and experiential aspects of in-person shopping and entertainment. Historic shopping districts were especially well-positioned because people often had long-standing personal attachments to them and were already in the habit of going there. Harvard Square had the added benefit of attracting visitors and tourists from around the world, given its proximity to the university.

In short, from the perspective of investors like Asana, they were not about to kill Harvard Square by placing a bunch of generic retailers no one wanted. Even if the reason some of the new stores could pay higher rents was because they also had robust online sales, these investors were still betting that people would come out to the Square to shop and eat. They merely thought the buildings and business mix needed a bit of a refresh if that was going to happen—and that they could profit on that in the process. One outside investor who bid on the Brattle Street properties defended his firm's high-level investment thesis by shifting to the street level for a moment. He told me that he had, in fact, sat outside some of the Square's existing stores to count how many people went in throughout the day (i.e., exactly what that local merchant said prospective owners should do). But, he said, "I counted a handful at most." The problem, in his opinion, was that the "concepts were irrelevant and dated. Maybe they were okay ten or twenty years ago but not now. Businesses run out of steam at a certain point, everything has a life cycle."

Asana's founder, Terry Brown, articulated his firm's strategy on a 2020 real estate podcast.[30] Brown spoke specifically about Asana's recent investments in Denver's Larimer Square, which he characterized as a well-known, historic shopping district. It was a place, Brown said, "where we could use our strengths, both in terms of access to capital to renovate" old buildings in need of upgrades, "as well as reinvent the merchandising." Near-term lease expirations also meant Asana could enact this strategy within a reasonable time frame. "It's very similar to the work we've done in other historic districts across the country," Brown explained, adding: "We think we have a very good plan to innovate and keep it current. It's been around for 150 years so we want to make sure we continue to help it evolve." He was not the first person to talk about keeping a square relevant by respecting its history of change.

And not all local merchants and residents disagreed with Brown's perspective, either. As usual, when the Harvard Square Death Discourse exploded, some spoke up to contest it, seeing the situation as nothing more than natural market evolution. In an article about recent business closings that was otherwise filled with laments, one unfazed twenty-nine-year-old told a *Boston Globe* reporter, "It's just a cycle. It's nothing out of the ordinary."[31] He sounded a lot like that outside investor who had concluded the Square's "concepts" had run their course.

Younger proprietors and those newer to the marketplace—in particular, those who felt secure in their current leases and whose businesses catered to a youthful clientele—were more likely than others to find the changes copacetic. Several told me that the new shops and restaurants might help rejuvenate the Square by drawing more young people. "We don't know how this will shake out by the time it's all settled," one local business owner said. "Who's to say what's bad now?" She admitted she would feel differently if her business was at risk of eviction and said she worried about the fate of independent businesses more generally, but, for now, she felt lucky to have found a place in the market she could afford and hoped the current wave of changes might help her venture succeed. She knew hers was a minority opinion, though, and did not want to appear unsupportive of other local establishments or lose favor with groups such as the Harvard Square Neighborhood Association, which were so upset over all the changes. After sharing her thoughts she asked I not quote her by name: "Please don't let people know that I don't think it's awful to have all these big businesses here!"

Yet even for those like her, who felt the Square might benefit from some fresh concepts, there was one thing almost no one at the street level liked, and that was all the vacancies. In the wake of the "global shock," some spaces were left empty for months or even years at a time. This sowed distrust. Empty storefronts seemed to suggest either the new landlords really were asking unreasonably high rents that not even chains wanted to pay or maybe the landlords just had so much capital and so many other assets in other locations to distract them, they could not be bothered to fill their spaces in a timely fashion. Either way, for those living and working at the street level, vacant storefronts were maddening. They left the market bereft of services and products consumers might like, created opportunities for vagrancy and vandalism, made portions of the Square feel dead, and depressed foot traffic for the enterprises that remained. As we've seen, a local market, like any platform, whether digital or physical, depends on network effects, and vacancies can create a negative feedback loop.

Some vacancies were more understandable than others, of course. It made sense that Regency would need its buildings empty in order to undertake the massive renovation planned for its JFK Street properties.[32] However, it struck many as bizarre that both Asana and Chan left some of their spaces empty for what seemed like unusually long periods of time. When there were prior tenants who would have liked to stay in the market at their old rent, and when there were new local ventures trying to find affordable spaces in the market, it all just seemed so illogical. A Cambridge resident looking to launch a new eatery in the Square told me he had reached out to at least one of the new landlords but never received a call back. He was baffled given the number of open spaces in the landlord's buildings. Local brokers and property managers wondered out loud about Asana and Chan's reasoning, asking, "From an owner perspective, why wouldn't you rent and get the cash," rather than let a space sit idle and earn nothing?

The new landlords had their reasons—just ones that were not all that visible or legitimate at the street level. As Asana's Terry Brown suggested, his firm sometimes undertook interior renovations after an old tenant vacated a space (and, indeed, few people in the local market knew that Asana was planning to renovate the office space above Black Ink). Investors like Asana were also willing and able to hold out until they found the sort of tenants they wanted. Leasing has always been a network-driven process: landlords cultivate and maintain relationships with relevant brokers and businesses so that when the time comes, they can activate those networks and find promising new tenants as efficiently as possible. This was as true for Harvard Square's new landlords as it was for older ones, like the local property manager who had leased the Dow and Stearns properties all those years before their sale. However, the networks of these new entrants were fundamentally different from the networks of most local landlords, and these differences made leasing unfold on a different timeline, with sometimes longer periods of vacancy between tenants.

Specifically, the networks of these new landlords tended to be national and global ones, not local ones. They were forged at a different level of the economy and composed of different brokers and businesses, who themselves had national or global strategies. It is telling that the local landlords with whom I spoke referred to tenants as "business owners," "shops," or "merchants," whereas in the real estate circles in which the Square's new landlords traveled, tenants were more commonly referred to as "brands." The leasing process looked different at this level of the economy, too. Here, it tended to involve a real estate investor's own internal leasing staff negotiating with the staff of a potential corporate tenant, which itself had multiple decision makers who needed time to familiarize themselves with Harvard Square and analyze whether it was one of the high-value locales in which the brand sought a physical presence.

It was also a part of some multi-market real estate investors' strategies to forge multi-market deals with their multi-market tenants. One private equity investor described to me how firms like Asana or Regency might start by pitching one of their properties in, say, Los Angeles or Atlanta to a prospective brand, and, then, in the same meeting, "turn the page of the brochure" and say, "you should be in Harvard Square, too." Striking such deals took time. Finally, because brand awareness was so central to tenants' corporate strategies, the tenants themselves often undertook substantial renovations before moving into a space. With access to capital—and often aided by "tenant improvement funds" and other incentives from landlords eager to secure these high-value lessees—they could afford to take more time and do more extensive buildouts than could most cash-strapped local merchants.

None of this is to say that the Square's new landlords were the first ever to leave locations vacant as they worked to secure long-term tenants on financially attractive terms. However, all this is to say that their business models and strategies led to a different leasing process than, say, when Susan Corcoran and her husband, Tim, first leased their Harvard Square space. Susan and Tim lived close to the Square and had often talked about wanting a shop there. One day in late 2000, they got a phone call from a friend who had heard of a space opening up in one of the Dow and Stearns buildings. Susan and Tim quickly met with the local property manager, negotiated terms and signed the lease, then began working day and night to renovate the interior as quickly as possible so they could open and start generating revenue to cover their expenses. Local entrepreneurs like them were unlikely to get a call like that from an Asana or Regency because they were not in those firms' networks; the market those investors saw from their heights was a different market. The local entrepreneur with the restaurant idea who never received a call back from one of the new landlords did eventually secure space in the market—in a building represented by a local broker, and the two of them hammered out the details of the deal in person. It was almost like there were two different markets now operating in this one little square.

Harvard Square's new landlords might have had other reasons that made them more tolerant of temporary vacancies as well. In some cases, a property owner's accounting practices could make it reasonable to hold off on leasing a space. For example, buildings are generally valued on the basis of the operating cash flows they can generate from some assumed *pro forma* rent. If a property owner began leasing out spaces at a lower rent than what it had assumed in its original valuation, it might have to write down the value of the asset on their books. This would be visible to its own investors, who might lose faith in the property owner's investment decision-making, and it would also make reselling the property at a profit more difficult because that lower rent would affect prospective buyers' own valuation assessments. So long as a space sat empty, however, the property could remain on the books at its estimated value for at least some period of time—until a tenant was secured at the desired rent or the property was sold to a new owner who believed the *pro forma* rent could be obtained.[33]

Both Asana and Regency made public assurances that they were long-term holders of their properties with no intent to sell them right away on the speculative market, but local actors could not assess the veracity of those claims. There was even less transparency into the plans of these outside firms than into the plans of local landlords, whose behavior often caught people by surprise as it was. To those at the street level, vacant spaces raised worrisome questions about the property owners' motives and contributed to suspicion that perhaps they really were just speculators who did not care about building the market for the long term and would soon sell their properties at a profit to another deep-pocketed investor, who would come in and disrupt things all over again.

By contrast, most people I spoke to in the marketplace did believe Chan was a long-term holder of his properties. However, they expressed frustration with vacancies in his buildings for a different reason. Noting his personal connection to the Square, they seemed to trust that he would eventually renovate and tenant his properties in a way that respected its historical character, and they pointed to his restaurant Parsnip as a good example of that. Nevertheless, they felt his substantial wealth led him to proceed at a pace that, in the meantime, left too many spaces empty and hurt the overall market. In 2017, Cambridge City Council went so far as to discuss seizing the Harvard Square theater building from Chan via eminent domain if he did not soon present plans for its re-use.[34] The property had sat empty since 2012, when AMC Loews stopped operating a movie theater there and a group of local investors purchased it for $6.5 million; Chan had stepped in to buy it in 2015 for $17.5 million, raising hopes that it might soon be reactivated.[35] As the years passed, however, it became a touchy subject in the community.[36] When Chan finally did present plans for the theater building, a member of the local neighborhood association felt reassured, telling me, "He's slow, but he seems genuinely to care about the Square."[37]

Others remained skeptical. Local merchants who worried about being displaced noted that when Chan did fill his buildings with new businesses, more often than not it was with well-capitalized chains such as Sweetgreen or David's Tea. Some felt Parsnip was too pricey, a far cry from the beloved Tasty and the socioeconomic diversity and sense of community that dingy little diner had symbolized. As for the vacancies in Chan's buildings, a few people speculated that he had so much personal wealth he might simply lack the necessary urgency and focus to fill his properties in a timely fashion. An individual at a local real estate advisory firm expressed frustration that Chan had "the power" to keep the Square special but was not doing that. Residents, merchants, and property owners theorized that his Harvard Square properties were luxury purchases to him, not unlike artwork a wealthy person might buy but then not get around to hanging on the wall. One person said Chan's buildings were "like Lego sets to a kid . . . he will build something eventually" and it might be great, but, in the meantime, he had a lot of other shiny toys to draw his attention away. Like this individual, Chan's critics worried most of all that he was too busy managing his various assets around the globe to focus on the Square and what it needed.

I came to see all the frustration over Chan—and all the attempts to theorize his motives—as reflective of the central questions the marketplace was facing: Was this going to be a marketplace made primarily by and for global actors, or local ones? Was it going to be exclusive, limited to only "sophisticated" investors, firms, and shoppers, or remain open to the broader community that had for so long loved it and claimed it as its own? Would it be rebuilt by outsiders who saw things from ten thousand feet, or those who spent their days living and working at the street level? Local individuals wanted Chan to act like one of them—they wanted him to see Harvard Square the way they did—and they grew worried and fearful when they sensed he might instead be seeing it differently.

The most common way people described Chan in interviews was as an "enigma," a "mystery," "hard to get," and sometimes "hard to get to." The *Boston Globe* described him and his investment strategy in Harvard Square as "elusive and mysterious."[38] This difficulty in placing Chan and his motives seemed to me to stem from his liminal status between insider and outsider, local and global, street-level participant and aerial observer. When Chan was in town he was a visible presence. He could be spotted riding his bike to and from the Square, stopping by Crimson Corner to pick up a newspaper, standing and chatting with people on the sidewalk, or sitting at an outdoor café. However, any sign that Chan was not a committed local seemed to provoke concern and frustration. A Cambridge city councilor expressed surprise upon learning I had secured a face-to-face meeting with him. She said he had rarely appeared at public hearings concerning his properties, sending his attorneys or staff members instead. I heard a member of the Harvard Square Business Association wonder out loud why, as of 2019, Chan had still not joined the group. It was unnerving when Chan did not seem to want to become more deeply embedded in the local community. "He seems to care about the Square . . . but why does he have no regard for the group?" the individual asked, adding, "Wouldn't he prefer to have everyone in the Square gushing about him?"

Asana and Regency did join the Business Association—and, yet, there was no gushing in those cases. Some of the very same people who said they wanted Chan more engaged were incensed to learn those firms had joined the group. Shortly after entering the marketplace, representatives from Asana and Regency took a seat on the association's board and contributed money to a special fund the group had for public-improvement projects in the Square. The Business Association had long lived with the tension of having both property owners and merchants in its fold. However, Asana and Regency were huge real estate investors with portfolios and strategies that spanned the country, and their membership heightened this long-standing tension. To critics, there seemed to be no question that these two firms were outsiders intent on remaking the Square in their image and that, therefore, they had no business being in the local business group.

To merchants growing increasingly fearful about their place in the market and to residents upset about the Square's changing character, the Business Association's decision to welcome these big firms into its ranks felt like a betrayal. Denise Jillson, the association's executive director, was criticized for the decision and, in general, for being too Panglossian in the face of the current market changes. "I'm sick of hearing Denise say the Square has always changed and we just have to embrace change," one shop owner in an Asana property told me. The Business Association's president, John DiGiovanni, came under fire as well, accused of benefiting from these changes because the high prices the new entrants had paid for their properties presumably drove up the market value of his own properties. "It's no longer a local business association," a city official and nearby resident said of the group, "It's become a property owner's association."

Several merchants let their association memberships lapse in protest, telling me they felt abandoned by the group's leadership. A citywide business organization called Cambridge Local First, which was part of a broader localism (anti-chain, anti-Amazon) movement and seemed to suffer less from divided loyalties, gained traction during this period. The Harvard Square Neighborhood Association formed a subcommittee on local businesses and invited local merchants to the 2019 meeting described in chapter 2 precisely because that group felt it could not trust the Business Association to protect the local market vis-à-vis these powerful new real estate investors. (It did not help for trust building that the Neighborhood Association was the Harvard Square Defense Fund's successor, while the Business Association's current president was the son of the Defense Fund's old archenemy, Lou DiGiovanni.)

Denise Jillson was not unaware of the criticisms. "I know some are disappointed the Business Association can't do more," she told me in the spring of 2019. But there was only so much she and the association could do, she said. So many of the changes were out of their hands: "We can't get the Dow and Stearns not to sell their buildings when they want to. We can't influence Asana or Regency buying property here." Like others with a long history in the Square, she worried that perhaps Asana and Regency, as well as the corporate brands they courted as tenants, did not fully "get what they were getting into" when it came to this special, little marketplace. But they were part of that marketplace now, so she wanted them to succeed for the sake of it. Did they really understand the local culture, she wondered? Did they really know who the customers were and what preferences they had? She too mentioned the two local taquerias that had outlasted the three chains.

Jillson wanted Asana and Regency to understand that sort of context and history, and to get to know more of the local businesses in the market. She invited the two firms onto the Business Association's board in hopes of getting them more embedded in the community: "I wanted [them] to commit to coming to each meeting and hearing what's going on. Business owners would have a channel to them this way, too. They'd be able to voice issues they were having." Said differently, Jillson wanted Asana and Regency to come down to the street level and see the market from that perspective.

Jillson was not naïve. She knew that these firms, like anyone, only joined a group like the Business Association because it served their interests in some way. Perhaps it was to learn a bit more about the street level of this particular investment; perhaps it was to keep an eye on and help maintain the public spaces upon which every landlord and tenant in the market depended; perhaps it was to cultivate some of the local connections their networks might otherwise lack, including those that could prove useful in securing special permits, waivers, or other approvals they might someday need from the city.

And Jillson was right when she said there was only so much she could do. When it did not serve these firms' interests to engage at the street level, they simply did not engage. When Susan Corcoran's Dear Asana Project launched, it did not seem to matter that Asana was a member of the Harvard Square Business Association. The firm never responded to the community outcry. After Corcoran mailed Asana pages and pages of messages left for the firm by local citizens and shoppers—after local reporters called the firm asking for comment—Asana still did not respond.[39] The firm was being called colonizers and robber barons and crooks responsible for killing the soul of the community, but it seemed entirely unmoved.

It is not uncommon for large, multi-market real estate firms to face criticisms from the local communities they enter. An investor with whom I spoke, whose firm faced similar criticism in another market, told me that it was rarely worth responding: "If this were the only thing we were doing in the world, maybe [we] would, but when you have projects around the world and you do the cost benefit [of engaging], it's not worth it."

Perhaps more than anything, this silence in the face of community criticism showed just how far apart the two worlds were. As angry as some people in the Square were with John DiGiovanni at the time—and as long-standing as the tensions were between local landlords and local merchants in this marketplace—whenever DiGiovanni or his dad, Lou, before him had faced criticism from the community, the two men always shot right back. There was the time Lou blasted the Defense Fund for criticizing him in one of its newsletters, and there were all the years John took heat and battled it out in local meetings, trying to keep Harvard Square from being designated an official Historic District. Those had been battles between different street-level actors vying for control in their little corner of the world. As nasty as things had sometimes gotten, there was something to be said for those who fought so vehemently—at least it showed they cared, at least it showed they saw themselves as fighting over the same market.

~

In an essay titled "The Moral Economy of the English Crowd in the Eighteenth Century," historian E. P. Thompson analyzed the so-called bread riots of that era.[40] Thompson wanted to understand what had driven common people to rise up and storm their local market houses, destroy the machinery of millers, and even steal grain straight from farmers' barns to distribute among themselves. He scoured firsthand accounts of the uprisings and poured over the hundreds of angry pamphlets and letters that had been dashed off at the time to convey people's grievances. Thompson concluded that the riots were not merely spontaneous outbursts in response to the high price of grain and peasants' resulting hunger. The uprisings reflected profound moral outrage that a new, "buoyant capitalist industry" was displacing the long-standing local market for bread—and the angry rioters felt increasingly powerless in this new world.[41]

Large-scale farmers, distributors, and millers had recently emerged and begun to dominate the market for bread. Those new actors tended to do business with one another. They often moved their products to whichever region offered the highest prices and profits. Theirs was a new market with different assumptions, norms, and practices from those that had operated in the traditional market—the market to which people had grown attached, the one around which they had organized their lives, the one that, over time, had come to reflect important community values.[42]

Reading Thompson's essay in 2019 and thinking about Harvard Square, it was hard not to hear the contemporary echoes. I heard echoes in the interviews I did with local market participants. I heard echoes in my own thoughts, as someone who lived in and loved and shopped in and had once run a business in a marketplace that seemed to be becoming less and less familiar to me.

I started to see the Dear Asana Project as a modern-day incarnation of those eighteenth-century pamphlets and letters. Of course, people were upset. There were new actors executing new strategies, upending old expectations. Did it matter if there was a logic to their actions that made sense to them? These new actors were operating through different networks, had different stakeholders, different sources of capital, different math, even. They had different values. Theirs was a different market, controlled by different people.

When I got to Thompson's description of a mob in 1740 led by a "lady with a stick and a horn," I thought of Susan Corcoran and her magic markers and the big white poster boards she hung in her shop so that people who wanted to express their anger could walk in from the street and do so. "They're wiping out anyone who isn't in their equity club," she told me when launching the Dear Asana Project. Susan could have started a change.org petition and let people comment online. But the market she was fighting to preserve did not live there. It lived at the street level, and she wanted to remind people of that.

Conclusion

Chapter Twelve

OUR MARKETS, OURSELVES

OUR DUAL, SOMETIMES DUELING INSTINCTS

Susan Corcoran and John DiGiovanni were both long-standing participants in the Harvard Square marketplace. However, that did not mean they saw things the same way. By the time I started my research, Susan felt let down by the Harvard Square Business Association, of which John was board president. In her opinion, the group better represented the interests of property owners like him than those of local merchants like her who were being driven out of the market. For his part, John balked at the notion that local shops like Black Ink defined Harvard Square any more than other types of businesses. He continued to see most changes in the Square's business landscape as the market's natural response to changing consumer preferences. If today's customers liked the shiny, new Warby Parker more than the Square's dusty, old optical houses, that's just the way things go. Talk that Harvard Square "wasn't what it used to be," whether in the local press or on the pages of Susan's Dear Asana Project, drove him nuts because he felt like it just made people less inclined to come to the marketplace.

I liked both Susan and John, but it did not surprise me that they did not see eye-to-eye. They were both deeply invested in Harvard Square but occupied different positions in the market. One was a business owner about to be displaced from it; the other, a longtime property owner whose stake in it remained secure. Those different positions gave them different perspectives on the changes unfolding at the time. And yet, as I got to know each of them personally, I came to believe they were more alike than different. Both were spirited individualists who also had strong collectivist instincts and cared deeply about community. Both were creative, strategically minded business-people who were also deeply, emotionally attached to Harvard Square and people in it. Both, in short, displayed the same qualities we have seen define the Harvard Square marketplace over and over throughout its history.

We are taught that markets are fueled by individual self-interest, but we tend to overlook the ways in which they also continually call forth, and even depend upon, that other human instinct—the one that makes us want to come together and find common cause. We assume that individualistic and collectivistic tendencies are always opposing instincts, and when we theo-rize markets, we think about the former, but not the latter. However, in our markets and our lives, both instincts are present, and they are not always in conflict. It's more complicated than that.

Sometimes a collective spirit emerges as a by-product of the individual pursuit of self-interest. Think of the Square's early twentieth-century busi-nessmen who decided it was in their best interest to come together and form an association to tackle the challenges of their day. Or consider how so many of the cherished connections that give our life meaning are formed in and around the for-profit projects of motivated individuals pursuing their own dreams. Black Ink, which came to symbolize a certain shared understanding of Harvard Square, was founded when Susan Corcoran decided to leave her former employer in search of greater independence, income, and creative freedom. The little shop that so many people would describe as a beloved part of the community on the pages of the Dear Asana Project was always, also, a reflection of a fiercely independent spirit.

At the same time, the sense of togetherness that surfaces in market life is not just a by-product of self-interest. People care about and value their connections to one another in ways that transcend their individual interests. It meant more to Susan than profits that Black Ink was a part of the local community. When she recalled some of the most joyful times in the store, like the holidays, she thought of the families who returned each year to do their shopping, and it gave her work meaning to be a part of their traditions. When she recalled the grueling period after her husband died, she spoke of the neighboring merchants and customers who stopped by to offer support for no reason other than to help another human being in pain. Even after Susan knew she would likely have to close her Harvard Square shop, she

helped launch a sticker and social media campaign to promote other independent businesses in the Square, called "Authentic Harvard Square." She
didn't have to do that; her fate in the marketplace was sealed. She also didn't
have to do the Dear Asana Project. Sure, it was cathartic to take a stand and
inflict some public shame on a firm she felt had wronged her, but she had
nothing practical to gain from it and assumed personal risk in the process.
Nevertheless, she wanted her business, even in its death, to do something
for the community, and she felt people had something they wanted to say.

John DiGiovanni, likewise, offers a case study in how individualism and
collectivism intermingle inside us and in the market in far more complex
ways than we normally contemplate. I first met John in early 2019, a few
months into my study of Harvard Square. By then, I had already heard a lot
about him. As president of the Harvard Square Business Association and an
owner of considerable commercial property in the Square, he was a well-
known figure and, I was learning, a rather controversial one. During my
interviews in the marketplace, I was told by one individual that John had
a "mafia-like hold" over the Business Association, leveraging it for his own
interests. A longtime local merchant told me he could be "very difficult" to
negotiate with on rent, then asked not to be quoted by name on that. Several
others were angry that John had welcomed the new, outside property owners
onto the association's board, noting he must have loved it when those new
investors entered the market because the high purchase prices they paid for
their properties pushed up the value of his.

Not everyone was critical, certainly. Many in the marketplace held John
in high regard, including a number of his longtime tenants, who described
him as a supportive landlord and friend. A number of property owners in
the Square credited John with spearheading public-improvement projects
that benefited landlords like themselves and their tenants. However, a few
seemed to resent how John always expected them to donate to those causes
and the Business Association right alongside him, feeling he must somehow
benefit more than they did.

Given everything I heard, I was not sure what to expect. Still, when I
was finally introduced to John on the sidewalk one day, I was surprised: He
reminded me of a mischievous Catholic schoolboy. Youthful-looking and
slight, he wore pressed khaki pants and a blue button-down shirt. He was
affable and animated and quick to laugh, while also exuding an unmistak-
able swagger and scrappiness that signaled readiness for a schoolyard fight
if provoked. After we made each other's acquaintance, we started to run into

one another often in the Square. He and his family lived in a nearby suburb, and his middle school–age son was a talented musician who liked to busk in the Square with his friends. "I'm their roadie," John quipped, when I spotted him one day standing off to the side while the band played nearby.

This is not to say others' impressions of John were wrong. When we met to talk about Harvard Square and real estate, it was obvious he could be a fierce negotiator and a take-no-prisoners competitor. He knew what his interests were, and he pursued them aggressively. However, his understanding of those interests was more nuanced than I had been led to assume, and, like Susan, his attachment to the Square ran deeper than just dollars and cents.

One of our first meetings took place in the Harvard Square offices of Trinity Property Management, the family real estate business John's father, Lou DiGiovanni, founded in 1960 and which John now ran. The first thing I noticed upon entering were all the photographs on the walls. Wrapping around the interior of Trinity's fifth-floor offices were dozens of large, framed photos of the Square starting in the 1800s and working their way up to present. As I waited for John to finish chatting with one of his tenants by the elevator, I wound my way around, following the pictures in chronological order. It was like turning the pages of a kineograph, those little illustrated books that create an illusion of time and motion when you flip them quickly. I saw buildings come and go from the scene, fashion styles change, carriages and trolleys turn to cars, and then cars evolve from one style to another through the years. The display conveyed a reverence for Harvard Square—specifically, a Harvard Square that had always been changing.

When John was ready to talk, we headed into his office. Not unlike the first time I met Gerald Chan, John was quick to talk about his father and the connection they had forged, in their case, over their many years of working together in the Square before Lou passed away of cancer. Family and legacy were clearly important to him. Hanging behind John's desk was a large painting of his Italian grandfather, Lou's father. Hanging near that was a copy of the Charter of the New Urbanism. New Urbanism was part of the broader movement in urban design inspired by people such as Jane Jacobs, and John had been an original signatory of the charter back in the 1990s. The charter defined urban design and development as a community-building project, and it read, in part: "We advocate the restructuring of public policy and development practices to support the following principles: neighborhoods should be diverse in use and population; communities should be designed for the pedestrian and transit as well as the car;

cities and towns should be shaped by physically defined and universally accessible public spaces and community institutions; urban places should be framed by architecture and landscape design that celebrate local history, climate, ecology, and building practice."[1]

A lot of time had passed since John signed that charter, and I was curious to hear how he reconciled the charter's principles with his own financial interests in the market. From old newspaper articles and public meeting minutes, I knew that he was unapologetic about having rented to chain stores over the years, even as others claimed those establishments degraded the historic character of Harvard Square. Also, it was undoubtedly true what people were saying, that the market value of his properties had gone up when Chan, Asana, and Equity One/Regency bought into the Square at the prices they did. Did he see the entrance of these new property owners and the spate of new global and national brands in their buildings as somehow consistent with the charter's community-building goals? Or were his critics right—was the charter on the wall just good optics at this point?

"You should know I will place anyone in my buildings—local, national, chain, whatever," John said to kick things off. "So, I won't sit and criticize [other landlords] for doing that." I was prepared for that, but his directness still disarmed me. He said he also did not care whether a building was owned by a global investor, national firm, or local individual. What he cared about, he explained, was that the Square's other property owners not be absentee landlords, that they not be disconnected from the marketplace. He cared whether they would invest in the Square's overall upkeep and, most of all, whether they would lease to tenants who appealed to shoppers and drew people to the marketplace.

It turned out John was, in his own way, concerned about the very same values as the Charter of the New Urbanism: he wanted the streets of Harvard Square to be filled with people; he wanted the Square to be a vibrant center of community life. As he saw it, there was no tension between the charter's goals and his financial interests. What made the Square a valuable real estate market was that diverse crowds of people all wanted to go there, hang out there, shop there, dine there. Years ago, the Harvard Square Defense Fund had fought him on putting a Dunkin' Donuts in one of his buildings, but that's where many cops and construction workers got their coffee each morning, he told me. John wasn't going to get hung up on local versus chain-store distinctions; both establishments could serve the same end, which was to bring people to the marketplace.

John was, however, concerned about the impact of the internet and e-commerce on markets like Harvard Square. Even before Chan, Asana, and Equity One/Regency arrived, he felt it was imperative for landlords to think strategically about what might keep people coming to the street level. This was why he had advocated for repurposing the kiosk into an event space. It was also why he spoke proudly of having put a live music venue in one of his buildings: he knew the crowds of concertgoers would not just come for a show; they might also grab a bite to eat in the Square before the show or head out for drinks after. Network effects like these were crucial for keeping this platform, the street-level marketplace, alive. At one point, John had even passed on the opportunity to put a bank in the old Sage Grocery building. When a different landlord leased to that same bank in a building nearby, John was incensed. He felt there were too many bank branches in the Square already.[2] They attracted few customers throughout the day, closed at 5:00 p.m., and left dead spaces at the street level during nights and weekends, which hurt neighboring businesses who depended on foot traffic.[3] That was not good for John's tenants, and it was not good for the marketplace as a whole.

If John had concerns about the Square's new real estate owners, it was that he did not yet know the people at these firms. Would they behave as if all their interests in the market were linked, as he believed they were? He was grateful that Asana and Regency had joined the Business Association right away and were contributing to public-improvement projects alongside him and other longtime property owners. However, it was still the early days of their and Chan's investments in the Square. He wasn't yet sure how these new entrants would perceive their individual self-interests and how committed they would be to the overall marketplace. He wasn't yet sure what sort of long-term partners they would make.

Pausing for a moment as if worried I might take all this talk of commitment, collective investment, and partnership the wrong way, John said: "Don't get me wrong, I'm a capitalist!" It was just that his networked theory of the market implied everyone would make the most money over the long term if they all thought of the marketplace as a connected whole. Sure, commercial banks were currently willing to pay high rent for street-level real estate, and that meant, in the short term, landlords could make a lot of money leasing to them. However, a street level blanketed with sleepy bank branches would stop attracting crowds, and, eventually, even bank branches would leave a ghost town.

Smart property owners, John said, thought beyond their individual properties. They thought about what would keep "the district, street, and location" *all* active and busy.[4] On the one hand, what he was saying sounded a
lot like what the Business Association's founders had said—i.e., that it was in
everyone's best interest to see themselves as joined in a collective enterprise.
On the other hand, he was saying something rather distinct. To John, the
most important collective was far broader than the existing merchants and
property owners. It was the community of potential consumers and visitors
who might be persuaded to come to the market—the people who would
keep it hustling and bustling for the long-term benefit of all. In his opinion,
everyone in the Square should always be thinking about what would expand,
nurture, and appeal to that collective.

Nothing got John more frustrated than when other property owners
failed to think of the market in this way. He criticized landlords who let
dying businesses stay too long in their buildings out of loyalty or laziness
or any other reason; even if an establishment had once been beloved, if it
stopped attracting customers, it was time for a change, John argued. There
was no love lost for those property owners who balked at contributing to
the various public-improvement projects or community events he and the
Business Association promoted; in his opinion, those individuals were too
narrow-minded to recognize that their interests were served by making
the marketplace as inviting as possible to visitors. Most of all, he hated it
when landlords let their storefronts sit empty; vacancies offered consumers
nothing and depressed foot traffic for everyone else. He understood that
buildings sometimes needed to be cleared out for renovations, of course,
but the number of vacancies in the Square had shot up after all the recent
property sales, and this disturbed him. It was almost unconscionable to
John that a property owner would allow a vacancy to persist for months or
even years at a time.

During my research, I stumbled upon an article from 2004 about a time
when John had an empty space in one of his buildings. Rents were running
between $50 and $150 per square foot then, and John's space was a highly
desirable location on our familiar block of JFK Street. He had not yet secured
a long-term tenant, however, and Sign of the Dove, an artist's cooperative
that had run a seasonal gift shop in Harvard Square for thirty-four years,
was struggling to find rent it could afford that year. Sign of the Dove's members were hoping to secure a short-term rental at a discounted rate of about
$20 per square foot, but they were striking out. To John, it was senseless to

let a property sit vacant when it could be put to use in the interim, so he rented his empty space to the cooperative at $12 per square foot for the holiday season. In a *Boston Globe* article entitled, "Miracle in Harvard Square," he explained that cultural offerings like Sign of the Dove helped retain the vibrant, rich street life of Harvard Square. Yet he also acknowledged that his decision had served his own interests. He joked to the reporter, "Don't make me sound too nice; I work at being a terrible guy."[5]

John knew that this act of goodwill was not pure charity. However, just as with Susan, it would be inaccurate to see his desire to do right by the community as merely an outgrowth of his self-interest. Retaining Harvard Square's vibrant, rich street life served John's financial interests as a property owner, but it also meant a lot to him personally. Ever since he was a kid parking cars in his dad's lot, John loved being in the Square on a busy day. As a teenager, he liked to swing by Cappy's Shoe Repair to listen to the old-timers and Cambridge cops who gathered there on cold days. Over the years, the Square's street performers had come to occupy a special place in his heart. When the puppeteer Igor Fokin—a Russian immigrant who hand-carved and painted his own quirky, charming wooden marionettes and sewed custom outfits for each—died suddenly in 1996, John helped raise money for a memorial to be placed on the corner of Brattle Street where Fokin had performed each day to adoring crowds. I could tell how happy it made John that his young son now busked in the Square, not far from Fokin's corner.

"It's not the specific shops or buildings or whatever else that makes this place authentic," John said to me one day as we walked through the Square. "It's the mass of human beings coming together. There's nothing more essential than that." The fact was, this former altar boy and graduate of St. Sebastian's Catholic School had a deeply rooted sense of community that was distinct from other motives that drove him, and it informed how he saw the world and how he behaved in it. John was a generous donor to community organizations beyond the Business Association, including local homeless shelters, churches, and a nearby hospital. He was the sort of guy who, after reading a book he found especially thoughtful, would head over to the Harvard Coop to buy extra copies to share with his friends. In 2020, he handed out a stack of copies of *The Tyranny of Merit: Can We Find the Common Good*, by the philosopher Michael Sandel.

Once, he sent me a journal article he had been discussing with a friend of his, a former priest turned academic. The paper was about the "Economy of Communion" movement in the Catholic Church that sees the profit motive as necessary for meeting society's needs but not a sufficient answer to the question of a business firm's purpose.[6] That answer, according to the movement, lay in the idea of "communion," i.e., of contributing to the common social good. John didn't claim to embrace the paper's view in its entirety, and when we caught up about it, he was quick to remind me that he would be "the last person in the world" to claim he didn't care about profits. But he said there was something to the ideas in the paper, and he wanted to know my thoughts. To see this man as someone who only ever thought about propping up his own property values was to miss the full person. John was more complicated than that; humans tend to be that way.

In *Dilemmas of the American Self*, sociologist John Hewitt writes that American culture has, from the start, been characterized by both communitarianism and individualism.[7] Those two values exist in our culture, and they exist inside both Susan and John, just as they exist inside each of us. According to Hewitt, however, these two orientations can create problems in our culture and our daily lives because we are constantly forced to navigate them, and, at times, they do pull us in quite different directions. Indeed, it is hard to ignore that many of the most heated debates in contemporary society (regarding taxation, gun control, masking during a pandemic, and more) concern conflicts between individual rights and collective responsibilities, and our often-competing conceptions of what each of those mean. As I dove through the archives of Harvard Square history and got to know people like Susan and John in the contemporary marketplace, I started to understand that this tension was also where the real trickiness has always lain in our relationship with markets. Both values are always at play.

Susan saw John's work at the Business Association as self-serving and felt it undermined her interests as a business owner and the sense of community she drew from the marketplace; John saw Susan's Dear Asana Project as propagating ideas about the death of Harvard Square that would drive people further away from the street level, undermining his interests as a property owner and the collective spirit he had always cherished there. Neither was wrong to see the other as motivated by self-interest, and neither was unusual in having found a meaningful sense of togetherness in the marketplace that went beyond self-interest. That's what makes this all so damn complicated.

It is easy to cast market conflicts in terms of "us versus them"—Asana versus Black Ink, property owners versus merchants, the Business Association versus the neighborhood Defense Fund, outsiders versus insiders, the new guard versus the old. However, the inherent conflict that causes so much grief in our market lives is a conflict that lives deep inside us all. Our markets are our constructions and our mirrors. Their tensions are our tensions. They both bring us together and channel our independent spirits. Our relationship with them is about our relationship with ourselves and with one another. How could this not be a tricky relationship? And yet, precisely because it is so tricky, perhaps we have not understood this relationship as well as we have thought.

AN ATTACHMENT THEORY OF MARKETS

Part 1 of this book highlighted the ontological security many of us derive from market routines such as my morning newspaper runs to Crimson Corner or Sunday bagels and book browsing with my father. We contemplated how all the little and big rituals and routines of market life—from daily coffee stops, to weekly dinners with families or friends, to holiday shopping traditions and annual festivals and fairs, to even just the predictable physical landscape of all the storefronts and signs we come to expect each time we pass through the marketplace—lend us a reassuring sense of stability and security in life. Part 1 also examined the complex array of market forces that are continually rolling through, disturbing the landscape, disrupting those very routines, and undermining our sense of ontological security in the process. We began to see what a tricky situation we are in. On the one hand, we tend to grow attached to a particular market and its particular institutions as we grow attached to the routines we forge in and around them. On the other hand, that market *will* change on us, often unpredictably and in ways we cannot control.

Live long enough, it seems, and you may find yourself one day feeling a little bit destabilized, saying what people have said about Harvard Square for hundreds of years: that a street-level market to which you had grown attached is "not what it used to be." Part 1 established that we have a relationship with these markets, even if we do not often think in those terms, and the book's early chapters probed this first layer of that tricky relationship: namely, that we seek and derive stability from something that is inherently unstable.

In part 2, we explored the even deeper ways we attach to markets and the deeper ways in which market change can destabilize us. To do this, we examined moments when people seemed to cling especially tightly to Harvard Square's past—when people got so upset about something changing in the

marketplace their behavior looked almost crazy on the surface. By unraveling the deeper logic of what was at stake, we discovered that, in each case
of "crazy love," market change was threatening some sense of togetherness
that had been built up around and supported by the marketplace in the past.
Whether it was a group of businessmen who came together to modernize the
shopping district but built bonds of friendship over cigars and scotch in the
process or a sense of neighborhood identity rooted in a shared way of life
that was both enabled by and reflected in the marketplace, what was at stake
in each instance was a sense of community and communal identity.

And therein lies the far more profound form of security and insecurity we
derive from markets: we attach to markets because of all the attachments we
form to one another in them; and the market changes that most destabilize
us are the ones that threaten to tear apart those precious attachments or that
signal our attachments have already begun to fray. Sometimes the attachments we feel cut off from are to specific individuals; sometimes they are to
a larger sense of community, a collective way of life and the set of relations
that seem to define it.

There is a psychological logic to all this. Attachment theory in psychology
suggests that the most significant source of ontological security in life comes
from the deep and enduring bonds we form with one another.[8] As infants,
we attach to consistent caregivers who are responsive to our needs and
engage with us in lively interaction. As adults, the attachments we form with
our partners, friends, family, colleagues, and neighbors—even the ones we
form with our favorite Reeboks-wearing waitress who serves us our weekly
bagel and cream cheese—continue to provide us with a sense of stability and
security. Our attachments make us feel seen, known, loved. They give life a
sense of meaning, purpose, and security. They help us define who we are,
provide us with the security to explore new things, and make us feel a part of
something bigger than ourselves—part of an ongoing and shared narrative.

Sunday mornings with my father were never just about the consistency of
our routine, never just about the bagel and cream cheese of it all. They were
always about the bond we were forming with one another, which deepened
and strengthened on all those walks through Harvard Square and all the
stops we made along the way to browse and shop and eat and talk. They were
also about the through-line that ran from my grandfather, to my father, to
me and which connected us all to each other. Those bonds are what made
Sunday mornings in the Square such a sacred ritual for us. Those bonds are
what made Harvard Square such a sacred place to me.

Writing this book drove that point home to me in more ways than one. Over the course of my research, I found myself growing attached to people like Susan Corcoran and John DiGiovanni—individuals who had started out as simply "research subjects" for the academic project I was undertaking. Some scholars will argue that that's how they should have stayed—that I should have kept my feelings out of this and that I sacrificed my academic objectivity in the process. However, I have always believed that our emotions are windows into life's deeper lessons if we just let ourselves follow them there. That has been this book's whole agenda, in fact. And, anyway, I couldn't help growing attached—I'm human, and that's the point.

The security we derive from our attachments to one another is even deeper than we tend to think. Psychological theory tells us that being connected to one another helps stave off fear of life's inherent uncertainty and our terrifying lack of control over so much that happens in it. As I tuned into my own evolving feelings as I researched and wrote this book, I came to realize that the attachments I was forming to Susan and John and others were also deepening my attachment to a version of Harvard Square that included them. I didn't want the Square to change if it meant losing my connections to them. I felt sick the day Susan closed Black Ink, for what she was losing but also for what I was losing. I started to worry about getting a call from John DiGiovanni telling me he was selling his properties and leaving the market. When he called one day with "big news," I held my breath until he revealed that the big news was a major renovation he planned for one of his properties, not the sale of it, as I'd feared (though I knew that day, too, would come). When Crimson Corner closed in May 2021, having been hit hard by the pandemic, I held back tears as I said goodbye to Chris Kotelly.

At some point or another, we all become aware of our existential dilemma: that we are alone in the world when it comes to facing the most fundamental insecurity life throws our way—our mortality. Our connections to one another help us navigate the messy, complicated feelings that arise from this. Our attachments help us feel more rooted in time and place, like that sturdy, spreading chestnut tree in Longfellow's poem. When we feel those attachments giving way, when we believe they are about to be ripped away from us, we feel uprooted and thrown back into the terrifying uncertainty of it all. For at least a moment, we are forced to confront that existential dread. Even if all this unfolds unconsciously, it can leave us feeling destabilized, a little bit disturbed, maybe even a little bit crazy.

When the Gap inevitably closes in Harvard Square because young people's tastes have moved on, it will not be the routine of going there that I will miss. I outgrew its styles long ago and haven't shopped there for years. Yet still I will feel it as a loss because it will remind me of when my best friend and I used to wander its aisles together, talking about boys and classes and what the future might hold. Its closure will remind me that we are not that age any longer, that hundreds of miles now separate us, that we speak infrequently these days because adult life is busy and messy, and that that future we imagined and are now living is filled with a little less wonder than it held for us back then.

Marketplaces and the shops and stores in them help anchor our connections to one another, and they anchor our memories of one another and the bonds we have shared. If we pay close attention when we replay the home videos stored in our minds, we can see how frequently the market is there, playing a supporting role–it's there in the after-school trips to the ice-cream parlor with our best friend or beloved grandparent, it's there in those late nights at the local grill with our college friends.

Yet we are not trained to see markets in this way. So, it is easy to miss just how many of the deep and enduring bonds we form with one another are forged in market settings—and how, because of that, we may even begin to feel a deep and enduring emotional bond with a market itself. Economists have begun to study the behavioral dynamics of markets, but they have not considered the emotional attachments we form *to* markets. Sociologists have studied our emotional attachments to place but often overlooked just how much of that attachment is derived in and through the commercial market in the place. The field of economic sociology has helpfully illuminated the many different sorts of relationships we form with one another through market transactions, but it is only when we begin to appreciate how markets—by being vehicles for our attachment to one another—can become *objects* of our attachment themselves, that we begin to see the crazy, complicated love story we have written for ourselves.

It is thrilling in the early days of romance with a marketplace like Harvard Square. We fall in love at a moment when the market is lively and responsive to our needs, when we see ourselves reflected in it and start to define ourselves through it, when it seems such a welcoming platform for forging the relationships that matter to us at that time. We begin to cherish it for all the cherished bonds we form in it—bonds that help ground us in a defining sense of self and comforting sense of belonging. We grow attached to the marketplace because of all that we get from it. We don't stop to think that what we are really attached to is the market in the place. And that's how the dagger slips between the ribs and pierces the heart—for the market we love does not stay attached to us. Eventually, inevitably, it begins to withdraw its attention. And, when it does, it stirs up a lot of complicated feelings, even those related to our mortality.

When markets change on us, they remind us that everything else does too, including ourselves. When markets mark the passage of time, they remind us how frustratingly little of it we each get with the ones we love. Like Fred Olsson who felt increasingly alienated from a market he had once loved— whose poems about that market were always poems about his friends and, eventually, became poems about the friends he had lost—we see in market change the bonds we formed but will someday lose, and it is hard not to feel we are losing a great love.

Years before I started this project, my father suggested that I write a book about Harvard Square. I dismissed the idea. I didn't get it at the time. Nor had the thought of writing a book about the Square crossed my mind earlier when I was a student and running a small business there, or even when I was standing outside the Tasty on its last night of operation, feeling a faint tug of something but concerned more about my outfit than with exploring what that something might be. Sure, I felt attached to Harvard Square and many of the businesses in it. But I had not yet lived through enough change or loss to really know what those experiences felt like. I certainly had no clue that, one day, those messy feelings might be surfaced just by looking out at Harvard Square and seeing something new where something old once had been. Back then, I felt in synch with the marketplace and the changes happening in it. I felt in synch with the world. I felt safe and secure and, dare I say, in control.

Then one day, I didn't as much. I found myself unsettled and upset and even a bit angry at something as predictable as a changing storefront. I found myself telling my husband that Harvard Square wasn't what it used to be. I saw myself reaching for a microphone in a basement meeting, about to yell at an investor from New York who was just doing his job. I heard myself sound like one of those "overly emotional Harvard Square types," to whom I had given just enough passing attention over the years to dismiss as crazy.

Psychologists tell us that accepting the inevitability of change is necessary for having a healthy emotional life. Damn is that hard to do, though. The Harvard Square Defense Fund wanted to preserve a version of Harvard Square its members loved, and there is nothing crazy about that instinct.

However, the Defense Fund had no real framework for accepting change. I'm not sure I do, either. That's the tough thing about markets: they are constantly forcing us to confront and accept change.

One issue with resisting market change is that we are often, in the process, defending some boundary around the definition of community. Because our attachment to markets is about our attachments to one another, whenever we fight to preserve a market we are ultimately fighting to preserve a particular set of attachments—often a particular collective and collective sensibility. And, like it or not, collectivism is not always the saint to self-interest's sinner. Like George Wright who saw immigrants as a threat to the community of merchants he had worked so hard to unite, or like members of Neighborhood Ten who worried that Middle American tourists would invade the marketplace and render existing residents strangers in their own land, attempts to stop change are often attempts to keep a beloved market to ourselves.

The problem is, we are never the only ones in a relationship with "our" market. There are always other people who see their interests, their attachments, their sense of collective identity in it as well. Even our own community, however we may define it, is never as uniform or stable as we feel it to be. Part of why markets are so rife with conflict—so capable of provoking love and outrage—is because they mean so much to so many.

It is not crazy for people to come together to defend a particular shared way of life to which they have grown attached—to defend *their* definition of community, the bonds that define it, and the sense of security they derive from it. It's human. But it can make us do crazy things if we do not also find some way to make peace with perspectives beyond our own. I'm sure I sounded crazy to the Equity One investors when I took the microphone in that basement meeting and told them in my own "overly emotional" way that they didn't understand the relationship people had with Harvard Square. Crazy, like love, is in the eye of the beholder. My problem was, I had forgotten for a moment that my special relationship with Harvard Square was just that: mine. I was speaking from my heart but not necessarily for others'.

It is unrealistic to expect us humans to stop drawing boundaries around ourselves. We derive too much meaning from the collectives around which we build our lives. But perhaps we can stop driving ourselves so crazy (and stop seeing one another as crazy)—perhaps we can accommodate more change with fewer calcifications and less friction—if we remind ourselves that we are all a part of an even larger collective. That larger human collective is the one that's always evolving and changing. It's the one in which our standpoint is just one among many. The one in which our precious attachments exist alongside so many others' precious attachments. After all, that's the collective the market is in a relationship with. If we don't appreciate that, we are just setting ourselves up for a lot of hurt.

This more expansive notion of community may help us meet change with greater equanimity but, of course, it will not eliminate all instability from our lives. The market, fueled by the individual pursuit of self-interest, will still be forever changing on us—because we will be forever asking it to. As consumers, we will pull away from once-cherished offerings when new ones serve our evolving tastes and needs better. As entrepreneurs, we will seize opportunities to profit by doing things differently or serving new groups of consumers with new preferences and habits. As property owners, we will seek new tenants to reinvigorate old spaces. As investors, we will spot new markets in which to deploy our capital for higher return. This is the nature of the system we have devised for ourselves. This is the crazy, complicated love story we have written for ourselves. What is our market society, after all, if not one big giant collective enterprise we have created and continually re-create together to serve our individual interests?

When we take the time to really reflect on ourselves and our markets, it becomes so obvious why we have such a tricky relationship with them. Our relationship with our markets reflects the unresolvable tensions that define us and our relationships to one another. Our markets are collectivizing and atomizing; they help us attach and they tear us apart; they offer a sense of security amidst the terrifying uncertainty that lies beyond comforting boundaries, while encouraging us to push boundaries and see what else there is to explore and create and claim for ourselves. In short, they give our lives stability and instability, security and insecurity, and, when we stop to think about it, we wouldn't really want it any other way.

Chapter Thirteen

RECLAIMING THE STREET LEVEL

COVID-19 and Beyond

"So this is a fucking disaster, huh?" I said, too thrown to censor myself. It was Friday, March 13, 2020, and I had just run into John DiGiovanni on the corner of JFK Street and Winthrop Park. John nodded and said, "That is the technical, official term for it, yes. A fucking disaster."

The Square was unusually busy that afternoon. Cars were double parked. Traffic was backed up. A few impatient drivers honked their horns. Students brushed past us on the sidewalk with moving boxes and suitcases. Some looked harried and anxious. Others looked like what I remember feeling as a kid after learning that a big snowstorm was coming so school was being let out early. The coronavirus had started to spread through Massachusetts. Two days earlier, Governor Charlie Baker had declared a state of emergency, and Harvard University announced it was sending students home for the year. Everyone needed to be off campus by the end of the weekend.

That night, my husband and I were awoken by the sound of students partying in the Square. As the evening wore on and the music died down, I heard some of the young revelers spill out onto the streets and shout their goodbyes. By Monday morning, there was only silence. The following week, Governor Baker issued a stay-at-home advisory and ordered all nonessential businesses in the state to close. Harvard Square's storefronts went dark.

Hastily printed signs reading "Temporarily Closed" were taped onto doors and windows to inform customers. But there were no more customers to read them. Nearby residents were hunkered inside, and the students were all gone, as were most of the workers, commuters, and tourists who typically passed through the Square each day. If ever there is doubt that our street-level markets are collective phenomena, we need only recall how they momentarily disappeared when we had to socially distance from one another.

Each morning, my husband and I walked our dog through an eerily empty Square. We started to photograph the signs on the shuttered storefronts. It felt like someone should bear witness. As the pandemic raged on and the lockdown continued (Massachusetts was hit hard in the first wave, and businesses did not reopen until the summer), John DiGiovanni and I got in the habit of chatting by Zoom or phone on most Friday afternoons.

John called the pandemic the "third fist." Harvard Square and marketplaces like it had been "taking lefts and rights" before the pandemic hit, but this was an even more powerful blow to street-level commerce and it seemed to come out of nowhere. It was like being in the ring, John said, dodging shots as best you could, "when all of a sudden a third fist comes at you." He worried this third fist might knock the Square to its knees.

In-person retail was on the ropes when the pandemic arrived; John had been seeing the effects of e-commerce for years in the declining sales figures of his retail tenants. Still, he had hoped that restaurants and service businesses, as well as live-music venues and other cultural offerings, could keep the marketplace active and commercially vibrant. As the pandemic bore down, however, everything felt uncertain.

Trends toward online shopping accelerated rapidly because of COVID-19. Would in-person retail return when this was over? And what about all the service businesses that had to close during the lockdown? Once restaurants, salons, gyms, and entertainment could finally reopen, would their customers return? How many businesses would die in the meantime? Neither John nor I knew the answers to any of these questions, but we spent a lot of Friday afternoons wondering about it out loud.

◦◦

For many of us, the pandemic highlighted just how much of our collective lives we still located in our street-level markets, just how many of our meaningful attachments were anchored there. Religious services were not the only sacred rituals—and houses of worship not the only sacred gathering spots—disrupted by COVID-19. It was disconcerting to see so many shops and restaurants closed and to have to forgo the daily, weekly, and seasonal routines we had built up around them: our morning coffee runs, our Friday night dates, our Sunday brunches. It was even more disconcerting to feel deprived of all the human contact and connections we accessed through those routines and in those spaces.

Unlike when the "Spanish flu" hit, however, we had more alternatives this time. Street-level establishments could stay closed for longer than they did back in 1918 because today's consumers could purchase so many of their essential goods online. We could connect with loved ones and colleagues online as well. When boredom hit, there were hundreds of shows to stream into the cozy confines of our private living rooms. Access to these alternatives undoubtedly saved lives by allowing people to safely distance, but it also opened up questions we would eventually have to confront once the pandemic was under control.

In places like Massachusetts, where businesses shut down for months to try to contain the virus's spread, we saw what it might be like if we no longer had street-level markets in our lives. After this forced break from our markets, what would our relationship be with them moving forward? Would absence make our hearts grow fonder for our dear old friend, the marketplace? Or, would it lead to a more complete parting of ways? Would we realize that we actually did not need the relationship as much as we once did and that we were okay with that?

For some, there was only one answer to these questions. Restauranteurs and retailers fought like hell during the pandemic to preserve this relationship. Street-level enterprises like theirs faced an existential threat. They needed the relationship to survive. They needed their customers more than their customers needed them at that moment, and they dug deep as they tried to adapt to the radically altered and disturbingly fluid environment.

When the pandemic hit, Kari Kuelzer, owner of the restaurant and pub Grendel's Den and a longtime member of the Harvard Square Business Association, decided it was time to reactivate the group's restaurant committee. She started holding weekly Zoom meetings for any restauranteur in the Square and the city who was interested. The purpose was to share best practices as they all tried to navigate this unprecedented situation and to come together when no one could come to them. I began attending the virtual meetings and was humbled by the individual ingenuity and collective spirit on display.

Kari's mother and father opened Grendel's in 1971, and now it was her operation. A late-forty-something badass with funky hair and a "don't fuck with me" vibe that suggests a punk past, Kari is tough, but also off-the-charts smart, loyal, and—like everyone with a high "EQ"—affiliation-driven. With Grendel's fiftieth anniversary approaching, Kari was not about to let her parent's legacy slip away. Having lived in Cambridge all her life, this was also about more than just her business. On the weekly calls, she shared tips with other restaurant managers and owners on how to apply for local and federal relief, led discussions of the ever-evolving pandemic protocols and how best to handle them, reported on the conversations she was having with mobile app developers working on a contact tracing system, and drew nuanced historical analogies to the AIDS epidemic and the role restaurants had played in disseminating public-health information during that crisis.

Like other restaurants, Grendel's had to shift to an entirely takeout business model when that was all the state permitted. Kari and her team tweaked Grendel's menu to better suit takeout. She upgraded the restaurant's website and kept Grendel's Instagram site active, updating it with new photos and promotions each week. She invested in company swag to build brand awareness and sell merchandise to loyal customers who wanted to know how they could help. She maintained a busy schedule of virtual events in lieu of the in-person ones Grendel's normally hosted. Each year Kari invited the storyteller and bard, Odds Bodkin, to deliver a rendition of *Beowulf* to Grendel's patrons. During the pandemic, my husband and I logged on to join a virtual audience and watch Bodkin's charmingly quirky performance online.

When Grendel's was able to reopen for indoor dining, Kari introduced a contact tracing system and encouraged other restaurant owners to adopt one as well. When vaccines were available, she instituted a vaccine requirement for customers and staff. She knew that everyone would need to feel safe if they were going to want to come back together again. As customers slowly began to return to the marketplace, the restaurant committee continued to meet and share information on things such as how to apply for city-sponsored heaters so that outdoor dining could continue even as the cold New England winter approached.

As street-level business owners like Kari Kuelzer fought for their livelihood, another population in the Square faced its own crisis. When the rest of us retreated into the safety of our homes, those who called the streets their home were left to fend for themselves. The most vulnerable among us, those who depended on the rest of us passing by each day and sparing a couple bucks, or a sandwich, or sometimes even just a smile, were now some of the only ones left out there. It was a powerful reminder that when we pull away from our street-level markets, we pull away from one another in more ways than one. It was a powerful reminder, too, of the unsung ways in which our street-level establishments serve the community, from their bathroom facilities to their warmth on a cold winter's day. Communities around the country scrambled to address the homelessness crisis amplified by the pandemic. When many shelters closed for fear of the virus spreading within them, some cities erected outdoor tent cities. Others turned empty hotels into single-occupancy shelters. There was no quick, easy solution to a social fabric unraveling.

In December 2020, a man named Alistair, whom I knew from around the Square and who had always interrupted his ukulele playing to offer my dog a friendly pat, wrote an article for the street newspaper *Spare Change*. Alistair's article was titled "They Were Locked In, We Were Locked Out," and it began by describing the day in March 2020 when the Harvard Square shelter in which he and twelve other individuals had been living closed.[1]

Alistair wrote, "We had no place to go. It would be my first day outside with nothing open, no restrooms, no place to sit and have a hot cup of tea, it really was hard out there." As the days turned into weeks and then months, Alistair continued, "I would sit with other homeless friends [and] watch the empty streets and read. Not a soul in sight, no cars, just the empty ghost buses picking up a few people."

Denise Jillson, executive director of the Harvard Square Business Association, was devastated by the pandemic's effect on the Square. For so long, her work had involved trying to get people to come out to the Square, but now she had to tell them to stay away. She also knew how much the homeless relied on the marketplace, and she had always seen it as part of her role at the Business Association to work with and advocate for the Square's unhoused individuals. In the past, she had collaborated on joint projects with area shelters and churches. As the pandemic bore down, she got to work. In concert with city officials and several other groups, she helped roll out a program in which restaurants in need of revenue were paid by the city to provide food for the area's homeless in need of sustenance. She had temporary public toilets installed in the Square. She worked with a group called Community Fridge, raising money for an outdoor refrigerator that residents could fill with items for those in need. Her husband built and painted an attractive wooden shed to house the fridge, and it was placed in front of one of John DiGiovanni's buildings in a prominent spot where, during non-pandemic times, hundreds of concertgoers lined up, waiting to head inside for a show.

When businesses began to reopen and customers began to return, some establishments came back to life. Manny Ramirez and Shoshanah Garber had kept their café, Black Sheep Bagel, running throughout even the darkest days of the pandemic. It was tough going early on, but they participated in the city's program to serve the homeless and shifted their operations to take-out. By early 2021, the business was on solid footing, and the young entrepreneurs even expanded, opening their second location, Black Sheep Market, in the nearby Cambridgeport neighborhood.

Other businesses struggled. Some vanished. By February 2021, approximately one hundred businesses in Harvard Square still had not reopened from the prior spring's shutdown.[2] No one knew how many of them might be gone for good. Chris Kotelly's Crimson Corner reopened for a while. I resumed my daily habit of stopping by to see Chris and pick up my morning paper. Only now he handed me my newspaper at the door, and we exchanged pleasantries from a distance, masked. He knew I had a medical condition that put me at high risk were I to catch the virus, and he had kindly offered to bring the paper out to me each day so that I did not have to go inside the small shop. He told me he was happy to be back in the store, but even with the mask obscuring his face, I could tell how hard things still were. His store was open, yes, but business was not coming back fast enough. Many of the Square's office and university workers were still working from home. Tourists had represented a large portion of Chris's customer base for the Harvard mugs, sweatshirts, and T-shirts he sold, but with restrictions on international travel still in place, those customers had not yet returned either. In May 2021, on the Sunday before Memorial Day weekend, Chris closed the family business his uncle had started nearly sixty years before.

That weekend, my husband and I stopped by for the paper and to say goodbye to Chris. We gave him a bottle of whiskey. He gave us a Harvard coffee mug from the shop. In the days that followed, Chris and I exchanged a few text messages. I told him how much he and his store had meant to me and how much I'd miss seeing him each morning. He replied, "It's the friends like you that have made it all worthwhile for all these years." I had grown attached not just to my morning routine but to Chris. His departure from the market felt like one more loss in a year full of them. He was losing his life's work and his family's business to which he'd given so much of himself. We were both losing the precious gift of starting off each day seeing a friend.

Susan Corcoran and I spoke a few times during the pandemic. Her Harvard Square shop had closed shortly before the virus began to spread through the United States, but she continued to operate her original Black Ink store in Boston's Beacon Hill neighborhood. She now spent her days alone in the shop. Some mornings, her daughter joined her. It reminded Susan of the period more than twenty years earlier when her daughter was just a baby and Susan would bring her to the store each morning while Susan's husband, Tim, headed off to class. After the state lifted restrictions on in-store sales, Susan decided to stick with curbside service for a while longer. It was too difficult to deal with customers who did not want to mask, she told me; but it also felt awful, she said, not to be welcoming customers back inside.

Susan was preparing to close this location at the end of 2021. Her Beacon Hill landlord was a nice, older woman who lived in an apartment above the store, and she had agreed to let Susan out of her lease. It had been a long few years, and Susan needed a break. She wasn't sure what she would do next. She told me she planned to keep running Black Ink's website from home as she figured it out. Susan sounded less fiery than during her fight with Asana and more philosophical these days. Perhaps something good would come of all this in the end, she said: "Maybe it will put the humanity back into it. Maybe people now see what it means to have all these empty spaces. I think some people are realizing 'oh god this is what it would be like if we lose this part of the community.'"

∼

Susan had a point. Perhaps because we have struggled to fully understand our relationship with markets in the past—perhaps because we have not always appreciated just how much we get from our street-level markets beyond their goods and services—we have not always treated this relationship with due respect. Perhaps, too, because we have been so caught up navigating all the changes constantly throwing us off our emotional equilibria, we have struggled to differentiate the sort of changes we have to live with, from the sort of changes that risk breaking the relationship apart for good and the broader social fabric it supports. Has the recent pandemic helped open our eyes to things that were harder to see before?

The months, now going on years, of the pandemic have given us all a lot to think about. Most important, we have been reminded of just how precious our limited time together is. We have confronted tough questions that we will have to reckon with as individuals and as a society in the days ahead. When it comes to our street-level markets, the question we need to ask ourselves is this: Where do we want to go from here?

We cannot stop our markets from changing on us, that much is clear. They change as the world changes and as our culture changes. Markets are a mirror not just of where we are in our individual lives but also of where we are as a society. They reflect back to us the prevailing preferences and values of our culture. They reflect the decisions we have made concerning how to regulate them and what to regulate in them. They reflect the collective choices we have made about how to prioritize the different things that matter to us (e.g., consumer prices, economic opportunity, job quality, competition and antitrust, equality, openness, and more). If we do not like the reflection we see when we look out on our markets, it is a sign that we may want to revisit some of those collective choices.

Before the pandemic, there was evidence of growing dissatisfaction with the reflection in the mirror. Localism movements were gaining traction in cities and towns around the country, including in Cambridge. Leaders of these movements hoped to remind people of the connections between local community and a thriving local economy, to get people to see it as in their individual and collective best interests to recommit to their local markets— and to one another in them. A rising chorus of legal experts and politicians, concerned about the long-term effects of declining economic competition, suggested the country needed to take a fresh look at its approach to antitrust enforcement and financial market regulation. On the ground in Harvard Square, the Death Discourse intensified to the point of becoming almost a reflex. Outpourings like we saw in the Dear Asana Project, while instigated by a single store closure, seemed to reveal heightening anxiety that something more precious than any individual store was being lost at the street level, something even more sacred to us than that.

From the seventeenth century, when Newtowne's settlers placed their first open-stall market on the top of the gentle slope that rose off the shores of the nearby river, through the days when Longfellow strolled around his local village marketplace, to our own era and whichever version of Harvard Square or Greenwich Village or Main Street we recall with fondness, street-level markets such as the Square have been a central, and centrally important, social institution in Americans' lives. As much as any church or temple or town hall, our markets have drawn us out of our homes and into communion with one another.

As we consider what sort of market society we want to live in, we should probably ask ourselves an even more fundamental question first: How do we want to relate to one another? Only by answering that will we sort out how we want to relate to our markets, because the two questions are inextricably intertwined. Do we want the spaces and places in which we come together to be decided by a few large corporations or a diversity of competing ones? How much of our social and economic lives do we want to spend separated from one another by our screens instead of meeting in person in our town centers and neighborhood markets? Do we want to meet one another for coffee only in the Metaverse? Do we want the Amazon marketplace to be the only marketplace we visit?

Part of answering these questions will be deciding what we want our relationship to be with the virtual platforms in our lives. I personally haven't quite figured that one out yet. When I'm away from my iPhone or email for an extended period of time, I feel either an overwhelming sense of relief or like an addict desperate for her next fix. By contrast, when the pandemic kept me away from Harvard Square, I simply longed to see the people and places I loved.

As painful a disruption as the pandemic has been, it has reinforced the importance of attending to the health of our social fabric. So long as we keep wanting to connect with one another in person, we are not likely to lose our street-level markets. Enterprising individuals will find new ways to keep the street level a relevant and appealing platform for those connections. But we can't expect it to look exactly the same as it has in the past. Today's street-level markets look different from those that existed before the advent of cars or malls. Tomorrow's will look different in response to the internet, the pandemic, and whatever lies beyond.

As we make our way forward in these unchartered times, however, there is one final thing we may want to keep in mind, and it is this: in all the great love stories, the camera always, inevitably swoops down from the clouds and lands at the street level. For it is there, on the streets of Harvard Square and Main Streets across America, where people have always gathered to meet and eat and shop and talk and fall in love—those simple acts through which we find comfort and communion and forge the bonds that last a lifetime.

CODA

In late July 2021, just as the coronavirus's Delta variant was making itself known and unsettling hopes for an easy return to pre-pandemic life, I found myself standing in a dark abandoned tunnel beneath Harvard Square. My street-level research had taken me underground.

I could see only what was illuminated by the small circle of light cast by my flashlight. Everything that popped into view looked gray and sepulchral. The uneven dirt floor was pocked with loose rocks and puddles. Stalactites hung off the concrete beams high above. On a side wall, a "Danger: Keep Out" sign was followed by a word cloud of graffiti in which "fuck" was by far the most common sentiment expressed. Yet the tall concrete arches bearing those inscriptions were still stunning; stately, even. I felt like I was standing inside an archeological site, having just unearthed the ruins of an earlier civilization. In a way, I was.

These tunnels were part of the original Harvard Square subway. They had gone unused for decades, as one or another renovation altered routes and opened up new tunnels. The long narrow puddle that ran alongside my right was where tracks had run. John DiGiovanni had been telling me about these tunnels for a while. "It might be crazy," he said each time he broached the subject, but he had an idea: the idea was that maybe this abandoned, subterranean space could be rebuilt into an exciting public space that would attract more people to Harvard Square. New York City had recently repurposed its old elevated railway line on the Lower West Side, creating the popular High Line. Why not think about repurposing unused, underground lines too?

It was hard enough to envision hundreds of people crowding into this catacombs-like space before the pandemic. It seemed even more bonkers to contemplate it as a highly contagious respiratory virus continued to ravage the globe. However, John did not abandon the idea after COVID-19 hit. He trusted that at some point, people would want to come back together. Whenever that happened, he wanted Harvard Square to draw the crowds it once had, and he knew that meant thinking outside of the box. My own thoughts on the subject wavered between dismissing the idea as insane, to realizing that I am just the sort of person who would have said putting trains underground was insane when that was first proposed.

John knew the whole thing was a long shot. It might prove physically impossible or prohibitively expensive to make the space safe and accessible to large crowds of people. All he wanted for now, however, was for some of the Square's property owners to chip in alongside him to pay for a feasibility study. Just maybe, this crazy idea would pan out. Or, who knows, maybe some better idea would emerge in the process.

Gerald Chan and John DiGiovanni had not always clicked, but that morning in the tunnels they were standing a few feet away from me, their own flashlights in hand, slowly making their way forward together. Gerald had been worried about the Square before the pandemic as well, and John invited him to come see the tunnels in hopes Chan might get excited about his crazy idea and contribute to the feasibility study. I was just tagging along, as were several others from the Business Association, Chan's staff, and the City of Cambridge.

The tunnels intrigued me, but I was more interested in watching John and Gerald. Born on opposite sides of the world and temperamentally quite different, both men were attached to Harvard Square, and that attachment was, in part, tied up with their attachments to their fathers and their pasts. I smiled when I saw that, by no act of coordination on their part, both men had brought their sons along to tour the tunnels with them that morning. John's school-age son was starting to show more curiosity about his father's work, but he also wanted to see what lay beneath his favorite busking spots in the Square. Gerald's adult son had fond memories of hanging out in the Square as a kid, and he was thinking of moving back to the East Coast to continue his work in urban design. He had been living out in Los Angeles, where he had converted an old factory into a funky arts and events center, and his dad thought the tunnels project might be of interest to him.

So much had changed since these tunnels were built, yet so much was still the same. The subway's construction all those years ago had been a massive disruption to the marketplace, but it had also alerted the Square's merchants to their shared interests and united them in common cause. Today, there were new challenges, new changes to adapt to, and here were John and Gerald being drawn together by their mutual self-interests, digging deep for ideas about how to give this street-level market a little boost. Maybe they would work together on this project. Maybe they would not. Maybe the project would go nowhere. Maybe, one day, John's son would play a concert down there to a crowd of screaming fans.

As we emerged from the tunnels into the center of Harvard Square, our eyes had to adjust to the bright sunlight. I was no more certain than before as to whether I thought this idea was crazy or not. But the tunnels had not been the most important thing I saw down there. I followed a few feet behind Gerald and John as they walked and talked their way through the Square. When they reached the Dunkin' Donuts and headed inside to keep the conversation going over coffee, I said goodbye and turned up JFK Street. Then I took out my phone and called my dad to see if he wanted to meet for a bagel in the Square.

ACKNOWLEDGMENTS

This book would not have been possible without the generosity and openness of so many members of the Harvard Square community. Fieldwork for the contemporary parts of this project entailed interviews with dozens of participants in the current market, plus my own participant observation in various local firms, nonprofits, community events, and public meetings. There is not space enough to list all the merchants, property owners, residents, community groups, and local officials who were kind enough to welcome me into their fold and share their Harvard Square experiences with me so I could see things from perspectives beyond my own narrow vantage point. But I am profoundly grateful to them all.

I would like to extend a special thanks to Susan Corcoran, John DiGiovanni, and Chris Kotelly for opening their personal and business lives to me and trusting me with their stories and their friendship. I will never be able to repay the debt of gratitude I owe them, but I hope this book goes a little way toward memorializing the contributions each has made to Harvard Square over the years.

I would also like to thank the following organizations and individuals: the Harvard Square Business Association, including its executive director Denise Jillson and board secretary Tod Beaty, who gave me access to current and past organizational records and introduced me to multiple contacts for this project; the Harvard Square Neighborhood Association, including its president Suzanne Blier and board member Chris Mackin, whose work on behalf of the neighborhood always kept me abreast of new developments in the Square, and Neighborhood Association member Pebble Gifford, who guided me to the Harvard Square Defense Fund's historical records early in my research process; Gerald Chan, who shared his insights on market trends in retail and real estate; Jan Devereux, who shared her insights on municipal governance; and, finally, Theodora Skeadas of Cambridge Local First and Jim McKellar of Harvard Student Agencies, who kept me connected to their organizations' activities in the market.

Two prior books on Harvard Square were inspirational touchstones and valuable resources for the historical aspects of this project: Susan Maycock and Charlie Sullivan's *Building Old Cambridge* and Mo Lotman's *Harvard Square: An Illustrated History Since 1950*. I am grateful for these impressive books and their supportive authors. The incomparable Charlie Sullivan, executive director of the Cambridge Historical Commission, met with me multiple times, directed me to key primary sources (even when it entailed dragging heavy file boxes out of back corners of the commission's offices so I could scour their contents), responded to queries at all times of the day concerning arcane details of Harvard Square history, and fact-checked a section of this book. Mo Lotman generously met with me at the start of my research, encouraged my early ideas, and, like Charlie, pointed me toward additional sources that would prove foundational for the analysis I present in this book.

The historical data on which this book relies include thousands of primary documents contained in organizational and personal archives, business directories, municipal reports, public-meeting minutes, and more, all preserved and cared for by Cambridge's historical institutions and their committed stewards. Charlie Sullivan of the Cambridge Historical Commission, Marieke Van Damme of History Cambridge/Cambridge Historical Society, and Alyssa Pacy of the Cambridge Room of the Cambridge Public Library helped me navigate their institutions' collections and showed great patience as I made my way through their contents.

I also draw on more than three thousand old newspaper articles covering events in the Harvard Square marketplace through the years. Cambridge Public Library's Historic Cambridge Newspaper Collection contains all Cambridge newspapers published between 1846 and 2015. The *Harvard Crimson* has also digitized its entire archive and made it available to the public. This project would not have been possible without those sources, and I thank those who did the hard work of preserving these materials for posterity. I would like also to thank the generations of *Crimson* reporters who covered the Harvard Square beat and left such a detailed record of life in the Square. One summer during college, I lived in a cramped sublet with half a dozen *Crimson* writers (and one rogue squirrel), and I saw how seriously the paper's staff took their work. I was reminded of that again during my research.

For the book's photos, I would like to thank Black Ink, Inc. and Susan Corcoran, Philip Borden, Chris and Mae Grimley, the Boston Public Library and Digital Commonwealth, the Cambridge Center for Adult Education, the Cambridge Historical Commission, Spencer Grant, the Harvard University Archives, and the JFK Presidential Library and Museum.

I could not have completed this project without the personal support I received from friends and colleagues. Peter Bearman of Columbia University was one of the first people whom I told about this project. His encouragement sustained me throughout. He invited me to present some of my early findings at Columbia's Interdisciplinary Center for Innovative Theory and Empirics. The feedback I received there from Peter and his Columbia colleagues, including Diane Vaughan, helped guide the next phase of my research. Later, in his capacity as friend, mentor, and faculty affiliate at Columbia University Press, Peter read an entire draft of the book, and his comments helped me sharpen the final manuscript.

Ezra Zuckerman was the other individual whom I told about this project when it was still just an inkling of an idea. Ezra was then—as he has been ever since my first day of graduate school—an indefatigable champion and cheerleader of my work. He too read and commented on the entire manuscript once I completed a draft, and I am grateful for both his comments and his many words of encouragement along the way.

I could not have asked for a more supportive and attentive editor than Eric Schwartz at Columbia University Press. I thank Eric, Peter, and the entire CUP team for taking such good care of a book that means so much to me.

Dedi Felman's close read of each and every part of the book helped sharpen my ideas and writing in innumerable ways. I am so grateful for all I have learned from her. Sarah Halpern-Meekin shared insights from the sociology of family and romantic relationships when I first began to think about the relationships people form with the markets in their lives. Karen Chitwood shared her expertise in psychology, giving me a primer on attachment theory as I contemplated the emotional attachments we form in and to markets. Jason Greenberg shared his expertise on small-business entrepreneurship and went above and beyond, diving into Massachusetts land records and census tract data to help me suss out details of the Harvard

Square marketplace. Lance Sallis walked me through the ins and outs of real estate financing. All these individuals and more—including Pilar Opazo, Alessandra Nicifero, and Judy Graham-Robey—offered friendship and support that sustained me as I slogged away on this undertaking.

Three incredible women from Wellesley College—Kerry Wells, Tara Wattal, and Neeraja Deshpande—served as undergraduate research assistants to me at different points in the process. Together, they helped me collect, sort, and analyze news on the Harvard Square marketplace, dig up facts about an earlier pandemic in the midst of a current one, and, most important, let me see my subject matter through their younger, fresher eyes. As I worked through this project, Orlando Patterson was also never far from my mind. My graduate school advisor, Orlando remains an inspiration and a model of the sort of scholar I hope to be.

Even with all that, I still could not have written this book without my family. My in-laws, Janellyn and Glenn Borden, offered weekly encouragement and cheer over Zoom when we could not be together in person. My mother, Joanne Turco, proofread every chapter draft as soon as I finished it, took my weary phone calls every afternoon, and offered love and understanding in ways only she can. My brother, Al Turco, listened to me talk through the entire outline of the book one day when I was sitting on my floor, surrounded by Post-its and chalkboards and poster boards and couldn't find my way forward. My father, Albert J. Turco, ever my wartime consigliere, was there to brainstorm whenever I encountered an obstacle. More important, he is why I could write this book, and he is why I did write this book. It is to him I dedicate it.

But we can't forget the dog. Or the husband. Winona, loyal patron to every Harvard Square establishment that offers Milk-Bones, did not help advance this project's forward momentum. However, she got me out on the streets of Harvard Square every day whether I liked it or not. Given her wild, joyful antics and the number of people who greet her by name on the street, I sense she is on her way toward becoming one of those beloved figures of Harvard Square lore. Philip Borden, my husband, lived every single (excruciating) moment of this project with me, and my greatest thanks go to him. He read every chapter multiple times over, told me to keep going when I did not want to, contributed a beautiful photo for the book cover, and showed patience when I woke him at 4 a.m. to talk out absolutely urgent (to me) issues pertaining to one or another footnote. Philip—thank you, I'm sorry I'm so crazy, I love you.

NOTES

ACRONYMS USED IN SOURCE CITATIONS

CHC   Cambridge Historical Commission

CHS   History Cambridge/Cambridge Historical Society

CPL   Cambridge Public Library

HSBA   Harvard Square Business Association

HSDF   Harvard Square Defense Fund

PCHS   Proceedings of the Cambridge Historical Society

PROLOGUE: SACRED SUNDAYS

1. Joshua Florence, "Curious George, Urban Outfitters Could Face Closures," *Harvard Crimson*, September 7, 2016.
2. In fact, that line from *The Godfather* had called to my mind a second relevant movie reference. In the 1998 film *You've Got Mail*, Meg Ryan plays the owner of a charming independent children's bookstore that is being run out of business by a chain. When the chain-store executive (played by Tom Hanks) quotes *The Godfather* by saying that the situation is "business, not personal," Ryan's character retorts: "All that means is it's not personal to you. It's personal to me. It's personal to a lot of people."

1. A LOVE STORY TOLD FROM THE STREET LEVEL

1. Susan E. Maycock and Charles M. Sullivan, *Building Old Cambridge: Architecture and Development* (Cambridge, MA: MIT Press, 2016), 117. It was also called "the Village"

during this time. The *Proceedings of the Cambridge Historical Society* (PCHS) contains multiple references to the early "Market-place" nomenclature as well, including Charles Eliot Norton, "Reminiscences of Old Cambridge," *PCHS* 1 (1905–1906): 11–23; George H. Kent, "Merchants of Old Cambridge in the Early Days," *PCHS* 8 (1913): 30–40; Lois Lilley Howe, "Harvard Square in the 'Seventies and 'Eighties," *PCHS* 30 (1944): 11–27.

2. Maycock and Sullivan, *Building Old Cambridge*, 7. It should be noted that the area comprising Newtowne (like the broader Massachusetts Bay Colony) was, of course, not new to the native people who had long occupied the land. Maycock and Sullivan contend that by the time Newtowne's settlers arrived, however, few Native Americans lived in the immediate settlement area, having been ravaged by disease and tribal warfare in previous years.

3. Local and national papers seem to keep stock aerial photos of Harvard Square to run alongside articles when newsworthy stories arise. See, for example, the 1988 and 1970 photos accompanying, respectively: Clancy Martin, "Taxi Driver," *New York Times*, May 5, 2013, https://www.nytimes.com/2013/05/05/books/review/harvard-square-by -andre-aciman.html; and Kathleen Conti, "Harvard Square Could Lose Iconic Out of Town News," *Boston Globe*, August, 25 2016, https://www.bostonglobe.com/business /2016/08/25/out-town-news-could-pushed-out-iconic-harvard-square-location /fuoJPz8OfNH2fofpgkxgzN/story.html. Movies set in Harvard Square that include aerial shots include *Good Will Hunting* (1997), *Legally Blonde* (2001), *The Town* (2010), and *The Social Network* (2010).

4. The aerial picture I paint in this paragraph was inspired by details of Newtowne offered in *Building Old Cambridge*, 5–6.

5. I stopped counting after seven horns in *Love Story* (1970) and after the same in real life, during a stroll I took one morning in 2019 with the express purpose of paying attention to the ambient traffic noise to see how it compared to that of the movie.

6. Michel de Certeau, "Walking in the City," in *The Practice of Everyday Life*, trans. Steven Rendall (Berkeley: University of California Press, 1984), 93.

7. Google Maps, accessed December 14, 2021. The measurement by Google Maps is broadly consistent with the City of Cambridge Park's Guide that lists it as 0.3 acres. My own measurements made with an admittedly uncooperative tape measure one windy day suggested something a bit more petite (approx. 133 feet by 72 feet), the difference likely owing to how sidewalks are or are not being counted.

8. Details of the marketplace as it existed from the seventeenth century through the mid-nineteenth century included here and on the pages that follow in this section are drawn primarily from Maycock and Sullivan, *Building Old Cambridge*, chap. 1–3, 5, 8. Maycock is an architectural historian and the long-time survey director of the Cambridge Historical Commission (CHC). Sullivan is a city planner and has served as the CHC's executive director since 1974. *Building Old Cambridge* is a comprehensive, 944-page history of early Cambridge that brings together decades of research compiled by them at the CHC. I draw upon *Building Old Cambridge* heavily in this section as it contains the most definitive description of the early Harvard Square marketplace I have found. In researching this period, however, I also examined files and archives at the CHC, traced down several of the primary sources cited in *Building Old Cambridge* relevant to this project, and triangulated what I found in their book with archival collections held at the city's other historical institution, History Cambridge/Cambridge Historical Society (CHS), as well as the Cambridge Public

Library (CPL). I note supplemental sources in these notes where relevant. Through-out, however, Maycock and Sullivan's excellent work remained my guiding source for early Cambridge history.

9. General facts about the operation of early markets like this one and their centrality in townspeople's daily lives are also drawn from Fernand Braudel, *Civilization and Capitalism, 15th–18th Century*, vol. 2, *The Wheels of Commerce*, trans. Sian Reynolds (New York: Harper Collins, 1979).

10. Kent, "Merchants of Old Cambridge in the Early Days," 30–34.

11. References to the Blue Anchor Tavern's founding can be found in Chauncey Depew Steele, "A History of Inns and Hotels in Cambridge," *PCHS* 37 (1957–1958): 29–44; George Hanford, *For the Entertainment of Strangers: The Inns and Pubs of Cambridge* (Cambridge, MA: CHS, 1997); and Maycock and Sullivan, *Building Old Cambridge*, 681.

12. Jasper Dankers and Peter Sluyter, *Journal of a Voyage to New York and a Tour of Several American Colonies in 1679–1680*, trans. Henry C. Murphy (Brooklyn, NY: Long Island Historical Society, 1867), quoted in Maycock and Sullivan, *Building Old Cambridge*, 14. Dankers (whose full name, Danckaerts, seems to have been short-ened by his translators) also expressed dismay at finding the main college house occupied by a handful of students sitting amid a cloud of their own tobacco smoke and seemingly unable to converse with his companion in Latin. The translation can be accessed here: https://babel.hathitrust.org/cgi/pt?id=nnc2.ark:/13960/t8bg5fd31&view=1up&seq=9&skin=2021.

13. According to Maycock and Sullivan, by 1770 there were seven shops located near the central market, and the surrounding area as a whole supported at least one of each of the following tradesmen: barber, blacksmith, brickmaker, carpenter, cooper, currier, distiller, glazier, hatter, saddler, shoemaker, tailor, tanner. *Building Old Cambridge*, 17–18.

14. Andrew Schlesinger, *Veritas: Harvard College and the American Experience* (Chicago: Ivan R. Dee, 2005), 25. Additional references to commencement festivities during this period can be found in: John Bartlett, *A Collection of College Words and Customs* (Cambridge, MA, 1851), quoted in Maycock and Sullivan, *Building Old Cambridge*, 16; Michelle Kurilla and Matteo Wong, "The History of Harvard's Commencement, Explained," *Harvard Crimson*, May 11, 2020; and Albert Matthews, "Harvard Com-mencement Days, 1642–1916," *Publications of the Colonial Society of Massachusetts*, vol. 18, *Transactions, 1915–1916*, 309–84. Matthews's chronicle suggests that managing the formal ceremony alongside the public frivolity was not always easy; he also notes years in which commencement was canceled on account of smallpox or other disease outbreaks, as it would be again in 2020.

15. Commencement seems to have had much in common with the sort of large, raucous fairs common in Europe at the time described by Braudel in *Civilization and Capitalism*. According to Braudel, these fairs had a schedule unto themselves, each with "its rhythm, its calendar and its code" (2:82). They would come to town for a short period and then move on. "During the intervals between these tumultuous, and cele-brated gatherings," the towns that hosted them were often "sleepy little" places, which returned to their normal affairs until the next cycle brought back the fair and all its wild commotion (2:83).

16. The elephant attended Harvard commencement in 1796, when the holiday had resumed after the Revolutionary War ("America's First Elephant at Harvard Graduation

Exercises in 18th Century Tour of the Continent," *Harvard Crimson*, October 6, 1934). Yet commencement was already quite the wild affair in the decades leading up to the war. Maycock and Sullivan note that by the mid-1700s, it was common knowledge in the colonies that to say something "resembled a Cambridge commencement" was to imply a crazy, chaotic affair. *Building Old Cambridge*, 16–17.

17. It also buzzed with British troops right before. The April 18, 1775, diary of a local woman notes, "Today, nine Redcoats stopped at Bradish Tavern [what the Blue Anchor Tavern was temporarily called before returning to its original name] and then galloped on toward Lexington. I wonder what mischief is in the wind now!" (Steele, "A History of Inns and Hotels in Cambridge," 32). The Battle of Lexington and Concord took place the next day.

18. Maycock and Sullivan, *Building Old Cambridge*, 61.

19. Maycock and Sullivan, *Building Old Cambridge*, 44.

20. James Russell Lowell, "Cambridge Thirty Years Ago: A Memoir Addressed to the Edelmann Storg in Rome" (1854), *Fireside Travels* (London and Cambridge: Macmillan, 1864), describes the 1820s village of the poet's youth as "quiet, unspeculative" and "sufficing itself" (19). Lowell recalls with fondness a local brewer named Lewis—"a grave and amiable Ethiopian"—who sold his stock off a hand-pushed cart and whose bottles of spruce and ginger beer sometimes exploded upon opening but were a rite of passage for boys in the area (26); as well as a Dutch barber, whose skills with the shears were questionable, but whose museum-like shop was filled with fascinating curios including "New Zealand paddles and war-clubs" and "whales' teeth fantastically engraved" (30–31). (Howe, "Harvard Square in the 'Seventies and Eighties,'" describes similar attractions in the 1870s marketplace of her youth.) In the 1820s, Harvard commencement—or what Lowell calls "the festival of Santa Scholastica" (21)—continued to draw "all the wonders of the world" to the area each year, from a fortune-teller named Wisdom to flying horses, which Lowell admits were turned by a man with a crank (58). A portion of Lowell's essay was published in the *Cambridge Chronicle*, April 29, 1854; above page numbers refer to the full-length piece that appeared in *Fireside Travels*.

21. Maycock and Sullivan, *Building Old Cambridge*, 57–61.

22. Maycock and Sullivan, *Building Old Cambridge*, 47–48. According to *Building Old Cambridge*, around this time some of the conservative mercantile and university elite of "Old Cambridge"—what the wealthy residential area just west of the Market-place was now being called—began to feel increasingly out of step with the more rapidly growing and industrializing areas of the city, East Cambridge and Cambridgeport. In the 1840s and '50s, Old Cambridge residents made several attempts to secede from the city. Their insistence that their newly independent town should rightly be called "Cambridge" did little to change the area's reputation as the stodgy, elitist part of the city. The secession attempts failed but the reputation lingered.

23. Maycock and Sullivan, *Building Old Cambridge*, 61.

24. Multiple biographies of Longfellow cover his time in the area, including Nicholas Basbanes, *Crosses of Snow: A Life of Henry Wadsworth Longfellow* (New York: Knopf, 2020); Craig Calhoun, *Longfellow: A Rediscovered Life* (Boston: Beacon, 2004); and Edward Wagenknecht, *Longfellow: A Full Length Portrait* (London: Longmans, Green, 1955).

25. "Amee Brothers Bookshop Now Only Memory to Harvard Men," *Boston Globe*, August 2, 1936.

26. Maycock and Sullivan, *Building Old Cambridge*, 62.

27. Henry Wadsworth Longfellow, *The Letters of Henry Wadsworth Longfellow*, vols. 5–6, ed. Andrew Hilen (Cambridge, MA: Belknap Press, 1982), 609, quoted in Maycock and Sullivan, *Building Old Cambridge*, 62–63.

28. Henry Wadsworth Longfellow, "The Village Blacksmith," in *Longfellow: Selected Poems*, ed. Lawrence Buell (New York: Penguin Books, 1988). Longfellow is said to have modeled the blacksmith in the poem on Dexter Pratt, the local smithy who lived and worked at 54 Brattle Street and whose workshop was marked by a large chestnut tree which stood nearby (Basbanes, *Crosses of Snow*; Wagenknecht, *Longfellow*). Longfellow also appears to have been paying tribute with the poem to an ancestor named Stephen Longfellow, who had been a blacksmith in Newbury, Massachusetts, in the seventeenth century (Wagenknecht, *Longfellow*; Calhoun, *Longfellow*). Calhoun describes the poem as "a genre-scene, a nostalgic evocation of the age of the citizen-artisan, proud, independent, pious, productive—a New England myth-in-the-making as the small towns began to become industrialized" (140).

29. André Aciman, *Harvard Square* (New York: Norton, 2013), 125.

30. For a discussion of case selection in qualitative research, see Mario Small, "How Many Cases Do I Need: On Science and the Logic of Case Selection in Field-Based Research," *Ethnography* 10, no. 5 (2009): 5–38.

31. Robert Campbell, "Showdown on Main Street," *Boston Globe*, September 17, 1996; and Robert Campbell, "Squeezing the Square," *Boston Globe*, October 27, 1991.

32. In the details that follow, we will see that many of the characteristics that have historically defined Harvard Square are those which Jane Jacobs, writing about Greenwich Village in the 1950s and early '60s, argued make for rich, lively urban neighborhoods. Jane Jacobs, *The Death and Life of Great American Cities* (New York: Random House, 1961).

33. Kerry Flynn, "Out of Town News Founder Sheldon Cohen Honored in Retirement," *Harvard Crimson*, January 11, 2012; and Cambridge Community Television, "Honoring Sheldon Cohen (the Unofficial Mayor of Harvard Square)," January 10, 2012, https://www.cctvcambridge.org/node/89402.

34. "Felix Caragianes, Aided Harvard Men," *New York Times*, March 21, 1951.

35. "Watch and Ward Hounds Descend Upon Felix, Bootlegger of Mercury's 'Hatrack,'" *Harvard Crimson*, April 1, 1926.

36. "ICO Honor Felix in Name Day Feast," *Harvard Crimson*, January 1, 1950.

37. "Felix Caragianes, A Harvard Square Celebrity Dies," *Cambridge Chronicle*, March 22, 1951.

38. "Max Keezer, of Harvard Fame, Passes Away," *Cambridge Chronicle*, February 6, 1941.

39. "Max Keezer Is Dead; Harvard Character," *New York Times*, February 2, 1941.

40. "If You Get Into a Jam at Harvard, See Max," *Boston Globe*, February 9, 1941.

41. Thomas Jack, "Return to Casablanca," *Boston Globe*, September 5, 1991.

42. Federico Muchnik, *Touching History: Harvard Square, the Bank, & the Tasty Diner*, 2005, https://vimeo.com/18973913. The Tasty and the battle to save it is also discussed in Mo Lotman, *Harvard Square: An Illustrated History Since 1950* (New York: Stewart, Tabori & Chang, 2009).

43. Jeffrey Mayersohn (owner of Harvard Book Store), email to author, October 20, 2020; also reported in Gabrielle Pesantez, "October Is the New December," *Harvard Crimson*, October 29, 2020. The Harvard Book Store's 2020 public appeal also drew the attention of the local businessman and philanthropist John Henry (owner of the

Boston Red Sox and *Boston Globe*), who eventually invested and became a co-owner of the bookstore to help put it on more solid financial footing. Janelle Nanos, "Harvard Book Store Gets a New Backer: John Henry," *Boston Globe*, December 17, 2021.

44. Mark Granovetter, Viviana Zelizer, and others in the field of economic sociology have explored the ways in which economic activity is deeply embedded in meaningful social relations and the often complex intermingling of market transactions and actors' intimate, personal relationships. See, for example, Viviana Zelizer, *Economic Lives: How Culture Shapes the Economy* (Princeton, NJ: Princeton University Press, 2011); and Mark Granovetter, *Society and Economy: Framework and Principles* (Cambridge, MA: Belknap Press, 2017). My book builds on that earlier work but will also reveal something new and distinct. While Zelizer's "connected lives" approach has persuasively demonstrated that people intermingle their intimate lives with their economic activities, her foundational assumption is that our culture continues to perceive intimacy and the market as incompatible. She thus focuses her analytical gaze on all the interactional, rhetorical, and relational work people do to navigate that tension—that is, on how people make and mark their personal relations in the market *despite* feeling that the market stands in opposition to them. This study of Harvard Square will explore how the market is the setting and source material for human connections of all kinds and how, precisely because of that, people develop a deep personal relationship *with the market itself*. It will unravel the complexity of that relationship, including why a market can mean so much to us that we may even fall in love with it and why, at times, this relationship seems to drive us all a bit crazy.

45. For a discussion of urban subcultures, see Claude Fischer, "Toward a Subcultural Theory of Urbanism," *American Journal of Sociology* 80, no. 8 (May 1975): 543–77.

46. The Brattle's frequent showings of *Casablanca* have been credited with helping the film remain in the American consciousness in the decades after its release.

47. Lotman, *Harvard Square*, 30.

48. Both the Brattle Theater and Club Passim eventually converted from for-profit businesses to nonprofit institutions in order to better sustain and support their cultural activities. However, both remain a part of the local marketplace, selling tickets and refreshments to their paying customers.

49. Michael Rosenwald, "To Chapman, Underground Music Is Pure Performance," *Boston Globe*, November 26, 2003, http://archive.boston.com/news/local/articles/2003/11/26/to_chapman_underground_music_is_pure_performance/.

50. Patti Hartigan, "Showtime in Harvard Square," *Boston Globe*, September 11, 1986; and Alexander Cohn, "Self-Taught Fiddler Sharpens Up Square," *Harvard Crimson*, October 20, 2006.

51. Ray Oldenburg, *The Great Good Place: Cafes, Coffee Shops, Bookstores, Bars, Hair Salons, and Other Hangouts at the Heart of a Community* (Cambridge, MA: Da Capo, 1989).

52. Ellen Mills, "Main Street or Mall Street?," *NewEnglandFilm.com*, December 1, 2005, https://newenglandfilm.com/magazine/2005/12/main-street-or-mall-street.

53. *The Firm* (1993) also starts off in the Square, where we meet a poor but scrappy law school student played by Tom Cruise who rushes out of an interview with a top law firm to make his shift waiting tables in a Harvard Square burger joint.

54. Linda Laban, "What to Know Before the Thai Festival Takes Over Harvard Square on Sunday," September 13, 2019, https://www.boston.com/culture/events/2019/09/13/what-to-know-tastes-of-thailand-festival.

1. A LOVE STORY TOLD FROM THE STREET LEVEL

55. Jane Thompson and Alexandra Lange, *Design Research: The Store That Brought Modern Living to American Homes* (San Francisco: Chronicle, 2010). Design Research and its trendsetting Marimekko prints are also discussed in Lotman, *Harvard Square*; and Maycock and Sullivan, *Building Old Cambridge*.
56. Neil Miller, "Out with the Old: Harvard Square Goes Squaresville," *Boston Phoenix*, February 19, 1985, quoted in Maycock and Sullivan, *Building Old Cambridge*, 156.
57. Braudel, *Civilization and Capitalism*.
58. Stanley Milgram, "The Small-World Problem," *Psychology Today* 1 (May 1967): 61–67.
59. Different works in this tradition include Richard Francaviglia, *Main Street Revisited: Time, Space, and Image Building in Small-Town America* (Iowa City: University of Iowa Press, 1996); Alison Isenberg, *Downtown America: A History of the Place and the People Who Made It* (Chicago: University of Chicago Press, 2004); Miles Orvell, *The Death and Life of Main Street: Small Towns in American Memory, Space, and Community* (Chapel Hill: University of North Carolina Press, 2012). Jane Jacobs's depiction of Greenwich Village's buzzing, vibrant sidewalk life has also been critiqued as offering an overly romantic, and since-commoditized, notion of an urban village; see, for example, Sharon Zukin, *Naked City: The Death and Life of Authentic Urban Places* (New York: Oxford University Press, 2010).
60. Ryan Poll, *Main Street and Empire: The Fictional Small Town in the Age of Globalization* (Piscataway, NJ: Rutgers University Press, 2012).
61. Aciman, *Harvard Square*, 25.
62. Aciman, *Harvard Square*, 57.
63. Aciman, *Harvard Square*, 7.
64. Francaviglia, *Main Street Revisited*; Orvell, *Death and Life of Main Street*.
65. Joe McCarthy, "Cultured Cambridge," *Holiday*, June 1956, 116.
66. McCarthy, "Cultured Cambridge," 117.
67. A few examples from economic sociology include White's 1981 discussion of production markets, Burt's theory of structural holes, Zelizer's study of the life insurance industry, and Fligstein's discussion of "markets as politics." Harrison White, "Where Do Markets Come From?," *American Journal of Sociology* 87, no. 3 (November 1981): 527–47; Ronald Burt, *Structural Holes: The Social Structure of Competition* (Cambridge, MA: Harvard University Press, 1995); Viviana Zelizer, *Morals and Markets: The Development of Life Insurance in the United States* (New York: Columbia University Press, 1979); and Neil Fligstein, "Markets as Politics: A Political-Cultural Approach to Market Institutions," *American Sociological Review* 61, no. 4 (August 1996): 656–73.
68. Fernand Braudel, *Afterthoughts on Material Civilization and Capitalism*, trans. Patricia Ranum (Baltimore, MD: Johns Hopkins University Press, 1977), 35.
69. Braudel, *Civilization and Capitalism*, 2:22.
70. Harvey Molotch and colleagues have done fascinating work on the "character" of place; for example, Harvey Molotch, William Freudenburg, and Krista Paulsen, "History Repeats Itself, but How? City Character, Urban Tradition, and the Accomplishment of Place," *American Sociological Review* 65, no. 6 (December 2000): 791–823.
71. For urban politics, see John Logan and Harvey Molotch, *Urban Fortunes: The Political Economy of Place* (Berkeley: University of California Press, 1987). For gentrification, see Sharon Zukin, "Gentrification: Culture and Capital in the Urban Core," *Annual Review of Sociology* 13 (August 1987): 129–47. For small-town decline, see Robert Wuthnow, *The Left Behind: Decline and Rage in Small-Town America* (Princeton,

NJ: Princeton University Press, 2018). For racial inequality, see Elijah Anderson, *The Cosmopolitan Canopy: Race and Civility in Everyday Life* (New York: Norton, 2011). For consumer culture and mass consumption, see George Ritzer, *The McDonaldization of Society: An Investigation into the Changing Character of Contemporary Social Life* (Thousand Oaks, CA: Pine Forge Press, 1993). For global capitalism, see Saskia Sassen, *The Global City* (Princeton, NJ: Princeton University Press, 1992) and *Cities in a World Economy* (Thousand Oaks, CA: Pine Forge Press, 1994).

2. NOT WHAT IT USED TO BE

1. Tom Meek and Mark Levy, "Harvard Square Isn't Losing Defense Fund, It's Just Gaining Neighborhood Association," *Cambridge Day*, June 12, 2017, https://www .cambridgeday.com/2017/06/12/harvard-square-isnt-losing-defense-fund-its-just -gaining-neighborhood-association/.
2. According to reports at the time, Crema's sales had dropped in recent years, and the new landlord chose not to renew the café's lease when it expired. Erin Kuschner, "Crema Café Will Say Goodbye to Harvard Square After 10 Years," boston.com, December 5, 2018, https://www.boston.com/food/restaurants/2018/12/05/crema-cafe -will-say-goodbye-to-harvard-square-after-10-years/; Isabel Kendall and Ema Schumer, "Crema Café to Leave Harvard Square in Late December," *Harvard Crimson*, December 7, 2018.
3. "About Us," Bluestone Lane, https://bluestonelane.com/about/, accessed December 17, 2021; "Bluestone Lane Secures Growth Capital from RSE Ventures," PR Newswire, June 11, 2018, https://www.prnewswire.com/news-releases/bluestone-lane-secures -growth-capital-from-rse-ventures-300678940.html; Kendall and Schumer, "Crema Café to Leave Harvard Square."
4. Kathleen Conti, "More of the Square for Sale," *Boston Globe*, July 20, 2017; Oset Babur, "An Uncertain Future for Harvard Square," *Harvard Magazine*, July 28, 2017, https://www.harvardmagazine.com/2017/07/harvard-square-redevelopment.
5. Crimson Editorial Board, "The Transformation of Harvard Square," *Harvard Crimson*, May 25, 2017.
6. Andrew Aoyama and Jane Li, "The Neighborhood Where Nothing Ever Changes," *Harvard Crimson*, February 14, 2019.
7. All quotes and details from this meeting, held March 3, 2019, are drawn from my ethnographic field notes taken during the meeting. Harvard Square Neighborhood Association meetings like this one are typically open to the public and often attended by at least some public officials and members of the local press.
8. Joshua Florence, "Vote Delayed, Famous Curious George Store to Stay—For Now," *Harvard Crimson*, September 9, 2016.
9. Brush co-founded the Harvard Square restaurant with Felipe Herrera in 2004. The two subsequently partnered with other independent restauranteurs in New Orleans and Florida to open several more locations; see https://www.felipestaqueria.com /katrina-10/.
10. Brush's account of Crema's closure at this meeting was consistent with his and others' comments in the press about the café's 2018 departure from the market. Kuschner, "Crema Café Will Say Goodbye"; Kendall and Schumer, "Crema Café to Leave Harvard Square."

11. In September of 2019, Brush announced Flat Patties was closing. In a news article at the time, he was quoted as saying, "I don't think it was our choice to close. If we had been able to continue the lease on the current terms, we would have stayed." Brush indicated that, in the case of Flat Patties, the decision to leave was due to rising rents not weak sales, but he said he understood the landlord's desire to maximize its revenue by finding a tenant who could pay higher rent than the burger joint could. Ellen Burstein and Sydnie Cobb, "Flat Patties Flips Out of Harvard Square," *Harvard Crimson*, September 19, 2019.

12. Deanna Pan, "Businesses Exiting, Talk of Mall-ification, Empty Stores. Some Fear What's Next for Harvard Square," *Boston Globe*, June 5, 2019.

13. "The Changing Face of Harvard Square," *Greater Boston*, hosted by Adam Reilly, WGBH TV, June 10, 2019, https://www.wgbh.org/news/local-news/2019/06/10/the-changing-face-of-harvard-square.

14. "New York Syndicate Buys Read Property," *Cambridge Chronicle*, February 14, 1920; "Transfer of Read Property to New York Syndicate," *Cambridge Chronicle*, March 20, 1920.

15. Multiple articles during this period reported on the property sale and subsequent rent increases, including: "Harvard Square Rents," *Cambridge Tribune*, April 10, 1920; "No Theatre Will Be Built on the Read Property," *Cambridge Chronicle*, April 10, 1920; untitled report of Wright & Ditson moving from Read Block properties on account of rent increase, *Cambridge Tribune*, April 17, 1920; "Local Merchants Are on the Move," *Cambridge Tribune*, May 8, 1920.

16. "James H. Wyeth Co. Has Determined to Go Out of Business," *Cambridge Tribune*, April 17, 1920.

17. "James H. Wyeth Co. Has Determined to Go Out of Business," *Cambridge Tribune*.

18. "Amee Brothers Are to Move June First," *Cambridge Chronicle*, May 8, 1920; "Amee Brothers Move After 50 Years' Stay," *Cambridge Tribune*, May 8, 1920.

19. "Amee Brothers Bookshop Now Only Memory to Harvard Men," *Boston Globe*, August 2, 1936.

20. "Amee Brothers Are to Move June First," *Cambridge Chronicle*.

21. Details and quotes from this meeting come primarily from "The Business Men Discuss Solution of Rent Problem at Their Annual Meeting," *Cambridge Tribune*, April 17, 1920. In the early years of the Harvard Square Business Men's Association, the *Cambridge Tribune* regularly published comprehensive minutes of the association's meetings. For this general time period, I also consulted the Harvard Square Business Association Collection (HSBA Collection) and the George Wright Collection, Courtesy of CHS, Cambridge, Massachusetts.

22. As was true in many parts of the United States, during the 1920s and 1930s there was debate about the value and meaning of chain stores in Harvard Square. Some individuals like Hadley saw chains as a healthy part of market evolution and development—a mark of progress and sign that Harvard Square must be "on the map" if sophisticated modern establishments wanted to locate there. Those who remained skeptical of chain stores were, at times, even mocked by chain-store advocates for their narrow-mindedness. In 1920, for example, someone submitted a fictionalized skit to the *Cambridge Tribune* titled "What Is the Matter with Harvard Square?" In it a woman complains about a new chain grocery store in the Square saying, "if those colors are not the worst you ever saw" and "I think it is a disgrace and an insult to put such a thing next to a real nice grocery store." Her male interlocutor responds in

a patronizing tone, noting that she is wrong to be skeptical: the chain "is bound to be one of the great booms which Harvard Square has seen for years," he says, explaining that chains like it are popular and will attract many new shoppers to the marketplace. "What Is the Matter with Harvard Square," *Cambridge Tribune*, March 13, 1920. For a discussion of chain-store debate across the United States during this period, see Paul Ingram and Hayagreeva Rao, "Store Wars: The Enactment and Repeal of Anti-Chain -Store Legislation in America," *American Journal of Sociology* 110, no. 2 (September 2004): 446–87.

23. That new building would be one of the ones causing heartache almost one hundred years later. The family trusts of those early twentieth-century developers held onto it until 2017 when finally they sold it to Corcoran and Brush's new landlord.

24. "Passing of Famous Rendezvous of Harvard Students," *Boston Herald*, August 2, 1936.

25. "Amee Brothers Bookshop Now Only Memory," *Boston Globe*.

26. "A Change in Harvard Square," *Cambridge Tribune*, August 7, 1936.

27. Frederic Olsson, "Our Historian Looks Back Forty Years," Harvard Square Business Men's Association Anniversary Meeting Program, CHS, HSBA Collection, Cambridge, Massachusetts.

28. Robert Reinhold, "Holiday Inn Near Kennedy Library Fought," *New York Times*, September 27, 1972.

29. Dick Swanson, "Harvard Square Task Force Appointed by Corcoran," *Cambridge Chronicle*, March 30, 1972; Memorandum of John Corcoran, "Message from City Manager to the Harvard Square Development Task Force," March 28, 1972, CHC, File "Harvard Square Study, Dept. P&D, Task Force, etc. 1972," Box "Harvard Square Planning Studies."

30. Elizabeth Samuels, "Harvard Square," *Harvard Crimson*, July 3, 1972.

31. Paul Hirshson, "Harvard Square Losing Funky Look," *Boston Globe*, August 25, 1987.

32. Paul Hirshson, "The Death of Harvard Square or Maybe It's a Rebirth in Brick. The Debate Rages On," *Boston Globe*, December 6, 1987.

33. Hirshson, "Death of Harvard Square."

34. Lisa Kocian, "Living in the Shadows of Giants," *Cambridge Chronicle*, March 15, 2000.

35. Kocian, "Living in the Shadows of Giants."

36. Steve LeBlanc, "Denizens Decry Harvard Square Decline. High Rents, Chains Drive Out Tenants," Associated Press, December 28, 2005.

37. Ann Downer, *Hatching Magic* (New York: Atheneum, 2003), 60.

38. John Hawkinson, "Forced Closing of Crimson Corner for Pizza Typifies Churn of Harvard Square," *Cambridge Day*, January 4, 2017, https://www.cambridgeday.com /2017/01/04/forced-closing-of-crimson-corner-for-pizza-typifies-churn-of-harvard-square -business/.

39. Tim Logan, "A Mall in Harvard Square? Not if Some Neighbors Get Their Way," *Boston Globe*, December 21, 2016. Another example of this contemporary reflexivity came when I was given the opportunity to describe my research agenda at a Harvard Square Business Association board meeting. When I explained that one of my emerging research questions was "Why has Harvard Square *always* been 'not what it used to be,'" my phrasing of the puzzle drew a knowing laugh from the membership, resonating so much that the board's president made sure the secretary entered my research question into their board meeting minutes. (And, in a subsequent meeting's review of those minutes, the board president made sure the record was corrected when he noticed the secretary had inadvertently recorded the phrase incorrectly the

first time.) After that first meeting, my research question and the tag line "always not what it used to be" became a popular phrase the Business Association and others picked up and used when discussing changes in the Square, including in the press. Denise Jillson, executive director of the Business Association, put my research question on a set of mugs to present to me at the association's March 6, 2020, annual meeting, which was attended by several hundred individuals, including local officials, business owners, and residents. When the local TV show *Chronicle* ran its next segment on whether Harvard Square was losing its character in the face of national chains and rising rents, the show's host profiled a set of the mugs Jillson had kept to display in the association's offices, and, against that backdrop, the host admitted that the *Chronicle* staff had looked back and discovered their own show had run similar segments on the Square's demise in both 1998 and 2015 ("Is Harvard Square at a Tipping Point," *Chronicle*, WCVB TV, May 18, 2020).

40. Hirshson, "Death of Harvard Square."

3. THE TIMES THEY ARE (ALWAYS) A-CHANGIN'

1. A description of the house's architecture and history can be found in Sarah Zimmerman, *Landmark Designation Study Report* (Cambridge, MA: CHC, 1988).
2. A blacksmith by the name of Torrey Hancock built the house and forge at 54 Brattle Street in 1808 and sold them to Pratt in 1827. Zimmerman, *Landmark Designation Study Report*; Susan E. Maycock and Charles M. Sullivan, *Building Old Cambridge: Architecture and Development* (Cambridge, MA: MIT Press, 2016), 180–84.
3. Maycock and Sullivan, 183–84; "Nelson Buys Property at 52 Brattle Street," *Cambridge Chronicle*, June 9, 1949. For the list of businesses of this address, I consulted: Cambridge City Directories (1954–1972), Cambridge Room, CPL; HSBA "Guide to Harvard Square" maps, 1995–2018, Hedberg Maps (Minneapolis, MN) with research assistance from InCase, LLC (Minneapolis, MN); as well as advertisements for businesses at this address run in the *Cambridge Chronicle*, for example a December 3, 1959, ad for Coolidge Cleansers and a May 23, 1968, ad for an auction of stock from The Versailles antique shop.
4. References to the tree's fate appear in multiple places, including: Nicholas Basbanes, *Crosses of Snow: A Life of Henry Wadsworth Longfellow* (New York: Knopf, 2020), 308; Maycock and Sullivan, *Building Old Cambridge*, 256; "Under a Spreading Chestnut Tree: The Village Smith Stands," A Cambridge Room Exhibit, CPL, https://thecambridgeroom.wordpress.com/2013/08/30/under-a-spreading-chestnut-tree-a-cambridge-room-exhibition/.
5. Details of Mary Walker's life are drawn from Sydney Nathans's fascinating biography of her, *To Free a Family: The Journey of Mary Walker* (Cambridge, MA: Harvard University Press, 2012).
6. According to Nathans's *To Free a Family*, Walker was a light-skinned woman, as were a number of slaves on that North Carolina plantation. She worked as a domestic servant inside the plantation owner's house, learning to read and write when accompanying his daughters to their lessons. But hers was, of course, a very different life than theirs. At age fourteen she gave birth to her first child, a fair-skinned, blue-eyed, freckled boy, the father of which Nathans was not able to confirm. Nathans speculates that Walker escaped after having a dispute with the plantation owner and mounting

threats from him to separate her from her family. In Massachusetts, a local family offered her refuge and work when she first arrived, and she immediately began trying to free her mother and three children who remained enslaved on the North Carolina plantation. Each attempt ended in heartbreak, and she was only reunited with her two youngest children after the Civil War, her mother having died in the interim, and her eldest having made his own escape years earlier. *To Free a Family*, chapter 1 (on Walker's early life and her escape, in particular pp. 16–18, 27–28), chapters 2 and 3 (on her arrival and life in Cambridge), chapters 4–10 (on her multiple attempts to free her family), and chapter 11 (on her reunion with her children and the family's life in Cambridge).

7. According to Nathans, Walker enlisted the aid of a prominent Boston broker for whose aunt Walker had served as caretaker. He purchased the property and then immediately deeded it to her. Because of the rule against perpetuity, Walker could not bind all future generations of her family from selling the property, but she was able to put it in trust until her youngest living relative reached maturity. *To Free a Family*, 239, 247.

8. "Cock Horse Tea Room at Blacksmith House: Frances D. Gage, a Kentucky Gentlewoman, Lover of Antiques, Its Founder," *Cambridge Tribune*, March 31, 1923. Additional details on Gage and the Cock Horse come from: "Jarvis Field House," *Cambridge Tribune*, December 31, 1904; "Circling the Square: The Cock Horse," *Harvard Crimson*, June 19, 1941. It is interesting to note that modern Gage displayed a fondness for the past—or at least recognized the marketing value of nostalgia: she filled her restaurant with antiques of all kinds, including brass tea kettles, candlesticks, and high-backed mahogany rockers, and reports at the time suggest customers appreciated the décor for its old-timey charm.

9. "The Cock Horse Changes Ownership," *Cambridge Chronicle*, August 22, 1930; "Cock Horse Inn Changes Owners," *Cambridge Chronicle*, November 9, 1939.

10. "Wants Bigger Space to Feed Navy and Waves," *Cambridge Chronicle*, March 11, 1943. For the sale to these new owners, see "The Cock Horse Purchased by the Duguids," *Cambridge Chronicle*, February 4, 1943.

11. Details on the Window Shop are drawn from Ellen Miller, Ile Heyman, and Dorothy Dahl, *The Window Shop: Safe Harbor for Refugees* (New York: iUniverse, 2006). I also consulted news articles written about the Window Shop during its tenure in the Square, including: Frances Burns, "10-Year-Old Window Shop Finds New Folk to Help," *Boston Globe*, May 14, 1949; "Refugees' Training Ground," *Boston Globe*, July 3, 1949; Dorothy Crandall, "Refugees Mold Futures in Cambridge Workshop," *Boston Globe*, July 14, 1957.

12. Miller et al., *Window Shop*; Ellen Goodman, "Curtain Falls for Window Shop," *Boston Globe*, December 27, 1972.

13. "The Cambridge Center for Adult Education, Est. 1871," prepared by Gavin Kleespies and Katie MacDonald, CHS, http://harvardsquare.com/History/Glimpses/The-Cambridge-Center-for-Adult-Education.aspx.

14. Personal communication with Hi Rise Bread Company staff, December 22, 2021; see also "Hi-Rise Bread Company in Cambridge Closing Brattle Street Location, Opening on Mass. Ave," *Boston Restaurant Talk*, March 14, 2011, https://bostonrestaurants .blogspot.com/2011/03/hi-rise-bread-company-may-be-opening-on.html.

15. The Longfellow at Alden and Harlow, online menu as of January 2021.

16. Maycock and Sullivan, *Building Old Cambridge*, 47.

17. While sitting on the corner of our block, Amee's address was 1380 Massachusetts Avenue (the street its entrance faced) according to the 1905 Cambridge Directory. Later directories (e.g., 1919) list its address as just "Harvard Square," in reference to its central location and address conventions at the time. Because of both address conventions over the years and the way the three streets intersect, some of the businesses located at the start of our block have not always had a JFK (Boylston) Street address, most notably those located in the 1380–1390 Mass Ave building on the corner. Because I rely primarily on business directories for ascertaining what businesses lay along this stretch of JFK Street at different times, however, most of the businesses I describe on the subsequent pages not only sat along this stretch to the naked eye, but also bore JFK/Boylston Street addresses during their lives.

18. In discussing the death and life of businesses, I'm drawing inspiration from Jane Jacobs's canonical work: Jane Jacobs, *The Death and Life of Great American Cities* (New York: Random House, 1961). More specifically, the idea of looking at one block over time—in addition to several of the specific examples of late twentieth-century businesses I discuss—owes a great debt of gratitude to Mo Lotman's photographic and oral history, *Harvard Square: An Illustrated History Since 1950* (New York: Stewart, Tabori & Chang, 2009). Lotman maps the businesses along multiple streets in the Square by decade, from the 1950s to early 2000s, offering photographic snapshots of the Square's commercial landscape as well as profiles of some of the iconic businesses from each era. To create as comprehensive a list as possible of the businesses located along this particular block of JFK Street since the turn of the twentieth century, I relied on the following sources: Cambridge City Directories (1890–1910, 1916, 1917, 1919, 1920, 1922, 1925, 1926–27, 1930, 1931, 1937, 1944, 1946, 1954, 1961, 1963, 1968, 1972), available through the Cambridge Room of the CPL as well as at the CHC; Lotman, *Harvard Square* (for the 1950s to early 2000s); HSBA "Guide to Harvard Square" maps (for 1995–2018); membership listings and minutes from the HSBA Collection, CHS, which extend back to the organization's founding in 1910; news articles and business advertisements in Cambridge newspapers starting in the early 1900s, accessed through the Cambridge Room, CPL; and annual editions of various twentieth-century circulars and publications such as the *Unofficial Guide to Life at Harvard* (Cambridge, MA: Harvard Student Agencies/Let's Go, Inc).

19. Arthur Stinchcombe, "Organizations and Social Structure," in *The Handbook of Organizations*, ed. James March (Chicago: Rand McNally, 1965), 142–93.

20. Details of Cardullo's life are drawn from his autobiography: Frank N. Cardullo, *Peeking Through the Hole of a Bagel or Behind a Hot Pastrami: The Life and Times of a Restauranteur*, as told to Elena Whiteside (n.p., 1990).

21. Cardullo, *Peeking Through the Hole of a Bagel*, 10.

22. Today, it is called "Cardullo's Gourmet Shoppe." The "Shoppe" seems to have been an old-timey flourish added sometime after the old days. References in the *Harvard Crimson* in the 1970s-90s also use "shop," suggesting this was not just a function of Cardullo narrating his autobiography to a scribe.

23. Maria Shao, "Landmark Wursthaus Closes Doors, Creditors Shut Down Harvard Square Eatery," *Boston Globe*, August 1, 1996.

24. In addition to profiles written in the local press at the time of the Wursthaus's closing, Lotman's *Harvard Square* offers a rich description of the restaurant and its cultural significance.

25. Sara Feijo, "Cardullo's Gourmet Shoppe Sold After Six Decades," *Wicked Local*, July 15, 2015, https://www.harvardsquare.com/cardullos-gourmet-shoppe-sold-after-six -decades/. Frances Cardullo was given the name Francis at birth and transitioned to Frances in the early 2000s. Although a number of the historical sources I draw upon in this book reference "Francis" or "Frank," I use Frances even when referring to events prior to the individual's transition, in keeping with guidance from LGBTQ advocacy groups.

26. Details of Rosen's life and Mandrake are drawn from the obituary of Irwin Rosen, "Irwin Rosen, 93, Harvard Bookshop Owner," *New York Times*, June 30, 1997.

27. Katharine Day, "Landlord Forces Stores to Move," *Harvard Crimson*, February 18, 1971.

28. Saskia Sassen, *The Global City* (Princeton, NJ: Princeton University Press, 1992) and *Cities in a World Economy* (Thousand Oaks, CA: Pine Forge Press, 1994); John Logan and Harvey Molotch, *Urban Fortunes: The Political Economy of Place* (Berkeley: University of California Press, 1987); Sharon Zukin, *The Innovation Complex: Cities, Tech and the New Economy* (New York: Oxford University Press, 2020).

29. Leases vary, of course. Some are structured with options to extend or renew the lease at its expiration date. These options can include pre-specified rent increases (e.g., tied to the Consumer Price Index), though more often they specify that the landlord and tenant will negotiate new terms (e.g., rent) at the time the option is exercised. Some leases specify that tenants show landlords regular financial statements and may include provisions that allow the landlord to cancel or void the option-to-extend or renew if business has slipped below some threshold.

30. Details on Bertha Cohen are drawn from: "Bertha E. Cohen," Cambridge Women's Heritage Project, https://www2.cambridgema.gov/historic/cwhp/bios_c.html#CohenB; "Mme. Bertha Cohen, Retail Milliner," *Women's Wear*, December 24, 1924; "Bertha Cohen, 67, Realty Financier: Woman Some Called 'Owner of Harvard Square' Dies," *New York Times*, February 3, 1965; "Bertha Cohen, Real Estate Tycoon, 67," *Boston Globe*, February 2, 1965; "Miss Cohen, Local Landlady Dies; Her Estate Is Valued at $20 Million," *Harvard Crimson*, February 3, 1965; Gail Perrin, "She Was Born Penniless . . . and Died a Multimillionaire: The Bertha Cohen Story," *Boston Globe*, February 7, 1965; Anthony Yudis, "Cambridge Firm Buys Late Bertha Cohen Estate," *Boston Globe*, October 24, 1970; "The Witch of Harvard," *Harvard Crimson*, December 2, 1970; Lotman, *Harvard Square*, 38, 81; Maycock and Sullivan, *Building Old Cambridge*, 152, 153.

31. Lotman, *Harvard Square*, 39.

32. "Miss Cohen, Local Landlady Dies," *Harvard Crimson*.

33. "Tenant Says That Wasserman Is Forcing Her Out of Business," *Harvard Crimson*, December 2, 1970; Day, "Landlord Forces Stores to Move"; "High Rents Force Stores from Square: Owners Blame Local Developer," *Harvard Crimson*, October 18, 1972; Maycock and Sullivan, *Building Old Cambridge*, 152; Lotman, *Harvard Square*, 38.

34. Robert Campbell, "Squeezing the Square: The Real Threat to Harvard Isn't Just Growth but the Danger It'll Become like Everywhere Else," *Boston Globe*, October 27, 1991.

35. John DiGiovanni, personal communication with author, April 6, 2021. DiGiovanni's family real estate business owned "the Garage" after Wasserman.

36. Maycock and Sullivan, *Building Old Cambridge*, 149. Maycock and Sullivan date the eviction in 1948. News articles from this period suggest some of the businesses did not vacate until 1949.

37. Day, "Landlord Forces Stores to Move"; "Charlesbank Trust Opens Harvard Square Branch," *Cambridge Chronicle*, May 20, 1971.

38. Cambridge City Atlases (1873, 1886, 1894, 1903) available at the CHC show stables extending from Brattle Street to JFK Street during this period. Maycock and Sullivan discuss these stables and the subsequent sale and redevelopment of that land in the early 1900s. *Building Old Cambridge*, 137.

39. Cambridge City Directories (1926, 1930). Maycock and Sullivan provide a history of the garage property: *Building Old Cambridge*, 133, 147.

40. Maycock and Sullivan, *Building Old Cambridge*, 147.

41. Joseph Schumpeter, *Capitalism, Socialism and Democracy* (1942; repr., New York: HarperCollins, 2008), 87.

42. Cambridge City Directories (1919, 1926). "Tailor Brennan Moves," *Cambridge Chronicle*, September 23, 1916; "Oldest Tailor in Harvard Square," *Cambridge Tribune*, September 17, 1937; Obituary of John J. Taylor, *Cambridge Chronicle*, November 23, 1944; "Harvard Tailor Dies: William Brennan Made Clothes for Two U.S. Presidents," *New York Times*, November 16, 1944. (It is unclear why the *Times* lists Brennan's first name as William, but the paper is clearly describing the same individual as the Cambridge papers.) Shoe-makers such as Patrick "Pat" Toohy were also common fixtures in the marketplace in those days. Toohy was born in Cork, Ireland, learned shoemaking in a London bootery, and then came to Cambridge in his twenties and opened up shop in Harvard Square making shoes-to-order: "Pat Toohy, King of Harvard Square Shoe Makers, Passes—Was Harvard Institution for Many Years," *Cambridge Chronicle*, April 18, 1946.

43. "Corcoran's Plans Branch Store in Harvard Square," *Cambridge Chronicle*, January 28, 1949. For Corcoran's earlier history, see "J.H. Corcoran Company Planning a New Store," *Cambridge Chronicle*, October 26, 1939.

44. "Harvard Square Going Out of Business: Corcoran's, Valeteria Are Closing This Week," *Boston Globe*, December 25, 1987; "Corcoran's to Relinquish Space to Urban Outfitters: Century Old Notions Give Way to New Age Dinosaurs," *Harvard Crimson*, December 15, 1987; Eliot Spalding, "Corcoran's to Close Harvard Square Store," *Cambridge Chronicle*, November 26, 1987.

45. Entry for Urban Outfitters, Inc., *Reference For Business*, Company Histories, https://www.referenceforbusiness.com/history/Ul-Vi/Urban-Outfitters-Inc.html, accessed December 23, 2021.

46. Cambridge City Directories (1919, 1920). Charles Lowry took over his brother James's business shortly after it opened and ran it for the next thirty years: "Charles F. Lowry, Veteran Optician Dies Here at 59," *Cambridge Chronicle*, May 7, 1953.

47. Alison Steinbach, "Warby Parker Eyewear to Open in Square," *Harvard Crimson*, September 27, 2017.

48. Lotman contains a nice discussion of this change and of Billings & Stover's overall evolution from which this paragraph draws. *Harvard Square*, 114. For more on the history of Billings & Stover, see: "Circling the Square: The Complete Apothecary," *Harvard Crimson*, October 15, 1940; "Billings and Stover: Leeches, Bleaches, and Drugs," *Harvard Crimson*, April 21, 1948; Eugenia B. Schraa, "After 140 Years, Sad Farewells," *Harvard Crimson*, February 15, 2002.

49. Pam Wasserstein, "Our Town: Do the Time Warp Again," *Harvard Crimson*, February 20, 1998.

50. Raghu Dhara and Samuel Vasquez, "New 24-Hour CVS to Open in April, Replacing Existing JFK Location," *Harvard Crimson*, January 27, 2015.

51. Lotman, *Harvard Square*, 125.

52. The Cambridge City Directories show Discount Records appearing in 1972 at the address where Western Union had been through at least the 1968 directory.

53. "National Chains Drive Out Discount Records," *Harvard Crimson*, March 11, 1996; Jennifer Burns, "Strawberries Closes Harvard Square Store," *Harvard Crimson*, February 26, 1997.

54. Cambridge City Directories (1890–1972); Melissa Hart, "No Bookstore Is the Same," *Harvard Crimson*, June 26, 1989.

55. The number of bookstores in Harvard Square was a fascination for some. See, for example, Lewis Burke Frumkes, "Shoppers World: At Cambridge, Bookstores in Volume," *New York Times*, May 7, 1989. In the 1980s and '90s, the *Harvard Crimson* also ran frequent pieces detailing the different focus and atmosphere of the Square's various bookshops; e.g., Paul Evans, "Whole Lotta Books," June 24, 1984; Charles Matthew, "Cambridge Stacks," June 23, 1985; Melissa Hart, "No Bookstore Is the Same," June 26, 1989; Joanna Weiss, "Bookstores Draw Bargain-Hunters and Browsers to Harvard Square," June 27, 1992. As of 1987, the *Boston Globe* put the number of bookstores at twenty-six ("Death of Harvard Square," December 6, 1987).

56. Maycock and Sullivan, *Building Old Cambridge*, 158. Amazon's list was publicized in Richard Florida, "The 20 Best-Read Cities in America," *The Atlantic*, May 27, 2011, https://www.theatlantic.com/entertainment/archive/2011/05/the-20-best-read-cities -in-america/239546/.

57. Sweetgreen's business model has been featured in the business press numerous times since its founding, including: Amy Farley, "The Winner of the Fast-Casual Salad Wars? Sweetgreen," *Fast Company*, February 19, 2019, https://www.fastcompany .com/90298904/sweetgreen-most-innovative-companies-2019; Eric Johnson, "Why Sweetgreen Thinks like a Tech Company," *Recode*, December 17, 2018, https://www.vox .com/2018/12/17/18144250/sweetgreen-jonathan-neman-fast-food-salad-delivery -blockchain-kara-swisher-decode-podcast.

58. In 2019, it raised another $150 million in institutional capital (Katie Roof, "Salad Chain Sweetgreen's Tech Focus Helps Push Valuation to $1.6 billion," *Wall Street Journal*, September 29, 2019), and in 2021 it went public (Chloe Sorvino, "Investors Feast on Sweetgreen IPO," *Forbes*, November 18, 2021, https://www.forbes.com/sites/chloesorvino/2021/11 /18/investors-feast-on-sweetgreen-ipo/?sh=2e4a307d2480).

59. Because of building demolitions and renovations as well as changing address conventions through the years, I refer here to establishments listed in the old Cambridge Directories as residing at or near Sweetgreen's current location on this end of the block.

60. Charlotte Silver, *Charlotte au Chocolat: Memories of a Restaurant Girlhood* (New York: Riverhead Books, 2012), has a nice discussion of the Square's changing restaurant landscape during this period.

61. Diane White, "Harvard Square Cafeterias: And Then There Was One," *Boston Globe*, June 28, 1984. The closing of Elsie's Sandwich Shop, which had served roast beef sandwiches on Mount Auburn Street for thirty years, was one of the notable closures in the 1990s. Andrew Green, "Landmark Elsie's Sandwich Shop Closes," *Harvard Crimson*, January 6, 1995.

62. King's first opened at 39 or 41 JFK Street, depending on which source you consult (the Cambridge City Directories or the *Cambridge Chronicle*). In 1947, it moved to 30 JFK Street where it seems to have stayed until it closed in 1969: "Moving-Time

for Several Harvard Square Stores," *Cambridge Chronicle*, Mach 13, 1947; Gene Goltz, "Landmark Men's Bar Dries Up," *Harvard Crimson*, February 11, 1970.

63. Goltz, "Landmark Men's Bar Dries Up."

64. Matthew DeShaw, "Square Abuzz with Entry of Good Vibrations Sex Shop," *Harvard Crimson*, February 16, 2017.

65. Carol Queen, "In Memoriam: Joani Blank," goodvibesblog.com, August 9, 2016, https://www.goodvibes.com/s/about/, https://goodvibesblog.com/memoriam-joani-blank/.

66. Lotman, *Harvard Square*, 21. For Varsity Liquor's founding story and history, see also Gawain Kripke, "We Need a Square Deal," *Harvard Crimson*, May 27, 1988.

67. Letter to members signed Pebble Gifford, May 1983, Harvard Square Defense Fund Collection (HSDF Collection), Courtesy of CHS. As one might imagine, the attempt to limit alcohol in the Square caught students' attention and was covered by *Crimson* reporters in articles such as Daniel Wroblewski, "All This for a Pint O'Beer," *Harvard Crimson*, September 23, 1985.

68. As testament to how morally contested some products can be as well as the role of evolving cultural beliefs, a JFK Street landlord tried to prevent this medical marijuana dispensary from opening near his property by filing a RICO lawsuit against the dispensary's owners. That suit resulted in a financial settlement for the landlord, which ultimately led to the sale of the medical dispensary. Later, however, this same landlord changed his mind on the topic and leased his own ground-floor retail space to a Cookies Cannabis franchise. This time, his decision met opposition from residents, who opposed a recreational cannabis shop in that location. For coverage of these events, see Marc Levy, "Owner of Crimson Galeria Has Cannabis Tenant After a Lawsuit Saying Pot Made 'Bad Neighbors,'" *Cambridge Day*, August 27, 2020, https://www.cambridgeday.com/2020/08/27/owner-of-crimson-galeria-has-cannabis-tenant-after-a-lawsuit-saying-pot-made-bad-neighbors/; Marc Levy, "Mixed Reception for Cookie Pot Shop Proposal, Complicated by Landlord's History of Opposition," *Cambridge Day*, August 28, 2020; Dan Adams, "After Landlord's Change of Heart, West Coast Marijuana Brand Cookies Could Land in Harvard Square," *Boston Globe*, September 1, 2020.

69. City of Cambridge Planning Board Notice of Decision, Case Number 352, January 29, 2020, https://www.cambridgema.gov/-/media/Files/CDD/ZoningDevel/Special Permits/sp352/sp352_decision_20200129.pdf.

70. Goltz, "Landmark Men's Bar Dries Up."

71. The 1926 Cambridge Directory, for example, lists the barbers Raffaele Catalano, Thomas Day, Anthony Spadafora, and Alfonso Demerino at an address just a few doors down from Sweetgreen's current location.

72. "Barbers Hard Hit by Long Hair," *Harvard Crimson*, March 19, 1968; William Fripp, "Dis-Tressed? Long Hair Closes Harvard Barber Shop," *Boston Globe*, June 2, 1968; Jacquin Sanders, "Barber Trimmed by Longhair Trend," *Boston Globe*, November 1, 1970.

73. Richard Ray, "Harvard Sq. Businesses Adjust to New Clientele as Long, Hot Summer Ends," *Boston Globe*, August 30, 1970.

74. Lotman, *Harvard Square*, 19.

75. Johnson, "Why Sweetgreen Thinks like a Tech Company."

76. Sharon Zukin, *Naked City: The Death and Life of Authentic Urban Places* (New York: Oxford University Press, 2010), 7.

77. Maycock and Sullivan, *Building Old Cambridge*, 61.

78. The persistence of the Death Discourse over the past one hundred years also suggests changes in the marketplace cannot be fully explained by gentrification at any one particular time.

79. This paragraph's discussion of Harvard Square's early twentieth-century gentrification is drawn from Maycock and Sullivan, *Building Old Cambridge*, 128–31.

80. 1913 report, *Future Development of Harvard Square and Its Neighborhood*, quoted in Maycock and Sullivan, *Building Old Cambridge*, 143, and reviewed by the author in the HSBA Collection, CHS.

81. Demographic data on Harvard Square is tracked and regularly updated by the Harvard Square Business Association, https://www.harvardsquare.com/about-harvard-square /demographic-data/.

82. Victoria Hallett, "Cell Phone Sales Spike in Square," *Harvard Crimson*, September 4, 2001; Imtiyaz Delawala and Andrew Holbrook, "Taking Care of Square Business: While Cell Phone Stores Sprouted, Mom-and-Pops Folded—and Even Chains Found They Couldn't Sell," *Harvard Crimson*, June 5, 2003.

83. I observed a November 18, 2019, meeting at the Harvard Square Business Association offices, which included representatives of the Business Association and the Harvard Square Neighborhood Association. Both groups supported the proposed amendment to limit street-level frontage of banks. The landlord expressed concern to the two groups' leaders that, if passed, the amendment would scuttle his plans to rent to a commercial bank on JFK Street. He later leased the space to Cookies, a recreational cannabis dispensary.

84. Maycock and Sullivan, *Building Old Cambridge*, 137.

85. Maycock and Sullivan, *Building Old Cambridge*, 144.

86. Lotman, *Harvard Square*, 131.

87. "J.H. Wyeth & Co in a New Store," *Cambridge Chronicle*, December 3, 1898.

88. In fact, it is somewhat hard to figure out which specific businesses were felled by the Depression because the City of Cambridge did not publish its directories as regularly during those years on account of its own fiscal constraints and a sharp fall-off in advertising revenue for the directories.

89. Vidya Viswanathan, "Z Square Café Shuts Its Doors," *Harvard Crimson*, January 30, 2009.

90. "Passing of Famous Rendezvous of Harvard Students," *Boston Herald*, August 2, 1936.

91. Miller et al., *Window Shop*, 88.

92. "Under a Spreading Chestnut Tree: The Village Smith Stands," A Cambridge Room Exhibit, CPL, https://thecambridgeroom.wordpress.com/2013/08/30/under-a-spreading -chestnut-tree-a-cambridge-room-exhibition/, accessed May 26, 2022.

93. Henry Wadsworth Longfellow, "From My Arm-Chair," available online from the Maine Historical Society, https://www.hwlongfellow.org/poems_poem.php?pid=267, accessed May 26, 2022.

4. A TRICKY RELATIONSHIP

1. See, for example: David Grazian, *Blue Chicago: The Search for Authenticity in Urban Blues Clubs* (Chicago: University of Chicago Press, 2003); Sharon Zukin, *Naked City: The Death and Life of Authentic Urban Places* (New York: Oxford University Press, 2010).

2. "Passing of a Cambridge Institution," *Cambridge Tribune*, April 17, 1920.
3. "A Change in Harvard Square," *Cambridge Tribune*, August 7, 1936. By the time it closed, Amee Brothers had relocated from the corner of JFK Street and Mass Ave to 21 Brattle Street, but that was still "just around the corner" from our block given the street geography.
4. Anthony Giddens, *The Constitution of Society* (1984; repr. Berkeley: University of California Press, 1991), xxiii.
5. In *The Structure of Sociological Theory*, Jonathon Turner helpfully extracts these mechanisms from Giddens's dense text. Jonathan Turner, *The Structure of Sociological Theory*, 7th ed. (Belmont, CA: Wadsworth/Thomson Learning, 2003), 485–87.
6. Emile Durkheim, *The Elementary Forms of Religious Life*, trans. Karen E. Fields (1912; repr. New York: Free Press, 1995). Durkheim and others have argued that these sorts of religious events and cultural rituals take on a sacred status, in part, because they are set apart from and kept distinct from the more mundane—more profane—everyday routines of market life, such as hunting, gathering, transacting, etc. As this book goes on, we will find we need to reconsider this long-accepted dichotomy: because many of the sacred ties we forge with one another are forged in our everyday market lives, the supposedly profane market can *itself* become a sacred object to us.
7. See, for instance: Thomas Gieryn, "A Space for Place in Sociology," *Annual Review of Sociology* 26 (2000): 463–96. In his insightful article, Gieryn discusses the concept of "place attachment," and how the emotional bonds people form with particular physical places (e.g., neighborhoods) can facilitate a sense of security and well-being, define group boundaries, and stabilize memories. He also discusses the loss of meaning people can feel when being displaced or when watching a sacred place be desecrated. The canonical example Gieryn uses of "place" is the pseudonymous English village of Childerley, featured in Michael Mayerfeld Bell's *Childerley: Nature and Morality in a Country Village* (Chicago: University of Chicago Press, 1994). Gieryn, like Bell, identifies Childerley's Horse & Hound pub as a part of the village's social and cultural milieu along with multiple other aspects of village life. However, both authors are focused on the overall meanings of place, and the commercial market in the place is outside the scope of their inquiries; neither attempts to theorize the market's broader role.
8. Cultural sociologist Ann Swidler distinguishes "settled" from "unsettled" settings and periods, noting that in unsettled times, once-taken-for-granted understandings and meanings are exposed and destabilized. Ann Swidler, "Culture in Action: Symbols and Strategies," *American Sociological Review* 51, no. 2 (April 1986): 273–86. The previous chapter suggested that markets may be thought of as continually unsettled settings.
9. In his discussion of ontological security, Giddens draws on *The Informed Heart* by Bruno Bettelheim. Bettelheim describes his experiences as a prisoner at Dachau and Buchenwald, including the radical ontological insecurity inflicted by the guards' erratic disruption of prisoners' routines and the resulting dissolution of any orderly, predictable unfolding of life for them. Giddens, *Constitution of Society*, 62.
10. Kotelly's landlord at that time, Colliers International, announced it was offering Kotelly an alternative location one day after the *Globe* reported that Colliers was forcing Crimson Corner out of its longtime home for a pizza chain. Kathleen Conti, "Harvard Square's Famous Crimson Corner Is Closing," *Boston Globe*, February 13,

2017; "Harvard Square Newsstand, on Verge of Eviction, Gets Offer for New Location," *Boston Globe*, February 14, 2017.

11. Jack Katz, "Pissed Off in L.A.," in *How Emotions Work* (Chicago: University of Chicago Press, 1999), 18–86.

5. CRAZY LOVE

1. Quotes from Susan Corcoran and other biographical details come from a four-hour interview held on March 20, 2019, as well as numerous follow-up conversations between Corcoran and the author (including in-person, telephone, and email communications).

2. Susan loved Joni Mitchell and played her music often in Black Ink. For me, this was another example of art imitating life, as I thought back to the film *You've Got Mail* in which the shopkeeper losing her store turned to the very same soulful singer-songwriter to process her feelings.

3. In this and the next paragraph, I am relying on Susan's description of her interactions with Asana. The account she provided me of those interactions was consistent with what she described at the March 3, 2019, Harvard Square Neighborhood Association public meeting, as well as what was reported in subsequent news articles about her store's closing—e.g., Ellen Burstein and Sydnie Cobb, "A Dark Blot in Harvard Square: Black Ink to Close," *Harvard Crimson*, September 9, 2019; Ellen Burstein and Sydnie Cobb, "Flat Patties Flips Out of Harvard Square," *Harvard Crimson*, September 19, 2019; Marc Levy, "Black Ink Closing Its Doors in Harvard Square After Rent Increase from Out-of-Town Landlord," *Cambridge Day*, September 5, 2019, https://www.cambridge day.com/2019/09/05/black-ink-closing-its-doors-in-harvard-square-after-rent -increase-from-out-of-town-landlord/; Dialynn Dwyer, "An 'Unsustainable' Rent Increase Is Forcing Black Ink to Close in Cambridge," boston.com, November 25, 2019, https://www.boston.com/news/business/2019/11/25/black-ink-closing-harvard -square-cambridge/; Dialynn Dwyer, "Black Ink Opens Its Doors for a Final Day of Business in Harvard Square," boston.com, December 31, 2019, https://www.boston .com/news/local-news/2019/12/31/last-day-business-black-ink-harvard-square/. Several of these articles indicated that reporters had tried to reach Asana Partners but that representatives of the firm could not be reached for comment. As part of my broader research on Harvard Square, I reached out to Asana, and the representative with whom I spoke asked not to be quoted on the record.

4. Quotes are from the Dear Asana Project. While the Dear Asana Project was under way, I made periodic visits to Black Ink to photograph the growing pile of messages. After her project was complete, Susan mailed some of the pages to Asana. However, there were so many by then that Susan hung on to a number herself, and she also gave me a large portfolio of them to store in my files and use in my research and analysis along with the more complete corpus I had photographed along the way.

5. Burstein and Cobb, "A Dark Blot in Harvard Square"; Dwyer, "An Unsustainable Rent Increase Is Forcing Black Ink to Close."

6. Viviana Zelizer, *Morals and Markets: The Development of Life Insurance in the United States* (New York: Columbia University Press, 1979).

7. Viviana Zelizer, *Pricing the Priceless Child: The Changing Social Value of Children* (Princeton, NJ: Princeton University Press, 1985); Viviana Zelizer, *The Purchase of*

Intimacy (Princeton, NJ: Princeton University Press, 2005); Keiran Healy, *Last Best Gifts: Altruism and the Market for Human Blood and Organs* (Chicago: University of Chicago Press, 2006); Arlie Hochschild, *The Commercialization of Intimate Life* (Berkeley: University of California Press, 2003); Rene Almeling, "Gender and the Medical Market in Genetic Material," *American Sociological Review* 72, no. 3 (2007): 319–40.

8. Alvin Roth, "Repugnance as a Constraint on Markets," *Journal of Economic Perspectives* 21, no. 3 (Summer 2007): 37–58.

9. Philip Tetlock, Orie Kristel, S. Beth Elson, et al., "The Psychology of the Unthinkable: Taboo Trade-Offs, Forbidden Base Rates, and Heretical Counterfactuals," *Journal of Personality and Social Psychology* 78, no. 5 (2000): 853–70. See also: Alan Page Fiske and Philip Tetlock, "Taboo Trade-Offs: Reactions to Transactions That Transgress the Spheres of Justice," *Political Psychology* 18, no. 2 (June 1997): 255–97; Philip Tetlock, "Coping with Trade-Offs: Psychological Constraints and Political Implications," in *Elements of Reason: Cognition, Choice, and the Bounds of Rationality*, ed. Arthur Luipa, Matthew McCubbins, and Samuel Popkin (Cambridge: Cambridge University Press, 2000), 239–63; Peter McGraw and Philip Tetlock, "Taboo Trade-Offs, Relational Framing, and the Acceptability of Exchanges," *Journal of Consumer Psychology* 15, no. 1 (2005): 2–15; Philip Tetlock, Barbara Mellers, and Peter Scoblic, "Sacred Versus Pseudo-Sacred Values: How People Cope with Taboo Trade-Offs," *American Economic Review: Papers & Proceedings* 107, no. 5 (2017): 96–99.

10. Mark Barabak, "Wealth and Struggle in a Liberal Bubble That Elizabeth Warren Calls Home," *Los Angeles Times*, February 7, 2020.

6. EVERYBODY GET TOGETHER

1. "Harvard Square Business Men," *Cambridge Chronicle*, March 19, 1910; "Soon to Organize: Business Men of Harvard Square Hold Preliminary Meeting—Very Encouraging Showing," *Cambridge Tribune*, March 19, 1910.

2. "Business Interests of Harvard Square District Will Be Advanced by a Proposed Organization—First Meeting," *Cambridge Tribune*, March 8, 1910.

3. "Soon to Organize," *Cambridge Tribune*.

4. "Soon to Organize," *Cambridge Tribune*.

5. The Citizens' Trade Association of Cambridge, Mass. 1893, Charter and By-Laws, George Wright Collection: Clubs, CHS, Cambridge, Massachusetts. The Citizens' Trade Association later became the Cambridge Board of Trade, and eventually the Cambridge Chamber of Commerce. Its founding and evolution are discussed in Robert Remer, "Chamber of Commerce Is Keeping Pace with Dynamic Growth of University City," *Cambridge Chronicle*, October 5, 1967.

6. Biographical details on Wright are drawn from primary materials reviewed by the author in the George Wright Collection, CHS (including personal essays, scrapbooks, and files pertaining to Wright's numerous group memberships, including the Harvard Square Business Men's Association and the Citizens' Trade Association), as well as the portrait of Wright's life presented by Stuart Crawford to the CHS on November 4, 1958: Stuart Crawford, "The George G. Wright Collection," *PCHS* 37 (1957–1958): 90–106. Descriptions of Wright's father's bakery and the marketplace of

Wright's early years appear in: Charles Eliot Norton, "Reminiscences of Old Cambridge," *PCHS* 1 (1905–1906): 11–23; Lois Lilley Howe, "Harvard Square in the 'Seventies and 'Eighties," *PCHS* 30 (1944): 11–27; and George Wright, "Gleanings from Early Cambridge Directories," *PCHS* 15 (1921): 30–40.

7. A photo of Wright appeared in "Harvard Square Merchants Alert," *Cambridge Chronicle*, March 25, 1911.

8. Wright's favorite was Lowell's 1854 essay, "Cambridge Thirty Years Ago."

9. Crawford, "George G. Wright Collection."

10. "Harvard Square Business Men Active," *Cambridge Sentinel*, April 30, 1910.

11. Debra Reynolds, "The Harvard Square Business Association: The Past Seventy-Five Years" (1985), available at the Harvard Square Business Association offices as well as in the HSBA Collection of the CHS. Reynolds's essay was prepared for the association's seventy-fifth anniversary, and it offers a valuable synopsis of the conditions just prior to the group's founding and its first seventy-five years. Because I draw upon many of the same primary sources as Reynolds (e.g., the association's annual reports as well as Cambridge newspapers held by the Cambridge Public Library), the history that follows dovetails with hers in places, and I checked my own interpretations of the primary materials against Reynolds's throughout, making it a particularly useful secondary source. Another good reference for early market conditions and the original impetus for the association's founding is the group's first advertising bulletin: "Bulletin of the Harvard Square Business Men's Association," Committee on Advertising, Harvard Square Business Men's Association (1911), https://live-harvard-square.pantheonsite.io/wp-content/uploads/2019/11/HSBMA-1911-Bulletin.pdf, accessed May 27, 2022.

12. "Harvard Square," *Cambridge Tribune*, October 23, 1909. According to this report, debris traveled "as high as the steeple of the First Parish Church."

13. "Italian Strikers Riot: Throw Sones and Injure Workmen in the Cambridge Subway," *New York Times*, April 2, 1910.

14. "Scenes at Harvard Square," *Cambridge Chronicle*, July 7, 1894. Also quoted in Susan E. Maycock and Charles M. Sullivan, *Building Old Cambridge: Architecture and Development* (Cambridge, MA: MIT Press, 2016), 141.

15. The difficulties surrounding credit were so great they were mentioned in the March 8, 1910, announcement inviting merchants to attend a meeting to discuss the formation of a Harvard Square business association.

16. The loss of business to Boston markets and the formation of the Boston Chamber of Commerce were also mentioned in that March 8, 1910, recruitment notice.

17. For this chapter's discussion of the association's early decades, the author reviewed all available annual reports and meeting minutes from 1911 to 1929 in the HSBA and George Wright Collections of the CHS.

18. "Report of the Credit Committee," April 16, 1912, *1912 Annual Report*, HSBA Collection, CHS.

19. "Bulletin of the Harvard Square Business Men's Association," Committee on Advertising.

20. "George Wright, President's Report, April 1914," *1914 Annual Report*, HSBA Collection, CHS; "New Lights Burn at Last," *Harvard Crimson*, March 23, 1914.

21. He wrote an essay on his graveyard strolls, which was eventually published in the *Cambridge Tribune*: "Country Graveyards Have Much of Interest Says George G. Wright," *Cambridge Tribune*, October 18, 1919.

22. *The Future Development of Harvard Square and Its Neighborhood* (1913), HSBA Collection, CHS.

23. "George Wright, President's Report, April 1911," *1911 Annual Report*, HSBA Collection, CHS.

24. A number of these dinners were reported in the local papers in articles such as "Harvard Square Merchants Alert," *Cambridge Chronicle*, March 25, 1911. They are also described in the association's annual reports and meeting minutes through the decades.

25. "Harvard Square Business," *Cambridge Tribune*, July 9, 1910.

26. "Business Men Dine and Talk," *Cambridge Chronicle*, November 9, 1910.

27. Remarks of George Wright, 1911, George Wright Collection (Clubs-HSBA-Internal), CHS. A portion of his remarks were also reprinted in "Harvard Square Merchants Alert," *Cambridge Chronicle*.

28. "George Wright, President's Report," *1911 Annual Report*. My review of his personal collection suggests that Wright's prepared remarks often became the basis for his written annual reports.

29. "Business Men's Association," *Cambridge Tribune*, June 18, 1910.

30. Wright's and several others' frustration on this point bubbles up throughout the 1911–1915 annual reports.

31. "George Wright, President's Report," *1911 Annual Report*.

32. "George Wright, President's Report, April 1912," *1912 Annual Report*, HSBA Collection, CHS.

33. "Women Confer with Harvard Sq. Merchants," *Cambridge Chronicle*, May 11, 1912; "To Boom Harvard Square," *Cambridge Tribune*, May 11, 1912.

34. "Trading in Harvard Square from the Women's Point of View" (1912), HSBA Collection, CHS.

35. In this paragraph and the next, all quotes are drawn from "Trading in Harvard Square from the Women's Point of View" (1912), which includes extensive quotations recorded during the women's luncheon.

36. "Quips & Quirks," *Cambridge Chronicle*, June 8, 1912; "Dollar Day Will Be Monday," *Cambridge Chronicle*, September 16, 1916.

37. "Discount Stamps: Proposal of F. A. Olsson Will Be Considered by Harvard Square Business Men's Association," *Cambridge Tribune*, February 6, 1915; "The Business Men: How the Discount Coupon Plan Is Regarded," *Cambridge Tribune*, June 12, 1915; "Profit-Sharing Coupons of the Harvard Square Business Men's Association," advertisement of the Harvard Square Business Men's Association, *Cambridge Tribune*, October 23, 1915.

38. "George Wright, President's Report," *1914 Annual Report*.

39. "Fred Olsson, Committee on Advertising, April 1915," *1915 Annual Report*, HSBA Collection, CHS.

40. Olsson's window display competition is mentioned in "George Wright, President's Report, April 1915," *1915 Annual Report*, HSBA Collection, CHS.

41. Olsson's photo appears in "Mr. Burnstead Says," *Cambridge Tribune*, February 22, 1919.

42. "In Night Robe: Thus Clad, F. A. Olsson Fled from Home," *Boston Globe*, September 21, 1900.

43. "Married," *Cambridge Chronicle*, January 4, 1902.

44. His father's obituary mentions Fred's 1906 departure from the firm to start his own shop: Obituary of John F. Olsson, *Cambridge Tribune*, January 9, 1915.

45. "Pardon Me, But Can You Tell Me Where Mr. Smith Lives?," *Cambridge Tribune*, January 30, 1915. Olsson's father died on January 8, 1915: Death Notice of John F. Olsson, *Cambridge Chronicle*, January 9, 1915; Obituary of John F. Olsson, *Cambridge Tribune*.

46. "Stand for Sex Equality," *Cambridge Tribune*, June 5, 1915; "They Say Women Now Allowed," *Cambridge Chronicle*, June 5, 1915.

47. "After Their First at Home," *Cambridge Tribune*, February 20, 1915. Fred Olsson had run ads like this, instructing shoppers to pay attention to the initials and shop at F. A. Olsson's—and presumably not J. F. Olsson's—before his father's death, and he kept up the practice afterward.

48. "John Amee, President's Report 1917–1918, April 1918," *1918 Annual Report*, HSBA Collection, CHS.

49. "J. Lee Robinson, Secretary's Report, April 1918," *1918 Annual Report*, HSBA Collection, CHS.

50. "George Wright, Committee on Municipal Affairs, April 1919," *1919 Annual Report*, HSBA Collection, CHS.

51. For description of the flu outbreak in Cambridge, including business and school closures, see: "Board of Health and Influenza: Local Health Authorities Are Exerting Every Effort Possible to Control the Disease," *Cambridge Chronicle*, September 28, 1918; "Grippe Epidemic Closes Schools," *Cambridge Chronicle*, September 28, 1918; "Mayor Quinn Acts to Check Influenza," *Cambridge Chronicle*, September 28, 1918; "Epidemic Has a Firm Hold," *Cambridge Chronicle*, October 5, 1918; "Fighting the Plague," *Cambridge Sentinel*, October 5, 1918; "Liberty Loan Work Impeded: Influenza Causes Canvassing to Progress Very Slowly," *Cambridge Chronicle*, October 5, 1918; "How Cambridge Is Fighting the Grippe," *Cambridge Chronicle*, October 12, 1918. In late October 1918, the *Cambridge Chronicle* optimistically declared the outbreak over: "Epidemic at End," *Cambridge Chronicle*, October 26, 1918. The Harvard Square Business Men's Association resumed their dinners by December of that year: "Business Men Meet," *Cambridge Sentinel*, December 7, 1918. However, as of January of the next year, the *Harvard Crimson* reported that, even though the situation had improved since the fall, it remained serious. The *Crimson* advised readers to don "proper clothing" (which may have entailed masks; photos of Harvard football games during the fall and winter show masked spectators) and to avoid streetcars, churches, and theaters: Marshall Henry Bailey, "Influenza Epidemic Kept Well Under Control Here," *Harvard Crimson*, January 8, 1919. For a history of the 1918–1919 pandemic in Cambridge that was prepared amidst the 2020 coronavirus pandemic: "The Influenza Epidemic of 1918–1919 in Cambridge," *Cambridge Life* (Fall 2020) [a publication of the City of Cambridge, Massachusetts].

52. Obituary of Harold S. Moore, *Cambridge Chronicle*, December 21, 1918.

53. "Cameron & Knowles Succeed Moore & Hadley," *Cambridge Tribune*, March 22, 1919.

54. "J. Lee Robinson, Report of the Secretary, April 1919," *1919 Annual Report*, HSBA Collection, CHS.

55. For example, real estate broker Edward Andrews had to leave his office for several months owing to a slow recovery from a serious bout of influenza, as reported: "Old Cambridge," *Cambridge Chronicle*, June 21, 1919.

56. "Amended By-Laws, April 24, 1919," *1919 Annual Report*, HSBA Collection, CHS.

57. "Fred Olsson, Advertising Committee, April 1919," *1919 Annual Report*, HSBA Collection, CHS.

58. "To Improve Harvard Square Is the Object of This Association" [remarks by Fred Olsson], *Cambridge Tribune*, January 11, 1919.

59. "Fred Olsson, Advertising Committee, April 1921," *1921 Annual Report*, HSBA Collection, CHS.

60. "To Improve Harvard Square Is the Object of This Association" [remarks by George Wright], *Cambridge Tribune*, January 11, 1919.

61. John Gregory, "The Coming City," *World Work*, May 1913; quoted in "George Wright, Municipal Affairs Committee, April 1919," *1919 Annual Report*, HSBA Collection, CHS.

62. "George Wright, Municipal Affairs Committee, April 1919," quoting Gregory, "The Coming City."

63. "Bulletin of the Harvard Square Business Men's Association," Committee on Advertising.

64. These criticisms were raised in the April 17, 1920, meeting described in chapter 2 and reported on in "The Business Men Discuss Solution of Rent Problem at Their Annual Meeting," *Cambridge Tribune*, April 17, 1920.

65. Concerns over outside real estate investors were raised in various meetings and articles, including: "Beneficial to Harvard Square," *Cambridge Tribune*, March 11, 1922; "Local Building Pride," *Cambridge Tribune*, July 1, 1922.

66. "George Wright, Committee on Municipal Affairs, April 1923," *1923 Annual Report*, HSBA Collection, CHS.

67. Maycock and Sullivan discuss the structure and controversy surrounding it. *Building Old Cambridge*, 144.

68. The George Wright Collection, CHS, contains a file kept by Wright documenting some of his many communications with the El and local and state officials.

69. "George Wright, Committee on Municipal Affairs, April 1919," *1919 Annual Report*, HSBA Collection, CHS.

70. "George Wright, Committee on Municipal Affairs, April 1919," *1919 Annual Report*.

71. The back-and-forth squabble with the El over Christmas decorations unfolded across months and is recorded in the 1937 Meeting Minutes, HSBA Collection, CHS.

72. *Annual Reports*, 1919–1929, HSBA Collection, CHS.

73. Reference to the "Cigar Budget" first appears in the *1916 Annual Report*. The line item grew from $16.25 that year to more than $100 by the mid-1920s (*Annual Reports*, HSBA Collection, CHS).

74. "Voices a Protest Against Cheap Public Servants—President at Annual Meeting of Harvard Square Business Men's Association Sounds Call to Civic Duty," *Cambridge Tribune*, April 26, 1924; similar reference to the night's entertainment found in HSBA Scrapbook, George Wright Collection, CHS.

75. "N. Russell Cazmay, Report of the Secretary, April 1921," *1921 Annual Report*, HSBA Collection, CHS.

76. Quoted in "George Wright, Committee on Municipal Affairs, April 1923," *1923 Annual Report*, HSBA Collection, CHS.

77. "George G. Wright Expresses Disgust at Action of Harvard Sq. Business Men," *Cambridge Chronicle*, December 16, 1922.

78. "George Wright, Report of the President, April 1924," *1924 Annual Report*, HSBA Collection, CHS.

79. "R. Currie Grovestein, Report of the Retiring President, April 1927," *1927 Annual Report*, CHS.

80. *1928 Annual Report*, printed in "Harvard Square Business Men's Annual Meeting," *Cambridge Tribune*, April 28, 1928.
81. *1928 Annual Report*. The original source of these words was not actually Sage himself but Merle Thorpe, "Competition and Change," *Nation's Business: A Magazine for Business Men* 16, no. 4 (1928): 9 [a publication of the U.S. Chamber of Commerce]. Sage quoted at length from Thorpe's piece, although the newspaper's reprint of his remarks did not include any attribution to Thorpe.
82. Sage, quoting Thorpe, "Competition and Change."

7. FOREVER YOUNG

1. Details of the event included in this paragraph and the next paragraph are drawn from: "Harvard Square Business Men to Hold 40th Anniversary Dinner on Tuesday," *Cambridge Chronicle*, October 12, 1950; "Mayor Tells Harvard Square Merchants of Plans for Parking Area," *Cambridge Chronicle*, October 19, 1950; Meeting Minutes, October 17, 1950, HSBA Collection, CHS.
2. Meeting Minutes, March 15, 1953, HSBA Collection, CHS.
3. Mo Lotman, *Harvard Square: An Illustrated History Since 1950* (New York: Stewart, Tabori & Chang, 2009), 26.
4. "Corcoran's Opens Its New Harvard Square Store Friday," *Cambridge Chronicle*, March 11, 1949.
5. Meetings Minutes, 1950, HSBA Collection, CHS; "Mayor Tells Harvard Square Merchants of Plans," *Cambridge Chronicle*.
6. All quotes from Olsson's remarks in this and succeeding paragraphs come from Fred Olsson, "Our Historian Looks Back Forty Years," 40th Anniversary Meeting Program, HSBA Collection, CHS.
7. Meetings Minutes, 1930–1935, HSBA Collection, CHS. This chapter was informed by the author's reading of the annual reports and meetings minutes, 1930–1950, HSBA and George Wright Collections, CHS.
8. "Edwin Sage, Report of the President, 1928 Annual Meeting," printed in *Cambridge Tribune*, April 28, 1928.
9. Meetings Minutes, 1930–1934, HSBA Collection, CHS. Some such talks were covered in the local papers, for example: "Present Aspects of Business Discussed by Joseph Snider," *Cambridge Tribune*, May 17, 1930; "Industrial Association: Harvard Professor Spoke on Business Conditions," *Cambridge Chronicle*, May 16, 1930.
10. Joint meetings with the Cambridge Industrial Association appear to have been held in 1930, 1933, and 1935, including May 13, 1930, October 18, 1933, and March 6, 1935: Meetings Minutes, 1930s, HSBA Collection, CHS; "Some aspects of the Business Situation," *Cambridge Tribune*, May 17, 1930; "Buy Now Parade," *Cambridge Tribune*, October 27, 1933.
11. Debra Reynolds, "The Harvard Square Business Association: The Past 75 Years," (1985), available at the Harvard Square Business Association offices as well as in the HSBA Collection of the CHS, includes a nice discussion of the parking and traffic issues over the years. Annual reports and meetings minutes of the association document its seemingly never-ending struggle to wrestle the traffic and parking situation into some sort of order.
12. "Harvard Square Business Men Discuss Civic Problems in Their Vicinity," *Cambridge Chronicle*, October 30, 1931; "Meeting of Harvard Square Business Men's Association,"

Cambridge Tribune, October 31, 1931; "Fred Olsson Outlines Plans for Traffic," *Cambridge Tribune*, November 28, 1931; "Many Views on Harvard Square Traffic Problem," *Cambridge Tribune*, December 5, 1931.

13. "Harvard Square Business Men Discuss Civic Problems," *Cambridge Chronicle*, October 30, 1931.

14. Meeting Minutes, May 4, 1936, HSBA Collection, CHS.

15. As the Depression deepened so did this problem, and in 1936 the association dropped eleven members for nonpayment of dues: Meeting Minutes, April 13, 1936, HSBA Collection, CHS.

16. Meeting Minutes, June 25, 1934, HSBA Collection, CHS. Olsson was vice president of the group at this time.

17. Details of the golf event were reported in: "Harvard Square Business Group Holds an Outing," *Cambridge Tribune*, June 29, 1934; "Business Men Play Golf at Arlmont," *Cambridge Chronicle*, June 29, 1934; Meetings Minutes, 1934, HSBA Collection, CHS.

18. Meeting Minutes, November 21, 1934, HSBA Collection, CHS.

19. Meeting Minutes, November 20, 1935, HSBA Collection, CHS; "Harvard Sq Men Met Last Night," *Cambridge Chronicle*, November 21, 1935.

20. Larrabee was a professor at Burdett College and gave motivational speeches like this at multiple local business and social groups during the 1930s, including the Kiwanis Club (reported in *Cambridge Chronicle*, June 14, 1930) and the Mount Olivet Lodge (reported in *Cambridge Chronicle*, March 30, 1934). At the November 1935 Harvard Square dinner, he told a parable about two brothers supposedly from Larrabee's own hometown. According to Larrabee, one brother was a brilliant scholar but ultimately unsuccessful. The other, considered dull as a boy, had "the power of right thinking" and became a great success. The story was recounted here: "Employees Guests of Business Men of Harvard Square: Speaker Stresses Value of Human Understanding in Business," *Cambridge Tribune*, November 22, 1935.

21. Meeting Minutes, January 1937, HSBA Collection, CHS.

22. The poem is included in the files for Meeting Minutes, March 17, 1937, HSBA Collection, CHS. The moment of silence for Olsson was held at a February 17, 1937, meeting.

23. Meeting Minutes, March 18, 1936, HSBA Collection, CHS.

24. Meeting Minutes, October 21, 1936, HSBA Collection, CHS. Parking and parking meters (whether to have them, how to finance them, how to manage them if they eventually got them) were topics of discussion through the 1940s.

25. Meetings Minutes, November 15, 1938, November 18, 1941, January 20, 1942, March 17, 1942, HSBA Collection, CHS.

26. Meeting Minutes, October 17, 1939, HSBA Collection, CHS.

27. Olsson's remarks and poem are included in the files for Meeting Minutes, April 16, 1940, HSBA Collection, CHS.

28. Fred Olsson, "Albert F. Amee: A Memory," included with Meeting Minutes, January 20, 1941, HSBA Collection.

29. This poem appears to have been untitled. It was read at the association's annual outing in June 1940. Meeting Minutes, June 24, 1940, HSBA Collection, CHS.

30. "George Wright, Report of the President 1924–1925, April 1925," *Annual Report*, HSBA Collection, CHS. Subsequent quotes in this paragraph refer to the same George Wright report.

31. Upon his retirement, Olsson was elected a lifetime member of the association: "Harvard Square Merchants Elect Slate President—Fred Olsson Elected as Life

Member," *Cambridge Chronicle*, April 28, 1949. Maycock and Sullivan note Olsson's eviction by Dow, though they write that Olsson relocated his shop to Brattle Street at the time. In fact, Fred retired and closed up his shop. The store on Brattle Street was J. F. Olsson's, which his sister had taken over from her late father and which she relocated to Brattle Street in 1925 from its original location at 1414 Massachusetts Avenue. Susan E. Maycock and Charles M. Sullivan, *Building Old Cambridge: Architecture and Development* (Cambridge, MA: MIT Press, 2016), 149. A history of J. F. Olsson's ownership changes and relocations can be found here: "Olsson Co. Celebrates Centennial Anniversary," *Cambridge Chronicle*, December 19, 1985.

8. OUTSIDE AGITATORS

1. Andrew Schlesinger, *Veritas: Harvard College and the American Experience* (Chicago: Ivan R. Dee, 2005). Schlesinger quotes a Harvard College classmate of JFK's: "He knew all the tailors and the soda jerks and all the people that worked in the stores." *Veritas*, 183.
2. "President Inspects Sites for Library," *Harvard Crimson*, May 13, 1963; Charles Claffey, "Kennedy Inspects Three Sites for Library," *Boston Globe*, May 12, 1963; "Kennedy Library: Brighton," *Boston Globe*, May 24, 1963; Joe Pilati, "Two Visits By President Kennedy Led to the Library-Site Controversy," *Boston Globe*, January 30, 1975.
3. In this and subsequent paragraphs, details on JFK's October 19, 1963, visit and attendance at the Harvard-Columbia game are drawn from newspaper accounts of it at the time including: "Boston Awaits JFK," *Boston Globe*, October 19, 1963; Richard Connolly, "Plaza Crowd's Loss Was Harvard-Columbia Gain," *Boston Globe*, October 20, 1963; Frank White, "JFK Team Defeats Harvard, Columbia," *Boston Globe*, October 20, 1963; Leonard Koppett, "Columbia Is Tied by Harvard," *New York Times*, October 20, 1963; Associated Press, "Harvard Rooters Have President on Their Side," *New York Times*, October 20, 1963. I also draw on retrospective accounts, some written right after his assassination, others years later, including: "Kennedy and Harvard: A Complicated Tie," *Harvard Crimson*, November 26, 1963; Steven Brown, "John F. Kennedy's Final Footsteps at Home," WBUR, October 18, 2013, https://www.wbur.org/news/2013/10/18/jfk-last-trip-home.
4. White, "JFK Team Defeats Harvard, Columbia."
5. Photos from the game can be found in the JFK Presidential Library Archives: Cecil Stoughton, White House Photographs, John F. Kennedy Presidential Library and Museum, Boston, https://www.jfklibrary.org/asset-viewer/archives/JFKWHP/1963/Month%2010/Day%2019/JFKWHP-1963-10-19-C?image_identifier=JFKWHP-ST-473-11-63.
6. Quotes from Harshbarger are drawn from his WBUR interview: Brown, "John F. Kennedy's Final Footsteps at Home."
7. My description of Harvard Square on the day of JFK's assassination is drawn directly from the poignant report of student journalists there at the time: "Death of President Shocks Cambridge," *Harvard Crimson*, November 22, 1963.
8. "'Mayor' Cohen of Harvard Square Marks his 25th Year of Business," *Harvard Crimson*, September 1, 1972.

291

9. "Kennedy Album Proceeds Aid JFK Library," *Cambridge Chronicle*, January 16, 1964; Christopher Lydon, "Harvard Square Friend Helps," *Boston Globe*, March 3, 1964.
10. Garrett Graff, "The Men & the Boys: How Veterans Altered the Campus Fabric," *Harvard Crimson*, June 5, 2000. For a discussion of postwar Harvard, see also Schlesinger's *Veritas*.
11. Jane Thompson and Alexandra Lange, *Design Research: The Store That Brought Modern Living to American Homes* (San Francisco: Chronicle Books, 2010), 19. Details on Design Research in this and the following paragraphs are drawn from Thompson and Lange's biography, which includes, among other things, oral history interviews with former employees of the store and reprints of newspaper and magazine articles written about Thompson and the business, including the very first profile of Design Research, in which Thompson talks about his motivation for founding the store: "US Retailer Looks at Foreign Design," *Industrial Design*, September 1957. Design Research is also discussed in: Mo Lotman, *Harvard Square: An Illustrated History Since 1950* (New York: Stewart, Tabori & Chang, 2009), 113; Susan E. Maycock and Charles M. Sullivan, *Building Old Cambridge: Architecture and Development* (Cambridge, MA: MIT Press, 2016), 152.
12. Cover photo, *Sports Illustrated*, December 26, 1960.
13. Lotman, *Harvard Square*, has wonderful photographs and descriptions of Harvard Square establishments during the 1950s, including a number of those discussed in this chapter such as the Brattle Theater, Club Casablanca, and Club 47.
14. Details of Genevieve McMillan's life and Henri IV included in this chapter are drawn from *In Remembrance: Genevieve McMillan*, ed. Nancy Murray, designed by Jody Lee (2008). *In Remembrance* is a fifty-page booklet compiled by McMillan's friends and associates after her death. It includes tributes from dozens of individuals who knew McMillan; reprints of *Boston Globe* and *Harvard Crimson* articles written about her and Henri IV through the years; McMillan's own words describing her life, businesses, and passions (including those from an interview conducted by Mo Lotman); and her obituary (Gloria Negri, "Genevieve McMillan, at 85: MFA Donor," *Boston Globe*, May 24, 2008). A link to this booklet can be found on McMillan's biography page of the McMillan Stewart Foundation website: http://mcmillanstewart.org /founder/biography/. Other sources consulted include: Ellen Goodman, "Africa-with a French Accent," *Boston Globe*, January 5, 1968; The McMillan Stewart Foundation, http://mcmillanstewart.org.
15. McMillan went on to become an avid collector and world traveler for the rest of her life, and her Harvard Square home was eventually filled with hundreds of objects of indigenous art and artifacts bought on her yearly trips abroad. She donated her expansive collection to the Boston Museum of Fine Arts. During her life, she also founded a nonprofit foundation, whose mission was to support the end of racism and the promotion of civil and human rights, in particular through the arts. The foundation, which lives on, has endowed a lecture series and professorship at MIT in the study of women in the developing world.
16. In the 1960s, McMillan also opened the area's first discotheque, a concept that had recently taken off in Europe. It was located in the basement of Henri IV and called Club Nicole: Kay Shreve, "Where the Action Is: Our Drowsy Little Village Has Discotheque—It Swings," *Cambridge Chronicle*, February 24, 1966.
17. Specific details about the restaurant's interior and menu are drawn from: Michael Finkelstein, "Club Henri IV," *Harvard Crimson*, April 28, 1953; and "In Genou's Voice:

In Conversation with Josefina and Interviewer Mo Lotman," February 24, 2005. Both sources are in *In Remembrance*.

18. Maycock and Sullivan describe this era of the market similarly, observing that "new stores coexisted with traditional retailers and services." *Building Old Cambridge*, 154.

19. The combined merchant-police crew apparently had good times together. Things got so rowdy at their June 1953 outing they were asked by the country club to take their socializing elsewhere in future years. The businessmen blamed their guests. Meeting Minutes, December 14, 1953, HSBA Collection, CHS. Debra Reynolds, "The Harvard Square Business Association: The Past 75 Years" (1985), also found this noteworthy in the group's historical record. (As in earlier chapters, Reynolds's summary of the association's meetings dovetails with mine as we rely on the same primary materials in the archives; here, the HSBA annual reports and meetings minutes, 1950–1973, HSBA Collection, CHS.)

20. Meeting Minutes, March 15, 1955, HSBA Collection, CHS; U.S. Chamber of Commerce, "It's Everybody's Business" (1954), https://www.c-span.org/video/?435063-1 /its-everybodys-business, accessed May 28, 2022.

21. Meetings Minutes, January 15, 1952, March 16, 1954, January 21, 1959, HSBA Collection, CHS.

22. Meetings Minutes, 1954, 1955, 1956, 1960, 1961, HSBA Collection, CHS.

23. Reynolds, "Harvard Square Business Association," offers a nice analysis of the association's waning membership during this period.

24. Meetings Minutes, April 27, 1960, and January 16, 1962, HSBA Collection, CHS.

25. Meeting Minutes, October 5, 1961, HSBA Collection, CHS.

26. Meeting Minutes, January 16, 1962, HSBA Collection, CHS.

27. The history and influence of Club 47 (and its successor Club Passim) have been profiled in multiple books as well as commemorative articles and events, including: Lotman, *Harvard Square*, 80–81; Jim Rooney, *In It for the Long Run: A Musical Odyssey* (Champaign: University of Illinois Press, 2014); Rachel Lipson, "Club 47 Revisited," *Harvard Crimson*, November 19, 2009; Noah Guiney, "Group Celebrates Local Folk Music Legacies," *Harvard Crimson*, November 30, 2010; Stuart Munro, "At Passim's 60th Anniversary Show, an Evening of Memories and Music," *Boston Globe*, November 15, 2019; Jed Gottlieb, "Folk Music Hotspot Passim Marks 60 Years with Benefit Concert," *Boston Herald*, November 10, 2019.

28. Details of Baez's time in Harvard Square are drawn from Joan Baez, *And a Voice to Sing With: A Memoir* (1987; repr. New York: Simon and Schuster, 2009).

29. Baez, *And a Voice to Sing With*, 50.

30. Baez, *And a Voice to Sing With*, 50.

31. Bob Spitz, *Dylan: A Biography* (New York: Norton, 1989), 158. Perhaps referring to the same night or a different one, *From the Heart of Cambridge: A Neighborhood Portrait*—a compilation of oral history interviews with residents of the city's Mid-Cambridge neighborhood—includes an essay by George Bossarte, in which he recalls an evening in the early '60s when Baez and Dylan stopped by Club 47 late one night and played an informal set together. George Bossarte, "Harvard Square: A Folk Music Mecca," in *From the Heart of Cambridge: A Neighborhood Portrait*, ed. Paula Lovejoy (Cambridge, MA: Longfellow Neighborhood Council and Community School, 2011), 130.

32. Lipson, "Club 47 Revisited"; Lotman, *Harvard Square*.

33. Lipson, "Club 47 Revisited."

34. Baez, *And a Voice to Sing With*, 315.

35. Baez, *And a Voice to Sing With*, 315.

36. "Senator Urges Group 'Purge' Reds," *New York Times*, May 26, 1960; "Back Sane Against Eastland," *Harvard Crimson*, March 21, 1961.

37. The case went to court, and the club was eventually allowed to reopen. The saga, which entailed protests and counterprotests, was covered extensively by the *Harvard Crimson* in such articles as: Rudolf Ganz, Jr., "Pickets Jeer 'Sing Along with SANE,'" October 24, 1961; "Management of Club Mount Auburn Enters Building in Defiance of Order," *Harvard Crimson*, November 10, 1961; "Club, Organizer Await Hearing on 'Sing Out,'" *Harvard Crimson*, November, 15, 1961; "Superior Court Hears Case This Morning Against Club 47," *Harvard Crimson*, January 4, 1962; Lawrence Feinberg, "Absence of Witnesses Forces New Delay in Club 47 Case," *Harvard Crimson*, January 5, 1962.

38. Rooney, *In It for the Long Run*, 26.

39. Meeting Minutes, October 21, 1964, HSBA Collection, CHS.

40. Marian Christy, "Stroll Through Harvard Square," *Boston Globe*, May 21, 1961.

41. Marylin Bender, "Fashion Wins High Marks at Harvard Weekend," *New York Times*, October, 19, 1964.

42. Paula Cronin, "Tourist View of Harvard Square," *New York Times*, October 25, 1964.

43. Anne Moore, "Harvard Square—Where the Action Is," *Cambridge Chronicle*, November 10, 1966.

44. Gregory McDonald, "It's Soho . . . It's Greenwich Village . . . It's the Left Bank . . . IT'S HARVARD SQUARE," *Boston Globe*, May 22, 1966; "The Front of Holyoke Center Becomes a Hippie-Drome," *Harvard Crimson*, August 11, 1967.

45. Alexander Auerbach, "Business Really Swings in Harvard Square," *Boston Globe*, February 12, 1967.

46. Robert Samuelson, "Cambridge Police Begin Square Button Struggle," *Harvard Crimson*, March 3, 1967.

47. Samuelson, "Cambridge Police Begin Square Button Struggle"; James Beniger, "Krackerjacks Faces Court Action, Lacks License to Sell Old Clothes," *Harvard Crimson*, April 28, 1967.

48. Auerbach, "Business Really Swings in Harvard Square."

49. Meeting Minutes, October 26, 1966, HSBA Collection, CHS.

50. Moore, "Harvard Square—Where the Action Is." The *Chronicle*'s editors felt the need to preface Moore's piece, introducing it with the following: "Teenagers in Harvard Square have been a major problem concerning Cambridge parents and police for some time. The *Chronicle-Sun* asked feature writer Anne Moore, a senior at Radcliffe, to browse about the Square, to find out why teenagers gathered there, and what they had in mind. This is her story."

51. "Mayor Hayes Hits at Hippies: Urges Landlords Keep Them Out," *Cambridge Chronicle*, September 28, 1967. Subsequent quotes from Hayes in this paragraph refer to this same article.

52. Maycock and Sullivan, *Building Old Cambridge*, 154–55.

53. Robert Remer, "Council Asks Dope Squad; Two Raids Made During Vote," *Cambridge Chronicle*, April 20, 1967.

54. Remer, "Council Asks Dope Squad."

55. All of *Avatar*'s issues from 1967 to 1968 and an indexed list of articles could be found here as of December, 2021: https://www.trussel.com/lyman/avatar/avatar.htm.

56. Mel Lyman, "I'm Going to Fuck the World," *Avatar*, no. 15 (December 22, 1967): 11.

57. "Rudolph Tells City Council Traffic Signals May Cost \$1 Million," *Cambridge Chronicle*, October 19, 1967. Apparently, City Councilor Sullivan also declared the newspaper, "the dirtiest, filthiest material I've ever read": Robert Remer, "Councilors Plan Private Session on City's Future," *Cambridge Chronicle*, November 16, 1967.

58. "Stop the War on Avatar," *Harvard Crimson*, December 7, 1967.

59. Meeting Minutes, November 30, 1967, HSBA Collection, CHS.

60. Mark Rasmuson, "5 Students Convicted for Selling 'Avatar,' " *Harvard Crimson*, March 1, 1968.

61. Meeting Minutes, February 29, 1968, HSBA Collection, CHS.

62. Meeting Minutes, October 31, 1969, HSBA Collection, CHS.

63. Meeting Minutes, May 28, 1968, HSBA Collection, CHS.

64. Meetings Minutes, April 8, 1969, and October 31, 1969, HSBA Collection, CHS.

65. William Davis, "Occult: Oddly Enough, It's Thriving," *Boston Globe*, November 23, 1969.

66. "Police Raid Sit-In at Dawn; 250 Arrested, Dozens Injured," *Harvard Crimson*, April 10, 1969; see also Declan Knieriem, "Haunted by the War: Remembering the University Hall Takeover of 1969," *Harvard Crimson*, May 27, 2019.

67. The account of the April 15 protest and riots in this and subsequent paragraphs is drawn from several sources including: Donald Jansson, "Damage Estimated at \$100,000 After Harvard Riot," *New York Times*, April 17, 1970; Rachelle Patterson, "Harvard Square Is Written Up," *Boston Globe*, April 20, 1970; Garrett Epps and the Crimson Staff, "Rioting Devastates Harvard Square; Windows Smashed, Scores Injured," *Harvard Crimson*, April 16, 1960. I also consulted retrospective accounts in *From the Heart of Cambridge*, as well as Maycock and Sullivan's discussion (*Building Old Cambridge*, 154) and Lotman's (*Harvard Square*, 98–99).

68. Epps and the Crimson Staff, "Rioting Devastates Harvard Square."

69. Arrest and injury counts as well as tabulation of damages are obtained from Jansson, "Damage Estimated at \$100,000." Lotman provides a similar tabulation ("April 15, 1970, By the Numbers," *Harvard Square*, 99).

70. Patterson, "Harvard Square Is Written Up."

71. "In Harvard Square, 'Street People' Are Challenging Liberal Ideas," *New York Times*, August 19, 1970.

72. Local officials and others were quoted using these terms throughout this period, including in: Remer, "Council Asks Dope Squad"; "Mayor Hayes Hits at Hippies," *Cambridge Chronicle*.

73. Meeting Minutes, May 19, 1970, HSBA Collection, CHS.

74. Meeting Minutes, May 19, 1970, HSBA Collection, CHS.

75. David Ignatius, "What Can They Do to Cool the Square?" *Harvard Crimson*, July 31, 1970.

76. Bennett Beach, "Felix and the Square: The End of an Era," *Harvard Crimson*, June 11, 1970; Maycock and Sullivan, *Building Old Cambridge*, 154–55.

77. Maycock and Sullivan, *Building Old Cambridge*, 154–55.

78. David Ignatius, "The Harvard Square Mess," *Harvard Crimson*, August 7, 1970. Maycock and Sullivan discuss this tense year in the market, including merchant and customer reactions to it. *Building Old Cambridge*, 154–56.

79. Meeting Minutes, August 5, 1970, HSBA Collection, CHS. Sunday Concerts on Cambridge Common were a big deal at the time. Bands played throughout the day and crowds gathered on the lawn to hear them. In *From the Heart of Cambridge*,

Cambridge resident Ken Bowles recalls the Common being "filled with hippies . . . in the thousands, I would say" on those days. Hare Krishnas chanted, and drug use was not uncommon: "You could get high just walking across Cambridge Common," Bowles notes. Ken Bowles, "Be-ins and Poetry: The 1960s Culture," in *From the Heart of Cambridge: A Neighborhood Portrait*, ed. Paula Lovejoy (Cambridge, MA: Longfellow Neighborhood Council and Community School, 2011), 133.

80. Meeting Minutes, August 5, 1970, HSBA Collection, CHS.

81. Ignatius, "Harvard Square Mess."

82. Declining sales figures are cited in: "Bringing Order to Cambridge," *Boston Globe*, July 30, 1970; "In Harvard Square: Street People Are Challenging Liberal Ideas," *New York Times*.

83. Mrs. Keith F. Adams, "Shopper Comments on Square," Letter to the *Cambridge Chronicle*, August 27, 1970.

84. This postcard, like so many other preserved details of Cambridge history, was found and saved by the diligent effort of Charlie Sullivan of the Cambridge Historical Commission. Sullivan presented it (and a treasure trove of other historical details) in a 2017 talk on radical politics in Cambridge: Charles Sullivan, "Radical Events (and Bad Behavior) in Cambridge, 1819–2000," CHC, July 20, 2017, https://www.cambridgema.gov/-/media/Files/historicalcommission/pdf/slideshows/ss_radical.pdf.

85. Mark Frazier, "JFK Library: Future Shock in the Square," *Harvard Crimson*, June 15, 1972; Alvin Toffler, *Future Shock* (New York: Bantam, 1970).

86. For a high-level chronology of the proposed project and subsequent controversy, see "History of John F. Kennedy Library," *Boston Globe*, November 25, 1975. Hundreds of contemporaneous articles in the local and national press documented the unfolding project and controversy and serve as my main source for the history that follows, along with archival material from the Cambridge Historical Commission, Cambridge Historical Society, and Cambridge Public Library, cited below. In addition, Maycock and Sullivan discuss the controversy (*Building Old Cambridge*, 160–64), and several academic articles provide useful overviews as well, including: Mark Francis, "Urban Impact Assessment and Community Involvement: The Case of the John Fitzgerald Kennedy Library," *Environment and Behavior* 7, no. 3 (September 1975): 373–403; Dan Fenn, "Launching the John F. Kennedy Library," *American Archivist*, 42, no. 4 (October 1979): 429–42.

87. Initial trustees of the Corporation included JFK's brothers Bobby and Ted as well as his close political advisors Robert McNamara and Arthur Schlesinger. A history of the corporation can be found here: https://www.jfklibrary.org/about-us/about-the-jfk-library/history/history-overview.

88. Robert Reinhold, "Holiday Inn Near Kennedy Library Fought," *New York Times*, September 27, 1972.

89. Ada Louise Huxtable, "What's a Tourist Attraction Like the Kennedy Library Doing in a Nice Neighborhood Like This?," *New York Times*, June 16, 1974. Mark Francis includes a useful overview of the various publics affected by the proposed memorial and their specific concerns (Francis, "Urban Impact Assessment"); Francis was a student at Harvard's Graduate School of Design at the time and participated firsthand in the debate around the library. Another thoughtful contemporaneous overview of the various arguments against and for the library (and the different groups making them) was "Getting Ready for the John F. Kennedy Library: Not Everyone Wants to Make It Go Away," *Architectural Record*, December 1974, 98–105.

90. The corporation's estimates, based on a 1965 study it commissioned, are cited in Richard Weintraub and Joe Pilati, "Kennedy Library, Plans Grew and Grew," *Boston Globe*, November 18, 1973. Maycock and Sullivan provide similar estimates of Arlington Cemetery attendance and expected attendance at the proposed memorial. *Building Old Cambridge*, 161.

91. Quotes in this paragraph are drawn from Frazier, "JFK Library: Future Shock in the Square."

92. Dick Swanson, "Harvard Square Task Force Appointed by Corcoran," *Cambridge Chronicle*, March 30, 1972.

93. In 1970, 9,824 people resided in Cambridge's Neighborhood 10 (out of a total population of approximately 100,000). A 1975 profile of the neighborhood revealed its residents to be among the city's most affluent and educated. Median family income there was higher than in any other part of the city ($14,922 compared to the city median $9,815), and single-family homes represented a larger percentage of its housing stock than in other areas. Five percent of the Neighborhood 10 residents were black, compared to 6.8 percent in the city as a whole. Neighborhood 10 Profile, Cambridge Community Development Department (1975), Cornelia Wheeler Collection, Neighborhood Ten Files, CPL, Cambridge, Massachusetts. Wheeler, a longtime Cambridge resident and member of the Neighborhood Ten Association, was active in Cambridge politics and civic life from the 1930s to 1990s and served on the Cambridge City Council in the 1960s.

94. Local newspaper articles about Neighborhood Ten from the decade prior to the library controversy list various group members and leaders, including individuals such as James Burr Ames, a senior partner at the elite Boston law firm Ropes and Gray and grandson of a former dean of Harvard Law School; a senior executive at a tobacco company; and a textbook editor whose husband was on the faculty at Boston University.

95. Local and national reports of the controversy include: "Bankers Ask Legislature to Save Sycamore Trees," *Record American*, January 15, 1964; "Memorial Drive War Nears Decisive Battle," *Cambridge Chronicle*, February 4, 1964; "A Little Green Space," *Time*, February 14, 1964, 64. The Cornelia Wheeler Collection, Save Memorial Drive Files, CPL, includes, among other things: pamphlets the group produced and circulated for their campaign to save the trees; a February 22, 1965, Dahl cartoon depicting a young George Washington being scolded by his father for chopping down a tree with the caption, "I'll forgive you for the cherry tree but if I ever catch you fooling around those Sycamores—!"; remarks that Wheeler delivered to state officials at the Massachusetts State House at a hearing about the underpass project; and a song composed by the local Mother's Discussion Club, sung to the tune of "Oh Tannenbaum" with lyrics like "Oh woodman dear, please save our trees!"

96. "M.D.C. Spares the Trees," *Boston Globe*, October 3, 1964; "Axe to Spare Most of Memorial Drive Sycamores," *Record American*, October 2, 1964.

97. Martha Lawrence, "A Statement on Harvard Square," April 14, 1972, endorsed by Neighborhood Ten Association Executive Committee on April 18, 1972, Neighborhood Ten Association Collection 1963–1985 (hereafter Neighborhood Ten Collection), CHC.

98. Thaddeus Beal Memo to Harvard Square Task Force, In Re: Proposed Letter from Task Force to City Manager John Corcoran, June 21, 1972, Harvard Square Development Task Force Committee, Neighborhood Ten Collection, CHC.

99. Letter from Paul Lawrence, "Mail from Our Readers—Don't Let It Be a Blot," *Cambridge Chronicle*, July 13, 1972.
100. "Pei, Planners Discuss Inn," *Cambridge Chronicle*, November 2, 1972. A photo of Neighborhood Ten members collecting signatures ran alongside this article.
101. Ronald Lee Fleming, "Letter to Mayor on Holiday Inn," *Cambridge Chronicle*, November 2, 1972, documents the multiple community groups that aligned in opposition to the inn. See also "Bulldozer Kicks Up Opposition to Inn," *Cambridge Chronicle*, September 21, 1972. Among those who joined the opposition were the Harvard Square Development Task Force, several city officials, the Cambridge Conservation Commission, the Cambridge Chamber of Commerce, the Harvard Square Business Association ("Men's" having been dropped from the group's name in early September 1972), and the Boston Industrial Mission (an organization of businessmen, bankers, and clergy interested in technological change with offices in Harvard Square).
102. Reinhold, "Holiday Inn Near Kennedy Library Fought."
103. Anne Raver, "City Digs in to Change Holiday Inn," *Cambridge Chronicle*, September 28, 1972.
104. "Evaluation of Kennedy Library, February 1973," Memo from Robert A. Bowyer, Director Cambridge Planning & Development Department, to John H. Corcoran, City Manager, Planning Board, and Harvard Square Development Task Force, February 20, 1973, Cornelia Wheeler Collection, Harvard Square Development Task Force Files, CPL.
105. Jeff Robison, "JFK Library Plans Unveiled," *Cambridge Chronicle*, May 31, 1973.
106. Robert Reinhold, "Kennedy Library Plans Are Unveiled," *New York Times*, May 30, 1973.
107. Robert Campbell, "Library Is Fine by Itself but . . . ," *Boston Globe*, June 10, 1973.
108. Joe Pilati, "Cambridge Groups Oppose Plans for JFK Library Complex," *Boston Globe*, June 5, 1973.
109. Neighborhood Ten Association newsletters and pamphlets distributed during this period had headlines such as: "Let's Stop Being Ostriches! Let's Face Up to the Kennedy Library" (October 1973), "KENNEDY ALERT!" (August 1974): Cornelia Wheeler Collection, Neighborhood Ten Files, CPL. In 1974, three neighborhood groups (spanning wealthy to working-class areas of the city) joined forces to produce and distribute a highly professionalized fifteen-page booklet laying out their opposition to the project: "Cambridge, Harvard Square, and the Kennedy Memorial," sponsored by Neighborhood Ten Association, Neighborhood Nine Association, Riverside/Cambridgeport Community Corporation (1974), HSDF Collection, CHS.
110. Specifically, opponents wanted an Environmental Impact Statement to assess the effects of the museum on not just the physical but also the social environment surrounding it. In their letters to the Kennedy Library Corporation (KLC) and the General Services Administration (GSA), they offered extensive (often unsolicited) feedback on what precise data should be collected in such an assessment. They wanted assurances that the Square would not be so overrun by burdensome crowds and traffic that there would be no room for them or the merchants who serviced them. See, for example: "Citizens Seek Kennedy Help for Solving Library Problems," *Cambridge Chronicle*, June 14, 1973; "CCA Statement on Library," *Cambridge Chronicle*, June 14, 1973. The Cornelia Wheeler Collection, Harvard Square Development Task Force Files, CPL, contains multiple communications between, on the one side, the chair of the Harvard Square Development Task Force, and, on the other, officials

at the KLC and GSA about this issue—communications that grew increasingly tense with time. A sampling of these include: Oliver Brooks (Chairman, Harvard Square Development Task Force) Letter to Arthur Samson (Administrator, GSA), June 6, 1973; Oliver Brooks Letter to Stephen Smith (Chairman, KLC), June 7, 1973; Oliver Brooks Letter to Albert Gammal (Regional Administrator, GSA), July 26, 1973; Albert Gammal Letter to Oliver Brooks, August 2, 1973; Letter from Harvard Square Development Task Force, signed Oliver Brooks, to Robert Griffin (Special Assistant to Administrator, GSA), October 12, 1973. Brooks's internal memos to the Task Force during this period also report tense phone calls with KLC and GSA representatives.

111. A common theme of criticism during these years was that the project's managers were evasive about their plans and insufficiently transparent and responsive when it came to addressing public concerns. In early 1974, the GSA selected a consulting firm to conduct the desired Environmental Impact Study (EIS). Shortly after, the *Boston Globe* reported that the firm hired to do the EIS may have, on a prior engagement, bowed to pressure from political insiders and switched its final recommendation. This set off a new uproar. Local opponents of the project held yet another large, multiparty press conference, this time demanding the GSA investigate the *Globe*'s accusations and replace the firm if need be. See: Ken Botwright, "Massport Pressure May Have Caused Switch in Terminal Report," *Boston Globe*, February 26, 1974; "Five Groups Call for Investigation of Firm Doing Library Impact," *Cambridge Chronicle*, February 28, 1974. The Cornelia Wheeler Collection, Harvard Square Development Task Force Files, CPL, contain communications between the Task Force and the KLC and GSA pertaining to this as well.

112. A 1975 newsletter of the Neighborhood Ten Association references its team of technical consultants, who appear to have been first engaged in early 1974: "News About the Kennedy Library/Museum," *Neighborhood Ten Association Newsletter*, January 18, 1975, Cornelia Wheeler Collection, Neighborhood Ten Files, CPL.

113. Mark Penn, "Task Force Names Seven to Library Study Team," *Harvard Crimson*, March 8, 1974.

114. Martha Lawrence wrote up her notes from this trip and published them in the *Crimson* upon her return. Quotes and details included in this paragraph are drawn from Lawrence's firsthand account: Martha Lawrence, "The Other Presidential Libraries," *Harvard Crimson*, October 15, 1974.

115. Ruth Murphy, Letter to the Editor, "Kennedy Museum Snobbery, Build Library in Cambridge," *Cambridge Chronicle*, February 6, 1975. The *Chronicle* ran a letter from another local woman accusing project opponents of "snobbery of the worst kind": Sheila Russell, Letter to the Editor, "Kennedy Museum Snobbery, Build Library in Cambridge," *Cambridge Chronicle*, February 6, 1975.

116. "Wooden Souvenir Offered," *Record American*, September 3, 1964.

117. Jeff Robison, "Library Supporters Form Committee," *Cambridge Chronicle*, May 30, 1974.

118. In the late 1960s, Thompson had moved Design Research across Brattle Street, into a new, modern building he designed. In 1970, however, he ran into financial difficulty and lost control of the store. Nevertheless, at the time of the awards dinner on May 15, 1974, he remained a prolific architect with offices in the Square and was a distinguished faculty member in the Harvard Graduate School of Design's Department of Architecture. A complete transcript of Thompson's May 15 remarks was circulated to

Neighborhood Ten members on May 24 as: Boston Society of Architects, "Remarks on Harvard Square and the Kennedy Memorial by Award Recipient—For Release; Remarks by Benjamin A. Thompson," Cornelia Wheeler Collection, Neighborhood Ten Files, CPL. The quotes and description of Thompson's remarks in this and the following paragraphs are drawn from this transcript.

119. See, for example: Letter from Michael Mazur (Neighborhood Nine Committee on the JFK Library/Museum), Paul Lawrence (President, Neighborhood Ten Association, and David Clem (President, Riverside Cambridgeport Community Corporation), "Community Fears," *Boston Globe*, June 26, 1974.

120. Quoted in Nick King, "Harvard Square Development Limit Urged," *Boston Globe*, January 15, 1975. Portions of the report were excerpted in multiple articles at the time. The Task Force's report was drafted in consultation with the city's Community Development Department and an architectural consulting firm. More than five hundred copies of it were distributed at the time.

121. Quoted in "Separate Museum, Library Task Force Plan Urges" *Cambridge Chronicle*, January 16, 1975. After the Kennedy controversy was over, a final version of the report was published as a forward-looking policy plan for development in the Square. The "People in Harvard Square" section contained much the same content as the 1974 draft. It began by noting that the population of the Square had grown increasingly youth-oriented, stating "Young adults and young professionals now constitute about 65 percent of the population of the area around Harvard Square. The desirable pattern of development to offset these trends is set forth below." It went on to emphasize that the Square should serve a variety of different groups of people. *Harvard Square Comprehensive Policy Plan* (May 1976), adopted by votes of the Harvard Square Development Task Force, prepared by City of Cambridge Community Development Department, assisted by Monacelli Associations, Cambridge, Massachusetts, Neighborhood Ten Collection, Harvard Square Policy Plan File, CHC.

122. "The Library and the City" [excerpts from the GSA EIS], *Harvard Crimson*, January 7, 1975. See also Mark Penn, "Environmental Study Says JFK Library Will Have Minimal Impact on Square," *Harvard Crimson*, January 7, 1975; Robert Rosenthal, "Environment Study Favors JFK Library," *Boston Globe*, January 7, 1975.

123. Mark Penn, "JFK Officials Saw GSA Drafts," *Harvard Crimson*, February 3, 1975. Robert Campbell of the *Globe* called the study a "red herring" and a "whitewash": Robert Campbell, "The Impact Study as Red Herring," *Boston Globe*, January 26, 1975.

124. "The Kennedy Library and Museum," *Washington Post*, January 15, 1975.

125. "More EIS Facts Sought by Group Through Courts," *Cambridge Chronicle*, January 16, 1975; "Judge Ponders EIS Challenge," *Cambridge Chronicle*, February 6, 1975. The Cornelia Wheeler Collection includes a January 19, 1975, letter from Oliver Brooks of the Task Force to the GSA requesting a delay of the public hearing scheduled to discuss the EIS. Brooks complained that the GSA had failed to provide a sufficient number of copies of the EIS to distribute to all the interested parties and that the GSA was refusing to release the data on which the EIS's conclusions were based. The Wheeler collection also includes a draft response to the EIS by the Task Force as well as a January 18, 1975, memo prepared by the Neighborhood Ten Association that attempts to lay out some of the EIS's (flawed, in Neighborhood Ten's opinion) assumptions.

126. Maycock and Sullivan, *Building Old Cambridge*, 163.

127. Quoted in Campbell, "The Impact Study as Red Herring"; Campbell was not himself accusing the opponents of elitism but characterizing another *Globe* columnist's opinion. Campbell himself seems to have felt the memorial's opponents had every right to defend the Square and its unique character as they did. In this piece, he wrote, "There isn't anything elitist about hoping that one place can remain different from other places, that it doesn't have to get swamped with Winnebagoes and MacDonald [sic] stands in a homogenized worldwide sprawl." Of those lobbing accusations of elitism, Campbell asked, "Have they forgotten that JFK himself was a Brattle Street elitist to his toes? Imagination fails to conjure up a picture of Jackie in curlers on Boylston Street."

9. WHOSE SQUARE? THE BATTLE FOR CONTROL

1. Federico Muchnik, *Touching History: Harvard Square, the Bank, & the Tasty Diner* (2005), video, 33 min., https://vimeo.com/18973913.
2. Amy Miller, "Bank Buys Chunk of Historic Harvard Square," *Cambridge Chronicle*, January 27, 1994.
3. Charles Sullivan, *Final Landmark Designation Report* (Cambridge, MA: Cambridge Historical Commission, June 5, 1997).
4. Details in this paragraph on the history and physical state of the buildings are drawn from several sources: Jason Lefferts, "Vote Moves Historic Harvard Sq. Block Closer to Landmark Status," *Cambridge Chronicle*, April 10, 1997, in which Lefferts describes a tour he took through the properties and in which Cambridge Savings Bank's senior vice president for administration describes some of the slapdash modifications made throughout the years; Sullivan's *Final Landmark Designation Report* as well as a March 29, 2021, personal communication with Sullivan; Tom Bracken, "Memorandum to Gifford, Moot & Medwed, Re: Cambridge Savings Bank Read Block Proposed Development," June 17, 1996, HSDF Collection, CHS, in which the report of a structural engineer named Wayne King is summarized and noted for identifying the building's sagging wooden beams and rooftop billboard that acted "like a sail which continuously shakes the building."
5. When presenting the bank's initial demolition plans, Ingram indicated the bank had hired consultants who advised the buildings were unsalvageable and that the best path was demolition and redevelopment. The bank's position was quoted in numerous reports at the time including: Amy Miller, "Historic Harvard Square Blocks Face Wrecking Ball or Landmark Status," *Cambridge Chronicle*, May 9, 1996; Amy Miller, "Razing, Rebuilding Harvard Sq. History," *Cambridge Chronicle*, July 20, 1995; Howard Manly, "Harvard Sq. Battle Lines Being Drawn—Preservationists Fear Bank Will Demolish Wursthaus-Tasty Site," *Boston Globe*, October 1, 1995.
6. Amy Miller, "Bank Floats Plan, Seeks Opinions on Fate of Key Harvard Square Corner," *Cambridge Chronicle*, July 27, 1995.
7. Miller, "Razing, Rebuilding Harvard Square History."
8. A 1983 profile of the Tasty in the *Boston Globe* provides a nice description of both the physical and social attributes of the Tasty from which I draw in this and the next paragraph: Paul Hirshson, "Little Changes at the Tasty, Except the Year," *Boston Globe*, January 22, 1983.

9. Quotes from Coney in this paragraph are from Hirshson, "Little Changes at the Tasty."

10. Hirshson, "Little Changes at the Tasty."

11. "Groups Rally to Preserve Restaurants," *Harvard Crimson*, August 2, 1996.

12. Amy Miller, "Watchdogs Do Best to Preserve Wursthaus Block, Save Old Facade," *Cambridge Chronicle*, August 24, 1995.

13. Miller, "Watchdogs Do Best to Preserve Wursthaus Block"; Miller, "Historic Harvard Square Blocks Face Wrecking Ball."

14. Joe Matthews, "The Battle for Harvard Square; Endangered: Preservationists Are Fighting a Holding Action as Quirky Eateries and Unique Buildings Give Way to Starbucks and Chain Stores in This Outpost of Urban Eclecticism," *The Sun* (Baltimore, MD), December 13, 1996.

15. "Groups Rally to Preserve Restaurants," *Harvard Crimson*, August 2, 1996.

16. The multiple public meetings held to discuss the bank's plans are featured in Muchnik's film and were covered at the time in news reports such as "Decision on Fate of Tasty Delayed," *Harvard Crimson*, January 8, 1997.

17. Matthews, "The Battle for Harvard Square."

18. Susan E. Maycock and Charles M. Sullivan, *Building Old Cambridge: Architecture and Development* (Cambridge, MA: MIT Press, 2016), 164.

19. For businesses entering and exiting the market during the 1980s and 1990s, mentioned here and below, I consulted various sources including: *Crimson* articles about store openings and closings; Mo Lotman, *Harvard Square: An Illustrated History Since 1950* (New York: Stewart, Tabori & Chang, 2009); HSBA "Guide to Harvard Square" maps, 1995–1999, Hedberg Maps; Richard Curran and Allan Curran, *All About Harvard Square: A Guide: Historic Walking Tours, Museums, Restaurants, Shopping & Entertainment* (Cambridge, MA: Basement Graphics, 1989); and issues of the *Unofficial Guide to Life at Harvard* (Cambridge, MA: Harvard Student Agencies/Let's Go, Inc).

20. A sample of articles from the 1980s include: Paul Hirshson, "Harvard Square Losing Funky Look," *Boston Globe*, August 25, 1987; Paul Hirshson, "The Death of Harvard Square or Maybe It's a Rebirth in Brick. The Debate Rages On," *Boston Globe*, December 6, 1987; Gawain Kripke, "We Need a Square Deal," *Harvard Crimson*, May 27, 1988. A sample of articles from the early 1990s includes: Jon Marcus, "Harvard Square Neighbors Fight Change," *Los Angeles Times*, April 28, 1991; Gady Epstein, "The New Guard of Harvard Square," *Boston Globe*, August 29, 1992; "Square Change," *Harvard Crimson*, March 3, 1993; Leondra Kruger, "Old Days of Quiet Neighborhood Die," *Harvard Crimson*, February 17, 1995; Richard Thomas, "Vestige of 'Yesterday's Village' Worthy of Preservation in Heart of Harvard Sq," *Cambridge Chronicle*, January 23, 1997.

21. George Ritzer, *The McDonaldization of Society: An Investigation into the Changing Character of Contemporary Social Life* (Newbury Park, CA: Pine Forge Press, 1993).

22. For books that touch on this theme, see, for example: Ritzer, *McDonaldization of Society*; James Coleman, *The Asymmetric Society* (Syracuse, NY: Syracuse University Press, 1982); Robert Bellah, Richard Madsen, William Sullivan, et al., *Habits of the Heart: Individualism and Collectivism in American Life* (Berkeley: University of California Press, 1985); Michael Sandel, *Democracy's Discontents: America in Search of a Public Philosophy* (Cambridge, MA: Belknap Press, 1996).

23. One of the largest undergraduate classes at Harvard at the time was "Social Analysis 10: Principles of Economics"—or "Ec 10" as it was known. From the mid-1980s on, it was taught by Martin Feldstein, a free-market economist who had served as Reagan's chief economic advisor. A December 1994 opinion piece in the *Harvard Crimson* suggested that groups such as the Harvard Square Defense Fund that were upset about changes in Harvard Square and wanted to protect it from "the forces of evil" should, instead, take Ec 10. "Whether some residents of Cambridge like it or not, this nation runs on the capitalist model," the *Crimson* writers declared, "As any Ec 10 student knows, we keep this system because it does the best job of allocating goods and services and meeting consumer needs": The *Crimson* Staff, "Square Guardians Should Take Ec 10," *Harvard Crimson*, December 16, 1994.

24. Meeting Minutes, September 7, 1972, HSBA Collection, CHS.

25. Paul Ingram and Hayagreeva Rao, "Store Wars: The Enactment and Repeal of Anti-Chain-Store Legislation in America," *American Journal of Sociology* 110, no. 2 (September 2004): 446–87.

26. This seems to have been discussed at various points in the 1980s and '90s, for example: "Ideas Fly at Retailers Meeting," *Harvard Square Business Association Newsletter*, February 1994, Tod Beaty Collection, Cambridge, Massachusetts (Beaty generously shared his personal collection of newsletters from the early 1990s to early 2000s with the author; hereafter cited as *HSBA Newsletters*, Beaty Collection).

27. Even when chain-store managers or franchisees joined the Harvard Square Business Association, they had fewer decision rights over their stores' operations than did independent proprietors. Salaried managers also had less incentive to give themselves over to time-consuming collective endeavors.

28. For Cohen's comments, also quoted in chapter 2, see Hirshson, "Death of Harvard Square." Cohen described the market changes during this period as a result of the organic growth and development of the marketplace. In 1994, Cohen took advantage of the opportunities afforded by such growth when he sold his business to Hudson News, a New Jersey–based chain that operated newsstands around the country. Reports at the time suggest Cohen was in financial trouble on account of a pending lawsuit and had to sell; he also noted personal reasons for wanting to retire. Meg Vaillancourt, "Landmark Newsstand to Be Sold, NJ Firm to Purchase Harvard Square Newsstand," *Boston Globe*, July 10, 1994; "Harvard Square Kiosk Is Sold", *Harvard Crimson*, July 12, 1974.

29. Debra Reynolds, "The Harvard Square Business Association: The Past Seventy-Five Years" (1985), available at the Harvard Square Business Association offices as well as in the HSBA Collection of the CHS. In 1993, a new executive director was hired, and the announcement indicated the group had specifically sought someone with strong marketing and public-relations experience, including events planning. "New Executive Director Kristin Sudholz," *HSBA Newsletter*, September 1993, Beaty Collection.

30. The first Oktoberfest was held in 1979, and by the mid-1980s, the one-day event was drawing crowds of nearly fifteen thousand. The first Mayfair was held in 1984, and it soon began to draw thousands as well. "Octoberfest Brings Crowds, Contest to Harvard Square," *Harvard Crimson*, October 9, 1984; "Thousands Converge on Square for Mayfair," *Harvard Crimson*, May 6, 1991.

31. *HSBA Newsletter*, September 1993 and September 1995, Beaty Collection.

32. The 1994 seminar was mentioned in a 1995 recap of the prior year's activities: *HSBA Newsletter*, March 1995, Beaty Collection.

33. This project got going in earnest in the 1990s. "Caring for the Square: Property Owners, HSBA, and DPW Team Up," *HSBA Newsletter*, June 1995, Beaty Collection.
34. Articles of Organization, Harvard Square Defense Fund, Inc., Filed with Commonwealth of Massachusetts, 1979, HSDF Collection, CHS; and "Save Our Square," *Harvard Square News* 1, no 1 (July 1979), published by the Harvard Square Defense Fund,
HSDF Collection, CHS. *Harvard Square News* was a newspaper-format publication
put out by the Defense Fund during its most active years to keep members up-to-date
on pertinent issues and generate awareness of and support for the group's activities.
Related to this section's subheading, the group explicitly cast itself as essential guardians of the Square; see, for example: Priscilla McMillan Letter to Michael Robert,
March 15, 1993, HSDF Collection, CHS.
35. This and the paragraph's subsequent quote from Gifford to the author are from Conversation with Gladys Gifford, March 3, 2019, Harvard Square Neighborhood Association meeting, Cambridge, Massachusetts. After I introduced my research project
to Gifford there and she shared some of her history with the Defense Fund, she generously pointed me to the Defense Fund's archives as a resource for the project. I later
had two follow-up conversations with Gifford in summer 2021 after I had reviewed
those records.
36. Maycock and Sullivan discuss the Defense Fund's activities during this period.
Building Old Cambridge, 164–74. Other profiles of the group that chronicle its battles
include: Adam Hickey, "The Defense (Fund) Never Rests Its Case," *Harvard Crimson*,
March 5, 1997; Howard Manly, "Playing Hardball on the Home Turf Harvard Sq.
Defense Fund Puts Its Stamp on the Area," *Boston Globe*, October 9, 1994.
37. Jeremy Hirsh, "Group Opposes Development," *Harvard Crimson*, December 5, 1988;
Jay Weaver, "Group Floats Curb to Square Development," *Cambridge Chronicle*, January 12, 1989.
38. Maycock and Sullivan, *Building Old Cambridge*, 164.
39. Letter from Priscilla McMillan, Treasurer of the Harvard Square Defense Fund, to
Michael Robert, March 15, 1993, HSDF Collection, CHS; also referenced in "Carpenter Lawsuit vs. Us" File, HSDF Collection, CHS.
40. Gladys Gifford, telephone conversation with the author, July 24, 2021.
41. Details on Lou DiGiovanni's biography in this and subsequent paragraphs are drawn
from interviews and conversations with Lou's son John during the course of my
research in 2019–2021, as well as a 1987 *Boston Globe* profile of the developer: Paul
Hirshson, "Developer Stays Out of Public Eye," *Boston Globe*, March 25, 1987.
42. John DiGiovanni, interview by the author, September 5, 2019.
43. Pamela Varley, "Razing Blocked; City Goes to Court," *Cambridge Chronicle*, May 20,
1982; "Suit, Countersuit Filed in Demolition Attempt," *Cambridge Chronicle*, October
7, 1982.
44. Letter from Louis F. DiGiovanni to Olive Holmes, President of the Harvard Square
Defense Fund, May 13, 1987, HSDF Collection, CHS. DiGiovanni repeated this criticism of the Defense Fund publicly in Hirshson's *Boston Globe* profile of the developer.
Hirshson, "Developer Stays Out of Public Eye."
45. Letter to Friends of Harvard Square from Pebble Gifford, May 1983, HSDF Collection, CHS. See also Paul Hirshson, "Opposition to Cambridge Video Arcade," *Boston
Globe*, November 15, 1982.
46. Letter to Friends of Harvard Square from Pebble Gifford, May 1983. See also "Liquor
Permits Stir Controversy," *Cambridge Chronicle*, November 18, 1982.

47. Among the issues over which the Defense Fund and DiGiovanni (first Lou, then John) butted heads was the placement of a Dunkin' Donuts franchise in DiGiovanni's property at 65 JFK Street. In May 21, 1997, the Defense Fund's attorneys sent a letter to the Cambridge Commission of Inspectional Services stating that the Dunkin' Donuts at that location was operating in violation of conditions stipulated by the city's Board of Zoning Appeal. The letter noted the store's failure to display nondisposable cups, plates, and utensils and criticized it for, instead, having a "massive stacking" of paper cups on the counter. Letter to Commissioner Robert Bersani, City of Cambridge, from Thomas Bracken as counsel for the Harvard Square Defense Fund, March 21, 1997, HSDF Collection, CHS.

48. "Save Our Square," *Harvard Square News*.

49. For discussion of the "highest and best use" paradigm, including its dominance by the 1980s, see Mark Dotzour, Terry Grissom, Crocker Liu, and Thomas Pearson, "Highest and Best Use: The Evolving Paradigm," *Journal of Real Estate Research* 5, no. 1 (Spring 1990): 17–32.

50. It was not just landlords who thought this way. The assumption that markets are allocatively efficient is a mainstay of neoclassical economics. The writers of the December 16, 1994, *Crimson* article, "Square Guardians Should Take Ec 10," articulated the logic when they wrote: "The Square does not need to be defended against capitalism and the forces of the free market. . . . The stores in the Square that serve their customers well, providing quality merchandise at good prices will flourish. Success means that people have made their voices heard: this is a store they want in the Square. The stores that can't pay their rents are those stores that haven't done a good job of delivering value to consumers. Their departure from the Square is no great loss. . . . In fact, any business that satisfied the needs of the local population will survive. Frivolous businesses . . . deserve to be pushed out by the invisible hand. Ultimately, of course, Squaregoers will determine the definition of 'frivolousness.'"

51. Amy Miller, "What's in Store for Harvard Square," *Cambridge Chronicle*, April 1, 1993.

52. Miller, "What's in Store for Harvard Square."

53. James Coleman's most famous treatment of this is *Asymmetric Society* (1982). However, he began developing these ideas earlier, and his concise discussion in *Power and the Structure of Society* (New York: Norton, 1974) of the alienation people experience when forced to interact with distant corporate actors instead of other individuals is highly relevant to this discussion. I thank Diane Vaughan for pointing me to this earlier work.

54. This is not to say the Square was immune from the economic cycles affecting other markets at the time. The U.S. economy experienced a recession in the early 1980s and again in the early 1990s, both of which were felt by businesses in the Square. Nevertheless, those years were also active periods for new development, and the Square continued to be a popular shopping destination during these decades.

55. When I presented an early version of my research on Harvard Square at Columbia University in 2019, a member of the audience told me he'd grown up going to regular family dinners at the Harvard Square Chili's in the 1980s and '90s. When Bertucci's closed in 2013, among those disappointed were members of Harvard's Classics Department who had some years before begun a tradition of holding Friday dinners there: Nikki Erlick, "Bertucci's Closes After 25 Years on Brattle Street," *Harvard Crimson*, August 24, 2013.

56. Douglas M. Bailey, "USA to Buy Janus, Harvard Square Theaters," *Boston Globe*, August 5, 1986; Desiree French, "USA Cinemas to Be Sold for $165 Million," *Boston Globe*, January 23, 1988.

57. The Square's street life has been commented upon and profiled numerous times. The "philosopher for rent" was mentioned in passing in Diane White, "Cute Food Ruins Appetite," *Boston Globe*, February 26, 1983. Several years later, the *Globe* ran a feature article on the Square's street performers: Patti Hartigan, "Showtime in Harvard Square," *Boston Globe*, September 11, 1986.

58. "In Pursuit of A SOUND POLICY," *HSBA Newsletter*, June 1994; and "Summer Sounds," *HSBA Newsletter*, July/August 1995, Beaty Collection.

59. Robert Campbell, "Showdown on Main Street, At Stake Is More than Just a Corner of Harvard Square," *Boston Globe*, September 17, 1996.

60. Muchnik discusses his motivation for the project and the process by which he filmed and produced it in Ellen Mills, "Main Street or Mall Street," interview with Federico Muchnik, NewEnglandFilm.com, December 1, 2005, https://newenglandfilm.com /magazine/2005/12/main-street-or-mall-street.

61. Amy Miller, "Historic Harvard Sq. Blocks Face Wrecking Ball."

62. The *Crimson* Staff, "Keep the Tasty; Gut the Building," *Harvard Crimson*, June 2, 1997. It seems even the *Crimson* staff may have been divided by this controversy. Presumably the student journalists who advocated that the bank keep the Tasty or be punished with a Historic District designation did not see exactly eye to eye with the *Crimson* writers who had, just a couple of years earlier (December 16, 1994, "Square Guardians Should Take Ec 10"), insisted that rental decisions be left up to the free market (see notes 23 and 50).

63. Amy Miller, "Bank Plans to Save Historic Asset, Citizens Cheer Preservation Victory," *Cambridge Chronicle*, June 12, 1997.

64. Amy Miller, "Bank Plans to Save Historic Asset."

65. In Muchnik's film, Haddad says of this period, "It's difficult to deal with the bank when the key person who's calling most of the shots, Pete Ingram, doesn't even speak to you." News reports at the time suggest that Haddad and the community were still holding out some hope that the Tasty might be able to return after construction, and both Haddad and bank representatives are quoted in February 1999 news articles as saying that the bank did ultimately offer him the opportunity to return to the space after construction but at a rent the business could not afford. In Muchnik's film, Haddad offers his interpretation of the bank's behavior during this process: "The bank portrayed themselves as being the good neighbor, they want to do the right thing by the community, and it was all a farce." For news reports of the ongoing negotiations: Jeremiah Leibowitz, "Tasty Owner Makes Second Run at Old Spot," *Cambridge Chronicle*, February 5, 1998; "Clothing Shops Confirm Move to Read Block in Harvard Square," *Cambridge Chronicle*, February 4, 1999; Jason Goins, "Tasty Owners Will Not Reopen Famous Diner," *Harvard Crimson*, February 9, 1999.

66. Jeremiah Leibowitz, "No Temporary Home for the Tasty," *Cambridge Chronicle*, November 27, 1997.

67. Amy Miller, "Tasty Evicted, Future Uncertain," *Cambridge Chronicle*, November 6, 1997.

68. Jeremiah Leibowitz, "Residents, City Rally to Save Tasty," *Cambridge Chronicle*, November 20, 1997.

69. Muchnik, *Touching History*.

70. Jeremy Leibowitz, "Business Group: City Should Stay Out of Tasty Affairs," *Cambridge Chronicle*, November 27, 1997.

71. "Historic District in Harvard Square?," *Cambridge Chronicle*, August 17, 1995.

72. The Cambridge Historical Commission has an entire box containing just the meetings minutes and correspondence of the Historic District Study Committee's work from 1997 to 1999. Having read through some of this material, I can attest to both the patience and passion of all the participants involved in this process.

73. Covered in Part 1, Title VII, Chapter 40C, Sections 1–17 of Massachusetts General Law, https://malegislature.gov/Laws/GeneralLaws/PartI/TitleVII/Chapter40C, accessed May 31, 2022.

74. Part 1, Title VII, Chapter 40C, Section 2 of Massachusetts General Law, https://malegislature.gov/Laws/GeneralLaws/PartI/TitleVII/Chapter40C/Section2, accessed May 31, 2022.

75. A 1998 document listing the pros and cons of a Historic District designation for the different interest groups indicates the Defense Fund was disappointed that such a designation "still does not guarantee 'non-chain' tenants" in the Square. "Harvard Square Historic District with Zoning Amendments," ca. 1998, HSDF Collection, CHS.

76. Seth Harwood, "Save the Square Effort Continues," *Cambridge Chronicle*, December 10, 1998.

77. Harwood, "Save the Square Effort Continues."

78. DiGiovanni articulated his position in Historic District Study Committee meetings and public hearings as well as to the local press. In November 1999, he sent an open letter to every member of the city council explaining his opposition: Lisa Kocian, "Harvard Square Set to Make History, Vote on Historic District Likely Next Month," *Cambridge Chronicle*, November 24, 1999.

79. "Getting and Giving Perspective: A Discussion About Historic Districts," *HSBA Newsletter*, December 1996/January 1997, Beaty Collection.

80. "Maintaining Balance: Past, Present, Future," *HSBA Newsletter*, September 1996, Beaty Collection.

81. "Maintaining Balance: Past, Present, Future," *HSBA Newsletter*.

82. The Business Association ribbed the Defense Fund in a series of April Fool's newsletter articles. In its April 1995 newsletter, for example, the Business Association ran a fictional piece announcing that a McDonald's was opening in the Square and quoted a fictional Pebble Gifford welcoming the change enthusiastically. The next year's April Fool's issue reported that the Tasty was going to remain in the Square but would be transforming itself into a fast-food soft pretzel vendor, with a parking garage atop its building and two mega-bookstore chains as its neighbors. Again, a fictional Pebble Gifford was quoted as welcoming the change, this time saying she was "delighted that Cambridge Savings Bank has heard the community's concerns and are demonstrating such flexibility in its innovative plan." "McDonald's Not Clowning; Square Location Proposed," April 1995, *HSBA Newsletter*; and "One Harvard Square: Final Plans Unreal!," *HSBA Newsletter*, April 1996, Beaty Collection.

83. "November 1999 Letter from Richard. R. Beaty to Mr. Sullivan," published in *HSBA Newsletter*, November 1999, Beaty Collection.

84. "November 1999 Letter from Richard. R. Beaty to Mr. Sullivan," *HSBA Newsletter*. In April 2000, just before a final city council vote was set to be held on the issue, members of the Harvard Square Business Association including DiGiovanni rallied

again and circulated a letter opposing the Historic District, saying it would "freeze Harvard Square in time" and "make change too difficult": Lisa Kocian, "Businesses Not Buying Historic District, Thirty Owners Sign Petition Against Designation for Harvard Square," *Cambridge Chronicle*, April 26, 2000.

85. Harwood, "Save the Square Effort Continues."

86. Harwood, "Save the Square Effort Continues."

87. Leigh Hornbeck, "Preservation vs. Innovation in Harvard Square," *Cambridge Chronicle*, June 13, 2001; Zachary Heineman, "Protecting, Not Petrifying, Harvard Square," *Harvard Crimson*, February 21, 2001.

88. *Crimson* writers were on-site that night as well and reported that the souvenir photographs were going for $20 per snapshot. Jennifer Lee, "Tasty Closes but May Move," *Harvard Crimson*, November 3, 1997.

10. PULLING AWAY

1. Quotes from Corcoran and details about her experiences at Black Ink are drawn from the author's multiple interviews and personal communications with Corcoran during the research for this project in 2019–2021.

2. "New Members," *HSBA Newsletter*, March 1995, Tod Beaty Collection, Cambridge, Massachusetts (hereafter cited as Beaty Collection).

3. Elizabeth Angell, "Under the Cushions of Cyberspresso," *Harvard Crimson*, February 9, 1995.

4. Angell, "Under the Cushions of Cyberspresso." The new café concept was apparently so noteworthy that its Harvard Square opening received coverage across the country in the *Los Angeles Times*: Richard Lorant, "Harvard Square Café Offers Cyberspace, Hot Coffee Too," *Los Angeles Times*, February 26, 1995. In its first year of operation, crowds reportedly gathered outside some days just to watch the people inside playing "virtual reality" video games on the terminals: R. Alan Leo, "Cybersmith Nets First Year Success," *Harvard Crimson*, February 10, 1996. Its opening-day crowd that wrapped around the block was recalled a few years later when the café closed: Patti Hartigan, "Cybersmith Logs Off for the Last Time," *Boston Globe*, March 19, 1999.

5. "Harvardsquare.com, Building Our On-Line Community," *HSBA Newsletter*, July/August 1996, Beaty Collection.

6. Tod Beaty, conversation with the author, October 17, 2019.

7. A full-page promotion in the January 1997 *HSBA Newsletter* advertised an upcoming workshop being held at Cybersmith to help Business Association members learn how to edit their webpages on harvardsquare.com. It also noted members could receive additional training through Cybersmith's "Hour Intro to the Internet" workshop, for which they would receive a discounted rate. "Internet: Learn How to Edit Your Web Page," *HSBA Newsletter*, January 1997, Beaty Collection.

8. "Harvardsquare.com, Building Our On-Line Community," *HSBA Newsletter*.

9. "Click to the Heart of Harvard Square! www.harvardsquare.com," *HSBA Newsletter*, October 1996, Beaty Collection.

10. Hartigan, "Cybersmith Logs Off for the Last Time."

11. Details on Harvard Book Store's activities during this period come from communications with Frank Kramer, who owned the store until 2008, Jeff Mayersohn, who purchased it from Kramer that year and has operated it since, and Carole Horne, a

longtime manager of the store. Interviews and discussions with Kramer took place on May 13, 2019 and May 29, 2019; with Mayersohn on October 20, 2020, via Zoom; and with all three on August 7, 2019.

12. "Meet Rebekah Brooks of Rebekah Brooks Jewelry in Beacon Hill and Harvard Square," *BostonVoyager*, May 30, 2017, http://bostonvoyager.com/interview/meet-rebekah-brooks-rebekah-brooks-jewelry-beacon-hill-harvard-square/.

13. By 2004, Little Russia's owners were old and ready to retire. By then, eBay had become a powerful platform for purchasing the sort of interesting goods stores like Little Russia sold. Jessica Rubin-Wills, "After 25 Years, Little Russia to Close Its Doors, Mt. Auburn Institution Sells Slavic Jewelry, Trinkets," *Harvard Crimson*, March 2, 2004; Chris Berdik, "A Little Bit of Russia Is Vanishing from Harvard Square," *Boston Globe*, February 15, 2004.

14. Mary Hurley, "In Square, Another Sad Corner Turned," *Boston Globe*, July 10, 2005.

15. Shifra Mincer, "Camera Shop Shutters, Its Long Kodak Moment Over," *Harvard Crimson*, October 16, 2006.

16. A search of articles finds that the internet was mentioned as a precipitating factor in articles about bookstore and newsstand closings during the first decade of the twenty-first century, reflecting the publishing industry's relatively early disruption. However, the internet and e-commerce were rarely invoked in more general pieces about the demise of Harvard Square or in many of the reports of other business closings until the middle to end of the following decade. Even then, as we saw in chapter 3, chains and rents remained the primary focus of local discourse.

17. Gifford cites 2008 as the approximate date of the Defense Fund's dissolution in Tom Meek and Marc Levy, "Harvard Square Isn't Losing Defense Fund, It's Just Gaining Neighborhood Association," *Cambridge Day*, June 17, 2017.

18. Mary Hurley, "In Square, Another Sad Corner Turned," *Boston Globe*, July 10, 2005.

19. The financial crisis of 2008 dealt yet another blow that could manifest as an inability to cover rent and obscure the impact of online competition.

20. Jay Fitzgerald, "80-Year-Old Newsstand May Close," *Boston Herald*, November 20, 2008; Michael Levenson, "At Kiosk, Dire News—Plan to Shutter Newsstand Pierces Heart of Harvard Square," *Boston Globe*, November 20, 2008; "Out of Town News 1955–2009," *Cambridge Chronicle*, November 20, 2008; Abby Goodnough, "A New Sign of Change at the Gates of Harvard," *New York Times*, November 22, 2008; Ed Symkus, "Writer Remembers His Out of Town News Ritual," *Cambridge Chronicle*, November 27, 2008. These articles tended to note the internet as a cause of Out of Town News's demise, while also giving voice to people's grief over the loss of that Harvard Square institution and the cherished routines and rituals it had once supported in their lives.

21. Levenson, "At Kiosk, Dire News."

22. Jenna Nierstedt, "Good News! Corporation Rescues Out of Town Stand," *Boston Globe*, January 29, 2009; Associated Press, "Harvard Square Newsstand Is Saved," *New York Times*, January 30, 2009.

23. According to Chris Kotelly, owner of the Square's other newsstand at the time, cigarettes had long been a part of the newsstand business, and declining sales of that product had also affected these establishments over the years. For reports of the new owner stepping in to run the kiosk newsstand: Liyun Jin, "Square Kiosk Finds New Owners," *Harvard Crimson*, January 28, 2009; Associated Press, "Harvard Square Newsstand Is Saved."

24. Kerry Flynn, "Business Owners Draft Construction Plan to Model Harvard Square on Times Square," *Harvard Crimson*, May 23, 2012; Ashley Studley, "Biz Group Looks to Give Square a Makeover," *Cambridge Chronicle*, May 31, 2012.

25. Joshua Florence, "Out of Town News Planned Renovations Provoke Local Outcry," *Harvard Crimson*, August 31, 2016. A consistent theme of the criticisms was that city officials and the Harvard Square Business Association were not allowing sufficient public participation in decisions about how the kiosk would be renovated and used, including the fate of Out of Town News. At one city council meeting, a local resident spoke up to say that she felt those powerful actors had "monopolized" the process and, as a result, "our Harvard Square is increasingly becoming dehumanized, sanitized, homogenized, institutionalized, and corporatized": Joanna Duffy, "Plans for Kiosk Draw More Fire," *Cambridge Chronicle*, October 20, 2016. Even some city councilors seemed to feel that the Business Association and the city officials working with that group were moving too fast and without enough community input: Natalie Handy, "Harvard Square Kiosk Plan Gets Mixed Review," *Cambridge Chronicle*, March 3, 2016. Meanwhile, a group of Harvard Square residents convened to discuss the situation and contemplate what action might be taken, and a local burger joint put a chalk sign outside its front entrance saying, "Save Out of Town News": Florence, "Out of Town News Planned Renovations Provoke Local Outcry." Amidst all this debate, the internet often receded from focus. A guest columnist for the *Cambridge Chronicle* wrote, "The real question facing the city isn't one of keeping up with the times or presenting a modern face. No, the real question is one of character." Out of Town News was the "manifestation" of the community's character. Accordingly, this writer argued, the community must "Keep Out of Town News in town, on the peninsula, within the intact kiosk,"—"whether or not one ever steps foot inside that business, or buys print from somewhere in the reaches of the world": James Mahoney, "The In-Town Argument for Out of Town News," *Cambridge Chronicle*, November 24, 2016.

26. Sounding much like the owner of the Tasty when that business was being evicted by Cambridge Savings Bank, the owner of the newsstand told the *Boston Globe* that he wanted to keep running the business in the kiosk but said, "What can you do? We don't own the property": Kathleen Conti, "Out of Town News Could Be Pushed Out of Harvard Square," *Boston Globe*, August 25, 2016.

27. Travis Anderson, "Public Input Sought for Project to Redesign Harvard Square," *Boston Globe*, June 24, 2016.

28. Adam Sennott, "Group to Study Harvard Square Kiosk," *Cambridge Chronicle*, March 30, 2017. A timeline of the city's formal evaluation process for the kiosk's renovation and reuse can be found here: https://www.cambridgema.gov/CDD/Projects/Parks /HSquarePublicSpace. The working group's final report (which was the result of multiple meetings of the group itself, plus numerous community meetings, a public call for ideas, a survey, stakeholder interviews, and several workshops) can be found here: City of Cambridge Report, *Harvard Square Kiosk and Plaza Final Report*, October 2018, https://www.cambridgema.gov/-/media/Files/CDD/ParksandOpenSpace /ParkProjects/HSquarePublicSpace/hsq20181018kioskworkinggroupfinalreport1.pdf.

29. Suzanne Blier, Kathleen Coleman, Tom Conley, Joseph Koerner, Timothy McCarthy, and Steven Pinker Letter to the Editor, "Preserving the Harvard Square Kiosk," *Harvard Crimson*, August 30, 2016. That same month, one of those professors, Suzanne Blier (who would go on to form the Harvard Square Neighborhood Association the following year), teamed up with another woman to form a group called "Our Harvard

Square." They started a change.org petition calling for the kiosk to be granted historical landmark status so that significant physical modifications to it could not be made. The kiosk had been listed on the National Register of Historic Places since 1978, but the group wanted additional protections for it. Focused on the fate of the physical structure, Blier acknowledged that the newsstand business was likely to go, saying, "It's a time when media are changing. It's a sad event but these things happen": Kathleen Conti, "Out of Town News Founder Heartbroken," *Boston Globe*, August 29, 2016.

30. Quotes from Denise Jillson and description of her perspective included in this and subsequent paragraphs are drawn from a June 10, 2019, interview with Jillson on a range of subjects, including the kiosk and the overall effects of online commerce on the Square.

31. Conti, "Out of Town News Could Be Pushed Out of Harvard Square." Jillson was not the only individual to offer this perspective. When Out of Town News finally closed in 2019, the Rev. John F. Hudson composed a tribute to the fallen establishment and a thoughtful take on market change. Hudson acknowledged that, yes, the city had decided to renovate a valuable piece of real estate and, as a result, Out of Town News no longer had a home in the kiosk; but "what really killed Out of Town News," Hudson wrote, "is me, and you, and millions of other folks who still consume the news, read the news, follow the news but now do so on our screens. . . . We don't buy the news at Out of Town News anymore": John F. Hudson, "Out of Time for Out of Town News," *Cambridge Chronicle*, September 19, 2019.

32. These are year-end 2017 numbers, i.e., Amazon's size at the approximate time Asana became Corcoran's landlord. By the end of 2017, Amazon had more than 100 million subscription-paying Prime members, which is a conservative customer count that does not include individuals without Prime memberships who also purchased things from Amazon. By the end of 2019, when Corcoran's store closed, Amazon's market value had risen to almost $1 trillion, and the company now had 200 million Prime subscribers. Sources: Amazon's annual reports for 2017 and 2019, "Annual Reports, Proxies and Shareholder Letters," Amazon.com, https://ir.aboutamazon.com/annual-reports-proxies-and-shareholder-letters/default.aspx, accessed June 1, 2022; "Amazon Market Cap 2010-2022 | AMZN," macrotrends, https://www.macrotrends.net/stocks/charts/AMZN/amazon/market-cap, accessed June 1, 2022.

33. In his piece on the closure of Out of Town News, the Rev. John F. Hudson made a similar observation about the appeal of disruptive innovations, though he offered a more religious than romantic perspective. He wrote, "We humans are a restless lot, created by a God who gives us the power to think, to change, to grow, to innovate, and to reach for the stars. Along that path, as we shift from one way of doing things to another, it can be hard to bid farewell to the familiar and the comfortable and the known. But the truth is that innovation and disruption happen and not just because some vague outside force wrenches us into the future. Disruption happens because of us." Hudson, "Out of Time for Out of Town News."

11. DIFFERENT MARKETS, DIFFERENT PERSPECTIVES

1. Edward Mason, "Billionaire Buying into Harvard Square," *Boston Globe*, April 5, 2014. In the years after this *Globe* article, Chan continued to acquire properties in

and around the Square, so the article's 2014 estimate may undervalue his total portfolio. For example, in 2018 he purchased 52 Brattle Street, the building next door to the village blacksmith's old house, for a reported $24 million: Joe Clements, "Dr. Gerald Chan Seen Paying $24M for Legacy Harvard Sq. Asset via HFF," *Real Reporter*, December 27, 2018.

2. Mason, "Billionaire Buying into Harvard Square."

3. Details on Chan in this and subsequent paragraphs are drawn from personal conversations with Chan during my research as well as profiles written about him and his real estate acquisitions in local media, for example: David Harris, "Billionaire Hong Kong Native Buys into Cambridge," *Banker and Tradesman*, February 23, 2014; Ivan Levingstone, Celeste Mendoza, and Caroline Zhang, "Billionaire Buys Up Harvard Square Real Estate," *Harvard Crimson*, March 5, 2014; Mason, "Billionaire Buying into Harvard Square"; Neil Swidey, "Meet Boston's Invisible Billionaire," *Boston Globe*, May 3, 2015; Christopher Muther, "Could Clues to Harvard Square's Future Be Found in Stunning New English Hotel?," *Boston Globe*, July 13, 2019.

4. "A Gift Unsolicited, Unrestricted, and Unexpected," *Harvard School of Public Health Magazine*, September 8, 2014, https://www.hsph.harvard.edu/magazine/magazine_article/a-gift-unsolicited-unrestricted-and-unexpected/; Christine Cahill and Matthew Clarida, "With Naming Rights on the Table, Harvard Gave Its Price," *Harvard Crimson*, September 10, 2014.

5. "Equity One Reports Fourth Quarter and Year End 2015 Operating Results," *Business Wire*, February 24, 2016, https://www.businesswire.com/news/home/20160224006285/en/Equity-One-Reports-Fourth-Quarter-and-Year-End-2015-Operating-Results; the 2015 sale was also reported the following year when the fate of some of the building's tenants became a topic of discussion: Joshua Florence, "Curious George, Urban Outfitters Could Face Closures," *Harvard Crimson*, September 7, 2016.

6. "Regency Centers and Equity One Announce Closing of Merger," Regency Centers Company Release, March 1, 2017, https://investors.regencycenters.com/news-releases/news-release-details/regency-centers-and-equity-one-announce-closing-merger.

7. Kathleen Conti, "Harvard Square Properties Sell for $108 Million," *Boston Globe*, December 19, 2017; Henry Burnes, Franklin Civantos, and Katherine Wang, "Properties Housing Felipe's, Crema, Cardullo's Sold for More than $100 Million," *Harvard Crimson*, December 20, 2017.

8. Brie Buchanan, Ellen Burstein, and Peter O'Keefe, "Urban Outfitters and Sweet Bakery Close Ahead of Renovations," *Harvard Crimson*, January 15, 2019.

9. Alex Green and Judith Rosen, "New Owner and Move for Curious George," *Publishers Weekly*, May 16, 2019, https://www.publishersweekly.com/pw/by-topic/childrens/childrens-industry-news/article/80084-new-owner-and-move-for-curious-george-store.html. The store relocated briefly but closed in 2021 according to an April 28, 2021, post on its Facebook page, https://www.facebook.com/CuriousHSq, accessed December 30, 2021.

10. In fact, some of the market's new entrants such as Sweetgreen and Warby Parker, both in Chan properties, opened in buildings where chains and national businesses (e.g., CVS and Amex Travel) had previously operated. For businesses coming and going during this period, I rely on news articles of store openings and closings in the *Harvard Crimson*, *Boston Globe*, and other media sources as in earlier chapters, as well as my own ethnographic observations of the market during the course of my research. For discussion of the Atlanta-based REIT's purchases in the early 2000s, see "Wells REIT

Makes Second Cambridge, Mass., Acquisition," *Atlanta Business Chronicle*, February 26, 2004, https://www.bizjournals.com/atlanta/stories/2004/02/23/daily40.html.

11. Quotes in this chapter are drawn from forty-five formal interviews I conducted in 2019–2020 concerning happenings in the marketplace at that time. For my analysis, I also draw upon my participant observation fieldwork, which included hundreds of informal conversations with individuals in the marketplace during this period and attendance at dozens of public meetings. Prior chapters have carried us back in time to reconstruct how earlier market participants experienced the economic forces affecting their lives. In this chapter, we will see how people made sense of what was happening to them in real time. Some local business owners, residents, and property owners/managers asked for anonymity for certain of their comments, afraid to irk those with whom they now had to share the market (and those who, in some cases, were—or might become—the individual's new landlord). I have honored those requests below in keeping with both the ethics of ethnographic research and my university's Institutional Review Board policies. Representatives for Asana and Regency preferred not to speak on the record, but I was able to observe their participation in public meetings and took a number of steps to ensure I understood and could accurately portray their perspectives as well: I supplemented my interviews with analyses of those firms' public statements and disclosures, interviewed individuals at similar real estate firms in other geographic markets (whose requests for anonymity I also honor), consulted with real estate industry experts at several top business schools to confirm my understanding of certain features of the market, and followed real estate industry news and discourse in several trade publications and podcasts.

12. Real estate investors can generate returns by selling properties at a higher valuation than they paid for them; however, the length of time investors hold onto properties before reselling varies. REITs like Regency are restricted in how much of their property holdings they can sell in any given period, and their annual returns are thus highly dependent on rental income from their existing assets. Private equity firms investing out of "closed-end" funds (which have a fixed life) tend to sell their investments before the end of the fund's life; private equity firms like Asana that also invest out of "open-ended" funds may have longer hold periods.

13. For references to Chan's investment firm and entities through which some of his real estate purchases were made, see: Harris, "Billionaire Hong Kong Native Buys into Cambridge"; Mason, "Billionaire Buying into Harvard Square"; Swidey, "Meet Boston's Invisible Billionaire."

14. Dianne Lee, "Square Property Values Nearly Doubled in Last Five Years," *Harvard Crimson*, November 2, 2017.

15. Harris, "Billionaire Hong Kong Native Buys into Cambridge"; Mason, "Billionaire Buying into Harvard Square."

16. The families appear to have agreed on the 2015 sale to Equity One. However, in 2017, members of the Stearns family did not want to sell the Brattle Street properties while members of the Dow family did. The issue went to court, and ultimately the buildings were sold. See: Brattle Square Properties LLC v. Stearns Brattle Street LLC and Marshall W. Stearns Trust LLC, Commonwealth of Massachusetts, Land Court Department of the Trial Court, Case Nos. 17 MISC 000179-RBF and 17 MISC 000180-KCL; John Hawkinson, "Family Clash Over Sale of Brattle Buildings Could Be 'Destabilizing' for Harvard Square," *Cambridge Day*, July 16, 2017 with update on July 17, 2017, https://www.cambridgeday.com/2017/07/16/family-clash-over

-sale-of-brattle-buildings-could-be-destabilizing-for-harvard-square/; Conti, "Harvard Square Properties Sell for $108 Million."

17. Kevin Gotham, "The Secondary Circuit of Capital Reconsidered: Globalization and the US Real Estate Sector," *American Journal of Sociology* 112, no. 1 (July 2006): 231–75.

18. This was a common sentiment among real estate investors with whom I spoke in 2019. However, a commercial real estate bubble (pertaining to both office and retail properties) had been a topic of discussion for at least several years before then. As early as 2012, the *Wall Street Journal* quoted a REIT CEO who said retail rents in New York City were skyrocketing to such an extent that, "It's almost unbelievable. Maybe it's a bubble, maybe it's not": Laura Kusisto, "A Breeze on Fifth Avenue," *Wall Street Journal*, July 16, 2012. In 2015, the *Journal* reported mounting concerns about a global commercial real estate bubble: Art Patnaude and Peter Grant, "Surge in Commercial Real-Estate Prices Stirs Bubble Worries," *Wall Street Journal*, August 12, 2015. In 2018, Bloomberg reported that a number of financial market experts were now cautioning that the commercial real estate sector looked overvalued, including Janet Yellen, Jerome Powell, analysts at Goldman Sachs, and executives at Wells Fargo and U.S. Bancorp: Noah Buhayar, "Bankers Are Worried About Sky-High Commercial Real Estate Prices," Bloomberg.com, October 11, 2018, https://www.bloomberg.com/graphics/2018-commercial-real-estate-bubble/. By 2019, *Forbes* reported with confidence that the market was in a "dangerous bubble": Jesse Colombo, "Why U.S. Commercial Real Estate Is Experiencing a Dangerous Bubble," Forbes.com, July 31, 2019, https://www.forbes.com/sites/jessecolombo/2019/07/31/why-u-s-commercial-real-estate-is-experiencing-a-dangerous-bubble/.

19. In previous chapters we've seen how generational turnover can affect the street level (e.g., the influx of hippies in the late '60s and early '70s). By 2019, generational dynamics were playing themselves out at this other level of the economy as well: many pension funds had looming liabilities on account of all the aging baby boomers, and managers of those pension funds were in search of high returns to meet those obligations.

20. Speaking to a local reporter, one of the brokers that listed the Dow and Stearns Brattle Street properties described the 2017 sales process as "extremely competitive" and having moved "at lightning speed": Conti, "Harvard Square Properties Sell for $108 Million," *Boston Globe*, December 19, 2017. Several real estate investors familiar with that sales process confirmed to me there had been significant interest in the properties and multiple bidders.

21. For an incisive discussion of how real estate violates many of the assumptions necessary for an efficient market, see: John Logan and Harvey Molotch, *Urban Fortunes: The Political Economy of Place* (Berkeley: University of California Press, 1987).

22. Leases can have small annual increases in rent built into them, and some derive at least a portion of the rent from a percentage of the tenant's sales (usually, a percentage of sales over some prespecified benchmark). Nevertheless, unlike prices on, say, a commodity trading floor, rent does not immediately and fluidly adjust to changing supply and demand conditions because of how (and for how long) most leases are structured.

23. "The Abbot," Property Brochure, Regency Centers and Boston Realty Advisors, accessed and downloaded from Regency Centers website, October 15, 2021, https://www.regencycenters.com/pdfdocuments/GetPropertyPdf/80098. An earlier version of this brochure downloaded in 2019 included a similar map and also touted the

area's "excellent demographics": "The Abbott," Property Brochure, Regency Centers and Boston Realty Advisors, accessed and downloaded from Regency Centers website, October 8, 2019.

24. The "showroom" function of physical stores seems initially to have had a negative connotation in some corners of the retail world. It referred to customers going to a department store or big-box retailer to check out products in person but then buying the products online from whichever site offered the lowest price: Ann Zimmerman, "Can Retailers Halt 'Showrooming?,'" *Wall Street Journal*, April 12, 2012. However, with the evolution of "clicks-and-mortar" and "omni-channel" strategies (especially among own-brand retailers such as Warby Parker) the experiential, showroom aspect of physical stores has been embraced by firms able to leverage it.

25. James Scott, *Seeing Like a State* (New Haven, CT: Yale University Press, 1998).

26. Scott, *Seeing Like a State*, 19–20.

27. Scott, *Seeing Like a State*, 8.

28. Quotes in this paragraph are from the Dear Asana Project, 2019.

29. Eric Johnson, "Why Sweetgreen Thinks Like a Tech Company," *Recode*, December 17, 2018, https://www.vox.com/2018/12/17/18144250/sweetgreen-jonathan-neman-fast-food-salad-delivery-blockchain-kara-swisher-decode-podcast.

30. Quotes from Terry Brown in this paragraph are from "A Question of Balance: The Changing World of Urban and Mixed-Use Retail," *The Weekly Take from CBRE*, hosted by Spencer Levy, March 1, 2021, https://anchor.fm/cbre/episodes/A-Question-of-Balance-The-Changing-World-of-Urban—Mixed-Use-Retail-eraanp.

31. Deanna Pan, "Businesses Exiting. Talk of Mall-ification. Empty Stores. Some Fear What's Next for Harvard Square," *Boston Globe*, June 5, 2019.

32. This did not mean everyone found the situation unproblematic, but vacancies were only part of the issue in that case. By the time construction began, Regency's modified design plans had won community support, and the firm was credited with upgrading old buildings in need of repair. Nevertheless, nearby businesses would still have to operate next to empty, hollowed-out buildings and in the middle of a construction zone for the project's duration. Regency was aware of the rocky start its predecessor, Equity One, had had with the community, and it made an effort to improve relations: during construction, Regency wrapped its fencing and scaffolding in tarps that bore ads for the neighboring businesses most affected by their project; and its construction was presumably no more or less disruptive than that of other landlords' major renovations in the past. Still, just like in the early 1900s when Boston Elevated Railway's subway project complicated the lives of existing merchants and shoppers by tearing up the streets, rerouting traffic, and making the place a generally noisy and chaotic place for several years, Regency's project was a sizable disruption to the marketplace, and the firm was an outsider with no track record of trust upon which to lean, so it took a while for some to come around.

33. This may be less of a consideration for REITs such as Regency, which need to return operating income to their public shareholders every year, than it is for private equity firms such as Asana.

34. Kathleen Conti, "Theater Site Is Sore Spot for City," *Boston Globe*, February 28, 2017; Alison Steinbach and Katherine Wang, "City Council Pressures Harvard Square Theater Owner to Make Plans for Property," *Harvard Crimson*, March 1, 2017.

35. The transaction history was reported in Mark Shanahan, "Chan Silent About Harvard Square Theatre," *Boston Globe*, March 5, 2015.

36. Shanahan, "Chan Silent About Harvard Square Theatre"; Conti, "Theater Site Is Sore Spot for City"; Alison Steinbach and Katherine Wang, "Former Harvard Square Theater Still Without Plans," *Harvard Crimson*, March 31, 2017.

37. In May 2017, Chan announced his plan to replace the original theater building with a new mixed-use building. The design plans were still in development and working their way through the Cambridge Historical Commission approval process in 2019: Dan Adams, "Harvard Square Theater Would Be Replaced with New Building, Cinema," *Boston Globe*, May 31, 2017; Amanda Su, "Billionaire Gerald Chan Presents New Harvard Square Theater Design," *Harvard Crimson*, June 3, 2019.

38. Muther, "Could Clues to Harvard Square's Future Be Found."

39. Dialynn Dwyer, "An 'Unsustainable' Rent Increase Is Forcing Black Ink to Close in Cambridge. Hundreds Have Written to the Landlord in Outrage," boston.com, November 25, 2019, https://www.boston.com/news/business/2019/11/25/black-ink -closing-harvard-square-cambridge/; Ellen Burstein and Sydnie Cobb, "A Dark Blot in Harvard Square: Black Ink to Close," *Harvard Crimson*, September 9, 2019.

40. E. P. Thompson, "The Moral Economy of the English Crowd in the Eighteenth Century," *Past & Present*, no. 50 (February 1971): 76–136.

41. Thompson, "Moral Economy of the English Crowd," 79.

42. According to Thompson, in the old model small farmers took their grain to the local market and sold directly to consumers. Norms and expectations had developed over the years concerning when and how such sales should generally transpire. Also, millers, to whom people brought their grain for grinding, were known to be out for a buck, but since they depended on local business, there was generally enough transparency to keep them from charging exploitative prices. This was still a market, and there was inequality and friction, but it worked well enough and people organized their lives around it. Eventually, things began to change, although enough pockets of the old market remained so as to live on as an ideal in many people's minds. Some farmers grew larger and more powerful, as did some dealers and bakers. Those farmers would sometimes hold back their stocks from the local market in order to sell to those larger entities at higher prices. Sometimes farmers or dealers would export grain to other regions where prices were higher, even when there was local need. Millers, too, became a whole "different order of entrepreneur" ("Moral Economy of the English Crowd," 104) than they once had been. Now, they were often too busy grinding orders from those large bakers and dealers to be bothered with consumers. As grain passed through more complex networks of larger players, the market as a whole became less transparent to local individuals. People grew increasingly angry. They dashed off pamphlets and wrote letters to the press. They issued threats and, at times, turned to mob violence. Rioters destroyed millers' machinery, took over market houses until given what they considered to be a fair price for the grain, and sometimes even carried away stocks of grain and meal to distribute among themselves.

12. OUR MARKETS, OURSELVES

1. The full text of the Congress for the New Urbanism's "Charter of the New Urbanism" can be found online at: https://www.cnu.org/who-we-are/charter-new-urbanism, accessed June 2, 2022.

2. This was something John had been saying for years. For example, in 2004 he expressed disappointment in Cambridge Savings Bank's decision to put a Citizens Bank branch in the space being vacated by Abercrombie & Fitch: Joshua Rogers, "Abercrombie Closes Doors: Clothing Retailer to Be Replaced by the Square's Fourth Major Bank," *Harvard Crimson*, July 2, 2004.

3. He rented a tiny space next to Dunkin' Donuts to a bank for its ATMs, but at the time of my research he did not have any bank branches in his buildings.

4. Like the issue of bank branches, this, too, was something John had been advocating for years in conversations with other landlords, in meetings of the Business Association, and in his comments to the press. See, for example, a 2006 *Boston Globe* article in which John was quoted as saying, "Landlords should think about the overall leasing of the Square and not just one space at a time. We all need to be good stewards of the Square. This really is a very unique and special place in the country": Kristen Green, "Can It Again Be Hip to Be in the Square?," *Boston Globe*, March 25, 2006.

5. Susan Diesenhouse, "Miracle in Harvard Square: Landlord Extends Rock-Bottom Rent to Artist Co-op for Its Seasonal Store," *Boston Globe*, December 15, 2004.

6. The paper John DiGiovanni shared with me was: John Gallagher, "Communion and Profits: Thinking with the Economy of Communion about the Purpose of Business," *Revista Portuguesa de Filosofia*, 70, no. 1 (2014): 9–27.

7. John Hewitt, *Dilemmas of the American Self* (Philadelphia: Temple University Press, 1989).

8. I thank Dr. Karen Chitwood for her helpful comments on attachment theory as I worked out the ideas for this chapter and for her directing me to the work of the psychologists John Bowlby and Mary Ainsworth. Bowlby and Ainsworth have done the most to deepen our understanding of the role of attachments in human development. See: John Bowlby, *Attachment and Loss, Volume 1* (1969; repr., New York: Basic Books, 1982), *Separation: Anxiety and Anger, Volume 2* (1973; repr., New York: Basic Books, 1976), *Loss: Sadness and Depression, Volume 3* (1980; repr., New York: Basic Books, 1982); Mary Ainsworth, Mary Blehar, Everett Walters, and Sally Wall, *Patterns of Attachment: A Psychological Study of the Strange Situation* (1978; repr., New York: Routledge, 2015).

13. RECLAIMING THE STREET LEVEL: COVID-19 AND BEYOND

1. "They Were Locked In, We Were Locked Out: A Story of Lockdown and Homelessness in Harvard Square," *Spare Change*, December 18, 2020, http://sparechangenews .net/2020/12/they-were-locked-in-we-were-locked-out-a-story-of-lockdown-and -homelessness-in-harvard-square/.

2. Meghan Ottolini, "Historic Harvard Square Devastated by Year-Long Coronavirus Pandemic," *Boston Herald*, February 13, 2021, https://www.bostonherald.com/2021/02 /13/historic-harvard-square-devastated-by-year-long-coronavirus-pandemic/.

INDEX

Page numbers in *italics* indicate photos.

of the Square for Sale" in, 44; on F.
Olsson, 120; on the Tasty, 186, 300n8.
See also specific citations in notes
Boston Herald: on Amee Brothers closing,
53; on COVID-19 pandemic, 85. *See
also specific citations in notes*
Boston Industrial Mission, 297n101
Boston Society of Architects, 165
Boston Transcript, on automobiles, 125
Bowlby, John, 316n8
Bowles, Ken, 294n79
bowling alleys, Spanish flu and, 121
Boylston Street, 64, 275n17; Designers 3
on, 151; proposed underpass at, 161;
renaming of, 167. *See also* JFK Street
Bradish Tavern, 266n17
Brattle Florist, 26, 209
Brattle Street, 20; Asana Partners on, 208;
Billings & Stover on, 65, 72, 74, 277n48;
Café Algiers on, 63; Cambridge Center
for Adult Education (CCAE) on,
62–63; the Cock Horse on, 61, 61–62,
274n8; Design Research on, 32, 144–
145, 146, 298n118; Dow and Stearns
Family Trust on, 312n16; Episcopal
Divinity School on, 43; J. F. Olsson's
on, 120, 289n31; street widening of,
82–83; Tories on, 21; Tory Row and, 22;
Woolworth's on, 130; Zecropia on, 151.
See also Amee Brothers; blacksmith;
Cardullo's Gourmet Shoppe;
Longfellow, Henry Wadsworth;
Walker, Mary; Window Shop
Brattle Theater: *Casablanca* at, 10, 30,
268n46; foreign films at, 30, 32, 37, 146;
on Harvard Square Development Task
Force, 161; as non-profit, 268n48
Braudel, Fernand, 38–39, 265n9, 265n15
Brennan, John, 66, 73, 277n42
brickmaker, 265n13
Briggs & Briggs, 74
Brooks, Rebekah, 198–199
Brown, Terry, 219
Bruegger's Bagels, 12, 174, 184
Brush, Tom, 46–47, 270nn9–10, 271n11.
See also Felipe's Taqueria
Building Old Cambridge (Maycock
and Sullivan), 17, 19, 65, 72, 264n8,

265nn12–13, 266n22, 276n36. *See also
specific citations in notes*
building restrictions, HSBMA and, 116
"Buy Now" parade, 132

Café Algiers, 24, 35, 63
Café Pamplona, 32
Cambridge: Office of Tourism of, 177;
population increase in, 21–22. *See also
specific topics*
Cambridge Board of Trade, 283n5
Cambridge Center for Adult Education
(CCAE), 62–63; Great Depression
and, 84
Cambridge Chamber of Commerce,
283n5; on Holiday Inn, 297n101
Cambridge Chronicle: Caragianes's death
in, 27; on counterculture, 151–152, 158;
on Harvard Square changes, 56; on
Holiday Inn, 297n101; on Larrabee,
289n20; on Out of Town News,
309n25, 309nn28–29; on subway
construction, 115. *See also specific
citations in notes*
Cambridge City Council: Boylston Street
name change by, 167; Chan and, 223;
during 1960s and 1970s cultural unrest,
152–153, 157; during the Kennedy
memorial controversy, 162, 164, 167;
Harvard Square Historic District Study
Committee and, 189; Historic District
and, 192; HSBMA and, 157; recent
market changes and, 9, 52, 56–57; the
Tasty and, 187–188
Cambridge Common, 1, 20; in American
Revolution, 21; commencement
festivities on, 20; Sunday concerts in,
157, 294n79
Cambridge Conservation Commission,
on Holiday Inn, 297n101
Cambridge Directories, 65, 278n59
Cambridge Historical Commission
(CHC), 264n8; Historic District and,
192; the Tasty and, 187; zoning and,
189. *See also specific citations in notes*
Cambridge Historical Society, 49; Wright
in, 113, 127. *See also specific citations
in notes*